International Political Economy Series

Series Editor
Timothy M. Shaw
University of Massachusetts Boston
Boston, USA

Emeritus Professor
University of London
London, UK

The global political economy is in flux as a series of cumulative crises impacts its organization and governance. The IPE series has tracked its development in both analysis and structure over the last three decades. It has always had a concentration on the global South. Now the South increasingly challenges the North as the centre of development, also reflected in a growing number of submissions and publications on indebted Eurozone economies in Southern Europe. An indispensable resource for scholars and researchers, the series examines a variety of capitalisms and connections by focusing on emerging economies, companies and sectors, debates and policies. It informs diverse policy communities as the established trans-Atlantic North declines and 'the rest', especially the BRICS, rise.

NOW INDEXED ON SCOPUS!

More information about this series at
http://www.palgrave.com/gp/series/13996

Robin Mills · Li-Chen Sim
Editors

Low Carbon Energy in the Middle East and North Africa

palgrave
macmillan

Editors
Robin Mills
Qamar Energy
Dubai, United Arab Emirates

Li-Chen Sim
Abu Dhabi, United Arab Emirates

ISSN 2662-2483 ISSN 2662-2491 (electronic)
International Political Economy Series
ISBN 978-3-030-59553-1 ISBN 978-3-030-59554-8 (eBook)
https://doi.org/10.1007/978-3-030-59554-8

This Palgrave Macmillan imprint is published by the registered company Springer Nature Switzerland AG
The registered company address is: Gewerbestrasse 11, 6330 Cham, Switzerland

Acknowledgments

This book pointedly avoids a multi-disciplinary approach to studying energy. Its focus on politics—the process, the stakeholders and their wider networks, the institutions, the informal practices—is born of the conviction that energy is above all a political matter.

This work would not have been possible without the contributing authors. They have endowed the book with their expert knowledge and exercised endless patience and good humor throughout the entire process. We hope you will learn as much from them as we have.

We are also grateful to the following individuals who generously gave up their time to review portions of the book during its development. Their invaluable feedback has strengthened its quality. They are: David Scott, Ahmad Ali, Tom Moerenhout, David Butter, Neil Quilliam, Laura El-Katiri, Morgan Bazilian, Jonathan Walters, Gulmira Rzayeva, Ellen Wald, and a reviewer who prefers to remain anonymous.

Finally, we would like to thank the team at Palgrave, including Timothy Shaw and Anca Pusca for supporting the project, as well as Thangarasan Boopalan and Keerthana Muruganandham for ably guiding us through the labyrinth of the publishing process.

Robin Mills
Li-Chen Sim

Contents

Notes on Contributors

Faris Al-Sulayman is a Research Fellow in the Political Economy Unit of the King Faisal Center for Research and Islamic Studies in Riyadh. He is also a cofounder and director at Haala Energy, a Saudi based solar EPC and developer working at the commercial and industrial scale. Before Haala Energy, Faris held a number of research positions at Georgetown University, the Wilson Center, and Arabia Monitor, focusing on the political economy of the GCC states generally, and the challenges facing private sector development in Saudi Arabia more specifically. Faris holds a B.Sc. from Georgetown's School of Foreign Service, and an M.Sc. from the London School of Economics.

Oksan Bayulgen is an associate professor of political science at the University of Connecticut. Bayulgen has published numerous articles on foreign investment, oil politics, public opinion on renewable energy, politics of clean energy reforms as well as democratization, and microfinance. Her book *Foreign Investment and Political Regimes: The Oil Sector in Azerbaijan, Russia and Norway* was published by Cambridge University Press in 2010. She has conducted extensive fieldwork in Azerbaijan, Russia, Norway, Kazakhstan, and Turkey. She is currently working on a book project analyzing the politics of renewable energy development in Turkey.

Michael Hochberg is a renewable energy project developer at Hecate Energy, a leading US-based independent power producer (IPP) focused on the development of solar, wind, and battery storage capacity across North America and internationally. Michael is also a 2020 fellow at the Clean Energy Leadership Institute and is a Research Associate at the Oxford Institute for Energy Studies, where he was formerly the OIES-Saudi Aramco Fellow. He previously spent five years as a management consultant in the Global Energy & Utilities practice of PA Consulting Group, where he helped launch and grow the firm's Mexico City office from two to more than ten consultants, and worked with utilities, IPPs, private equity, and other investors on market and regulatory challenges facing the energy industry. Prior to consulting, Michael worked at the Delaware Department of Natural Resources & Environmental Control, the White House, and was a Fulbright Scholar. He holds a master's degree focused on energy economics from Universidad Pontificia Comillas (Iberdrola Scholar), and graduated summa cum laude with a B.A. in Political Science from Tulane University.

Jim Krane, Ph.D. is the Wallace S. Wilson Fellow for Energy Studies at Rice University's Baker Institute for Public Policy. He specializes in energy geopolitics, with a focus on oil-exporting countries and the challenges they face from energy subsidies, internal demand, and climate change. Jim spent nearly 20 years as a journalist, six of them in the Middle East. He is the author of two books. His acclaimed 2009 volume *City of Gold: Dubai and the Dream of Capitalism* is widely recognized as the seminal work on the iconoclastic city-state, while his 2019 book *Energy Kingdoms: Oil and Political Survival in the Persian Gulf* is the definitive study of energy demand in the region. As a journalist, was a longtime correspondent for the Associated Press, based in New York, Baghdad, and Dubai. He has written for myriad other publications including The *Washington Post*, *Wall Street Journal*, and *Financial Times*. He is the winner of several journalism awards, including the 2003 AP Managing Editors Deadline Reporting Award, for coverage of Saddam Hussein's capture in Iraq. Jim earned a bachelor's degree from City College of New York and a master's from Columbia University prior to receiving his Ph.D. from Cambridge University. He lives in Houston with his wife and two children.

Mari Luomi is a Senior Research Fellow at the Emirates Diplomatic Academy, where she leads the research program on Energy, Climate Change, and Sustainable Development. Specializing in the politics and political economy of natural resources and the environment, she is an expert in international climate politics, and sustainable development in the Gulf. Dr. Luomi holds a Ph.D. degree in Middle East Politics from Durham University. Previously, she has worked as Research Associate at the Oxford Institute for Energy Studies, Post-Doctoral Fellow at Georgetown University's Center for International and Regional Studies and Researcher at the Finnish Institute of International Affairs. As part of a team of thematic experts, she provides independent on-site reporting from UN climate change negotiations and has written hundreds of news stories on the global governance of sustainable development for the International Institute for Sustainable Development. Dr. Luomi's research publications include a broad range of working and briefing papers, academic journal articles, essays, books, and book chapters.

Paasha Mahdavi is Assistant Professor of Political Science at the University of California, Santa Barbara. He is the author of *Power Grab* (Cambridge University Press, 2020), which shows how leaders maintain their grip on power by seizing control of oil, metals, and minerals production. His research on energy governance and political economy has appeared in top political science and general interest journals, and has received media attention from *The Financial Times*, *The Wall Street Journal*, and *The Washington Post*. Mahdavi earned his B.A. in Economics from Columbia University, M.A. in International Policy from Stanford University, and M.S. in Statistics and Ph.D. in Political Science from UCLA. He has held fellowships at the Initiative for Sustainable Energy Policy, the Payne Institute, and the World Economic Forum, and is a Term Member at the Council on Foreign Relations.

Robin Mills established Qamar Energy in 2015 to meet the need for regionally based Middle East energy insight. He is an expert on energy strategy and economics. Prior to this, he led major consulting assignments for the EU in Iraq, and for a variety of international oil companies on Middle East business development, integrated gas and power generation and renewable energy. Robin worked for a decade for Shell, concentrating on new business development in the Middle East. He subsequently worked for six years with Dubai Holding and the Emirates National Oil Company (ENOC), where he advanced business development efforts in the Middle East energy sector. He is a Fellow at the Columbia University Center on Global Energy Policy, and Senior Fellow of the Iraq Energy Institute, spent two years as the Non-Resident Fellow for Energy at the Brookings Doha Center, is columnist on energy and environment at *The National* and Bloomberg, and the author of the influential report on

Middle East solar, *Sunrise in the Desert*, and two books, *The Myth of the Oil Crisis*, and *Capturing Carbon*. He holds a first-class degree in Geology from the University of Cambridge and speaks Arabic, Farsi, Dutch, and Norwegian.

Sharlissa Moore is an Assistant Professor of International Energy Policy jointly appointed between James Madison College and the College of Engineering at Michigan State University. Her research interests focus on the policy, social equity, and security dimensions of energy systems, particularly those that cross nation-state borders and are undergoing dramatic change. Her recent book *Sustainable Energy Transformations, Power, and Politics: Morocco and the Mediterranean*, focuses on renewable energy cooperation between Europe and North Africa. The book examines renewable energy from a regional perspective, from the perspective of the national government in Morocco, and from the perspective of citizens living in desert landscapes in Morocco. She has co-led four study-abroad trips to Morocco for students. Dr. Moore also engages in social science–engineering collaborations to understand the social and governance aspects of emerging energy technologies, including solar power, advanced nuclear power, and socio-mobility transitions related to electric and autonomous vehicles.

Jessica Obeid is an electricity policy consultant. She's academy associate at the Royal Institute of International Affairs—Chatham House, energy environment and resources program, where she previously served as resident fellow 2017–2018. She's also non-resident fellow at the Lebanese Center for Policy Studies and senior advisor for Castlereagh Associates Consultancy. Formerly the chief energy engineer at the United Nations Development Programme in Beirut, Jessica had a decade experience in the deployment of renewable energy across the Middle East on the technical side prior to moving into policy. Jessica holds a bachelor's degree in Electrical Engineering and a masters' degree in Political Sciences with emphasis on Diplomacy and Strategic Negotiations.

Li-Chen Sim is an Assistant Professor at Khalifa University in the United Arab Emirates. She is a specialist in contemporary Russian politics, and in particular the Russian oil industry and its impact on the country's politics, economic development, and foreign policy. Her concurrent area of research centers on the political economy of energy in the Gulf and wider Middle East. Her books include *The Rise & Fall of Privatization* *in the Russian Oil Industry* and *External Powers and the Gulf Monarchies* along with other publications on energy, economic diversification, Gulf-Asia, and Russia-Gulf relations. Dr. Sim has also lectured on these issues as a guest speaker at INSEAD, Middle East Institute Singapore, Gulf Intelligence, the National Defense College, and the Emirates Center for Strategic Studies & Research. She holds a Ph.D. from Oxford University and a M.Sc. from the London School of Economics.

Noosha Uddin is a Ph.D. student at the University of California Santa Barbara, focusing on Political Economy and Energy Politics. Her prior research examines labor migration trends of working-class laborers in South and Southeast Asia to the Arabian Gulf and the transactionary relationships between sending and receiving states. She earned BAs in Political Science and in Economics from the University of Massachusetts Amherst.

Abbreviations

BCM	Billion Cubic Metres
CNG	Compressed Natural Gas
GCC	Gulf Cooperation Council
GDP	Gross Domestic Product
GW/GWh	Gigawatt/Gigawatt Hours
IPP	Independent Power Producers
kW/kWh	Kilowatt/Kilowatt Hours
LCOE	Levelized Cost of Energy/Electricity
LNG	Liquified Natural Gas
MBPD	Millions of Barrels (of oil) Per Day
MENA	Middle East and North Africa
MMBtu	One million British Thermal Units
MW/MWh	Megawatt/Megawatt Hours
NGO	Non-Governmental Organisation
OPEC	Organization of the Petroleum Exporting Countries
TW/TWh	Terawatt/Terawatt Hours
UNFCCC	United Nations Framework Convention on Climate Change

List of Figures

List of Tables

CHAPTER 1

Low Carbon Energy in the Middle East and North Africa: Panacea or Placebo?

Li-Chen Sim and Robin Mills

Introduction

A seismic transformation of the global energy system is currently underway. It involves a shift away from fossil fuels, which account for 85% of our primary energy consumption, toward a low carbon energy system. Not only is this process underway but it appears to have reached a 'critical inflection point'[1] where the technical performance and market penetration of solar and wind, in particular, may be rendering the transition almost irreversible. Two key trends are driving this transformation.

The first is the increasing use of low carbon sources of energy to generate power. By the end of 2019, for instance, 172 countries or

L.-C. Sim (✉)
Abu Dhabi, United Arab Emirates
e-mail: li-chen.sim@ku.ac.ae

R. Mills
Qamar Energy, Dubai, United Arab Emirates
e-mail: robin@qamarenergy.com

R. Mills and L.-C. Sim (eds.), *Low Carbon Energy in the Middle East and North Africa*, International Political Economy Series,
https://doi.org/10.1007/978-3-030-59554-8_1

four times the number in 2005 had adopted at least one type of renewable energy target, including those in the Middle East and North Africa or MENA (see Table 1.1). Electricity generation from renewables has grown substantially; it supplied 27.3% of global power production in 2019 up from 18% in 2000.[2] Its share is expected to rise to 38% by 2030 according to the International Renewable Energy Agency and to over 50% by 2035 as projected by McKinsey.[3] Anthropogenic climate change, negative externalities of fossil fuel energy, falling prices of equipment for renewable energy production, international funding for renewable projects, and electrification of transport, industry, work processes, buildings, and households underpin the global momentum in favor of low carbon energy.

The second trend is stagnant oil demand growth. This is driven in the short term by the COVID-19 pandemic and associated economic fallout; and in the longer term by increasing energy efficiency, uptake of electric and hybrid passenger vehicles, the rise of a 'sharing' economy, falling prices of renewable energy, the limits of China's export-led growth model, and the possible introduction of a carbon tax regime. Oil will continue to play a major role in the global energy mix but most likely at sustained prices far lower than $100 in a 'new normal' scenario of lower-for-longer prices.[4] This is because reduced oil demand will be coupled by abundant oil supply from relative newcomers like Brazil and Guyana as well as from stalwarts like Norway and Canada, while established oil producers such as Saudi Arabia, Iraq, and the UAE seek to monetize hydrocarbon resources lest they become 'stranded' assets.

As a major stakeholder in the current energy system, the MENA region will be greatly impacted by the transition to a low carbon world. While energy is the *sine qua non* of any state's economy, 'this is more pronounced in the MENA region than perhaps anywhere else in the world, as energy is central to political power, economic development, and foreign relations.'[5] Challenges abound but so do opportunities. Changes include geopolitical re-alignments[6] but also shifts in state-society relations and the distribution of influence among groups in society. This introduction will outline the main issues addressed by chapters in this volume and in so doing highlight their contributions to the extant literature.

Table 1.1 Renewable energy power targets in selected MENA countries

Country	*Overall Target*	*Electricity*	*Solar*	*Wind*	*Hydropower*	*Others*
Bahrain	5% by 2025 10% by 2035	710 MW by 2030	200 MW by 2025 400 MW by 2035	50 MW by 2025 300 MW by 2035		5 MW by 2025 (bio) 10 MW by 2035 (bio)
Egypt	20% by 2022 37–42% by 2035		17.3 GW by 2035 (PV) 11 GW by 2035 (CSP)	7.2 GW by 2022 21 GW by 2035	2.8 GW by 2020	
Iran			5 GW by 2020 (solar and wind)			
Iraq	10% by 2020		2.24 GW by 2020 (PV)			
Jordan	20% by 2020 30% by 2030	1.8 GW by 2020 3.22 GW by 2025	1 GW by 2020 2.5 GW by 2025	1.2 GW by 2020		50 MW by 2025 (bio)
Kuwait	15% by 2030		3.5 GW by 2030 (PV) 1.1 GW by 2030 (CSP)	3.1 GW by 2030		
Lebanon	12% by 0202 30% by 2030 100% by 2050			400–500 MW by 2020		
Morocco	42% by 2020 52% by 2030	6 GW by 2020 11 GW by 2030	2 GW by 2020 4.56 GW by 2030	2 GW by 2020 4.2 GW by 2030	2 GW by 2020	

(continued)

Table 1.1 (continued)

Country	*Overall Target*	*Electricity*	*Solar*	*Wind*	*Hydropower*	*Others*
Palestine	10% by 2020 100% by 2050		45 MW by 2020 (PV) 20 MW by 2020 (CSP)	44 MW by 2020		21 MW by 2020 (bio)
Qatar	2% by 2020 20% by 2030	500 MW by 2030	400 MW by 2030	50 MW by 2030		50 MW by 2030 (bio)
Saudi Arabia	30% by 2030	27.3 GW by 2023 58.7 GW by 2040	20 GW by 2023 (PV), 40 GW by 2030 (PV) 300 MW by 2023 (CSP), 2.7 GW by 2030 (CSP)	7 GW by 2023 16 GW by 2030		13 GW by 2040 (geothermal, bio, wind)
Turkey	65% by 2023		5 GW by 2023 (PV)	20 GW by 2023	34 GW by 2023	1 GW by 2023 (biomass) 1 GW by 2023 (geothermal)
UAE	44% by 2050					

Source Renewables 2020 Global Status Reports, REN21

MENA and the Global Energy System

The MENA region contains the world's largest reserves of oil and gas (see Table 1.2). More significantly, its oil resources are predominantly in large, conventional, high-quality reservoirs with well-developed infrastructure and close to export routes, resulting in much lower production costs than the big but costly resources of US shale/tight hydrocarbons, Canadian oil sands, or Venezuelan extra-heavy oil. As a result, MENA is also dominant in exports of oil and liquefied natural gas.

The MENA region has also become a significant energy consumer in its own right (see Table 1.2), although comprising only 5.9% of world population and 4.2% of global gross domestic product (GDP) in 2018.[7] Its share of global oil consumption increased from 9.1 to 12.2% between 2000 and 2019 while its share of global gas consumption rose from 10.1 to 18% over the same period.[8] This has been driven by a number of factors including the paucity of other traditional energy sources like hydropower and coal; the hot, arid climate with a high requirement for air-conditioning and desalination; the oil-driven economic boom of 2003–2014; policies of energy-intensive industrialization (oil refining, petrochemicals, aluminum, steel, cement, ceramics); and low, subsidized prices for energy which have encouraged inefficient and wasteful consumption.

This hydrocarbon bounty is distributed unevenly across the region. Some states, such as the six that comprise the Gulf Cooperation Council

Table 1.2 Energy in MENA by the numbers

Indicator	*Global share (%), 2019*
Oil reserves	51.9
Gas reserves	42.0
Oil production	35.1
Gas production	21.4
Oil exports	45.4
LNG exports	30.8
Pipeline gas exports	8.8
Oil consumption	12.2
Gas consumption	18.0
Carbon dioxide emissions	8.6
Electricity generation	6.9

Source BP Review of World Energy 2020

(GCC), and Libya, have small populations and large resources[9]; others like Iraq, Iran, Algeria, Yemen, Syria, and Egypt have significant resources but also relatively large populations. And then there are Lebanon, Jordan, the State of Palestine, Morocco, Turkey, and Tunisia, that have very little or no hydrocarbon production. Yet, even the oil and gas importers of the region are linked to their hydrocarbon-exporting neighbors by flows of labor, trade, remittances, foreign aid, and investment.[10] For example, just over 50 and 80% of banking assets in Lebanon and Jordan, respectively, are held by GCC-based banks and around half of all greenfield foreign direct investment in Egypt and Jordan originate from the GCC.[11] Hochberg and Moore highlight, within this volume, that companies and sovereign wealth funds based in the Gulf states participate actively in renewable energy projects in Egypt and Morocco. In Jordan, Dubai-based Yellow Door has designed, developed, and operated photovoltaic solar plants that supply electricity to supermarkets, malls, hospitals, and apparel manufacturers.

Low Carbon Energy in MENA

Countries in MENA remain almost entirely dependent on hydrocarbons for electricity, with low carbon sources accounting for only 11.1% of electricity generation, the lowest share among all regions in the world (Fig. 1.1). Demand-side explanations include the pre-existing fossil fuel-based infrastructure and stakeholder networks and corporate, cultural, political, and urban idiosyncrasies that favor hydrocarbon consumption. The supply-side of the equation includes relative resource endowments; concerns about the grid such as higher than average distribution losses and scale of power theft and non-payment issues; business and regulatory environment; and limited returns from investments due to subsidized electricity rates.[12]

Reflecting on this, Al-Sulayman in his chapter here posits a link between large hydrocarbon rents and the relatively belated uptake of renewable energy in the GCC states, compared to other countries in MENA. Furthermore, the type of fossil fuel on which rents are based is relevant: Qatar has not prioritized the development of renewables or of climate mitigation policies partly because of its abundant low-cost gas, which is the least polluting of all fossil fuels.[13] The variation in commissioning and installing low carbon energy facilities across MENA

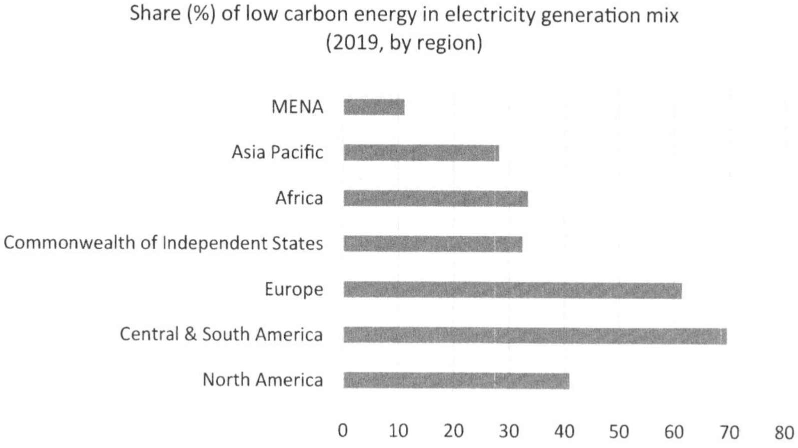

Fig. 1.1 Share of low carbon energy (including hydro) in Electricity Generation Mix (*Source* BP Review of World Energy, 2020)

is also a function of institutional capacity and coherence. In their chapters on Saudi Arabia and Lebanon, Al-Sulayman and Obeid highlight, respectively, the impact of bureaucratic infighting and political rivalry among domestic stakeholders that have impeded the progress of renewable energy; similarly, Mills notes the impact of political dysfunction and corruption in preventing progress in Iraq; in contrast, Sim notes that the UAE, which was successful in uniting stakeholders through crafting and managing coalitions, fared better in implementing nuclear power than Egypt, Jordan, and Turkey. Mahdavi and Uddin, in Chapter 9, offer another explanation of what determines the different pace of low carbon energy adoption, namely, the longer political time horizons of leaders coupled with the cost of energy imports.

The use of hydroelectricity is limited to Iran, Iraq, Turkey, Egypt, and Morocco; that of nuclear in Iran and by the end of 2020 in the United Arab Emirates; while solar and wind energy is making headway across most of MENA (Table 1.3). The choice of low carbon power generation technology, however, is not merely a technocratic decision informed by objective analyses of technology costs and country-specific factors such as grid size, solar irradiance, wind speed, or rainfall.[14] Moore's chapter is a reminder that energy choice is also shaped by historical narratives, in

Table 1.3 Actual installed capacity of low carbon power sources in selected MENA countries

	Solar PV	*Solar CSP*	*Wind*	*Hydro*	*Others*	*Total capacity (MW)*
Bahrain	6.35 (90.3%)		0.68 (9.7%)			7.03
Iran	367 (2.6%)		302 (2.2%)	13,292 (95.1%)	12 (^) 915 (6.5%)	13,973
Iraq	37 (1.5%)			2514 (98.5%)		2311
Kuwait	43.3 (40.9%)	50.0 (47.3)	12.4 (11.7%)			105.74
Oman	8.3 (100.0%)					8.3
Qatar	5.1 (11.8%)				38 (88.2%)	43.1
Saudi Arabia	344.4 (86.7)	50 (12.6%)	2.8 (0.7%)			397.2
UAE	1783 (94.6%)	100 (5.3%)	0.85 (^)		1.0 (^)	1884.9
Egypt	1647 (27.6%)	21 (0.4%)	1375 (23%)	2851 (47.7%)	79 (1.1%)	5.973
Jordan	998.1 (71.3%)		373.5 (26.7%)	16.2 (1.2%)	13 (0.9%)	1400.9
Lebanon	56.4 (17.5%)		3 (0.9%)	253 (78.7%)	9 (2.8%)	321.4
Palestine	43 (99.1%)				0.38 (0.9%)	43.4
Morocco	206 (5.5%)	530 (14.2%)	1220 (32.7%)	1770 (47.5)	2	3728
Turkey	5995 (13.6%)		7591 (17.2%)	28,503 (64.6%)	2049 (4.6%)	44,138

By volume (in megawatts or MW) and as a share (in %) of total low carbon power, end 2019
Note ^denotes a share below 0.1%
Source IRENA Renewable Capacity Statistics 2020 dataset

this case by Morocco's self-identification as a low carbon consumer originally of hydropower and more recently of solar power. Mills discusses the influence of political lobbies in driving the development of nuclear and hydroelectric power in Iran rather than wind and solar. Additionally, Hochberg's analysis of the poor economic case for nuclear power in Egypt compared to gas-fired plants underlines the role of geopolitical considerations—in this case building a relationship with Russia; this represents foreign policy hedging in the face of an unclear commitment from its traditional aid benefactor, the US.

The relatively minimal role of low carbon sources in MENA's power sector is likely to change substantially in the coming decades. A recent study projected that in the Middle East excluding Turkey, low carbon energy's share in the power mix could rise from 3.6 to 29.4% between 2017 and 2035.[15] It is clear that economic considerations incentivize the adoption of renewable energy in MENA on the back of strong electricity demand (Fig. 1.2). These include sharp declines of 82% in the global levelized cost of electricity of utility-scale solar photovoltaics since 2010, exposure to high fossil fuel import bills (for instance, for Jordan and to a lesser degree the UAE), and the costs of foregone crude oil and petrochemical exports due to wasteful domestic consumption (e.g., in Saudi Arabia).[16] The 'financeability' of renewable energy projects varies across MENA[17] but is generally not a major problem, as many of the contributors note, with the exception of sanctions-hobbled Iran. Yet, as Krane, Bayulgen, Moore, and Obeid highlight in their chapters in

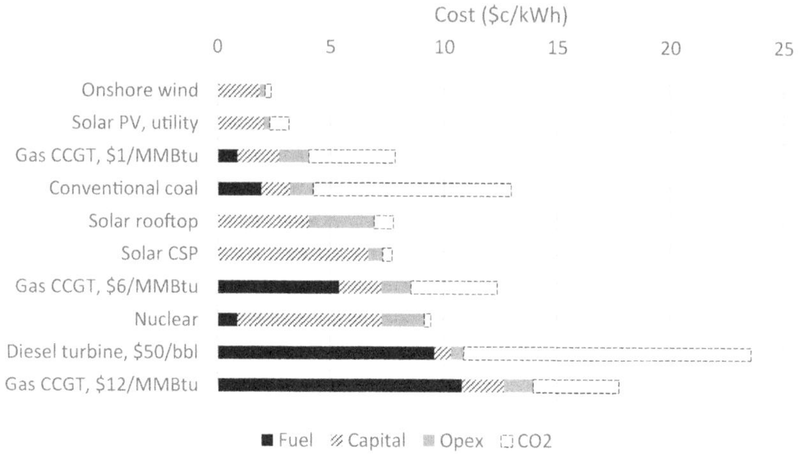

Fig. 1.2 Power generation costs (LCOE) under typical Middle Eastern conditions (*Source* Mills, Under a Cloud, 2020)

this book, non-financial considerations such as prestige, regime legitimacy, and sovereignty are equally significant drivers of low carbon energy adoption.

The Geopolitics of Low Carbon Energy in MENA

Oil has shaped international conflict for decades. According to one estimate, 25–50% of interstate wars between 1973 and 2012 had oil-related linkages.[18] In contrast, it is generally thought that a low carbon energy world is likely to reap a peace dividend in geopolitics.[19] This is partly because national energy security will be less contested; the limited number of countries endowed with hydrocarbon resources is trumped by indigenous production of readily-available low carbon energy. Trade in electricity is also assumed to be more interdependent and reciprocal than trade in oil, which in turn decreases the likelihood of interstate war.

Within MENA, Morocco and Jordan are consistently touted as winners in a low carbon world, given their credible potential to produce, consume, and export renewable electricity[20]; this could render them regional leaders. Despite their declared 100% renewable power target, Lebanon and the State of Palestine are highly unlikely to be in the same league as their regional peers largely due to political dysfunction and other reasons outlined by Obeid in her contribution. As for the oil-exporting states in the Gulf, they are typically identified as losers given the massive loss of revenues due to 'stranded' hydrocarbon assets and the slow progress in developing a non-oil export-oriented sector.[21]

Nevertheless, a strong case can be made that in the run-up to a low carbon world, some 'losers' will be able to adapt. Mahdavi and Uddin highlight in their chapter that the UAE is ranked among the countries best prepared for the energy transition in MENA given its credible project execution toward a 44% share of installed low carbon power by 2050. It was also the destination of nearly one-quarter of planned and committed investments in renewable power projects in MENA in 2019.[22] UAE-based private firms are also active investors in renewable energy in MENA, as noted earlier. In addition, the UAE has complemented its traditional petro-diplomacy with clean energy diplomacy by investing in overseas projects through Masdar, an Abu Dhabi-based parastatal, and through collaboration between the International Renewable Energy Agency and the Abu Dhabi Fund for Development.[23] Interestingly, however, the

UAE has not sought an active profile at UN climate change negotiations—an issue taken up by Luomi in her contribution in this volume. Her analysis of the disconnect between climate change and energy policies in Saudi Arabia also casts doubt on a proposal that the G20, of which the kingdom is a member, should take the lead in the energy transition.[24]

In the medium term during the period of transition to a low carbon world, it is not inconceivable that economic stress and struggles over remaining hydrocarbon resources, rents, and power may lead to more violent confrontations instead of a peace dividend.[25] Two scenarios are especially relevant. The first is the recovery of Iraq's oil industry and its success in wresting market share from Saudi customers in Asia; this will have implications for hegemony in the Persian Gulf and for influence within the Organization of the Petroleum Exporting Countries+.[26] The second concerns the relative ascendency of major gas producers Qatar and Iran (assuming the easing of sanctions) as the global demand for gas increases in the run-up to a low carbon world. This is because gas-fired power plants are easily paired with solar and wind energy for system balancing purposes. Likewise, geopolitics may trip up Morocco and Jordan; these include a renewed intensity in the simmering conflicts with Algeria and with Israel, respectively.

Low carbon power also raises the issue of the geopolitics of electricity trading. MENA countries that have successfully developed large amounts of low carbon power may seek to export surpluses at certain times. They may also rely on dispatchable capacity in other countries to reduce their need for balancing variable renewables. And time differences across the region can be exploited. Iraq's Ministry of Electricity, which already buys power from Iran, recently signed an electricity purchase agreement of up to 2 gigawatts with the GCC Interconnection Authority. Iraq shall receive power supplied by GCC countries (which have a pre-existing interconnection grid) from transmission lines from Kuwait. Egypt has also shown interest in a linking its national grid with Saudi Arabia's to meet peak demand with imports.

However, political rivalry has stymied robust intra-GCC exchanges. Consequently, only small volumes of trading take place among Gulf states on an emergency basis or during scheduled outages. Large-scale electricity exports from MENA to Europe are also unlikely in the medium term, although Morocco currently exports small volumes to Spain. From the Middle East, transmission lines would have to cross unstable areas in Syria, Iraq, or Lebanon. From North Africa, the distance is shorter and easier but the investment climate is mostly unfriendly, and all the North African countries have been prioritizing meeting their own demand. Europe would also, for reasons of local employment and security of supply, not wish to depend too heavily on its Mediterranean neighbors.

Low carbon energy projects have also broadened MENA's outreach beyond the region through interactions with new, non-oil, foreign stakeholders. Power developers and financiers from Asia (for example, Marubeni from Japan, KEPCO from South Korea, Jinko Solar and Silk Road Fund from China) and Europe (EDF from France, Abengoa from Spain, Rosatom from Russia, the European Bank for Reconstruction and Development) jostle with those from the region (the jointly-owned APICORP, Acwa Power from Saudi Arabia, Masdar from Abu Dhabi, Gulf Investment Corporation from Kuwait, and local banks). The Middle East therefore continues to be a 'penetrated system' subject to exceptional external influence, although the degree of local agency has grown significantly from when the observation was made in the 1980s.[27]

Low Carbon Energy and State-Society Relations in MENA

The dominance of the state in MENA is ubiquitous, be it in the hydrocarbon sector, the 'private' sector, domestic consumption, banking, media, or politics. The region's electricity market is no different. Historically, a designated state-owned or controlled monopoly generated, purchased, and transmitted electricity. For instance, in Kuwait the monopoly is the Ministry of Electricity and Water, in Iran it is Tavanir, a holding company. Since the early 2000s, independent power producers have been introduced in most regional countries, breaking the model of the vertically integrated, state-owned monopoly utility. However, privatization of distribution has remained very limited and true electricity markets do not exist; the 'single buyer' model persists and a state monopoly remains in charge of transmission. In a possible case of path dependency, MENA countries have preferred to introduce large-scale, centralized renewable power projects in contrast to the decentralized and distributed model pioneered in Europe. These have typically been awarded by tender by the state-owned utility, ministry, or energy regulator, with a decades-long offtake guarantee. Nuclear power projects replicate this centralized model.

For Al-Sulayman in Chapter 4, rentier states in the Gulf have expanded their traditional dominance to include the renewable energy sector, partly because of the latter's promise of job creation (the latter being a hot button issue in MENA).[28] The significant share by Acwa Power in the region's renewable energy projects seems an apt metaphor; it is a privately-owned Saudi company that now counts the kingdom's Public Investment Fund as a major shareholder. Bayulgen concurs that the Turkish state has been increasingly centralized and strengthened by the simultaneous pursuit of low carbon and fossil fuel energies. A less pessimistic view is expressed by Mahdavi and Uddin in Chapter 9. For them, the decline of hydrocarbon rents will necessitate the shift to taxation—VAT, tourism taxes, and municipality fees have already been introduced—and with it, a renegotiation by the state in favor of greater institutionalized societal influence over public expenditure. The impact of low carbon energy on the evolution of the state in the UAE is also a theme explored in the chapter by Krane; the deployment of coal, the most polluting fossil fuel, in Dubai's energy mix appears to run counter to the low carbon narrative in the neighboring emirate of Abu Dhabi which includes a 'gold standard' non-proliferation civilian nuclear program, yet both emirates are also regional leaders in large, centralized solar projects.

Social pressure and environmental concerns among domestic constituents play an insignificant role in shaping the MENA region's low carbon energy agenda. There were episodic protests against coal in Turkey a decade ago but, as Bayulgen explains, coal—because it provides cheap baseload power and employment—continues to be central in supporting economic modernization in Turkey. Moore and Sim note that there have also been protests around solar siting and gas stations in Morocco and plans for nuclear energy in Jordan, respectively; these grievances were, however, more to do with concerns about lack of consultation with local communities or compensation or government corruption than with objections to low carbon energy per se. Hydropower and its relation to water has been a complex local and regional problem in Iran, Iraq, and Egypt. Domestic conflicts over siting of solar and wind projects are likely to proliferate in tandem with their share in renewable energy targets[29]; their relatively low power density compared to fossil fuel plants means they will be more numerous and visible as sites of contestation particularly in North Africa, with a larger unsettled population than the Gulf.

The lack of sustained social activism in favor of low carbon energy and the limited integration of climate policies into economic development plans discussed in Luomi's chapter have implications for the energy transition in MENA. They suggest a continuation of the top-down pattern in state-society interactions and the perpetuation of the primacy of hydrocarbon-based interests and networks domestically and in foreign policy. The transition toward a low carbon future is likely to be gradual and incremental so as not to imperil existing energy stakeholders, with low carbon power included as an 'add-on' instead of the centerpiece of a new energy policy.

Scope of the Book

Before proceeding to the rest of the chapters, a few comments about scope of the book are necessary. First, throughout the book, the term 'low carbon' will refer to the deployment of non-hydrocarbon energy sources such as solar, wind, hydropower, and nuclear energy as part of the overall fuel mix. They emit no (during the operational phase) or low levels of carbon dioxide and other greenhouse gases (on a whole life-cycle basis) compared to fossil fuels. Energy efficiency measures, carbon capture and storage, a circular economy, electric vehicles and the use of hydrogen among others also inform the path toward a low carbon global energy system, but they are beyond the scope of this book. While the issue of low carbon energy waste—end-of-life wind turbine blades or solar panels or radioactive waste—is an important one, its salience is still some way off. This is because the average life span of solar panels and wind turbines average 20–25 years while that of nuclear plants built today is over 60 years.

Second, the objects of this volume are the countries within MENA. They share common characteristics such as the dominance of the state in economic and social patterns of interaction; and the outsize role of energy in underwriting political, economic, and social stability, as well as foreign relations. They also differ in many ways such as in terms of population size, resource endowment, governance, and integration into global economy. Consequently, seven country- or area-specific chapters at the beginning of the book are complemented by three chapters that deal with themes relevant across the region. The contributors are all experts in their respective fields and are a mix of energy practitioners and academics; each chapter was also rigorously peer-reviewed by distinguished specialists.

Third, the focus of this volume is the evolving impact of domestic and external stakeholders—such as the oil and gas industry, financiers, foreign governments, state-owned utilities, Ministries, power developers, and grassroots organizations—on the uptake of low carbon energy. The degree to which low carbon energy targets, policies, and actors have been institutionalized, mainstreamed, and embedded into development plans is also a central tenet of enquiry since this 'locks in' changes in energy policy and the role of the state. After all, and to paraphrase Milton Friedman, energy is always and everywhere a political phenomenon.

Notes

1. Rahmatallah Poudineh, Anupama Sen, and Bassam Fattouh, "Advancing Renewable Energy in Resource-Rich Economies of the MENA," *Renewable Energy* 123 (2018), http://dx.doi.org/10.1016/j.renene.2018.02.015.
2. REN21, *Renewables 2020: Global Status Report* (Paris: REN21 Secretariat, 2020), Table 10, p. 48, https://www.ren21.net/wp-content/uploads/2019/05/gsr_2020_full_report_en.pdf.
3. IRENA, *Transforming the Energy System—And Holding the Line on the Rise of Global Temperatures* (Abu Dhabi: International Renewable Energy Agency, 2019); McKinsey, *Global Energy Perspective 2019: Reference Case* (McKinsey, 2019), https://www.mckinsey.com/~/media/McKinsey/Industries/Oil%20and%20Gas/Our%20Insights/Global%20Energy%20Perspective%202019/McKinsey-Energy-Insights-Global-Energy-Perspective-2019_Reference-Case-Summary.ashx.
4. Spencer Dale and Bassam Fattouh, *Peak Oil Demand and Long-Run Oil Prices* (Oxford: Oxford Institute of Energy Studies, 2019), https://www.oxfordenergy.org/wpcms/wp-content/uploads/2018/01/Peak-Oil-Demand-and-Long-Run-Oil-Prices-Insight-25.pdf.
5. David Ramin Jalilvand and Kirsten Westphal, eds., *The Political and Economic Challenges of Energy in the Middle East and North Africa* (Abingdon, Oxon: Routledge, 2018).
6. Manfred Hafner and Simone Tagliapietra, eds., *The Geopolitics of the Global Energy Transition* (Cham, Switzerland: Springer, 2020).
7. WB, *World Bank Open Data* (Washington, DC: n.d.).
8. BP, *BP Statistical Review of World Energy 2020* (2020), https://www.bp.com/content/dam/bp/business-sites/en/global/corporate/pdfs/energy-economics/statistical-review/bp-stats-review-2020-full-report.pdf.
9. The Gulf Cooperation Council was formed in 1981 and comprise six members, namely, Saudi Arabia, Kuwait, Bahrain, Oman, United Arab Emirates, and Qatar.

10. Kamiar Mohaddes and Mehdi Raissi, "The US Oil Supply Revolution and the Global Economy," *Empirical Economics* 57 (2018), http://dx.doi.org/10.1007/s00181-018-1505-9; Adam Hanieh, *Capitalism and Class in the Gulf Arab States* (London: Palgrave Macmillan, 2011).
11. Adam Hanieh, *Money, Markets, and Monarchies: The Gulf Cooperation Council and the Political Economy of the Contemporary Middle East* (Cambridge: Cambridge University Press, 2018); MENA-OECD, *Fdi in Fragile and Conflict Affected Economies in the Middle East and North Africa: Trends and Policies* (Paris: OECD, 2018), http://www.oecd.org/mena/competitiveness/ERTF-Jeddah-2018-Background-note-FDI.pdf.
12. See, for example, Benjamin K. Sovacool and Steve Griffiths, "The Cultural Barriers to a Low-Carbon Future: A Review of Six Mobility and Energy Transitions across 28 Countries," *Renewable and Sustainable Energy Reviews* 119 (2020), http://dx.doi.org/10.1016/j.rser.2019.109569; OIES, *MENA Energy Pricing Reforms* (Oxford: Oxford Institute for Energy Studies, 2017), https://www.oxfordenergy.org/wpcms/wp-content/uploads/2017/04/OEF-108.pdf; Poudineh, Sen, and Fattouh.
13. Mari Luomi, *The Gulf Monarchies and Climate Change: Abu Dhabi and Qatar in an Era of Natural Unsustainability* (London: Hurst, 2012).
14. Hisham M. Akhonbay, ed., *The Economics of Renewable Energy in the Gulf* (Abingdon: Routledge, 2019).
15. Robin Mills, *Under a Cloud: The Future of Middle East Gas Demand* (New York: Center on Global Energy Policy, Columbia University, 2020), https://energypolicy.columbia.edu/sites/default/files/file-uploads/MiddleEastGas_CGEP-Report_042920.pdf.
16. IRENA, *Renewable Power Generation Costs 2019* (Abu Dhabi: International Renewable Energy Agency, 2020), https://www.irena.org/-/media/Files/IRENA/Agency/Publication/2020/Jun/IRENA_Power_Generation_Costs_2019.pdf; Andrea Gamba, *New Energy Sources for Jordan: Macroeconomic Impact and Policy Considerations* (Paris: International Monetary Fund, 2015), https://www.imf.org/external/pubs/ft/wp/2015/wp15115.pdf; IRENA, *Renewable Energy Market Analysis: GCC 2019* (Abu Dhabi: International Renewable Energy Agency, 2019).
17. Joel Krupa and Rahmatallah Poudineh, *Financing Renewable Electricity in the Resource-Rich Countries of the Middle East and North Africa: A Review* (Oxford: Oxford Institute of Energy Studies, 2017), https://www.oxfordenergy.org/wpcms/wp-content/uploads/2017/02/Financing-renewable-electricity-in-the-resource-rich-countries-of-the-Middle-East-and-North-Africa-A-review-EL-22.pdf.
18. Jeff Colgan, *Petro-Aggression* (Cambridge: Cambridge University Press, 2013).
19. See, for instance, Andreas Goldthau, Martin Keim, and Kirsten Westphal, "The Geopolitics of Energy Transformation," *SWP Comment*, 2018; n.d,

A New World: The Geopolitics of the Energy Transformation (Abu Dhabi: Global Commission on the Geopolitics of the Energy Transformation, 2019), http://geopoliticsofrenewables.org/assets/geopolitics/Reports/wp-content/uploads/2019/01/Global_commission_renewable_energy_2019.pdf.

20. Indra Overland et al., "The Gegalo Index: Geopolitical Gains and Losses After Energy Transition," *Energy Strategy Reviews* 26 (2019), https://doi.org/10.1016/j.esr.2019.100406; Stratfor, *How Renewable Energy Will Change Geopolitics* (Stratfor, 2018), https://worldview.stratfor.com/article/how-renewable-energy-will-change-geopolitics.
21. A New World, n.d., p. 29; Manal Shehabi, "Slowing the Pump? Why GCC Economies Have a Diversified Base but Remain Overly Hydrocarbon-Dependent," in *Economic Diversification in MENA*, ed. Anupama Sen et al. (Oxford: Oxford Institute of Energy Studies, 2018).
22. Personal e-mail communication between APICORP and co-author Sim, Li-Chen, 12 April 2020.
23. Courtney Weatherby and Brian Eyler, *UAE Energy Diplomacy: Exporting Renewable Energy to the South* (Washington, DC: Stimson Center, 2018), https://www.stimson.org/content/uae-energy-diplomacy.
24. Andreas Goldthau, "The G20 Must Govern the Shift to Low-Carbon Energy," *Nature* 546 (2017), https://www.nature.com/news/the-g20-must-govern-the-shift-to-low-carbon-energy-1.22099.
25. Kirsten Westphal and Susanne Dröge, "Global Energy Markets in Transition: Implications for Geopolitics, Economy and Environment," in *Global Trends 2015: Prospects for World Society*, ed. Tobias Debiel, Michèle Roth, and Cornelia Ulbert (Bonn: Stiftung Entwicklung und Frieden, 2015).
26. Li-Chen Sim, "Global Energy Markets and the Persian Gulf," in *Routledge Handbook of Persian Gulf Politics*, ed. Mehran Kamrava (Abingdon: Routledge, 2020).
27. Carl Brown, *International Politics and the Middle East: Old Rules, Dangerous Game* (London: I.B. Tauris, 1984).
28. I-Tsung Tsai, "Political Economy of Energy Policy Reforms in the Gulf Cooperation Council: Implications of Paradigm Change in the Rentier Social Contract," *Energy Research & Social Science* 41 (2018).
29. Lasse Eisgruber, "The Resource Curse: Analysis of the Applicability to the Large-Scale Export of Electricity from Renewable Resources," *Energy Policy* 57 (2013); Samantha Gross, *Renewables, Land Use, and Local Opposition in the United States* (Washington, DC: Brookings, 2020), https://www.brookings.edu/research/renewables-land-use-and-local-opposition-in-the-united-states/.

CHAPTER 2

The Politics of Low-Carbon Energy in Iran and Iraq

Robin Mills

Introduction

Iran and Iraq present curious paradoxes in their use—in fact—their lack of use of low-carbon energy. Both have suffered over the past forty years from well-reported wars, sanctions and political upheaval. Both, though in different ways, have experienced fast-rising electricity demand which has been a challenge to meet. Through a mix of circumstances and choice, they have relied primarily on domestic, and usually state, investment to build their power sectors. Both have large-scale, low-cost oil and gas resources, but also significant hydroelectric, solar and wind potential. Yet the use of the 'modern' renewables, solar and wind, has made little progress.

On closer examination, though, there are sharp differences in the underlying reasons for this limited penetration of low-carbon energy. Low domestic energy prices and a hydrocarbon-dominated mindset are part of

R. Mills (✉)
Qamar Energy, Dubai, United Arab Emirates
e-mail: robin@qamarenergy.com

R. Mills and L.-C. Sim (eds.), *Low Carbon Energy in the Middle East and North Africa*, International Political Economy Series,
https://doi.org/10.1007/978-3-030-59554-8_2

the story. But institutional capacity, high-level government strategic priorities, the interests of key players, and the ease or difficulty of accessing international finance and technology, differ between the two. Even if the raw statistics in terms of renewable deployment look quite similar, the processes of getting there have been unlike.

Iran

Background

Despite its large land-mass, wealth of renewable resources, heavy energy demand and technically-skilled population, Iran has made relatively little progress in renewables, with the exception of hydroelectricity. This is in sharp contrast with regional neighbours such as the UAE and Turkey.

On the other hand, it was the first Middle Eastern country to begin generating nuclear power. Nuclear forms only a small part of its future planned energy mix, yet has received disproportionate political attention and funding. Nuclear's low-carbon nature has not been an important factor in Iran's choice to adopt it.

By 2019, Iran's installed generation capacity amounted to 81 GW of gas and oil-fired generation, 16 GW of hydropower, 1 GW of nuclear, 0.35 GW of solar photovoltaic, 0.02 GW of solar thermal and 0.3 GW of wind. There are some limited plans for coal power in the Tabas mining area in eastern Iran.

Electricity generation growth was exceptionally rapid following the Iran-Iraq war (1980–1988), with a compound average growth rate of 7.6%, driven by economic reconstruction, fast population growth, the extension of the grid to more remote locations and low, subsidised prices. Annual growth slowed to 3.5% from 2010 to 2018, as most population centres had been connected to power, population growth slowed, the economy suffered two intense phases of sanctions, and subsidies were sharply reduced in late 2010. Nevertheless, keeping up with such fast growth without major nationwide power shortages was a significant achievement.[1]

Iran's complex and factionalised political system features a number of loosely organised groupings, which compete for power and financial resources under the supervision of the supreme leader, Ayatollah Ali Khamenei. Apart from material and social interests, ideological differences between these groups include statist versus more private enterprise-focussed approaches to the economy; self-sufficiency and the 'resistance economy' favoured by the supreme leader versus international openness and engagement; priority to national and regime security versus the economy; and looking to Europe as Iran's main trade partner versus China and Russia.[2] Note however that all factions co-opt the rather vague rhetoric of the 'resistance economy' since its promulgation by the supreme leader.[3] The 'moderniser' faction (grouping those often termed 'reformists' and 'moderates', including President Hassan Rouhani) is increasingly blamed for failing to deliver prosperity following the signature of the Joint Comprehensive Plan of Action (JCPOA), the 'nuclear deal' or 'Barjam' in Farsi in October 2015 and the US withdrawal in May 2018. The modernisers lost out heavily in the parliamentary elections of February 2020 to the 'Principlist' and 'Securocrat' (Islamic Revolutionary Guards Corps) groupings. This suggests a further shift towards economic self-sufficiency and trade with Russia and China. This was emphasised by the trade and political deal with China announced in July 2020, a purported text of which was 'leaked', but which originated with Chinese President Xi Jinping's visit to Tehran in January 2016. However, these countries are not willing, and Russia is not able, to replace Europe as a trade partner. The new Islamic Republic of Iran inherited after the revolution a large state-dominated energy sector. Its constitution, adopted in December 1979, has a statist orientation, with socialist influences.[4] It states (Article 44): 'The economy of the Islamic Republic of Iran is to consist of three sectors: state, cooperative, and private, and is to be based on systematic and sound planning. The state sector is to include all large-scale and mother industries, foreign trade, major minerals, banking, insurance, *power generation, dams* and large-scale irrigation networks…' [Author's emphasis]. Tavanir, the Iran Generation and Transmission Management of Electric Power Company, had been established in 1970 as a vertically-integrated, monopoly state utility, and continued in that role after the revolution.

This orientation changed somewhat following the Iran-Iraq War, in which 2210 MW of generating capacity was damaged, and under the administrations of then President Ali Akbar Hashemi Rafsanjani (1989–1997). Foreign investment in the upstream oil and gas sector, though not ownership of reserves or production, was allowed by a creative interpretation of the constitution and the introduction of 'buyback' contracts from 1997,[5] effectively a service contract. Widespread blackouts in the early

1990s strengthened awareness of the need for power sector expansion and reform. A wholesale electricity market with a regulator was established in 2003,[6] and in 2004, Tavanir was allowed to list 65% of subsidiaries on the Tehran Stock Exchange, and a separate (though 100%-Tavanir) entity was established to operate the electricity transmission system.[7] The privatisation decree of July 2008 permitted privatisation of major enterprises,[8] albeit excluding the upstream oil and gas sector. Electricity transmission and distribution remain state-owned, but private investment has been encouraged in independent power producers (IPPs) from about 2003, with investors entering the sector from 2005, including for renewable projects, and the majority of power plants have been privatised.[9] However, much of this privatisation, particularly under then President Ahmadinejad, was really pseudo-privatisation, with insiders and parastatal organisations taking control of state assets.[10] Though Quest Energy of Dubai was negotiating for an IPP in 2008, it was not until 2016 that the first foreign company, Unit Group of Belgium, was successful in signing an IPP agreement in Iran (in this case, 6020 MW of gas-fired plants).[11]

There have been attempts to privatise dams and their hydroelectric facilities, but these did not succeed because water resources are strictly property of the state, so they continue to be owned by the Iran Water and Power Resources Development Company, established in 1989.

By 2017, the Energy Ministry owed private producers the equivalent of $6.8 billion, because of non-payment by some of its users, particularly industries, and because of the gap between electricity supply costs and regulated prices.[12] Political opposition and fears of protests have prevented prices being increased sufficiently to cover costs.

From the late 1990s onwards, there was a lively debate in Iran concerning the best way to use the country's massive gas reserves, which the discovery of South Pars and other fields had by then elevated to the largest or second-largest (after Russia) in the world. This was reminiscent of the policy question in the 1970s concerning depletion of Iran's oil reserves (see below). Options for gas use including domestic power generation and industry (including petrochemicals), transport (compressed natural gas or CNG for vehicles), residential distribution for heating and cooking, reinjection in mature fields for improved oil recovery, and export either by pipeline or as liquefied natural gas (LNG).

This debate was partly couched in economic terms, but largely resolved by political exigencies. In rough descending order of priority, the competition at times of shortage was resolved as residential, transport, power, industry, reinjection, pipeline exports (with LNG exports last, had there been any). Residential use had the attraction of bringing gas even to relatively small and remote communities, and winning electoral support for local members of the Majles (parliament). The grid expansion also benefited IRGC-linked construction and steel companies, a positive point for then President Ahmadinejad. The length of gas distribution pipelines rose from 120,852 km in 2005 to 286,756 km in 2015,[13] before the growth rate slowed down as gasification was largely completed.

In transport, key aims were to reduce pollution, and to limit reliance on petrol (gasoline), and CNG use really accelerated from 2005.[14] Iran had to import gasoline and this vulnerability was targeted by US sanctions, though subsequently new refining capacity has eliminated imports. For power, gas was displacing oil which could then be exported. In industry, well-connected business groups were able to secure allocations, particularly under the administrations of then President Mahmoud Ahmadinejad (2005–2013). However, when at times gas supplies were limited, particularly during cold winters, industry has often suffered cut-offs.

Reinjection was lower-priority and fell far below planned rates (achieving only 40% in 2015[15]), affecting the country's oil export capacity, though when production was limited by the periods of US sanctions, this did not matter so much. The economic attractiveness of higher oil production was outweighed by the relatively long response time of the reservoirs, and therefore the temptation to divert gas to more urgent needs elsewhere.

Exports by pipeline to Turkey began in 2001 and to Iraq in 2017[16]; small amounts are also exported to Azerbaijan and Armenia. Iran has imported gas from Turkmenistan to serve its northern provinces, due to limited capacity to move gas from southern fields. These imports ceased in late 2016[17] due to a commercial dispute and Iran's own rising output and expanded pipeline and storage capacity to the north. But again, when domestic gas has been short, Iran has cut exports to Turkey and Iraq despite incurring commercial and reputational penalties. A pipeline was completed to the UAE emirate of Sharjah, but never functioned commercially after technical problems, sanctions delays and allegations of corruption and underpricing. Plans for pipelines to Pakistan and Oman have similarly been stymied by long commercial negotiations and American opposition. In this way, with the exception of Iraq, Iran lost its opportunity to create some mutual dependence with neighbours, which might have dampened down tensions and would have been hard for the USA to target with sanctions.

Finally, LNG exports have made little progress, despite long negotiations with Shell, Repsol, Total and China National Petroleum Corporation (CNPC), as well as smaller firms. The difficulty of accessing specialised equipment and financing under sanctions, a lack of commercial realism, shortages of gas until quite recently, and domestic political opposition, has made LNG exports particularly intractable.

Thus, most of growing gas output was directed to the domestic market, which grew rapidly because of deliberate policies and because of low, subsidised prices. Under the 2010 subsidy reform, gas prices were intended to rise to 65% of the export price, after taxes and transport costs, for industry and 75% for domestic use,[18] and electricity prices were also raised. With careful planning and the deposit of compensation in special bank accounts, this passed off with little unrest. Inflation and currency devaluation have required several subsequent rounds of price rises, while the improvement in the government budget has been limited by rising non-payment of residential bills. Despite or because of the difficulty of procuring equipment under sanctions, Iran's domestic industry became quite capable at building offshore gas production platforms and domestic pipelines. By 2019, its domestic primary energy mix was 65% gas, amongst the highest rates in the world. As a medium-sized country in economy and population, the volume of domestic gas consumption was the fourth highest in the world, behind only the USA, Russia and China.

Because of this rapid demand growth, Iran did suffer gas shortages, usually during the winter high-demand period. These mostly eased by 2017, due to the delayed completion of several phases of the South Pars development. However, shortages recurred in January 2020, possibly because of technical problems at South Pars, and potentially also because of the need to shut-in gas production to avoid over-production of condensate, which cannot be exported due to US sanctions or refined due to delays in refinery upgrades. In view of these issues, and the high reliance of the power sector on gas, alternative generation has again gained attractiveness.

Climate policy has not been a major contributor to Iran's energy plans. Its Nationally Determined Contribution (NDC) under the Paris Agreement (2015) refers to renewable and nuclear power quite generally.[19]

On the whole, the energy transition might be expected to favour a state with large gas resources, such as Iran, over neighbours whose hydrocarbon endowment is biased more to oil, such as Saudi Arabia, Kuwait and Iraq. Iran could indeed, in the longer term, expand gas exports by pipeline to neighbours, and perhaps develop some LNG exports. But because of internal bureaucracy and debate, high domestic consumption and the likely continuing impact of at least some level of sanctions and regional tensions, it is unlikely that Iran will become a major exporter of gas on the scale of Russia, Qatar or the USA.[20]

Nuclear Power

Iran's civil nuclear power plans date back to the 1950s, with the establishment of a programme under US President Eisenhower's 'Atoms for Peace' initiative. The Tehran Research Reactor was set up in 1967, and Shah Mohammad Reza Pahlavi launched a programme to build nuclear generation in 1974.

This was at a time of optimism over nuclear's future in Western countries (and the Soviet bloc[21]); nuclear power was seen as a sign of technological advance. The Shah was in a hurry to build his 'great civilisation', had ample oil revenues following the 1973–1974 price surge and had been diagnosed with cancer in 1974, although it is not entirely clear how aware he was of the seriousness of his condition.[22] Iran's crude oil production reached its all-time high of 6.02 million barrels per day in 1974,[23] and there were concerns its reserves would be depleted by the 1980s.[24] They were estimated at 58.8 billion barrels in 1979, which at the 1974 production level would have been totally exhausted within 27 years.

The country was flaring large quantities of associated gas, but again it was expected that would be captured and used productively by the 1980s, and major projects were planned to use gas for reinjection for improved oil recovery. The supergiant South Pars field, Iran's share of the structure known as North Field in Qatar, would not be discovered until 1990.[25]

The Atomic Energy Organization of Iran (AEOI) was set up in 1974 under Akbar Etemad,[26] and received lavish funding, with a budget in 1976 of $1.3 billion, larger than any public institution other than the oil industry.[27] Alumni of its training programmes include Ali Akbar Salehi, later head of the AEOI under the Islamic Republic (2009–2010, 2013–present). The plans were for 23 gigawatts (GW) of nuclear generation, via deals with France, West Germany and the USA. However, the

Ford administration was concerned about nuclear weapons proliferation, following some ambiguous statements from the Shah and India's first nuclear test, also in 1974.[28] At this point, Iran's installed generating capacity was only 14 GW, and observers questioned the very large size of the planned power programme.[29]

Iran also acquired an indirect 10% stake in the Eurodif enrichment consortium in France. The USA, at this point, was not particularly concerned about uranium enrichment, but was opposed to Iran's having a reprocessing facility, which could have allowed it to extract plutonium from spent fuel for possible use in weapons. Concepts were floated for Iran to invest in an enrichment plant in the USA, or somewhere else as part of an international consortium. Etemad felt from the start that the USA could be ruled out as a partner; a deal was initialled in 1978, when the Shah conceded on reprocessing, but then fell foul of the revolution. Yet Iran's insistence on its nuclear 'rights', including enrichment, and its view of nuclear power as a corollary of modernity have continued through into the post-revolutionary period.

Agreement had been reached in 1974 with Germany's Kraftwerk (which became Siemens) to build two pressurised water reactors of 1293 MW each at Bushehr on the northern end of the Persian Gulf. The first reactor was substantially complete and the second about half-complete when work was abandoned in 1979 as payment ceased after the revolution. Framatome of France had just started construction of two 910 MW reactors at Darkhovin, in the Khuzestan province near the Iraqi border, but this was abandoned in April 1979. AEOI continued in existence but many trained nuclear professionals also left the country at this time. Ayatollah Khomeini saw the nuclear programme as an expensive legacy of the Shah's programme of Westernisation, and annulled the power plant contracts, though nuclear work with a possible aim of developing weapons did resume in 1983.[30] The Iran-Iraq war denied the nuclear programme further resources, and the Bushehr site was severely damaged in Iraqi air raids during 1984–1988.[31]

Following the war's end in 1988, Iran's nuclear activities picked up again. However, the USA strongly opposed them because of concerns over proliferation, and persuaded Russia, China and Argentina to drop cooperation plans. Iran was reimbursed for its investment in Eurodif in 1991, but lost its right to enriched uranium from the plant. Instead, it began to develop a clandestine enrichment programme from about 1986, with the help of A. Q. Khan, the leader of Pakistan's nuclear weapons effort. Russia did commit in 1995 to complete the Bushehr-1 plant, using the Russian-model VVER-1000 but reusing the remaining infrastructure as far as possible. Russia agreed to supply fuel and to take back spent fuel, so that enrichment in Iran would not be required. After numerous technical problems, the reactor started up in May 2011 and began commercial operations in September 2013.[32]

Iran also pursued a variety of plans for additional nuclear power plants. This included up to four more VVER-1000 reactors at Bushehr and four at another unspecified site, to be built by Rosatom. Limited work on the site for the first two reactors was carried out between March 2017 and November 2019.[33] In March 2019, it was announced that construction of Bushehr-2 and Bushehr-3 was underway, to be operational by October 2024 and April 2026, respectively,[34] at a cost of $10 billion, financed by Iran.

A further string of announcements has come out between 2007 and 2014 for an indigenous 360 MW light water reactor at Darkhovin, two 100 MW reactors to be built by the China National Nuclear Corporation on the Makran (southern) coast, and possibly others on the Caspian Sea coast. Under the JCPOA, China also committed to reconstruct Iran's Arak reactor so that it could not produce or reprocess weapons-grade plutonium.

Russia and China are, of course, the two main diplomatic supporters of the Islamic Republic, and China is its sole remaining paying customer for oil. This presents an opportunity for Rosatom to market its reactors with little competition. Deals with China allow Iran to use barter or renminbi-denominated trade offset against oil sales. Iranian officials are frustrated with the actual practical support from these countries, which has done little to shield them from the effect of unilateral US sanctions, but have few alternatives.

During this period, Iran also carried out numerous nuclear activities not directly related to power production, including construction of a heavy water plant, the Arak research reactor and uranium enrichment. Various revelations of these projects led to growing international pressure, particularly from 2003 onwards, for more inspections and restrictions. Some of the justification for Iran's indigenous enrichment effort, and related endeavours such as domestic uranium mining, has been the need to guarantee a fuel supply for its reactors, partly because of the Eurodif experience, partly because of mistrust of various international offers to provide fuel or third-country enrichment and partly because of the experience of struggling for survival in the face of international isolation during the Iran-Iraq War. But Iran's own uranium resources do not appear sufficient in quality or quantity to fuel a large power generation fleet, and it still has difficulty manufacturing usable fuel rods, making imports of some kind a necessity.[35]

Iran's nuclear power programme has thus taken some forty years, of which about 22 years were spent in active work, to construct 1 GW of generating capacity, at an estimated direct cost in current dollars of $11 billion,[36] and a much higher cost in terms of sanctions and lost economic opportunities. For comparison, the country's total installed capacity as of 2019 amounted to about 99 GW and peak demand to about 61 GW. The UAE's nuclear programme started construction in 2012 and should have 5.6 GW operational by about 2024, a period of 12 years, at a construction cost of $24.4 billion. This can be seen either as a story of Iran's remarkable persistence in the face of revolution, war and sanctions, giving it a nuclear capacity that will now be able to yield a significant number of new reactors; or an odd and indecisive commitment to a very expensive programme which will eventually meet only a small part of the country's electricity needs.

However, the nuclear programme since its revival in the late 1980s, and indeed from its inception in 1974, has been about much more than power generation. Barzegar notes that, 'the Iranian nuclear program exceeds mere access to nuclear energy and economic growth and is concerned with more substantial issues, like mastering indigenous knowledge of nuclear technology; in other words, having access to an "independent nuclear fuel cycle". This is the embodiment of progress and regional and international prestige for Iran, as the nuclear program has become a symbol of national unity, the country's desire for development and advancement, as well as resistance to foreign powers' unacceptable demands'.[37] Li-Chen Sim, in this volume, further addresses the regional geopolitical implications of nuclear power programmes.

Indeed, technology transfer and the training of Iranian nuclear engineers have been an important part of the agreements with Russia. This narrative is therefore convenient for the leadership of the Islamic Republic, as it plays into the ideology of self-sufficiency and the 'resistance economy', while it also finds favour on nationalist grounds with Iranians who would not otherwise be supportive of the regime. In polling in October 2019, 75% said that Iran should not accept a deal requiring it to cease permanently any enrichment on its territory, even in return for the lifting of additional US sanctions.[38] Some influential groups within the country, notably the Islamic Revolutionary Guards Corps (IRGC), benefit from a continuing level of sanctions, which allows them to exploit lucrative smuggling opportunities and keep out foreign competitors. Their engineering firms have also benefited from contracts connected to the nuclear power programme.[39]

And, of course, although debate continues on Iran's past and current intentions, enrichment allows it to progress towards potential nuclear latency—the ability to produce a nuclear weapon on short order, as a means of ensuring regime survival. The fate of Saddam Hussein in Iraq (discussed below) and Muammar Qaddafi in Libya, who both gave up nuclear weapons ambitions, contrasts here with the continued survival of the nuclear-armed Kim dynasty in North Korea. Under the Joint Comprehensive Plan of Action (JCPOA), agreed in 2015 with the USA under the Obama administration, the other UN security council permanent members and the EU, Iran accepted stringent restrictions on enrichment, to the point of being useless either for weapons or reactor fuel, but it achieved international recognition of its right to domestic enrichment, a nationalist win for the regime.

Hydropower

Hydropower in Iran also has strong domestic and international political implications, if not to the same level as nuclear energy. These implications relate more to its control of water than of electricity. It is a major part of the power mix, reaching 1.8 GW immediately before the revolution,[40] and now standing at 12.252 GW of installed capacity, generating 9.1% of total electricity in 2019 (this was unusually high due to strong rainfall; the average over the past decade has been 5.3%). Hydro generation is highly variable because of changes in precipitation.

Domestic political factors have led Iran to overbuild dams in the 1990s and 2000s, with the process accelerating particularly under former President Ahmadinejad. These include the drive for food security and national self-sufficiency[41]; rural employment; and lobbying from local MPs. The IRGC, with whom Ahmadinejad was closely associated, has lobbied to build excessive numbers of dams to benefit from contracts awarded to its engineering subsidiary, Khatam Al Anbiya, often under its construction affiliate Sepasad. For instance, in 2012, a Chinese company building the

Bakhtiari Dam in Lorestan was muscled aside by Khatam Al Anbiya.[42] Similar stories have been noted in the conventional power sector, where the IRGC held up a deal for five gas-fired power plants with international investors until Ghadir Holdings, one of its affiliates, was given a stake in an oil-field development.[43] Saeed Mohammed, who became head of Khatam Al Anbiya Construction Base in 2019, earlier led an IRGC company that built dams in western Iran.[44] The poor location and construction of dams built by the IRGC not only wastes water through leakage and evaporation, and dries up fertile areas, but limits the amount of electricity they can generate.

Drought, urbanisation and over-abstraction have led to water shortages and drying out of water bodies such as Lake Orumiyeh in the north-west.[45] It is possible that growing awareness of the negative consequences of dams, and an increase in water tariffs, will lead to a slowdown in future construction. Farmers, who tend to be politically conservative, have come under increasing pressure from water shortages, which may turn opinion against more impoundments. The administration of President Hassan Rouhani, in his first term, did stop some dam projects, in line with its objective to reduce the role of the IRGC in the economy,[46] but dam-building still benefits from the self-sufficiency narrative and powerful political backing.

Dams also have international political consequences, most notable on Iran's western and northern borders. In October 2017 and June 2018, the Kurdistan Region of Iraq (KRI) announced that Iran had interrupted the flow of the Lesser Zab. Kurdish media claimed the first cut-off was to put pressure on the KRI over its referendum on independence, held in September 2017.[47] In October 2018, Iran interrupted flows from the Karun and Karkheh rivers into southern Iraq.[48] In the face of water and power shortages at home, exacerbated by a heatwave, and also possibly because of non-payment by Iraq, Iran also reduced its electricity exports. These factors contributed to the protests centred on Basra, and to Prime Minister Haidar Al Abadi's failure to win a second term in the 2018 elections.

Dam-building has extended into Iranian diplomacy. For instance, in December 2011, its government agreed to fund the Balaa Dam in Lebanon on the condition that an Iranian company was awarded the construction contract. This requirement was dropped due to concerns about links to Khatam Al Anbiya.[49] In May 2020, Iran completed two hydropower projects on the Aras River, forming part of the border between it and Azerbaijan. The construction sites were on Azerbaijani territory occupied by Armenia, and, in addition to their practical use, they form part of Tehran's complicated diplomacy with its Caucasus neighbours.[50] Iran has also contributed to building the controversial Roghun Dam in Tajikistan, as well as dams in Kyrgyzstan.

Non-hydro Renewable Energy

Iran's progress in non-hydro renewable energy presents a sharp contrast with its efforts in nuclear and hydropower. It has excellent solar and wind resources, and a strong base of technical skills and local industry. There is also domestic pressure for more renewable energy to improve air quality and save on the use of scarce water in thermal and hydroelectric power plants. Renewable energy would also address its concerns over self-sufficiency and the depletion of fossil fuel resources.

Renewable energy appeared in the 20-Year Economic Perspective, put forward in 2005, where the target was to meet 18% of energy (probably meaning electricity) from renewables, likely including hydropower.[51] The Third Development Plan (2000–2005) included plans for a 250 MW wind farm, while the Fourth Development Plan envisaged 1000 MW of wind.[52] The Fifth Development Plan (2010–2015) introduced 20-year power purchase agreements for renewables with feed-in tariffs, and bonuses for higher local content. The Sixth Development Plan (2016–2021) envisages installation of 5000 MW of renewables by 2021 and a further 2500 MW by 2030.[53] In 2017, the country planned to reach about 4 GW of non-hydro renewables by 2021.

Yet by 2019, it had an installed capacity of 'modern' renewables of only 302 MW of wind, 367 MW of solar photovoltaic (PV) and 12 MW of bioenergy. This contrasts strongly to a much smaller country such as Jordan, which had in 2019 374 MW of wind, 998 MW of solar PV and 13 MW of bioenergy.[54] The solar plants in Iran are also mostly of small size, 10 MW or less. The 20 MW Mokran plant was the country's largest when it was opened in the Kerman province in July 2017, financed by a Swiss company and supervised by a German firm.[55] Of course, renewables have struggled to compete economically against low-priced gas,[56] until dropping in cost over the last few years, but the same applies to nuclear power. Various scenarios can meet Iran's power needs with a mix of improved efficiency, gas and renewables with lower costs and CO_2

emissions than either the current system or with the planned 10 GW of nuclear power.[57]

Renewable energy installation has accelerated recently. The Ministry of Energy Renewable Energy and Energy Efficiency Organisation (SATBA) has signed power purchase agreements (PPAs) for 1427 MW of wind, 2685 MW of solar, 31 MW of biomass and 15 MW of small hydropower. Still, the average size of these projects (32 MW wind and 9 MW solar) is very small compared to the plants of hundreds of megawatts up to 2 GW being constructed in neighbouring countries such as Pakistan, the UAE, Oman and Saudi Arabia. Plans for larger plants, such as a 1 GW solar PV plant near Saveh in the central Markazi province announced in January 2019, and a July 2018 memorandum of understanding for a 0.5–1 GW plant near Yazd with an Italian-Chinese joint venture, are backed by foreign investors.[58] Progress must remain doubtful given the problems posed by sanctions and financing. The feed-in tariffs offered by SATBA apply only to wind, solar or small hydropower projects of up to 10 MW,[59] given limited financial resources. 25% of value-added tax on electricity bills is allocated to SATBA, but this amounts to only $25 million annually.[60] In 2016, state-owned organizations were obliged to install solar panels to cover at least 20% of their electricity needs, but again take-up has been limited.[61]

There are several reasons for slow progress in renewables. Despite government efforts to promote renewables, the investment environment in Iran for foreign investors remains bureaucratic, slow and opaque. The increasingly tight international and US sanctions established under President Obama during 2010–2015, then the greatly intensified US sanctions imposed by Donald Trump's administration after its withdrawal from the JCPOA in 2017, have deterred foreign investment and made access to international equipment more difficult. International financial institutions such as the European Bank for Reconstruction and Development and the World Bank, which had been important in establishing renewables frameworks in countries such as Morocco, Jordan and Egypt, were not able to bring financing and expertise to Iran. This increased the financial requirement and risk on investors.

There was considerable interest in the brief period the JCPOA was fully operational, including from Danish, Norwegian, Swedish, French, German, Austrian, Spanish, Italian, Greek, Turkish, Indian, South Korean and Chinese companies, who completed solar plants totalling more than 100 MW.[62] But following 2017, most of this activity ceased; for instance,

UK firm Quercus withdrew in August 2018 from plans to build a 600 MW solar plant.[63] The Trump-era sanctions are said to have tripled the price of imported photovoltaic panels, inverters and cables.[64] The governance of the PPA under Iranian law is a further deterrent for international companies. Additional problems have been caused by the Covid-19 outbreak, with suggestions that the high concentration of initial cases around the city of Qom, south of Tehran, was due to the presence of Chinese engineers who are building a 30 MW solar plant there.[65]

All of Iran's non-hydro renewables have been developed with private-sector investment,[66] during a period that non-state companies have generally been squeezed for finance and/or concentrating on short-term, high-return projects. Iranian banks do not offer project financing and corporate finance is at high rates and directed to politically-favoured entities. The National Development Fund (NDF) has very limited resources and these are focussed on high-priority projects. The Renewable Energy Organisation of Iran, SUNA (which was merged into SATBA in December 2016) committed to issue letters of credit, but these do not have a credit rating or sovereign guarantee. The high resulting cost of capital for developers contrasts with the very low cost of capital achieved by developers in the Gulf Cooperation Council countries, a major contributor to their extremely low reported levelised cost of electricity (LCOE).

Instead of the increasingly popular tender model, SUNA offered a range of feed-in tariffs to offset the low electricity sales prices. In 2018, these ranged from 3200 Iranian rials (IRR) per kWh for large projects up to 8000 IRR/kWh for very small projects, which were to be adjusted based on inflation and exchange rates. At the then prevailing exchange rate,[67] this was equivalent to 7.5–18.8 USc/kWh, which should have been attractive. However, the requirement for payments under the power purchase agreement to be made in rials would be unacceptable to most international investors. The feed-in tariff has fallen because of depreciation of the rial; although payment is meant to be made at the official rate, rather than the much lower market rate, this raises the uncertainty of investors about access to hard currency. The Central Bank of Iran had reportedly offered payment to foreign investors in yuan rather than euros, again unattractive to most.[68]

Bureaucracy and unclear regulations hamper projects, with an indicated seven months for the initial stages of qualification with SUNA in reality taking about a year, and the developer has to obtain all licences and pay the associated costs. The developer is responsible for grid connection, a difference with the typical GCC projects. Acquisition of land is also a slow and expensive process, although this is meant to be provided by the government.[69]

There have been turf wars between the Ministry of Energy, responsible for electricity, and the Ministry of Environment. The Ministry of Energy has less institutional power than the Ministry of Oil and the National Iranian Oil Company (NIOC), who have historically produced most of export earnings. Other organizations have also been active in renewables and receiving part of the allocated budget, including the Renewable Energy Initiative Council (REIC) under the Research Institute of Petroleum Industry, part of NIOC; the Iranian Fuel Conservation Company; the Iranian Research Organization for Science and Technology; and the Ministry of Industry and Mines. This dispersal of responsibility and budget is also likely to have retarded progress.[70]

Despite several rounds of subsidy reform, electricity prices remain very low in international terms because of inflation and currency depreciation. In 2019, power cost a reported 2 USc/kWh to generate (with gas priced at about $1/MMBtu, a low figure by international standards) but was sold at 0.7 c/kWh.[71] This makes private installation of solar power unattractive. Mohammad Ali Pouramiri, a board member of the Iran Renewable Energy Association, said that subsidies had to be lifted to make renewables attractive.[72] However, given the difficulties in exporting oil and gas, social unrest at rising prices and the attempt to export products such as petrochemicals instead, there are countervailing pressures to retain subsidies.

Chinese firms could take a larger role in the market, given that they could be paid in yuan, they have the expertise and remain relatively willing to take on sanctions risk. As noted, Chinese firms have been developing projects in Qom, as well as the central city of Yazd. But Iran has recently been disappointed with the lack of support provided from China to help it withstand the intensified American sanctions.

These obstacles could, of course, be partly overcome with different government policies, at least to encourage domestic investors. But with a smaller size, lower rents and less domestic manufacturing capacity than for hydropower and the oil and gas sector, renewables have not so far attracted so much political attention from influential business groups, including those linked to the IRGC. There are some exceptions. For instance, in 2017, a Greek engineering firm, Metka, and its Iranian partner, Ghadir Electricity, completed a 10 MW solar plant near

Esfahan.[73] Ghadir has also built solar plants at Yazd, Qom and Kerman, each about 10 MW.[74] Ghadir Energy Investment Company is owned 60% by Ghadir Electricity and Energy Investment Company and 40% by MAPNA. The ultimate parent, Ghadir Investment Company, has been identified by the US's Office of Foreign Assets Control (OFAC) as affiliated with the Execution of Emam Khomeini's Order (EIKO), also known as SETAD.[75] MAPNA, meanwhile, listed on the Tehran Stock Exchange, is mostly involved in building thermal power plants and is also on OFAC's list because of its part-ownership by Iranian government entities.

Iraq

Background

Iraq's power sector has experienced exceptional difficulties over the past thirty years. The lack of progress on low-carbon energy despite major resources and desperate need is one small part of an overall damaged and dysfunctional sector. However, there are also particular reasons why renewable energy has made less progress than fossil-fuelled power.

Before 1990, Iraq had 10.2 GW of generating capacity, which was more than adequate to meet demand.[76] The power infrastructure was significantly damaged and deteriorated during the 1990–1991 Gulf War and subsequent sanctions up to 2003, then by looting following the US-led invasion of that year. After the invasion, power demand has grown rapidly because of a rising population, reconstruction and the growing availability of modern appliances, particularly air-conditioning.

The electricity system in Iraq is effectively split in two, with the autonomous Kurdistan Region of Iraq (KRI) operating its own sector. Both 'federal' (non-KRI) Iraq and the KRI have a state-owned sector run by a ministry of electricity with a monopoly of transmission and distribution. However, most generation in the KRI is via independent power producers (IPPs) contracted to the ministry, whereas the federal Ministry of Electricity (MOE) operates most of its own generation, with a limited use of IPPs, which started to generate in 2017.

Generation rose from 30.7 TWh in 2004 to 131.5 TWh in 2019.[77] Of this, 2.5 TWh was hydropower, down significantly from the post-invasion peak of 5.7 TWh in 2004; solar was 0.057 TWh. Of the remainder, slightly more than half was generated from gas, and the rest from oil (fuel oil, diesel and limited amounts of crude oil). Despite progress in capturing associated gas, flaring has continued at high levels, an estimated 16.8 billion cubic metres (BCM) in 2018, with 11.5 BCM captured and used, because of inadequate facilities to process the gas, and lack of pipeline capacity to power plants.[78] Iraq also imports gas from Iran, reaching about 32 million cubic metres daily in April 2020.[79] The USA has repeatedly granted waivers for Iraq to import Iranian gas and electricity, recognising its indispensability, but has shortened the period of these waivers at times to give it leverage on Iraqi politicians, and repeatedly pressured Baghdad to find alternative supplies. In July 2020, Iraq completed its side of a 1 GW link to Kuwait which would enable it to tap into the GCC grid.[80]

The KRI had managed to establish reasonably reliable electricity service, mostly powered by gas and some diesel, but the fiscal burden has been heavy, with diesel for the Dohuk power plant estimated to cost $100 million per month more than gas would.[81] By 2020, fuel and generating capacity shortages and power theft had led electricity provision to fall to 14–15 hours daily, with completion of the new Khabat fuel oil-powered plant hoped to boost that to 16–17 hours.[82]

Federal Iraq has suffered from severe and continuing power shortages, as significant growth in generation and fuel supply has still failed to keep up with demand. Peak generation was about 18 GW in summer 2019, plus 1.4 GW of imports from Iran, compared to estimated peak demand of about 25.3 GW.[83] The difference is met by power cuts and the use of distributed neighbourhood diesel generators, which receive fuel at subsidised prices. Technical losses, mostly in the distribution networks, are estimated at 40% and non-technical losses (unofficial connections/theft) at 20%, exceptionally high levels that compromise the ability to meet demand.[84] For comparison, transmission and distribution losses in Iran are about 15% and the world average is around 8%.[85] Even customers who pay their bills are only covering about 10% of the real cost of electricity provision,[86] making it impossible for the MOE to stand on a commercial basis. In April 2019, the World Bank considered a $200 million loan to improve transmission, distribution and billing in four southern governorates.[87]

Subsidy reform has been almost impossible, because of political and public opposition. Political parties and influential individuals seek a cut of spending on MOE projects, and block them if corrupt payments are not forthcoming. They also have a strong influence on personnel choices at

MOE and other ministries, making it hard to place competent individuals in the right roles and empower them.

Climate policy has not been a major part of Iraq's plans. Its NDC under the Paris Agreement mentions solar equipment and appliances, but the only quantitative target for renewables is to raise hydroelectric plant capacity by 3.3%, a very unambitious goal.[88]

Renewable and Nuclear Energy

Iraq has a good variety of renewable resources, including exploitable hydropower, abundant sunshine on unused land and, in some areas, good wind speeds. Given endemic power and gas shortages, and frequent insurgent and criminal sabotage of transmission lines, distributed renewables should be an economic and practical part of the generation mix.

Iraq has had significant **hydropower** capacity since the 1950s. Its dams are all intended for flood control and irrigation water provision, and all the large ones except Duhok have hydropower generation attached, totalling 2.1 GW. The Dokan (1959) and Darbandikhan (1961) Dams, in what is now the KRI, the Hamrin (1981) and Adhaim (2000) Dams are on tributaries of the Tigris, and the Samarra Dam is on the Tigris itself. The Haditha Dam is on the Euphrates and was finished in 1987.

The Mosul Dam on the Tigris accounts for the largest share of generation capacity with 1062 MW nominal capacity. It was built between 1981 and 1984, but has significant safety concerns because of dissolution of the gypsum bedrock, requiring continuous application of grouting to prevent collapse. The Badush Dam downstream was intended to absorb any flood from Mosul, and began construction in 1989 but work stopped in 1991 because of the UN sanctions. The US suspected in 1991 that the unfinished dam could have been supplying power to a supposed secret uranium enrichment plant nearby.[89] Completion of the dam would cost $300 million, but expansion to hold any flood from Mosul has been costed at $10 billion.[90] Work did, however, resume in the summer of 2019, with the possibility of including 170 MW of generation capacity.

The Darbandikhan Dam also suffers from poor construction and was bombed both in the Iran-Iraq and First Gulf wars. Following the US-led invasion of 2003, these dams were partly rehabilitated. However, in August 2014, the Islamic State of Iraq and Syria (ISIS), or Da'esh in its Arabic nickname, seized control of the Mosul Dam, before being driven out. During their occupation of large parts of northern Iraq, they inflicted severe damage on the electricity generation and transmission networks.

The Bekhme Dam, on the Greater Zab river in what is now the KRI, was begun in 1986, but halted in 1991 by the First Gulf War. It would have 1500 MW of generation capacity. In 2005, Baghdad promised to fund the required $5 billion. However, no work has commenced, reportedly because it would flood the Barzan area, historic home to the Barzani family which heads the Kurdistan Democratic Party, the region's leading party.[91] Additional dams have been planned in the KRI, including Mandawa (764 MW), Taq Taq (270 MW), Bakrman (52.5 MW) and Deralok (37.6 MW).[92] These have not progressed, although a number of small dams have been built for water storage.[93] The KRG has repeatedly suffered from budgetary crises, particularly following its loss of the Kirkuk area to federal government control in 2017, and during the coronavirus pandemic and sharp drop in oil prices in 2020, and these constrain its ability to fund such large projects. The central government is unlikely to come up with the finance either, since most lucrative subcontracting opportunities would go to politically-connected KRI companies.

Iraq's dams have also suffered from falling water availability, because of regional drought and upstream dam construction by Turkey and Iran,[94] although this improved somewhat with higher rainfall in 2019. Iraqi MPs and the minister of water resources have complained over water shortages because of the filling of Turkish dams,[95] and Turkey did agree to slow down the filling. This was a contrast to the situation in the late 1980s and early 1990s, when Iraqi and Syrian tensions with Turkey over dams escalated almost to the point of military action,[96] but neither country is in any position to coerce Turkey today. The KRI and the federal government in Baghdad have several outstanding disputes, including over territory, the national budget and the KRI's management of oil resources on its territory.[97] The construction of further dams controlling water flows into the Tigris could give the KRI more leverage in these disputes, another reason for Baghdad to drag its feet on funding them.

Repair and rehabilitation of the dams has been slow, both post-2003 and post-ISIS. By early 2019, the maximum operational capacity of the federal Iraq dams appeared to be about 867 MW from a nominal total of 1904 MW.[98] After the initial post-invasion repairs, the hydroelectric sector has received little attention either from the Iraqi government or the international community, except with respect to water. The IEA report on Iraq of April 2019,[99] for instance, only mentions dams in the context of water shortages, while discussing solar and wind power at length, while the Iraqi government's post-ISIS list of investment projects has five solar opportunities but nothing in hydroelectricity.[100] This may also reflect some opinion in the international community against large hydropower because of its negative social and local environmental impacts, for instance in the withdrawal of Western financial institutions from supporting Turkey's Ilısu Dam. Yet hydropower remains by far the largest source of renewable energy in Iraq, with considerable room for rehabilitation and expansion.

Iraq's **nuclear** programme started in 1956, and it acquired a 2 MW research reactor from the USSR. However, from the early 1970s, under the direction of then vice-president Saddam Hussein, its efforts were solely directed towards gaining nuclear weapons. The country's power generation relied on its oil, gas and about 10% of hydropower, while large amounts of associated gas continue to be flared, so civil nuclear power was never required. Iraq bought two research reactors from France, as well as a plutonium separation laboratory. However, Israel bombed the larger reactor in June 1981 before it could come online. After that, Iraq relied on more clandestine approaches towards uranium enrichment, but its nuclear infrastructure was entirely dismantled during the 1990–1991 Gulf War and subsequent IAEA inspections.[101]

There has been no serious attempt to revive nuclear power in Iraq after the 2003 US-led invasion. In 2009, the government approached France about the possibility of rebuilding one of the research reactors destroyed during the First Gulf War,[102] and it repeated this call to the UN in 2017.[103] But the continuing availability of flared gas, concerns over instability, Iraq's lack of financial resources and institutional capacity, and the growing competitiveness of renewables, make it very unlikely a nuclear power generation programme would make progress.

Iraq has seen a number of plans to expand its use of **non-hydro renewables**. Global horizontal irradiation (GHI) is about 1900–2000 kWh/m^2/year over the central part of the country, and more than 2100 kWh/m^2/year in the western desert. This is not as good as some neighbouring countries such as Jordan, Egypt or the UAE, but is still as good or better than southern Spain or the south-western USA, and presents very attractive conditions for solar PV.

A small amount (36.5 MW) of solar photovoltaic was installed during 2013–2014,[104] and parts of Baghdad feature solar street-lighting. The Integrated National Energy Strategy of 2012 foresaw 2 GW of renewables by 2030, including new hydro,[105] amounting to 3% of total generation. However, it rejected large-scale solar on the grounds that it was (then) too expensive compared to Iraq's cheap and abundant gas, although the MOE planned at that point 50 MW of solar/wind hybrid plants in remote locations where they would be competitive with diesel generators. In October 2012, the MOE announced plans for 400 MW of solar and wind, but these did not proceed.[106]

Following the defeat of ISIS, in 2018 the Iraqi government issued a long list of projects for international investment and reconstruction, which including 410 MW of solar power in various sites, as well as a solar research and manufacturing centre.[107] MOE's own projections showed 2695 MW of solar PV being installed between 2017 and 2020, spread across most provinces of the country, though excluding the KRI and the northern provinces of Kirkuk, Ninewa and Salahuddin, which were still affected by ISIS activities.[108] Projects were awarded to some regional companies: 465 MW in five locations to Sama Baghdad, and 230 MW in four locations to Kuwait-based Al Dana International. However, in the absence of a clear plan, priorities and investment model, these also did not go ahead. MOE has consistently suffered from a high turnover of ministers, because of changes of government and because of dismissal following allegations of corruption (Raad Shalal in 2011) and summer power cuts and protests (Karim Waheed in 2010 and Qassim Al Fahdawi in July 2018).

During this period, numerous companies approached the MOE with offers for solar projects, but these were generally rejected as too expensive. A feed-in tariff of 3.5 USc/kWh was set, inspired by the low prices achieved in some neighbouring countries, but given the early stage of solar power in Iraq and its particular challenges, this was not attractive. For comparison, bids in Jordan in 2015 were around 6–7 USc/kWh,[109] and its Risha project tendered in 2017 was awarded at 5.9 USc/kWh. The Iraqi projects offered were individually relatively small, so not achieving economies of scale. Part of the intention appeared to be to spread development across most provinces, particularly poorer rural provinces with limited other investment and weak grid connections, as well as widening the opportunity for insiders to benefit through land leases and contracts. Although security in most parts of Iraq has improved significantly, it remains a concern, along with high levels of corruption. Importantly, because of low electricity tariffs, theft and very high levels of non-payment, the MOE is reliant on budget transfers (the same applies to the MOE in the KRI). This creates the concern for investors that they will experience delays and difficulty in receiving payment, particularly in the absence of a sovereign guarantee. Officials at the MOE, meanwhile, were concerned that awarding projects at prices significantly above those achieved in neighbouring countries would attract political scrutiny and allegations of corruption.

The government of Adel Abdel Mehdi, with the highly-regarded Luay Al Khatteeb as electricity minister, came into power in October 2018, and intended to add 1.5–2 GW of renewables during its 3–4 year term.[110] A Renewable Energy Law was drafted, and institutions and individuals have been given the right to generate renewable power for their own use, to 'wheel' it through the state grid to their other facilities, or to sell to MOE under a PPA. Low-interest loans are offered for rooftop solar installations.[111]

In May 2019, the MOE abandoned the feed-in tariff for projects above 10 MW, and instead launched a competitive tender for 755 MW of solar PV across several sites, and pre-qualified 45 bidders,[112] with interested companies including Total, Siemens and Acwa Power, a private Saudi developer with a strong regional track record and significant state backing. In November 2019, a Ministry adviser revealed plans for another 750 MW,[113] or 1000 MW to be launched in the first quarter of 2020. The longer-term intention was for renewables to account for 20% of generation (probably meaning capacity) by 2030. In late 2019, Acwa Power and Amea Power, a private UAE developer, were reportedly encouraged by their home governments to look at investments in Iraq as part of supporting the government and offsetting Iranian influence. Acwa Power proposed two 1 GW solar projects; one would be based in Saudi Arabia and export to Iraq at a tariff of 1.65 c/kWh; the other would be in Iraq with a tariff of 6.5 c/kWh.[114] This illustrates the difference in business risk between the two countries, given that the solar resource is very similar.

However, Iraq has experienced major turmoil since, with widespread anti-corruption protests starting in October 2019, the resignation of Abdel Mehdi's government and the lengthy process of selecting a new prime minister, involving the replacement of Al Khatteeb who had been in office for barely a year, then the arrival of the coronavirus pandemic and the crash in oil prices of March 2020. In this environment, the solar projects have not advanced.

Distributed solar power would seem to be an ideal initiative for Iraq, given its frequent power cuts and the high cost of electricity from generators. There has been some degree of adoption in the KRI in particular, where small private companies offer installations.[115] But in practice, 'rooftop' solar has made little progress. Part of this could be due to opposition from the 'generator mafia', politicians with stakes in the local diesel generators, who have been blamed for ending pilots of electricity tariff reform.[116]

Conclusions

The political and financial capital the Iranian state has invested in its nuclear programme, and in totemic features such as its right to domestic enrichment, make it extremely difficult to back down. Its nuclear activities have incurred very heavy diplomatic and economic costs, but at the same time, they have been convenient to some elements of the regime, particularly the IRGC. Similarly, hydropower offers rent-seeking opportunities to developers, and temporarily satisfies the demands of constituents such as farmers. Non-hydro renewables have not yet attracted the same level of interest, though they may as the sector grows. They have suffered from a lack of suitable incentives, the limited scale and experience of local developers, US-imposed sanctions and continuing subsidies.

Iraq's lack of progress in renewables is more straightforward. It is mostly a story of ineffective organisation and capacity, overbearing bureaucracy, unworkable financing and investment models, insecurity and war damage, vested political interests and corruption, government instability, and cheap, subsidised electricity and gas. The renewables sector is not unusual in these regards; most parts of the Iraqi economy post-2003 have similarly failed to attract international or domestic private investment.

Yet objectively, both countries could realise enormous benefits from exploiting their abundant solar and wind resources, given the vast improvements in performance and cost of renewable technologies over the past few years. They have several regional examples of success that could be used as models. Their lack of progress is also not unique; several other neighbours, under apparently more favourable conditions, such as Bahrain, Lebanon, Tunisia and Algeria, have also not managed to install much renewable capacity. Only one other Middle Eastern state, the UAE, has succeeded in completing a civil nuclear power programme.

For Iran, the key to developing large amounts of non-hydro renewables could proceed through an easing of sanctions via negotiations with the USA, and depending on the state of American politics. That would at least allow European, Indian and East Asian firms, and possibly even Middle Eastern neighbours, to get involved. International support for a large renewables programme would reduce the rationale for further growth in nuclear generation. Or, a decision by major politically-connected business groups to get involved in renewables could foster a more supportive set of policies, using a mix of locally-manufactured and imported, particularly Chinese, equipment. Key policy improvements would include reducing subsidies, simplifying procedures and improving access to finance at lower costs. These two routes are not necessarily mutually-exclusive, though as noted, the presence of IRGC-linked companies tends to deter and exclude foreign competition. Estimates of the IRGC's share in the economy range from one-sixth to two-thirds of the economy,[117] though references tend to be circular, with unclear methodology, and the higher figures are implausible given that most of the large oil, agricultural and services sectors are not under IRGC control.

For Iraq, domestic capability and finance is much more limited. Large-scale international investment is crucial. There is substantial interest from a wide range of firms and countries, including GCC neighbours with a political interest in building bridges to Baghdad. By starting with some smaller projects, the MOE could build confidence in its payment model and bring down costs before awarding larger projects,[118] so avoiding the risk of being locked into a big and high-priced PPA, or being accused of corruption for accepting bid prices much higher than those of regional neighbours. The IEA's report proposed 21 GW solar PV and 5 GW wind by 2030, generating 30% of Iraq's electricity. This pace of progress looks unattainable now, but Iraq's renewable sector could still advance quickly under the right contractual model and with sustained and consistent policies. This, in turn, would require the new government of Mustafa Al Kadhimi, or a successor, to be able to overcome vested interests and statist positions, in the face of the political and economic emergency engulfing Iraq since mid-2019.

Notes

1. There have been episodic power cuts, as in 2001 and again in 2019 and 2020, caused by technical faults, shortages of gas and low water levels at hydroelectric dams (Fallahi 2019).
2. (Geranmayeh 2020)
3. (Iranian Students' News Agency 2013)
4. (Arjomand 2020)
5. (Ebrahimi and Shiroui Khouzani 2003)
6. (Yousefi et al. 2017)
7. (Poudineh et al. 2021)
8. 5 Iran Privatization Organization, "General Policies of Article 44 of the Constitution of the Islamic Republic of Iran", http://www.en.ipo.ir/index.aspx?siteid=83&pageid=822.
9. (Chitchian 2017)
10. (Harris 2013)
11. (Parris 2016)
12. (Tasnim News 2016)
13. (Omidvar 2019)
14. (Sharifi and Gougerdchian 2012)
15. (Chow et al. 2018)
16. (Dehghanpisheh 2017)
17. (Eurasianet 2017)
18. (Iran Data Portal 2009)
19. (National Climate Change Committee 2015)
20. (Jalilvand 2013)
21. (Higginbotham 2019)
22. (Khoshnood and Khoshnood 2016)
23. (OPEC 1999)
24. (Fesharaki 1976)
25. (Esrafili-Dizaji and Rahimpour-Bonab 2013)
26. (Esfandiari 2015)
27. (Milani 2010)
28. (Burr 2009)
29. (Quester 1977)
30. (Coughlin 2009)
31. (Nuclear Threat Initiative 2017)
32. (World Nuclear Association 2020)
33. (Slivyak 2019)
34. (*Financial Tribune* 2019a)
35. (Vaez and Sadjadpour 2013)
36. (Vaez and Sadjadpour 2013)
37. (Barzegar 2012)

38. (Gallagher et al. 2019)
39. (AFP 2008)
40. (Mossavar-Rahmani 1981)
41. Iran became a net wheat exporter in 2018 (Badawi 2018).
42. (DW 2018)
43. (Bazoobandi 2019)
44. (Faucon and Rasmussen 2019)
45. (Embassy of the Kingdom of the Netherlands in Tehran 2019)
46. (Bozorgmehr 2017)
47. (Homa 2017)
48. (Aldroubi 2018)
49. (Sneddon 2015)
50. (Rahimov 2020)
51. (Kalehsar 2019)
52. (Atabi 2004)
53. (CMS Law 2016)
54. (International Renewable Energy Agency [IRENA] 2020)
55. (Euronews 2017)
56. (Azadi et al. 2017)
57. (Mills 2019)
58. (Bhambhani 2019)
59. (Ministry of Energy Renewable Energy and Energy Efficiency Organization (SATBA), n.d.)
60. (*Financial Tribune* 2020a)
61. (*Financial Tribune* 2016)
62. (Arefmanesh 2018)
63. (Karagiannopoulos 2018)
64. (Eghtesadonline.com 2019)
65. (AP 2020)
66. (Chitchian 2017)
67. (XE.com, n.d.)
68. (Arefmanesh 2018)
69. (Taherian 2018)
70. (Fadai et al. 2011)
71. (*Financial Tribune* 2019b)
72. (*Financial Tribune* 2020b)
73. (Al Bawaba 2017)
74. (Ghadir Energy Investment Company, n.d.)
75. (El Nakib 2018)
76. (Ahmad-Rashid 2017)
77. (BP 2020)
78. (International Energy Agency 2019b)
79. (Tehran Times 2020)

80. (Middle East Economic Survey 2020a)
81. (World Bank 2015)
82. (Wali 2020; Middle East Economic Survey 2020b)
83. (Ashwarya 2020)
84. (International Energy Agency 2019a)
85. (Poudineh et al., *Advancing Renewable Energy in Resource-Rich Economies of the MENA*, 2016)
86. (Al Khatteeb 2020)
87. (World Bank 2019)
88. (World Bank 2016; Government of Iraq 2015)
89. https://books.google.ae/books?id=EGlOBbPQpdYC&pg=PA99&lpg=PA99&dq=badush+megawatts&source=bl&ots=h88-YE7Lv2&sig=ACfU3U1NqvtZfbFoTC7lArvk19i4C-RpdQ&hl=en&sa=X&ved=2ahUKEwiUvI-R0P_pAhVtCWMBHYWEAl0Q6AEwAHoECAoQAQ#v=onepage&q=badush%20megawatts&f=false, p. 99.
90. https://www.washingtonpost.com/wp-dyn/content/article/2007/10/29/AR2007102902193.html?hpid=topnews.
91. (Qader and Hamid 2018)
92. (Kareem 2012)
93. (Abdullah 2019)
94. (Habib 2019)
95. (Karadeniz and Aboulenein 2018)
96. (Jongerden 2009)
97. E.g. (Mills, *A Rocky Road: Kurdish Oil and Independence*, 2018).
98. Qamar Energy analysis of Ministry of Electricity reported generation.
99. (International Energy Agency 2019a)
100. (Government of Iraq 2018)
101. (Nuclear Threat Initiative 2015)
102. (Chulov 2009)
103. (Nichols 2017)
104. https://public.tableau.com/views/IRENARETimeSeries/Charts?:embed=y&:showVizHome=no&publish=yes&:toolbar=no.
105. (booz&co 2012)
106. (Kami 2012)
107. (Government of Iraq 2018)
108. (Ministry of Electricity 2018)
109. (Maccagli 2015)
110. (Al Khatteeb 2020)
111. (Al Maleki 2020)
112. (Bellini 2019a)
113. (Bellini, Iraq Plans Second 750 MW Solar Tender, 2019b)
114. (MEED 2020)
115. (Fairley 2018)

116. (Al-Mawlawi 2020)
117. (Forozan and Shahi 2017)
118. (International Energy Agency 2019a)

Bibliography

Abdullah, Rawa. 2019. "KRG Restarts Work on Stalled Dam Projects." *Rudaw*, 24 December. Accessed June 27, 2020. https://www.rudaw.net/english/kurdistan/24122019.

AFP. 2008. "Iran Picks Firms to Hunt for New Nuclear Plant Sites." *AFP*, 19 August. Accessed July 9, 2020. https://www.energy-daily.com/reports/Iran_picks_firms_to_hunt_for_new_nuclear_plant_sites_999.html.

Ahmad-Rashid, Khalid. 2017. "Present and Future for Hydropower Developments in Kurdistan." *Energy Procedia* 112: 632–639. Accessed June 28, 2020. https://pdf.sciencedirectassets.com/277910/1-s2.0-S1876610217X00088/1-s2.0-S1876610217312559/main.pdf?X-Amz-Security-Token=IQoJb3JpZ2luX2VjEFUaCXVzLWVhc3QtMSJHMEUCIQDR4egj0LU3KtCpKo8PFSu4bW2Pqx1EZBdD2OqARM%2BpXwIgH%2Fn102%2BhmcjUgTWJvEpEG6nm3vr66bzvLg9%2F.

Al Bawaba. 2017. "Iran Launches Largest Solar Plant to Date, Announces Bids for Renewable Energy Projects." *Al Bawaba*, 27 April. Accessed June 29, 2020. https://www.albawaba.com/business/iran-largest-solar-power-plant-bids-renewable-energy-projects–968156.

Al Khatteeb, Luay, interview by Waylon Fairbanks. 2020. *Minister of Electricity* (15 May). Accessed June 29, 2020. https://www.mees.com/2020/5/15/geopolitical-risk/on-iraq-power-and-power-politics-mees-interview-with-luay-al-khatteeb/cf6ba480-96bc-11ea-9104-f105774a5b6c.

Al Maleki, Yesar. 2020. *Overview of Iraq's Renewable Energy Progress in 2019*. Iraq Energy Institute. Accessed June 29, 2020. https://iraqenergy.org/2020/02/20/overview-of-iraqs-renewable-energy-progress-in-2019/.

Aldroubi, Mina. 2018. "Turkey Steps in as Iran Cuts off Water Supplies to Iraq." *The National*, 10 October. Accessed June 28, 2020. https://www.thenational.ae/world/mena/turkey-steps-in-as-iran-cuts-off-water-supplies-to-iraq-1.779274.

Al-Mawlawi, Ali. 2020. *Public Sector Reform in Iraq*. Chatham House. Accessed June 28, 2020. https://www.chathamhouse.org/sites/default/files/2020-06-17-public-sector-reform-iraq-al-mawlawi.pdf.

AP. 2020. "Iran Now Says 5 Dead Out of 28 Infected with New Coronavirus." *Economic Times*, 22 February. Accessed June 28, 2020. https://m.economictimes.com/news/international/world-news/iran-now-says-5-dead-out-of-28-infected-with-new-coronavirus/articleshow/74256534.cms.

Arefmanesh, Sepehr. 2018. "Can Chinese Investment Bring Sunshine Back to Iran's Solar Industry?" *Bourse and Bazaar*, 4 September. Accessed June 28, 2020. https://www.bourseandbazaar.com/articles/2018/9/4/as-skies-darken-in-irans-economy-what-next-for-the-solar-industry.

Arjomand, Said Amir. 2020. *Constitution of the Islamic Republic.* 11 June. http://www.iranicaonline.org/articles/constitution-of-the-islamic-republic.

Ashwarya, Sujata. 2020. "Iraq's Power Sector: Problems and Prospects." *Georgetown Journal of International Affairs* (Georgetown). Accessed June 28, 2020. https://gjia.georgetown.edu/2020/01/13/iraqs-power-sector-problems-and-prospects/.

Atabi, F. 2004. "Renewable Energy in Iran: Challenges and Opportunities for Sustainable Development." *International Journal of Environmental Science and Technology*, 69–80. Accessed July 19, 2020.

Azadi, Pooya, Arash Nezam Sarmadi, Ali Mahmoudzadeh, and Tara Shirvani. 2017. "The Outlook for Natural Gas, Electricity, and Renewable Energy in Iran." Stanford Iran 2040 Project. Accessed June 27, 2020. https://iranian-studies.stanford.edu/sites/g/files/sbiybj6191/f/publications/the_outlook_for_natural_gas_electricity_and_renewable_energy_in_iran_5.pdf.

Badawi, Tamer. 2018. "Iran's Water Problem." Carnegie Endowment for International Peace. Accessed June 28, 2020. https://carnegieendowment.org/sada/77935.

Barzegar, Kayhan. 2012. "Iran's Nuclear Program." In *The Nuclear Question in the Middle East*, by Mehran Kamrava, 297. London: C. Hurst & Co.

Bazoobandi, Sara. 2019. *Iran's Revolutionary Guards: Four Decades of Expanded Business and Military Influence.* Washington, DC: Arab Gulf States Institute in Washington. Accessed June 28, 2020. https://agsiw.org/wp-content/uploads/2019/12/Sara-Bazoobandi_IRGC_ONLINE.pdf.

Bellini, Emiliano. 2019a. "Iraq Kicks off Huge 755 MW Solar Tender." *PV Magazine*, 3 May. Accessed June 28, 2020. https://www.pv-magazine.com/2019/05/03/iraq-kicks-off-huge-755-mw-solar-tender/.

———. 2019b. "Iraq Plans Second 750 MW Solar Tender." *PV Magazine*, 27 November. Accessed June 27, 2020. https://www.pv-magazine.com/2019/11/27/iraq-plans-second-750-mw-solar-tender/#:~:text=The%20Iraqi%20government%20is%20planning,prime%20minister%20Adil%20Abdul%2DMahdi.&text=The%20authorities%20want%20to%20build,30%20MW%20to%2050%20MW.

Bhambhani, Anu. 2019. "Iran's Markazi Province to Develop 1 GW Solar Power Plant with Funding From Unidentified UK Based Iranian Investor." *Taiyang News*, 9 January. Accessed July 9, 2020. http://taiyangnews.info/markets/iran-province-plans-1-gw-solar-project/.

booz&co. 2012. "Integrated National Energy Strategy (INES)." Baghdad, 174. Accessed June 28, 2020. http://documents1.worldbank.org/curated/en/

406941467995791680/pdf/105893-WP-PUBLIC-INES-Summary-Final-Report-VF.pdf.

Bozorgmehr, Najmeh. 2017. "Iran Cracks Down on Revolutionary Guards Business Network." *Financial Times*, 14 September. Accessed June 29, 2020. https://www.ft.com/content/43de1388-9857-11e7-a652-cde3f882dd7b.

BP. 2020. *BP Statistical Review of World Energy 2020*. BP. Accessed June 27, 2020. https://www.bp.com/en/global/corporate/energy-economics/statistical-review-of-world-energy.html.

Burr, William. 2009. "A Brief History of U.S.-Iranian Nuclear Negotiations." *Bulletin of the Atomic Scientists*, 21–34. Accessed June 11, 2020. http://www.nuclearfiles.org/menu/key-issues/nuclear-weapons/issues/proliferation/iran/A%20brief%20history%20of%20U.S.-Iranian%20nuclear%20negotiations.pdf.

Chitchian, Hamid, interview by Financial Tribune. 2017. *Energy Minister* (16 August). Accessed June 29, 2020. https://financialtribune.com/articles/energy/70500/power-plant-privatizations-reach-55-more-to-come.

Chow, Edward, Cyrus Ashayeri, and Andrew J. Stanley. 2018. *The Future of Iran's Oil and Gas Industry*. US Association for Energy Economics. Accessed June 27, 2020. https://dx.doi.org/10.2139/ssrn.3269898.

Chulov, Martin. 2009. "Iraq Goes Nuclear with Plans for new Reactor Programme." *The Guardian*, 2009 October. Accessed June 27, 2020. https://www.theguardian.com/world/2009/oct/27/iraq-nuclear-reactor-programme.

CMS Law. 2016. "Renewable Energy in Iran." Accessed June 29, 2020. http://www.satba.gov.ir/suna_content/media/image/2017/02/5196_orig.pdf?t=636219021775330000#:~:text=The%20Iranian%20government%20has%20now,additional%202%2C500%20MW%20by%202030.

Coughlin, Con. 2009. *Khomeini's Ghost: Iran Since 1979*. Pan Macmillan.

Dehghanpisheh, Babak. 2017. "Iran Starts Gas Exports to Iraq, Iranian Official Tells IRNA." *Reuters*, 21 June. Accessed June 27, 2020. https://www.reuters.com/article/us-iran-iraq-gas-idUSKBN19C2PT.

DW. 2018. "همدستی همه جناح‌های حکومت در سدسازی بی‌رویه در ایران." *DW.com*, 7 February. Accessed June 28, 2020. https://www.dw.com/fa-ir.

Ebrahimi, S. N., and A. Shiroui Khouzani. 2003. "The Contractual Form of Iran's Buy-Back Contracts in Comparison with Production Sharing and Service Contract." *Society of Petroleum Engineers*. https://www.onepetro.org/conference-paper/SPE-81547-MS.

Eghtesadonline.com. 2019. "Renewable Power Expansion Behind Schedule: Satba." *Eghtesadonline*, 2 December. Accessed June 27, 2020. https://www.en.eghtesadonline.com/Section-economy-4/31059-renewable-power-expansion-behind-schedule-satba.

El Nakib, Bachir. 2018. *OFAC—Iran Publication Re-Imposed Sanctions 700 Blocked Persons.* 11 May. Accessed June 29, 2020. https://calert.info/details.php?id=1710.

Embassy of the Kingdom of the Netherlands in Tehran. 2019. "Uniting Water Energy Food Nexus in Iran."

Esfandiari, Golnaz. 2015. "The Father of Iran's Nuclear Program Recalls How It All Began." *RFERL*, 3 July. Accessed June 11, 2020. https://www.rferl.org/a/father-of-iran-nuclear-program-recalls-how-it-began/27108228.html.

Esrafili-Dizaji, B., and H. Rahimpour-Bonab. 2013. "A Review of Permo-Triassic Reservoir Rocks in the Zagros Area, SW Iran: Influence of the Qatar-Fars Arch." *Journal of Petroleum Geology*, 257–279. Accessed June 11, 2020. https://onlinelibrary.wiley.com/doi/abs/10.1111/jpg.12555.

Eurasianet. 2017. *Turkmenistan, Iran Gas Dispute Serves as Ill Omen for New Year.* 2 January. Accessed July 9, 2020. https://eurasianet.org/turkmenistan-iran-gas-dispute-serves-as-ill-omen-for-new-year.

Euronews. 2017. "Largest Solar Power Plant in Iran Opens." *Euronews*, 31 July. Accessed July 9, 2020. https://www.euronews.com/2017/07/31/largest-solar-power-plant-in-iran-opens.

Fadai, Dawud, Zahra Shams Esfandabadi, and Azadeh Abbasi. 2011. "Analyzing the Cause of Non-development of Renewable Energy-Related Industries in Iran." *Renewable and Sustainable Energy Reviews* 15 (6): 2690–2695. Accessed July 19, 2020. https://doi.org/10.1016/j.rser.2011.03.001.

Fairley, Peter. 2018. "Rooftop Solar Takes Hold in Iraq in the Aftermath of ISIS." *IEEE Spectrum*, 23 May. Accessed June 28, 2020. https://spectrum.ieee.org/energy/renewables/rooftop-solar-takes-hold-in-iraq-in-the-aftermath-of-isis.

Fallahi, Ebrahim. 2019. "Iran Electricity Issue: Should We Expect Blackouts Again?" *Tehran Times*, 21 May. https://www.tehrantimes.com/news/436178/Iran-electricity-issue-should-we-expect-blackouts-again.

Faucon, Benoit, and Sune Engel Rasmussen. 2019. "Crushed by U.S. Sanctions, Iran Pins Economic Hopes on Mall Developer." *Wall Street Journal*, 9 July. Accessed July 19, 2020. https://www.wsj.com/articles/crushed-by-u-s-sanctions-iran-pins-economic-hopes-on-mall-developer-11562670006.

Fesharaki, Fereidun. 1976. "A Revaluation of the Middle Eastern Oil Reserves: the Case of Iran." *Pakistan Horizon* (Pakistan Institute of International Affairs) 29 (2): 13–32. Accessed July 9, 2020. https://www.jstor.org/stable/41403865?seq=1.

Financial Tribune. 2016. "Renewable Energy Scheme for State-Owned Property." *Financial Tribune*, 13 November. Accessed July 19, 2020. https://financialtribune.com/articles/energy/53506/renewable-energy-scheme-for-state-owned-property.

———. 2019a. "AEOI Elaborates on Work for Nuclear Power Plant's 2nd Unit." *Financial Tribune*, 15 October. Accessed July 9, 2020. https://financialtribune.com/articles/energy/100354/aeoi-elaborates-on-work-for-nuclear-power-plant-s-2nd-unit.

———. 2019b. "Rise in Electricity and Water Tariffs in Iran." *Financial Tribune*, 5 April. Accessed June 26, 2020. https://financialtribune.com/articles/energy/97278/rise-in-electricity-and-water-tariffs-in-iran#:~:text=Electricity%20is%20presently%20sold%20at,10.7%20cents)%20per%20cubic%20meters.

———. 2020a. "Green Energy Gets a Shot in the Arm From Majlis." *Energy Tribune*, 25 April. Accessed July 9, 2020. https://financialtribune.com/articles/energy/103016/green-energy-gets-a-shot-in-the-arm-from-majlis.

———. 2020b. "Iran's Energy Subsidy Policy Is Dysfunctional; Clean Energy a Far Cry." *Energy Tribune*, 28 February. Accessed July 9, 2020. https://financialtribune.com/articles/energy/102372/iran-s-energy-subsidy-policy-is-dysfunctional-clean-energy-a-far-cry.

Forozan, Hesam, and Afshin Shahi. 2017. "The Military and the State in Iran: The Economic Rise of the Revolutionary Guards." *The Middle East Journal*. Accessed July 9, 2020. https://www.researchgate.net/publication/313464589_The_Military_and_the_State_in_Iran_The_Economic_Rise_of_the_Revolutionary_Guards.

Gallagher, Nancy, Ebrahim Mohseni, and Clay Ramsay. 2019. *Iranian Public Opinion under "Maximum Pressure"*. School of Public Policy, Center for International & Security Studies at Maryland, 44. Accessed June 27, 2020. https://static1.squarespace.com/static/5525d831e4b09596848428f2/t/5dc045d33ef64d7e77410e79/1572881886712/Iranian+PO+under+Maximum+Pressure_101819_full.pdf.

Geranmayeh, Ellie. 2020. *Reviving the Revolutionaries: How Trump's Maximum Pressure Is Shifting Iran's Domestic Politics*. European Council on Foreign Relations, 40. Accessed June 29, 2020. https://www.ecfr.eu/page/-/reviving_the_revolutionaries_how_trumps_maximum_pressure_is_shifting_irans.pdf.

Ghadir Energy Investment Company. n.d. *Solar Power Plants*. Accessed June 29, 2020. http://en.geicgroup.com/products/page-30/page-44/.

Government of Iraq. 2018. "Iraq Reconstruction and Investment." 301. Accessed June 28, 2020. http://www.cabinet.iq/uploads/Iraq%20Reconstruction/Iraq%20Recons%20&%20Inves.pdf.

Government of Iraq. 2015. "وثيقة المساهمات المحددة وطنياً تجاه الإتفاق الجديد لتغير المناخ." 16. Accessed June 29, 2020. https://www4.unfccc.int/sites/submissions/INDC/Published%20Documents/Iraq/1/INDC-Iraq.pdf.

Habib, Mustafa. 2019. "In Iraq's Water Crisis, the Country with the Biggest Dam Wins." *Niqash*, 2 October. Accessed June 28, 2020. https://www.niqash.org/en/articles/economy/5995/.

Harris, Kevan. 2013. "The Rise of the Subcontractor State: Politics of Pseudo-Privatization in the Islamic Republic of Iran." *International Journal of Middle East Studies* 45 (1): 45–70. Accessed June 29, 2020. https://doi.org/10.1017/S0020743812001250.

Higginbotham, Adam. 2019. *Midnight in Chernobyl.* Simon & Schuster.

Homa, Ava. 2017. "Iran Reduces Water Flow to Kurdistan Over Referendum." *Kurdistan24*, 10 October. Accessed June 28, 2020. https://www.kurdistan24.net/en/news/bceb3e39-9983-43f3-a4e1-7350353cfb91#:~:text=Having%20joined%20Iraq%20and%20Turkey,Al%20Zab%20in%20the%20Region.

International Energy Agency. 2019a. *Iraq's Energy Sector: A Roadmap to a Brighter Future.* International Energy Agency, 59. Accessed June 28, 2020. https://www.connaissancedesenergies.org/sites/default/files/pdf-actualites/Iraq_Energy_Outlook.pdf.

———. 2019b. *Natural Gas Production and Flaring in Iraq, 2000–2030.* 18 November. Accessed June 28, 2020. https://www.iea.org/data-and-statistics/charts/natural-gas-production-and-flaring-in-iraq-2000-2030.

International Renewable Energy Agency (IRENA). 2020. "Renewable Capacity Statistics 2020." Abu Dhabi. Accessed June 25, 2020. https://www.irena.org/publications/2020/Mar/Renewable-Capacity-Statistics-2020.

Iran Data Portal. 2009. "Full Text of the Law for the Targeting of Subsidies." *Iran Data Portal.* December. https://irandataportal.syr.edu/full-text-of-the-law-for-the-targeting-of-subsidies-december-2009.

Iranian Students' News Agency. 2013. "سیاست‌های کلی «اقتصاد مقاومتی» ابلاغ شد." *Iranian Students' News Agency.* Accessed July 19, 2020. https://www.isna.ir/news/92113020882/%D8%B3%DB%8C%D8%A7%D8%B3%D8%AA-%D9%87%D8%A7%DB%8C-%DA%A9%D9%84%DB%8C-%D8%A7%D9%82%D8%AA%D8%B5%D8%A7%D8%AF-%D9%85%D9%82%D8%A7%D9%88%D9%85%D8%AA%DB%8C-%D8%A7%D8%A8%D9%84%D8%A7%D8%BA-%D8%B4%D8%AF.

Jalilvand, David Ramin. 2013. *Iran's Gas Exports: Can Past Failure Become Future Success?* Oxford Institute for Energy Studies. Accessed July 10, 2020. https://www.oxfordenergy.org/wpcms/wp-content/uploads/2013/06/NG-78.pdf.

Jongerden, Joost. 2009. *Dams and Politics in Turkey: Utilizing Water, Developing Conflict.* Middle East Policy Council. Accessed July 9, 2020. https://mepc.org/dams-and-politics-turkey-utilizing-water-developing-conflict.

Kalehsar, Omid Shokri. 2019. *Iran's Transition to Renewable Energy: Challenges and Opportunities.* Volume XXVI, Middle East Policy Council. Accessed July 19, 2020. https://mepc.org/journal/irans-transition-renewable-energy-challenges-and-opportunities.

Kami, Aseel. 2012. "Iraq Plans to Invest Up to $1.6 bln in Solar and Wind Energy." *Reuters*, 15 October. Accessed June 28, 2020. https://www.reuters.com/article/iraq-electricity-solar/iraq-plans-to-invest-up-to-1-6-bln-in-solar-and-wind-energy-idUSL5E8LFK7H20121015.

Karadeniz, Tulay, and Ahmed Aboulenein. 2018. "Turkey Halts Filling of Tigris Dam After Iraq Complains of Water Shortages." *Reuters*, 7 June. Accessed July 9, 2020. https://www.reuters.com/article/us-iraq-turkey/turkey-halts-filling-tigris-dam-after-iraq-complains-of-water-shortages-idUSKCN1J320X.

Karagiannopoulos, Lefteris. 2018. "Exclusive: UK's Quercus Pulls Plug on $570 Million Iran Solar Plant as Sanctions Bite." *Reuters*, 14 August. Accessed June 27, 2020. https://www.reuters.com/article/us-iran-sanctions-quercus-exclusive/exclusive-uks-quercus-pulls-plug-on-570-million-iran-solar-plant-as-sanctions-bite-idUSKBN1KZ0ZR.

Kareem, Yaseen H. 2012. "Energy Sources and Utilization in Iraqi Kurdistan Region." *Institute of Energy Economics Japan*. Accessed June 27, 2020. https://eneken.ieej.or.jp/data/4502.pdf.

Khoshnood, Ardavan, and Arvin Khoshnood. 2016. "The Death of an Emperor—Mohammad Reza Shah Pahlavi and His Political Cancer." *Alexandria Journal of Medicine*, 201–208. Accessed June 11, 2020. https://www.sciencedirect.com/science/article/pii/S2090506815000822.

Maccagli, Giulia. 2015. *Jordan, Second Round of Licensing Renewable Energy*. 8 June. Accessed June 29, 2020. http://www.eresenergy.net/news/2016/9/1/jordan-final-ranking-qualified-proposals-stage-ii-pv.

MEED. 2020. "Acwa Power Eyes Iraq Solar Schemes." *Power Technology*, 19 June. Accessed June 29, 2020. https://www.power-technology.com/comment/acwa-power-iraq-solar-schemes/.

Middle East Economic Survey. 2020a. "Iraq Advances Kuwait Power Link." *Middle East Economic Survey*, 3 July: 17. Accessed July 9, 2020.

———. 2020b. "KRG: Delayed Power Boost." *Middle East Economic Survey*, 17 July.

Milani, Abbas. 2010. "The Shah's Atomic Dreams." *Foreign Policy*, 29 December. Accessed June 26, 2020. https://foreignpolicy.com/2010/12/29/the-shahs-atomic-dreams/.

Mills, Robin. 2018. *A Rocky Road: Kurdish Oil and Independence*. Baghdad: Iraq Energy Institute. Accessed June 27, 2020. https://iraqenergy.org/2018/02/19/a-rocky-road-kurdish-oil-and-independence/.

———. 2019. *Iran Energy Needs and Nuclear Power*. Nuclear Proliferation Education Center. http://www.npolicy.org/article.php?aid=1374&tid=5.

Ministry of Electricity. 2018. "MOE Plan and Renewable Energy Plan." *Iraq Energy Forum*. Baghdad: Iraq Energy Institute, 29. Accessed June 29, 2020. https://iraqenergy.org/product/ministry-of-electricity-moe-plan-renewable-energy-plan/.

Ministry of Energy Renewable Energy and Energy Efficiency Organization (SATBA). n.d. *Guaranteed Feed in Tariffs (FiTs)*. Accessed June 27, 2020. http://www.satba.gov.ir/suna_content/media/image/2019/12/7999_orig.pdf.

Mossavar-Rahmani, Bijan. 1981. *Energy Policy in Iran: Domestic Choices and International Implications*. Pergamon Press.

National Climate Change Committee. 2015. "Intended Nationally Determined Contribution." Accessed June 29, 2020. https://www4.unfccc.int/sites/submissions/INDC/Published%20Documents/Iran/1/INDC%20Iran%20Final%20Text.pdf.

Nichols, Michelle. 2017. "Iraq Asks U.N. for Help to Build New Nuclear Power Reactor." *Reuters*, 24 September. Accessed June 27, 2020. https://www.reuters.com/article/us-iraq-nuclear/iraq-asks-u-n-for-help-to-build-new-nuclear-power-reactor-idUSKCN1BY0XY.

Nuclear Threat Initiative. 2015. *Iraq*. July. Accessed June 27, 2020. https://www.nti.org/learn/countries/iraq/nuclear/.

———. 2017. *Bushehr Nuclear Power Plant (BNPP)*. 10 July. Accessed June 11, 2020. https://www.nti.org/learn/facilities/184/.

Omidvar, Hedayat. 2019. "Iran, the Key Player of Transition." *International Journal of Petroleum Research* 3 (1): 255–261. Accessed June 27, 2020. https://madridge.org/international-journal-of-petrochemistry/ijpr-1000144.php.

OPEC. 1999. *OPEC Annual Statistical Bulletin*. Vienna: OPEC. Accessed June 11, 2020. https://www.opec.org/opec_web/static_files_project/media/downloads/publications/ASB1999.pdf.

Parris, Richard. 2016. *Clifford Chance Advising Unit Group on Ground Breaking Multi-Billion Euro IPP Power Projects in Iran*. 7 June. Accessed July 9, 2020. https://www.cliffordchance.com/news/news/2016/06/clifford-chance-advising-unit-group-on-ground-breaking-multi-bil.html.

Poudineh, Rahmatallah, Anupama Sen, and Bassam Fattouh. 2016. *Advancing Renewable Energy in Resource-Rich Economies of the MENA*. Oxford Institute for Energy Studies. Accessed July 9, 2020. https://www.oxfordenergy.org/wpcms/wp-content/uploads/2016/10/Advancing-Renewable-Energy-in-Resource-Rich-Economies-of-the-MENA-MEP-15.pdf.

———. 2021. "Electricity Markets in the Resource-Rich Countries of the MENA: Adapting for the Transition Era." *Economics of Energy & Environmental Policy* 10 (1). https://doi.org/10.5547/2160-5890.10.1.rpou.

Qader, Histyar, and Awara Hamid. 2018. "The Secret History Behind The Stalled Project To Solve Iraq's Water Problems." *Niqash*, 5 July. Accessed June 27, 2020. https://www.niqash.org/en/articles/politics/5950/.

Quester, George H. 1977. "The Shah and the Bomb." *Policy Sciences* 8: 21–32. https://www.jstor.org/stable/4531668?seq=1.

Rahimov, Rahim. 2020. "Iran Completes Controversial Hydropower Project on Aras River." *Eurasia Daily Monitor* 17 (91). Accessed June 29, 2020. https://jamestown.org/program/iran-completes-controversial-hydropower-project-on-aras-river/.

Sharifi, Keyvan, and H. Ali Gougerdchian. 2012. "Overview on Iran CNG Industry Status, Opportunities and Threats." *International Gas Union*. Kuala Lumpur. Accessed June 27, 2020. http://www.iangv.org/category/country/iran/.

Slivyak, Vladimir. 2019. *Dreams and Reality of the Russian Reactor Export*. Moscow: Ecodefense, 22. Accessed June 23, 2020. https://ecdru.files.wordpress.com/2019/03/rosatom-report2019.pdf.

Sneddon, Christopher. 2015. *Concrete Revolution: Large Dams, Cold War Geopolitics, and the US Bureau of Reclamation*. Chicago: University of Chicago Press. Accessed June 28, 2020.

Taherian, Sajjad. 2018. *Strong Solar Growth in Iran Though Still Challenges*. 25 May. Accessed June 26, 2020. https://www.pveurope.eu/solar-generator/strong-solar-growth-iran-though-still-challenges.

Tasnim News. 2016. "۸ ماهه ۱۰ هزار میلیارد تومان از بدهی وزارت نیرو پرداخت شد." *Tasnim News*, 6 November. Accessed June 28, 2020. https://www.tasnimnews.com/fa/news/1395/08/15/1231725/8-%D9%85%D8%A7%D9%87%D9%87-10-%D9%87%D8%B2%D8%A7%D8%B1-%D9%85%DB%8C%D9%84%DB%8C%D8%A7%D8%B1%D8%AF-%D8%AA%D9%88%D9%85%D8%A7%D9%86-%D8%A7%D8%B2-%D8%A8%D8%AF%D9%87%DB%8C-%D9%88%D8%B2%D8%A7%D8%B1%D8%AA-%D9.

Tehran Times. 2020. "Iran's Daily Gas Exports to Iraq at 32 mcm." *Tehran Times*, 17 April. Accessed June 28, 2020. https://www.tehrantimes.com/news/447238/Iran-s-daily-gas-exports-to-Iraq-at-32-mcm.

Vaez, Ali, and Karim Sadjadpour. 2013. *Iran's Nuclear Odyssey: Costs and Risks*. Carnegie Endowment for International Peace. Accessed June 29, 2020. https://carnegieendowment.org/2013/04/02/iran-s-nuclear-odyssey-costs-and-risks-pub-51346.

Wali, Zhelwan Z. 2020. "Unique Power Plant to Increase Electricity in Kurdistan Region by 10 percent." *Rudaw*, 14 July. Accessed July 19, 2020. https://www.rudaw.net/english/kurdistan/140720201.

World Bank. 2015. *The Kurdistan Region of Iraq: Assessing the Economic and Social Impact of the Syrian Conflict and ISIS*. World Bank Group. Accessed July 9, 2020.

———. 2016. *Iraq (Intended) Nationally Determined Contribution—(I)NDC*. World Bank Group. Accessed June 29, 2020. http://spappssecext.worldbank.org/sites/indc/PDF_Library/IQ.pdf.

———. 2019. "Project Appraisal Document on a Proposed Loan in the Amount of US$200 Million to the Republic of Iraq for an Electricity Services

Reconstruction and Enhancement Project." Accessed July 19, 2020. http://documents1.worldbank.org/curated/en/504001557108087756/pdf/Iraq-Electricity-Services-Reconstruction-and-Enhancement-Project.pdf.

World Nuclear Association. 2020. *Nuclear Power in Iran*. May. Accessed June 11, 2020. https://www.world-nuclear.org/information-library/country-profiles/countries-g-n/iran.aspx.

XE.com. n.d. Accessed June 27, 2020. https://www.xe.com/currencytables/?from=USD&date=2018-06-30.

Yousefi, G. Reza, Sajjad Makhdoomi Kaviri, Mohammad Amin Latify, and Iman Rahmati. 2017. "Electricity Industry Restructuring in Iran." *Energy Policy* 108: 212–226. https://fardapaper.ir/mohavaha/uploads/2017/09/32544564789765445634345455.pdf.

CHAPTER 3

Pairing Coal with Solar: The UAE's Fragmented Electricity Policy

Jim Krane

Introduction

The United Arab Emirates' transformation over the past decade into an interventionist player in regional and global politics has bled into domestic energy policy, incentivizing the diversification of fuels and technology choices for electricity generation. A country that once depended overwhelmingly on a single electricity source—thermal generation using domestic natural gas—is quickly building out a diversified power sector leveraging imports of gas in various forms, along with coal, nuclear, and solar power.

The UAE's fast-evolving power portfolio appears to have been assembled in a fragmented way, outside the reach of centralized planning and without fully exploiting the national electricity grid. Instead, changes in domestic energy policy revolve around questions of subnational autonomy, comparative cost, and political risk.

J. Krane (✉)
Rice University's Baker Institute, Houston, TX, United States
e-mail: jkrane@rice.edu

R. Mills and L.-C. Sim (eds.), *Low Carbon Energy in the Middle East and North Africa*, International Political Economy Series,
https://doi.org/10.1007/978-3-030-59554-8_3

Oil-rich Abu Dhabi has spent huge sums on clean power from nuclear and renewables, while investing in domestic natural gas production to replace imports from rival Qatar. Neighboring Dubai seeks to avoid dependence on Abu Dhabi with a cost-driven pairing of cheap and dirty Chinese coal with even cheaper photovoltaic solar. Sharjah, like Dubai, pursues autonomy from the national grid, while the four northern emirates move in the opposite direction, reinforcing dependence on power supplied by Abu Dhabi.

The inconsistent power sector strategy is reflected in the UAE's disunity in foreign relations, with Dubai's long-held neutrality and associations with Iran and Qatar coming under challenge from Abu Dhabi's increasingly interventionist role in the region. Energy policy in Abu Dhabi aims to increase freedom of maneuver in foreign policy through US-style 'energy independence' aspirations, which protect unfettered nationalist policies from being restrained by dependence on imports.

Further factors are coloring negative views of gas:

- The UAE has enjoined—or, arguably, instigated—regional political disputes with Iran and Qatar, the two countries holding the largest gas reserves in the region. Ongoing imports from Qatar are exposed to risk of cutoff or changes in contractual terms. Imports from Iran would be similarly exposed, had they started.
- Cost of solar power and battery storage continues to fall. Reduced costs, along with geographical advantages, have encouraged the UAE to leverage renewables for an increasing role in current generation and future plans.
- The UAE's natural gas imports have exposed it to fluctuating market prices on fuels that it sells domestically at low, fixed prices. Increases in domestic supply, until recently, were made more difficult by complex geology. Recent discoveries and increasing production of associated gas have moderated these factors.[1]

To mitigate the uncertainties associated with natural gas, utility planners have designated coal, nuclear, and solar to assume more than half of gas' current share in the national generation mix. If plans in Abu Dhabi and Dubai are followed through to fruition, utility planners forecast that natural gas demand would flatten or even decline.[2] Ultimately, policy-makers aim to end the UAE's status as a net importer of natural gas by 2030.[3]

This paper examines the political and strategic drivers for the UAE's shift toward coal, nuclear, and solar power. It finds that while coal and solar appear competitive with gas on the basis of cost, and nuclear and coal provide reliability of supply, the policy is also being driven by higher priority strategic rationales around power projection, external image enhancement, energy supply security, and ultimately the security and stability of the regime.

Background on UAE Power Sector

Electricity policy in the UAE is of vital importance due to two extremes: high average temperatures and high levels of demand. Per capita electricity consumption in the UAE is near world-leading levels, at 13,000 kilowatt-hours per capita in 2017.[4] Likewise, primary energy consumption averaged nearly 500 gigajoules per person in 2018, the world's 4th highest and nearly 7 times the world average (Fig. 3.1). High rates

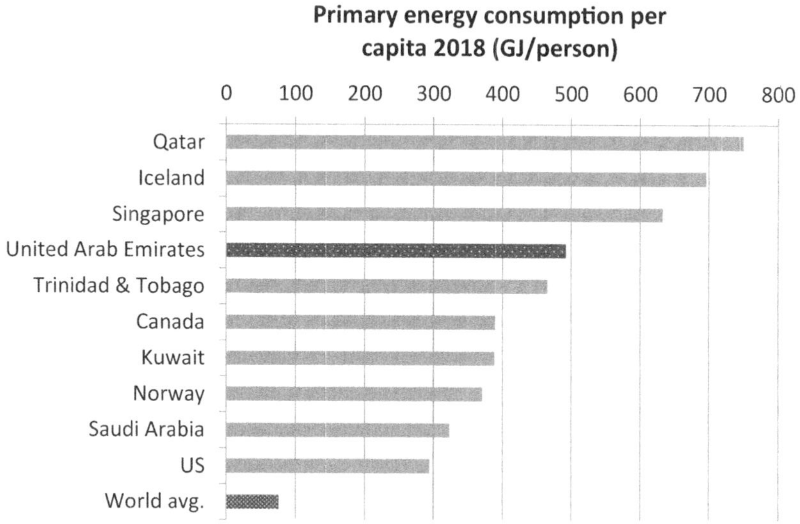

Fig. 3.1 Primary energy consumption per capita 2018 (*Source* BP 2019)

of demand are driven by high incomes, low fixed prices, high ambient temperatures, and inefficient designs of buildings and communities. Cooling buildings accounts for roughly 60% of power consumption.

Major disparities in demand occur between UAE nationals and generally poorer expatriates who make up 90% of the population. Emirati households in Abu Dhabi consume around three times more electricity than (typically smaller) expatriate households, and about five times more than a household in the US state of Arizona.[5] Further discrepancies exist among residents in the poorer northern emirates of Sharjah, Ajman, Umm al-Quwain, Ras al-Khaimah and Fujairah, and the dominant emirates of Dubai, the UAE financial capital, and Abu Dhabi, the political and economic capital. The disparities are bound up in constitutional provisions enshrining ownership of natural resources in individual emirates.

In 2018, fossil fuels made up 99% of primary energy consumption in the UAE. Oil, the dominant transportation fuel and a backup feedstock for power generation, held 40% of the overall energy market while gas retained nearly 60%.

Coal use, once nearly nonexistent in the UAE, rose by 22% per year over the decade to 2018, driven by substitution for natural gas in cement and ceramics manufacture outside Abu Dhabi. The UAE is destined to become a much more significant coal consumer upon the 2020 startup of Dubai's 2.4-gigawatt Hassyan coal-fired power plant. A planned expansion of the $3.4 billion Hassyan plant would push its capacity to 3.6 GW.[6]

The UAE's aspirational power mix calls for expanding coal-fired power to generate 12% of the country's electricity, an installation estimated at 11.2 GW of capacity,[7] more than coal capacity operating in Canada or Malaysia in 2019.[8] A quadrupling of coal capacity is unlikely, however, given the associated environmental and reputational damage, as well as the falling cost of competing technologies.[9] Since little coal is found in the Middle East, and none on the Arabian Peninsula, Middle Eastern coal is imported, mainly from Colombia (3.5 mtoe in 2018), Russia (1.7), and South Africa (1.5)[10] (Fig. 3.2).

Much of the diversification referenced in the introduction was yet to arrive at the time of writing. Some 98% of the UAE's electricity in 2018 was produced by combusting fossil fuels, nearly all of it from natural gas (41 bcm of a total 77 bcm consumed in the UAE 2018[11]) with small

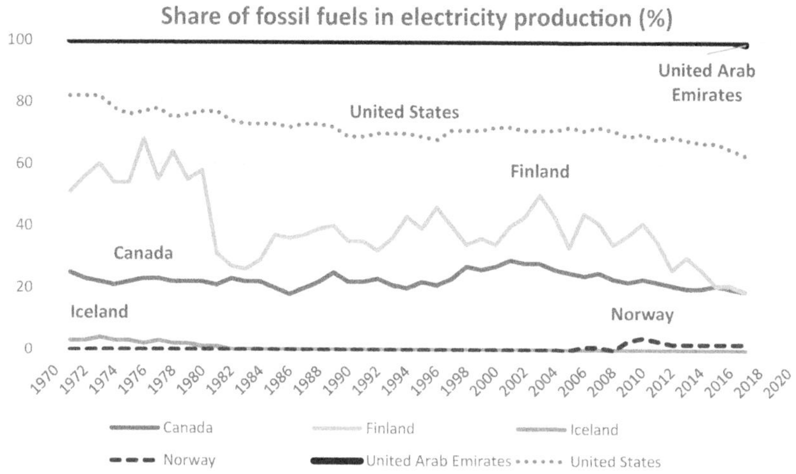

Fig. 3.2 Share of fossil fuels in electricity production. The UAE's electricity production is dominated by fossil fuels, in comparison with smaller amounts used in other high per capita consuming countries. However, much of the non-fossil generation depicted here depends on large hydropower and nuclear resources which are less intermittent than competing renewable technologies (IEA 2019)

amounts of oil-based fuel and an even smaller amount of solar power (Table 3.1/Fig. 3.3).

The power sector was to have been diversified by 2018 with the startup of Abu Dhabi's $25 billion Barakah nuclear power plant. However, problems emerged that delayed construction for three years. These included discovery of counterfeit parts supplied using forged safety documents[12] as

Table 3.1 UAE primary energy and power generation by fuel

	% of 2018 primary energy consumption	*% of 2018 power generation*
Natural gas	59	98
Oil	40	1.2
Coal	0.94	0
Renewables	0.19	0.7

Source BP 2019

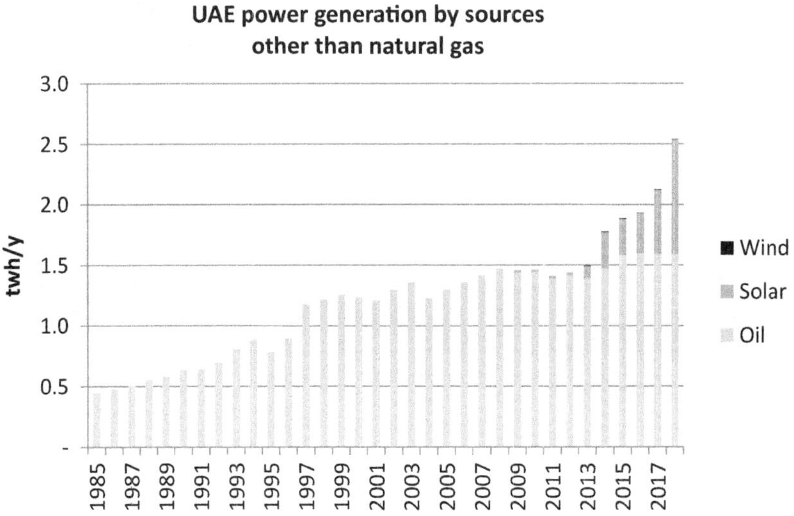

Fig. 3.3 Power generation by sources other than natural gas. Oil-based fuels were the main backup for natural gas, but solar power has increased since 2013 (*Source* BP 2019)

well as voids found in the concrete walls of two of the four units.[13] These issues prevented licensing and operation of the four 1.4 gigawatt nuclear generation reactors, the first of which was completed in 2018. Startup of the first reactor was achieved in 2020.[14]

Dubai and Abu Dhabi have also developed growing amounts of solar-powered generation (a combination of photovoltaic and concentrating solar power). These sources provided less than 1% of the UAE's electricity in 2018. Even so, growth in capacity nearly doubled over 2017, from 350 MW to almost 600 MW.[15] By 2019, capacity reached nearly 2.1 GW. A negligible amount of wind-generated electricity in the UAE is provided by a single 850 kilowatt turbine on Sir Bani Yas Island.[16]

As in other aspects of the UAE's energy profile, the national power sector is dominated by Abu Dhabi, with more than half the country's 30 GW of installed capacity, mainly gas-fired combined cycle gas turbine (CCGT) plants (Table 3.2). Abu Dhabi also supplies power to most of the other emirates, via the fully interconnected UAE national grid. Dubai, however, is fully self-sufficient in power generation. Once the Hassyan

Table 3.2 UAE installed power generation capacity by type, 2019

Power authority	*Total installed capacity*	*Solar*	*CCGT*	*Steam turbine*	*Gas turbine*	*Diesel*
EWEC Abu Dhabi (10 gas-fired, 3 solar*)	16,740	1780	14,678	1027	867	0
Dubai Electricity and Water Authority (DEWA) (10 gas-fired, 4 solar**)	10,703	713	7574	340	2076	0
Sharjah Electricity and Water Authority (SEWA) (6 gas/diesel)	2846	–	–	432	2382	32
Federal Electricity and Water Authority (FEWA) (3 gas/diesel)	703	–	–	–	703	0
Total (MW)	30,871	2493	22,252	1799	6028	32
%		8.1%	72.1%	5.8%	19.5%	0.1%

*50 MW CSP, 1.28 GW PV; **713 MW PV

Source Baker Institute, Ministry of Energy and Industry, MEES 2019

coal plant is complete, Dubai will have a generation-reserve margin that reaches 25% beyond 2020 peak demand. Dubai is not expected to import power from Abu Dhabi, even after the nuclear plants are online. Sharjah, too, is developing new CCGT plants that will allow it to become independent of Abu Dhabi power imports as soon as 2021.[17]

As may be apparent, planning for power generation expansions in Dubai, Sharjah and Abu Dhabi has been conducted independently and not coordinated through the central government. Dubai's decision to invest in coal was made when LNG prices were over $10 mmbtu and did not consider the scenario of falling LNG prices or a gas glut materializing in the region. Meanwhile, Abu Dhabi's 2008 decision to pursue nuclear power acknowledged that nuclear was not the most cost-competitive form of generation available at the time, and others—including coal—were cheaper.[18]

Clean Energy Goals Versus Reality

The onset of coal-fired power in the UAE runs counter to the 'green' energy narrative that policy elites have cultivated. In 2006, Abu Dhabi launched a strategic campaign to champion environmental initiatives, announcing it would build the world's first 'zero-carbon city'. Masdar City, as the development was called, was to receive $15 billion in government funding for zero-carbon housing for 40,000 residents and 1500 businesses, a carbon management unit, a clean technology investment fund, and a graduate school affiliated with the Massachusetts Institute of Technology, and sundry clean energy projects.[19] Amid worldwide accolades over the ambitious project, then-CEO Sultan Ahmed al-Jaber said in 2007 that Masdar enjoyed 'an unlimited budget for renewable energy projects.'[20]

Energy policymakers went further in 2009, declaring that Abu Dhabi would leverage its ample sunshine and vacant land to join the European clean energy vanguard. By 2020, the Abu Dhabi government announced, renewable energy sources were to account for at least 7% of the emirate's total electric power generation capacity (Table 3.3).[21] When bundled with its concurrent nuclear plans, Abu Dhabi pledged that zero-carbon sources would account for 24% of its electricity generation capacity. The

Table 3.3 Various 'green energy' targets announced in the UAE since 2006

Clean energy targets by emirate
Abu Dhabi
Create zero-emission city Masdar, operating on 100% renewable power
2020: Renewable power 7% of power mix
2021: Clean energy (solar + nuclear) 27% of power mix
Dubai
2020: 7% of power generation from renewables
2030: Reach 5000 MW solar capacity (25% of power mix)
2030: Burn waste to produce power, eliminate waste to landfill
2050: 75% of power from "clean" sources
Ras Al Khaimah
2040: 25–30% of power from "clean" sources
UAE
2050: 44% of UAE power generation capacity from renewables; 70% reduction in power sector carbon emissions from "business as usual" case

Source Compiled by author

two pledges appeared aimed to transform global public perceptions of the UAE from an autocratic petrostate that was an outsized producer, exporter, consumer, and subsidizer of fossil fuels, to a progressive haven for ambitious environmental goals.

The Masdar announcement came at a time when domestic production of associated natural gas—that produced in tandem with oil—began to lag growth in demand, and when oil prices were breaching new highs, driven by new consumption in China. Abu Dhabi was receiving an enormous windfall in oil profits while simultaneously grappling with a shortage of its main power generation feedstock.

Clean energy exuberance in Abu Dhabi was short-lived. Masdar's ambitions were scaled back after the 2009 recession, and several projects were cancelled or downsized. Among the victims was Masdar City itself, which saw its zero-carbon promise dropped as too expensive. The city's size was reduced and completion date pushed back. Also shelved was a 400 MW hydrogen power plant that was to have been built jointly with BP.[22] Construction and operating costs for concentrating solar power plant Shams 1 (50 MW of solar augmented by 50 MW of gas-fired generation) were so high that LCOE for the plant was estimated at 40 US cents per kilowatt-hour.[23] Two follow-on phases were cancelled.

The downsizing of Masdar, Shams, and Abu Dhabi's renewables ambitions did not reduce the reputational benefits that the emirate would accrue. In 2009, before virtually any of Abu Dhabi's clean energy plans had been realized, the emirate was selected for the prestigious opportunity to host the headquarters of a new United Nations agency, the International Renewable Energy Agency. IRENA, as it is known, remains the first and only UN agency with a permanent headquarters based in the Middle East.

On the other hand, the UAE's PV solar power ambitions turned out to have been underestimated in 2009. As panel prices fell, utilities in Dubai and Abu Dhabi secured ultra-low tariffs from developers—after providing free land and grid connections—and came close to meeting the 2020 renewables goal, in capacity terms at least. As 2020 arrived, Abu Dhabi's renewables installation had reached nearly 1 GW, 6% of its installed capacity of 16.7 GW, and sufficient to provide about 2–4% of the emirate's electricity. Installed renewables capacity in the UAE overall reached 2.1 GW by December 2019, equal to 7% of the country's roughly 30 GW of installed capacity, but—given the lower capacity factor for intermittent renewables versus thermal generation—producing 2–3% of nationwide power.[24]

Clean Energy Aspirations and Credibility

In 2017, the UAE launched an updated set of power sector goals, the National Energy Strategy 2050.[25] The strategy is focused on altering the electricity generation mix, rather than the overall energy balance including transport and industry. A full 50% of future electricity production is to be provided by 'clean' sources, i.e., nuclear and renewable power. The remaining 50% is to be split between fossil fuels, gas (38%), and coal (12%). The strategy implies a tripling in 2019 power capacity to 93 GW, including 11.2 GW of coal and 41 GW of renewables[26] (Fig. 3.4). As mentioned above, these targets remain aspirational and do not pertain to currently understood plans or proposals.

Given the high capacity factors of nuclear, coal, and gas—where plants typically produce power above 70% of their full capacity rating—the actual electricity output will differ markedly. Non-dispatchable solar, by contrast, produces power at about 20–25% of its peak output rating. If the UAE reaches its clean energy aspirations, gas, coal, and nuclear plants will produce around 78% of electricity in 2050 with solar, biomass, and wind producing the remaining 22%.[27] Therefore, fossil fuels will still produce around 70% of the UAE's electricity.

The 2050 strategy also envisions a 70% reduction in power sector carbon emissions from the business as usual level, an unattainable goal alongside such an enormous buildout of fossil capacity. Rather than a

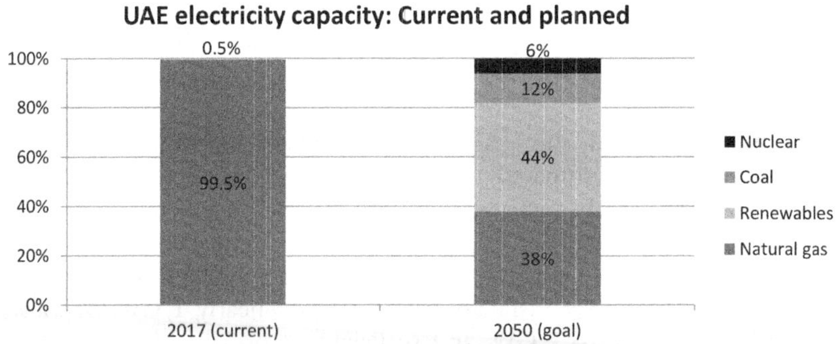

Fig. 3.4 UAE electricity capacity: current and planned. Natural gas-fired generation drops from 98% of capacity in 2017 to 38% by 2050 under the UAE's latest plan

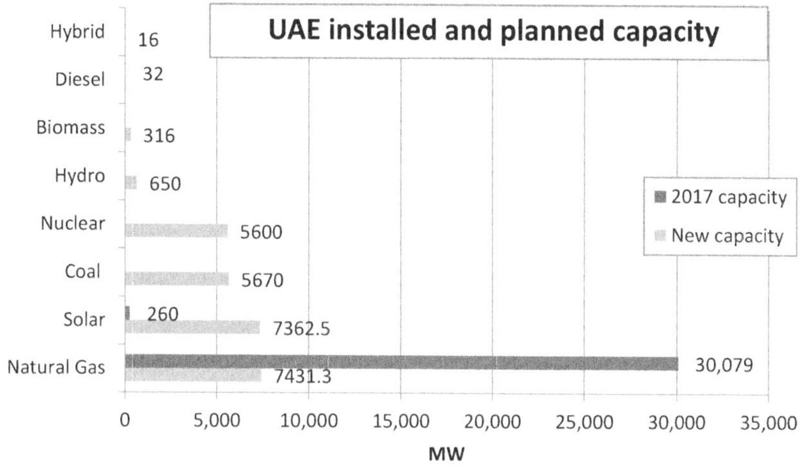

Fig. 3.5 UAE installed and planned capacity (*Source* Baker Institute compilation from project database in Annex)

decline in carbon emissions, adhering to the 2050 strategy implies the UAE's carbon emissions would rise well beyond 2018's level of 277 million tonnes.[28] The environmental NGO Climate Action Tracker has calculated that the UAE's GHG emissions, including those of transport and industry, would grow by 50% between 2010 and 2030.[29]

However, the list of planned and tendered projects, based on capacity, presents a different story (Fig. 3.5; see Annex for a full list). Gas appears certain to retain its dominance in the electricity mix, with some 7 GW of forthcoming capacity in the planning stages. Meanwhile, published plans suggest that nuclear, solar, and coal reach levels of capacity between 5 and 7 GW apiece.[30] Again, the far lower capacity factor of solar versus coal and nuclear suggests that solar will play a smaller role in electricity provision than that suggested by 'installed capacity' figures.

Diversification Away from Gas

Why would utility planners in the UAE trouble themselves to push through a diversification of the power sector, particularly one that includes a large commitment to renewables? Survey results in the Middle East suggest there is little grassroots pressure from society to embrace environmental goals or move away from fossil fuels, while civil society pressure groups are generally banned.[31]

Further, the UAE holds proven gas reserves of 6 trillion cubic meters of natural gas, roughly 3% of the global total and enough to produce at current rates for 90 years, according to BP. Even if domestic supply became an issue, the UAE lies within pipeline distance of some of the world's largest natural gas fields that happen to be controlled by neighboring states. These include the North Field/South Pars Field of Qatar and Iran; the Qeshm (Salakh and Gavarzin), Saru, Tabnak, Assaluyeh, Kish, Sarkhun, and Sirri fields of Iran; and the North and South Kidan fields of Saudi Arabia. All lie within a 250-mile radius of the UAE's main pipeline termini.

Examined from the perspective of a domestic electricity security standpoint, the state of natural gas supply looks more fraught.

First, the cost of producing gas in the UAE is rising. Marginal production costs for new fields were $3/mmbtu in 2015, rising to $7—the highest in the GCC—by 2030. Costs for new sour gas projects in the UAE were particularly high. Mills estimates a cost of $7–8/mmbtu for one forthcoming offshore sour gas project.[32]

Second, the UAE has since 2008 been a net importer of natural gas, importing nearly 20 bcm in 2017,[33] nearly as much gas as the total consumed in Kuwait that year.[34] The cost of imports is pushing up the overall cost of electricity. Between 2007 and 2014, Dubai paid an average $3.72 per mmbtu for fuels burned to generate power.[35]

Third, the UAE may lie within cost-effective pipeline range of major low-cost gas producers, including Iran and Qatar, but imports of gas from those countries have only been partly successful. Diplomatic relations with both have worsened under the more assertive regional policies of Mohammed bin Zayed al-Nahyan, the Abu Dhabi crown prince and de facto UAE ruler. Qatar supplies gas to the UAE through the undersea Dolphin Pipeline, but those imports eventually face the expiration in 2032 of the production sharing contract between the Dolphin Energy consortium and the Qatari government.

Fourth, regional gas trading is hampered by long-running government policies of fixing local prices below international benchmarks. Price levels in the UAE's six emirates vary widely, as do those in neighboring countries. These discrepancies could be overcome if the Gulf region developed a pricing hub that encouraged cross-border gas trading at prices based on an index that included futures pricing. But consumers in the GCC are unused to paying world market prices for natural gas. Most wholesale natural gas sales are done below the marginal cost of production, at fixed prices that range from $1.25 to $2.50/mmbtu.

Thus, while the average cost of gas looks reasonable, marginal increases in domestic production are increasingly costly, while import prices—and Qatari supplies—are uncertain.

Regional Gas Politics

As mentioned, the UAE lies close to two major potential suppliers, Iran—the world No. 2 holder of gas reserves—and Qatar, the No. 3 reserves holder. Both countries have long histories of commercial trade with the sheikhdoms that now make up the UAE. Dubai, in particular, harbors close ties to Tehran and Doha. However, the UAE's deteriorating relationship with both countries makes it unlikely that utility planners would choose to deepen their reliance on either state for critical energy needs.

Relations with Iran

The UAE has had shifting relations with Iran since the 1979 Islamic revolution. Dubai's historically warmer ties with Iran have been counterbalanced by those of Abu Dhabi, where initial estrangement was tempered in the 1990s when the UAE joined a collective agreement to reduce GCC-Iran tensions. At the time, Tehran developed its most constructive working relations with Qatar, Oman, and the UAE, although ties with Abu Dhabi were hampered by a territorial dispute over three Gulf islands. A high point came in 2007 when Iranian President Mahmoud Ahmedinejad made the first-ever state visit by an Iranian head of state to the UAE. Ahmadinejad gave a major public address in a stadium in Dubai, home to nearly half a million Iranian expatriates and thousands of Iran-owned businesses.

Since then, UAE relations with Iran have plummeted as Abu Dhabi's Crown Prince Mohammed bin Zayed has countered inroads of political Islam and Iran-backed Shia paramilitaries across the Middle East. The Abu Dhabi leadership opposed the US diplomatic outreach to Iran under US President Obama that resulted in the 2015 nuclear agreement. Abu Dhabi supported the Trump administration's pullout of the agreement and the re-imposed US trade embargo on Iran.

By late 2019, the UAE had backed away from confronting Iran, perhaps due to inconsistencies in the Trump administration approach of stoking conflict with Iran while seeking to avoid a major US role in any resulting war. The UAE therefore made concessions aimed at reducing the likelihood that the UAE would bear the brunt of any Iranian retaliation.

UAE-Iran Gas Trade

The UAE-Iran gas trade has paralleled the political relationship, with signs of promise undermined by dispute. Under a 25-year export agreement signed in 2001, Iran was supposed to supply a Sharjah-based firm with 600 million cubic feet of gas per day by 2005, via undersea pipelines between the UAE and multiple gas fields off Iran's Sirri Island. But Iranian parliamentarians protested what they saw as overly generous terms for UAE-based Crescent Petroleum. Iranian gas would have been sold at prices near $1/mmbtu, based on a crude-linked formula drawn up when oil prices were $18/bbl.[36]

Other than a brief test of the Sharjah leg of the pipeline in 2010—which found leaks during transmission—the pipeline has remained unused. Attempts to renegotiate have failed. An international tribunal in 2014 found in favor of Crescent Petroleum, which has begun pursuing damages from the National Iranian Oil Co.[37] Discussions revived in 2017 yielded hopes that Iran would finally start its exports.[38] But trade opportunity evaporated when the UAE backed Trump administration sanctions on Iranian exports.

Relations with Qatar

UAE relations with Qatar, like those with Iran, vary by emirate. Dubai's traditionally strong ties—cemented through ruling family intermarriage[39]—contrast with the historically cooler relationship between Doha and Abu Dhabi. Overall UAE-Qatar ties have deteriorated since the 1995 coup that brought Sheikh Hamad bin Khalifa al-Thani to power. Relations continued to decline as Qatar involved itself in regional politics that included support for opposition groups such as the Muslim Brotherhood during the Arab Spring. The dispute has continued under Sheikh Tamim bin Hamad al-Thani, who came to power in 2014.

In 2017, the UAE broke off diplomatic relations and launched a surprise trade embargo on Qatar, joined by Saudi Arabia, Bahrain, and

Egypt. The four closed airspace and borders, banned trade and travel, and ejected Qataris from their national territories. In the UAE, even Qataris married to Emirati citizens were forced to flee.[40]

One factor that appears to have prevented the UAE-Qatar conflict from escalating is the dependence of the UAE on imports of Qatari natural gas via the Dolphin Pipeline, a 50-mile undersea link that delivers about 2 bcf/day or 20 bcm/year, roughly half the UAE's annual requirement for power generation.

Despite the UAE-led blockade, Qatar has treated the gas exports as outside the bounds of the dispute, keeping the gas flowing at contracted prices around $2/mmbtu, below normal prevailing rates at most international hubs.[41] In fact, Dolphin's uninterrupted provision of gas has allowed Abu Dhabi to maintain its lucrative LNG exports at much higher prices. Qatari officials have long complained about the terms of the long-term contract (expiring in 2032), which, they argue, leaves Qatar in the position of cross-subsidizing the UAE.

Perhaps as a result, the UAE has never fully leveraged its access to Qatar's massive gas reserves. A third of the volume of the Dolphin Pipeline, with a capacity of 3.2 bcf/d, remains unused (Fig. 3.6). In the 1990s and 2000s, Qatar was unwilling to commit to increases in long-term supply at prices then on offer from the UAE.[42] But Doha has since sold so-called interruptible shipments during the UAE's peak summer demand period at prices around $5/mmbtu and has agreed to further higher-priced shipments to Ras al-Khaimah and Sharjah until 2026.[43]

The UAE's role in the blockade of Qatar leaves both countries cautious on the risks of expanding trade. Qatar appears unwilling to export further gas at prices inconsistent with its LNG netbacks. And the UAE's critical dependence on Qatari gas has exposed a weakness, while providing Doha a strategic trump card to deter the UAE from escalating hostilities against Qatar directly, and perhaps, against some Qatari interests in the region. In short, UAE dependence on Qatar serves as a dampener on Abu Dhabi's freedom of foreign policy maneuver in the Gulf region and therefore provides another rationale for the UAE's program of diversification in power generation.

Gas Trade with Saudi Arabia?

Another potential future source of supply that is often overlooked lies in neighboring Saudi Arabia. For the time being, the kingdom neither

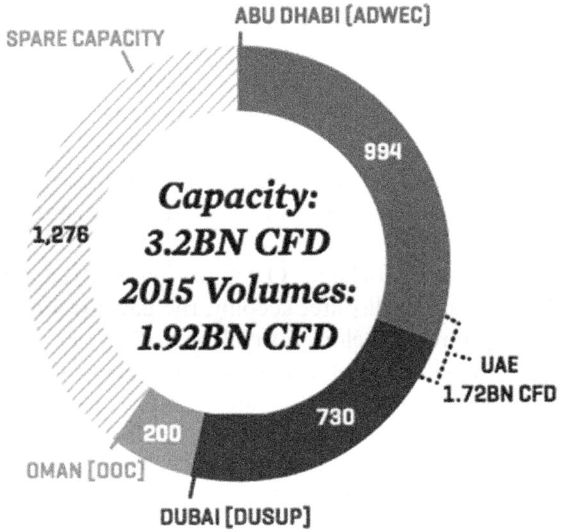

Fig. 3.6 Dolphin pipeline capacity. Some of the spare capacity depicted here has diminished as Qatar has begun gas shipments to Ras al-Khaimah and Sharjah (*Source* MEES 2019)

exports nor imports natural gas, but Saudi Aramco has invested heavily over the past decade to raise domestic output to supplant oil in power generation. Saudi energy officials have made suggestions about Saudi gas being exported via a GCC-wide gas grid.

Two major sour gas fields, North and South Kidan, sit in the Saudi Empty Quarter near the Abu Dhabi border, making them prime sites for future UAE-bound exports. The Kidan fields hold little in the way of valuable liquids to assist with costs, leaving lifting costs around \$6/mmbtu,[44] which makes the fields uneconomic sources of supply (albeit cheaper than LNG imports, at times) for any GCC state, all of which administer gas prices at lower levels.

Why Diversify?

Abu Dhabi's 2007–2008 Interagency Working Group on Energy laid out several reasons for diversifying the mix of power generation fuels and technologies, driven by a 13% increase in power demand in 2006 amid gas shortages that required expensive diesel backup. Criteria for the diversification included:

- Economic performance (including reducing the use of expensive backup fuels, particularly diesel, and reducing exposure to volatile commodity prices)
- A preference for domestic fuels (based on energy security concerns about potential for supply disruption)
- Dispatchability and flexibility of generation (versus intermittent or inflexible sources)
- Environmentally clean sources, technologies involving technical knowledge transfer and quality jobs.[45]

After the 2017 breakdown in UAE-Qatar relations, the UAE announced its intention to achieve self-sufficiency in natural gas prior to the 2032 expiration of the main Dolphin contract. Preexisting plans to diversify toward nuclear, coal, and renewables fit well within the self-sufficiency mandate and the UAE's more forceful regional and international political stance.

Further, for oil and gas exporters like the UAE, reduced gas demand at home—where prices are subsidized—allows more to be sold abroad at full international prices. At a minimum, the Gulf monarchies have been subject to enormous opportunity costs in providing subsidized domestic power, and in some cases, the domestic price for gas is insufficient even to cover costs.

Every gigawatt of solar power capacity offsets consumption of some 3 million barrels of oil equivalent, or roughly 0.5 bcm gas, per year.[46] For each gigawatt of dispatchable generation, the hydrocarbon savings are larger: 6 million barrels of oil equivalent/year (or 1 bcm/y) saved per gigawatt of coal-fired capacity (at 50% capacity usage) and as much as 10 million boe/y (2 bcm/y) per gigawatt for nuclear plants.

Regime Security and Nuclear Power

As mentioned, the first of Abu Dhabi's four 1.4 GW nuclear power plants was expected to begin providing power to the UAE grid in 2020. Levelized cost of electricity (LCOE) for Abu Dhabi's South Korean-built nuclear plants (including decommissioning costs) is estimated at the low end of the typical scale for nuclear of between 7.3 and 14 US cents per kWh.[47]

Abu Dhabi's experience with nuclear power has been difficult, and it appears that it will not be repeated in its current form. The emirate's ambitious completion deadlines fell by the wayside, while the complexity and cost of the Barakah plant have rendered them uncompetitive with competing options. However, mastery of the development process frees Abu Dhabi to consider a future array of nuclear options, such as small modular reactors, which might help the emirate cope with challenges from international climate action.

Nuclear power confers further benefits to Abu Dhabi beyond the 5.6 GW of firm, zero-carbon power generation capacity. These range from freeing domestic hydrocarbons for export, transfer of complex technology, and creating high-value employment.[48] Abu Dhabi's nuclear investment allows the state to leverage an oil windfall to meet essential long term power needs.[49] Nuclear power's long time horizon—the Barakah reactors may provide electricity until 2080—allows the state to transfer today's oil wealth to future generations.

From the perspective of an autocratic regime, there are further benefits from civil nuclear power. The nuclearization process tends to encourage a strengthening of the central state and the regime's control over society, through increased internal security measures and enhanced coercive apparatus, ostensibly justified by the technology's inherent hazards.[50] Vulnerabilities in nuclear systems also create new requirements for secrecy and surveillance, and less tolerance for dissent.[51] Protecting the fuel cycle does double duty in bolstering regime security.

Finally, for Abu Dhabi, 'going nuclear' may also increase the West's stake in the survival of the regime because a shift to anti-US governance could open the door to proliferation of nuclear technology. Gulf Arab rulers have had reason to fear that Washington may eventually seek to end its role as the GCC's long-term guardian. Nuclearization under those circumstances may offer an alternate path to maintaining the strategic interest of the United States and other global powers.[52]

The Political Economy of Gulf Solar Power

Early ambitions for solar technology to contribute materially to the UAE's power supply fell far short of initial expectations. But precipitous cost declines in solar reached a threshold by 2016 that allowed the technology to compete favorably in the Gulf. Reforms of subsidies on competing fuels also increased the relative attractions of solar.

In the UAE, solar is viewed as a clean power source that frees the state from dependence on imported fuel and associated political risks, while providing reputational benefits. But even in the sunny Gulf climate solar generation's intermittency requires backup from thermal generation or grid storage to render it a substitution option for gas.

The drop in cost has been dramatic. In 2016, solar bids came in under 6 US cents per kWh. A year later, bids halved to just under 3 cents/kWh and halved again in 2019 to around 1.5 cents/kWh. By comparison, gas purchased for $5/mmBtu produces electricity in a modern CCGT at 3.5–4.5 cents/kWh.[53] Current prices allow solar investments to underprice gas-fired generation on the basis of fuel savings alone.[54]

In unsubsidized markets with privately held gas generation—such as in parts of the United States—the idling of gas-fired power in favor of solar serves to reduce the capacity factor of the plants whose output is displaced. The idling undercuts the displaced plant's profitability and leaves investors holding a partially stranded asset. In the UAE, however, reducing demand for subsidized gas relieves government spending on imports. Amendments to subsidy accounting rules in 2016 provided further advantage to solar by requiring utility planners to consider the full opportunity cost of forgone hydrocarbon exports, rather than valuing gas as a waste product.[55]

In the UAE and Saudi Arabia, numerous PV solar installations–planned and under construction—have achieved power sales tariffs under 3 US cents per kWh. For instance, the Mohamed bin Rashid Solar Park Phase II array in Dubai reached a power purchase price of 2.99 cents per kWh, while the Sweihan solar project in Abu Dhabi reached 2.94 cents and Saudi Arabia's Sakaka project achieved 2.34 cents. In October 2019, Dubai announced it had accepted a bid to build 900 MW of solar PV within the fifth phase of the MbR plant selling power for just 1.7 cents per kWh.[56] Abu Dhabi was reported to have received a bid of 1.35 cents per kWh for a planned 2 GW PV installation.[57]

Ultra-low solar power purchase prices in the Gulf are a factor of the state bearing the costs of land and transmission, while reaping the effects of falling costs that have rendered PV modules just a third of the cost of a typical project. Apostoleris et al. have added further factors to this list for the Gulf, including zero sales tax, zero cost for environmental permits or grid connections, labor costs less than half those in developed states, low-cost financing, and high rates of debt to equity, all of which combine to achieve an LCOE in the UAE of 2.85 US cents, where a comparable US plant's LCOE would only reach 7.38 cents per kWh (including a 10% return for the developer).[58] It bears mentioning that LCOE estimates typically do not encompass the full costs of solar generation, including paying for backup generation to cover demand when solar is unavailable, along with required reinforcements to transmission networks.

Regardless, these cost advantages allowed the UAE's installed capacity to reach 2.1 GW by December 2019, meaning that 7% of the country's roughly 30 GW of installed capacity was renewable. However, given the lower capacity factor for intermittent renewables versus thermal generation, 2.1 GW of solar can be expected to produce around 2–3% of the UAE's electricity output.

Solar's unaccounted-for costs are balanced by off-books benefits in the form of reduced political risk. Once generating, solar plants produce electricity at zero variable cost, because the fuel (solar energy) is free. Solar 'fuel' is also not subject to embargo or trade risk, which provides an advantage over gas, coal, and nuclear, which involve fuel imports.

The Dash for Coal—To Replace Gas

The first-ever coal-fired power plant in the GCC was in the late stages of construction in late 2020. The first 2.4 GW phase of Dubai's Hassyan plant is scheduled to open in 2020 or 2021. If the Hassyan plant reaches its full 3.6 GW capacity as planned, it would be larger than the 2.8 GW Afsin-Elbistan Power Station in Turkey, currently the largest coal plant in the Middle East.

The nearby emirate of Ras al-Khaimah has also announced a pair of coal-fired plants, as has neighboring Oman. Neither had reached final investment decision.

The Dubai coal plant represents a contrarian watershed in Persian Gulf energy policy. The project leverages the only fossil fuel not found on the Arabian Peninsula to mitigate dependence on natural gas, a fuel so plentiful in the surrounding region that it is estimated to hold 40% of the world's proven reserves.[59] Dubai's power sector diversification will shift it away from the cleanest of the fossil fuels toward the dirtiest. In so doing, Dubai effectively reverses the 'dash for gas' pursued by the United Kingdom, United States and elsewhere that have achieved carbon and pollution benefits by replacing coal with gas.

Coal combustion in power generation emits roughly double the carbon per unit of electricity delivered versus natural gas, along with local pollutants such as sulfur dioxide, nitrogen oxides, and mercury. Coal ash is often mildly radioactive.[60] Coal soot drifting in the atmosphere becomes an agent of climate change when deposits darken surfaces of glaciers, ice caps, and sea ice, reducing the Earth's reflectivity while promoting warming and melting of those surfaces.

Dubai's investment in coal runs counter to more than a decade of 'clean energy' image-building and rhetoric from the highest levels of the UAE government. Abu Dhabi in particular has sought to establish itself as a 'green petro-state' through projects like low-carbon Masdar City, the hosting of the UN's renewable energy agency, and the solar power initiatives described above.

Perhaps accordingly, Dubai's embrace of coal is being done discreetly, with none of the fanfare afforded the UAE's investments into renewables or real estate. The discretion suggests that ruling elites are uncomfortable with coal.

Normally Dubai's media outlets can be counted on to trumpet the superlatives of the city's energy milestones. But coverage of Hassyan has been muted, overshadowed by solar projects and their record-low tariffs—even though the power output of Dubai's coal plant, if operated anywhere near nameplate capacity, will dwarf that of ***all the UAE's planned solar arrays combined***. Hassyan's 3.6 GW of coal capacity operated 60% of the time would generate almost 19 GWh of electricity in a year. That is nearly double the 11 GWh of power produced from the UAE's eventual 5 GW of solar installations operating at a 25% capacity factor.[61]

An indicator of the diverging levels of prestige between Dubai's solar parks and its coal plant is evident in their names. Dubai's ruler, Mohammed bin Rashid al-Maktoum, has named the solar development after himself, seeking to associate his legacy with clean energy. The uncommon name accorded the coal plant—Hassyan—suggests that Emirati elites were unwilling to be linked with it. Its location, too, is suggestive. Hassyan is being built on the least populated and furthest reach of Dubai's coastline, directly abutting the Abu Dhabi border.

The UAE government's energy policy documentation keeps Dubai's coal plant at arm's length. The government's online energy portal devotes multiple paragraphs to nuclear, solar, wind, and waste-to-energy projects. Coal is dismissed in just two sentences, with no links to further detail, even though the national Energy Strategy 2050 strategy envisions coal taking a 12% share of the UAE's power output.[62]

When official reports must mention the coal project, it is described as 'clean coal.' Although 'clean coal' is an ambiguous term, when used in energy circles it typically refers to plants equipped with carbon capture and storage (CCS) infrastructure, such as the W. A. Parish plant outside Houston or the Boundary Dam plant in Saskatchewan. The Hassyan plant will not be equipped with CCS. In Hassyan's case, 'clean' appears to be a reference to its use of ultra-supercritical boilers, contemporary technology, which operate with greater efficiency and lower particulate emission than those found in older plants. Since Hassyan's design requires it to be retrofitted for any future connection to CCS infrastructure, the plant does not meet standard criteria for 'clean coal.'[63]

The downplaying of coal in the UAE may become official policy. Disagreements between Abu Dhabi and Dubai over the wisdom of coal have cast doubt on the likelihood that coal capacity will be further expanded beyond Hassyan's 2.4 GW first phase, despite plans on record.[64]

Questions Around Coal

Why would a wealthy, energy-endowed country venture into imported coal at a time when the climate and pollution consequences are universally understood? Most commercial and development banks have halted coal lending, considering it inappropriate other than in very limited circumstances in energy-poor countries without alternatives. Besides not meeting these criteria, the UAE, and Dubai in particular, depend heavily on tourism, an industry sensitive to negative publicity and pollution. A 2015 World Bank statistical ranking found the UAE already had higher mean average particulate (PM 2.5) air pollution, mainly from airborne dust, than any other country in the world, including China and India, where coal combustion has created serious public health issues[65] (Fig. 3.7). Even low-particulate 'clean coal' will worsen air quality.

Why coal, then? There appear to be at least five reasons behind the UAE's 'dash for coal.'

The first is based on strategic calculations about energy security and diversity of supply and technology. The Middle East may hold the world's largest repository of natural gas, but it is also an arena for competition among great powers and regional autocracies, replete with ongoing

Environment and health	
$PM_{2.5}$ pollution, mean annual exposure (µg/cu. m)	80
$PM_{2.5}$ exposure (% pop. exceeding WHO guideline level)	100
Acute resp. infection prevalence (% of children under five)	..
Diarrhea prevalence (% of children under five)	..
Under-five mortality rate (per 1,000 live births)	8

Fig. 3.7 UAE air quality data from The World Bank's "Little Green Data Book," p. 219 (2015); https://openknowledge.worldbank.org/bitstream/handle/10986/22025/9781464805608.pdf

conflicts and proxy wars. The fact that Abu Dhabi has begun taking an active role in these conflicts exacerbates risks to its gas supply. Global coal reserves by contrast are so large and geographically dispersed that opportunities for political interference are limited. The fact that 99.9% of the world's coal is produced outside the Middle East[66] may actually enhance its attractiveness.

Cost factors are coal's second advantage. Dubai has managed to procure an extraordinarily low power purchase price for dispatchable coal-fired power. The tariff promised by the Hassyan plant's Chinese-led consortium was just 4.24 US cents per kWh at 2015 coal prices.[67] That price is slightly lower than those obtained in recent tenders for CCGT plants.[68] Estimates of Abu Dhabi's Barakah nuclear plant's LCOE, by contrast, run around 7 or 8 US cents per kWh.[69] As mentioned, however, Hassyan's cost analyses looked competitive with higher priced gas and renewables at the time planners made the final investment decision.

Third, coal can provide a source of baseload generation that can substitute for the UAE's natural gas-fired plants. Intermittent renewables cannot provide firm, dispatchable capacity without expensive add-ons, such as battery storage, pumped hydro storage, or gas backup. As such, coal represents an attractive alternative for times when gas is expensive or unavailable.

Coal may be dispatchable, but it does present a major disadvantage. Modern gas turbines can vary output within minutes. A gas 'peaker' plant can start up and dispatch power with an hour's notice. Coal's typical 8-hour startup makes it less appropriate for synergizing with renewables which vary their production based on weather.

Fourth, the Hassyan project represents a major overture to China, part of a growing strategic bilateral engagement. Political elites in the UAE have long felt comfortable with top-down Chinese autocratic state capitalism. That admiration now extends to the Chinese coal-driven energy backbone. China was the UAE's largest trading partner from 2014 to 2016, with some 300,000 Chinese residents and 4000 Chinese-owned businesses in the UAE in 2018.[70] The Chinese government has encouraged its construction and engineering firms to seek markets for new coal plants abroad due to declining demand in China.[71]

Fifth, diversification to coal either reduces gas imports or frees it up for higher-value uses in the UAE economy. These uses include those in industry, where gas is both feedstock and heat source and as exportable LNG.[72] Abu Dhabi exported 7.4 bcm as LNG in 2018.[73]

Discussion and Conclusion

The project mix shaping the UAE's electricity sector presents a fragmented mix of generation technologies, fuels, and geo-environmental messaging. The glaring disconnect in policymaking between Abu Dhabi's clean energy push and Dubai's more price-driven strategy raise the possibility of future inter-emirate disputes. While both emirates pursue diversification away from natural gas, Abu Dhabi's power mix appears to align with the future possibility of carbon taxation and border adjustment tariffs. Dubai's does not. Coal-driven carbon emissions from Dubai pose risks for the entire UAE, conceivably penalizing national exports by rendering them less competitive than those from countries with smaller footprints.

The Dubai-Abu Dhabi disconnect is the largest manifestation of a misalignment in electricity policy that has Abu Dhabi and the Northern Emirates ranking environmental criteria highly in their technology choices, while Dubai and Sharjah prioritize cost-driven solutions that increase autonomy from the central state. Also shaping the power portfolio are political rivalries with gas-rich Qatar and Iran, which appear to be predisposing the UAE's turn away from gas.

As these new power sources come online over the first half of the 2020s, one envisions the UAE increasing contributions from zero-carbon nuclear and solar power, with natural gas eventually relegated to peak periods and backup, a mix that comports well with the international climate action agenda. Indeed, Abu Dhabi plans to reduce the gas consumed by its power sector by as much as half, between 2018 and 2030.[74] However, if difficulties with intermittency and complexity cannot be overcome, the UAE appears destined to continued dependence on fossil fuel, including coal.

Solar installations have received outsized attention but had not, as of the end of 2019, contributed a material part of the UAE's power output. Going forward, contributions of solar will increase as plants under construction are completed and connected to the grid. If plants produce as advertised over the current decade, the realization of investment plans could push the UAE into a clean energy leadership position in the Middle East, albeit one tarnished by coal. It remained to be seen whether the response to COVID-19 resulted in project delays or cancellations.

The UAE's domestic solar projects have brought reputational and soft-power benefits, as have its overseas renewables investments.[75] Continued cost reductions in renewable energy, alongside flattening growth in domestic power demand, should enable PV solar to act as a fuel-saving daytime substitute for imported natural gas. It will take improvements to solar's dispatchability to allow it to substitute for the UAE's fossil generation capacity, particularly during peak periods after dark.

The prestige aspects of solar power are evident in Dubai's naming of a large solar initiative after its ruler, while the emirate's even larger coal-fired power investments are downplayed and misleadingly labeled as 'clean.' The 'greenwashing' of a carbon-intensive electricity strategy carries risks. The specter of an oil-rich emirate free-riding on climate actions elsewhere could generate sufficient opprobrium among the global public to expose the UAE to hostile actions such as boycotts, sanctions, trade penalties and other types of political and regulatory action from governments, non-government organizations, or international agencies.

Elsewhere, coal firms and government backers are coming under pressure from climate change movements to halt coal investment and reduce use of existing assets. It is hard to imagine the UAE evading international pressure over its coal pursuits, given the typical 40-year operating lifetime that could see Hassyan producing electricity until 2060. By that date, continued warming in the Gulf region could present life-threatening summer temperatures that might even trigger *domestic* opposition to coal use.[76] The combined trajectories of technological change in the power sector, physical changes in the climate, and pressure from the international public for action, could render carbon-intense assets stranded.[77]

High carbon intensity could also reduce the UAE's competitiveness in attracting foreign direct investment. As large multinationals pursue carbon reductions in their supply chains, they are igniting competition among countries to reduce emissions intensity of manufacturing sectors and electricity grids. Adding coal-fired capacity to an already fossil fuel-dominated power mix only reduces the UAE's carbon competitiveness.

Finally, the fragmentation of the UAE's 2050 energy strategy appears likely to undermine its longevity. A revision in strategy, particularly in regards to stated goals for expanded coal use, would be less painful if achieved before sunk costs increase the barriers to change.

Acknowledgements The author expresses his gratitude for research and data assistance from Rice University's Elsie Hung, as well as assistance from Geoffrey Lakings and Zainab Zamani of i2 Enabled in Houston, which provided data on power projects displayed in the Annex and cited in the narrative. Gratitude is also due to Robin Mills of Qamar Energy in Dubai, Li-Chen Sim at Khalifa University in Abu Dhabi, as well as two UAE energy officials who I will not name, all of whom read and provided comments and input on an earlier draft of this article.

Notes

1. In 2019, a major new offshore field straddling the Dubai-Abu Dhabi boundary near Jebel Ali was discovered that could reduce these costs.
2. Author interviews with UAE energy sector experts based on condition of anonymity, January 2020.
3. Anthony DiPaola, "U.A.E. Finds World's Biggest Gas Field Since 2005." *Bloomberg*, February 3, 2020; https://www.bloomberg.com/news/articles/2020-02-03/abu-dhabi-dubai-make-gas-discovery-in-push-for-self-sufficiency?sref=Q77DYrNe.
4. "Electricity Consumption per Capita." IEA Atlas of Energy, International Energy Agency, 2019; http://energyatlas.iea.org/.
5. Jim Krane, "Rationalizing Energy Demand Through End-User Prices in the GCC." *Oxford Energy Forum*, no. 101 (November 2015).
6. "Countries in and Around the Middle East Are Adding Coal-Fired Power Plants." U.S. Energy Information Administration, May 11, 2018; https://www.eia.gov/todayinenergy/detail.php?id=36172.
7. Mills, pp. 122–3.
8. Global Energy Monitor, "Coal Plants by Country (MW)." Database, Global Coal Plant Tracker (Global Energy Monitor, July 2019); https://docs.google.com/spreadsheets/d/1W-gobEQugqTR_PP0iczJCrdaR-vYkJ0DzztSsCJXuKw/edit#gid=0.
9. Author email and telephone conversations with UAE-based energy officials and analysts on condition of anonymity, 2019 and 2020.
10. BP 2019.

11. Robin Mills, "Appetite and Innovation: Natural Gas in the UAE." In *The Future of Gas in the Gulf: Continuity and Change*, ed. Jonathan Stern (Oxford: Oxford Institute for Energy Studies, 2019), p. 126. BP, "BP Statistical Review of World Energy 2019." Statistical report (London: BP, June 2019).
12. Max S. Kim, "How Greed and Corruption Blew Up South Korea's Nuclear Industry." *MIT Technology Review*, April 22, 2019; https://www.technologyreview.com/s/613325/how-greed-and-corruption-blew-up-south-koreas-nuclear-industry.
13. "Update to ENEC Announcement on 12.04.2018." Emirates Nuclear Energy Corporation (press release), April 10, 2019; https://www.enec.gov.ae/news/announcements/update-to-enec-announcement-on-12-04-2018/.
14. "UAE Nuclear Power Plant License in 2020." *Reuters*, November 27, 2019; https://financialtribune.com/articles/energy/100942/uae-nuclear-power-plant-license-in-2020.
15. All statistics from BP 2019.
16. "Sir Bani Yas UAE." Wind farm database, The Wind Power Wind Energy Market Intelligence, 2019; https://www.thewindpower.net/country_windfarms_en_103_united-arab-emirates.php.
17. Author interview with UAE energy sector executive on condition of anonymity, January 2020.
18. Ibid.
19. "Abu Dhabi Commits US$15 Billion to Alternative Energy, Clean Technology." *Middle East and North Africa Business Report*, January 21, 2008.
20. Himendra Mohan Kumar, "Phase One of Masdar City to Be Ready Before 2010." *Gulf News*, October 28, 2007; http://gulfnews.com/business/construction/phase-one-of-masdar-city-to-be-ready-before-2010-1.119793.
21. "Abu Dhabi Commits to 7 Percent Renewable Energy Target by 2020." *Emirates News Agency*, January 18, 2009; http://tinyurl.com/nlb5hjc.
22. "BP and Local Partner Shelve Hydrogen Power Project in Abu Dhabi." *The Oil Daily*, January 14, 2011. See also *Hydrogen Power Abu Dhabi (HPAD)*, accessed May 13, 2010, http://www.zeroco2.no/projects/masdar-precombustion-ccs-project.
23. "Saudi Arabia Awards 300 MW Sakaka PV, At Record Low Pricing." MEES, Vol. 61, Issue 6, February 9, 2018.
24. Data in this paragraph come from utility sources collected by the author, utility officials interviewed by the author, and data published in MEES.
25. "UAE Energy Strategy 2050." Government of the United Arab Emirates, May 30, 2019; https://government.ae/en/about-the-uae/strategies-

initiatives-and-awards/federal-governments-strategies-and-plans/uae-energy-strategy-2050.
26. "Abu Dhabi Eyes Innovative Approach to Energy Transition." MEES, Vol. 62, Issue 38, September 20, 2019.
27. Percentage totals are author's calculations based on capacity factor of 70% for nuclear, gas and coal, and 25% for renewables.
28. The UAE was the world's 24th largest emitter of CO2 in 2018. BP, "BP Statistical Review of World Energy 2019."
29. United Arab Emirates page, updated December 2, 2019, Climate Action Tracker; https://climateactiontracker.org/countries/uae/assumptions/.
30. An official suggested that plans for additional coal capacity beyond the 2.4 GW Hassyan plant would not come to fruition and that solar plans would be increased to 15 GW.
31. For instance, in the World Values Survey 2010–2014, less than a third of Kuwaitis and Egyptians agreed with the statement "Protecting the environment should be given priority, even if it causes slower economic growth and some loss of jobs" while 63% of Qataris agreed with the statement. Less than 6% of respondents in the three countries reported being a member of an environmental group, and more respondents (outside Qatar) had little or no confidence in environmental protective groups. World Values Survey (Wave 6), 2010–2014; http://www.worldvaluessurvey.org/WVSOnline.jsp.
32. Mills, p. 119.
33. "GCC Gas Integration: More Than Just a Pipe Dream?" MEES, Vol. 62, Issue 4, January 25, 2019.
34. BP, "BP Statistical Review of World Energy 2019."
35. Mills, p. 128.
36. Maximilian Kuhn, *Enabling the Iranian Gas Export Options: The Destiny of Iranian Energy* (Berlin: Springer, 2014), p. 243.
37. Kuhn, p. 243.
38. Jennifer Gnana, "Dana Gas Ready to Import Iranian Gas If Supplies Are Reliable." *The National* (Abu Dhabi), November 15, 2017; https://www.thenational.ae/business/energy/exclusive-dana-gas-ready-to-import-iranian-gas-if-supplies-are-reliable-1.676007.
39. Marriage ties between the ruling family of Qatar, the al-Thani, and that of Dubai, the al-Maktoum, include the marriage of Sheikha Mariam, the elder sister of Dubai's current ruler, who was married to the former Qatari Emir Sheikh Ahmad bin Ali al-Thani, who died in 1977. See J. E. Peterson, "Rulers, Merchants and Shaikhs in Gulf Politics: The Function of Family Networks." In *The Gulf Family: Kinship Policies and Modernity*, ed. Alanoud Alsharekh (London: SAQI, 2007), 24.
40. For a chronicle on the dispute, see Kristian Coates Ulrichsen, *Qatar and the Gulf Crisis* (London: Hurst, 2020).

41. Low gas hub prices at present notwithstanding. Volumes were contracted in the early 2000s at around $1.20–1.30/mmbtu with a small annual escalation in price.
42. Jim Krane and Steven Wright, *Qatar 'Rises Above' Its Region: Geopolitics and the Rejection of the GCC Gas Market* (London: London School of Economics, 2014).
43. "Qatar Finally Agrees to Boost Dolphin Gas Deliveries to UAE." MEES, Vol. 59, Issue 40, October 7, 2016; Dania Saadi, "UAE Holds Back from Qatari-Saudi Detente and Plans for Gas Independence." *S&P Global Platts*, December 23, 2019; https://www.spglobal.com/platts/en/market-insights/latest-news/natural-gas/122319-feature-uae-holds-back-from-qatari-saudi-detente-and-plans-for-gas-independence.
44. "Shell Calls Time on Saudi Gas Project." MEES, Vol. 57, Issue 28, July 11, 2014.
45. Author interview with UAE energy policymaking official by email January 2020 on condition of anonymity.
46. Hisham Akhonbay, "The Economics of Renewable Energy in the Gulf." KAPSARC slide presentation, 2018; https://www.ief.org/_resources/files/events/third-ief-eu-energy-day/5.-hisham-akhonbay---kapsarc.pdf. Oil to gas conversion uses BP's oil-gas conversion tables, with 1 m barrels of oil = 0.17 bcm of natural gas.
47. Abu Dhabi LCOE estimate provided by UAE energy policymaker in 2020; cost range is from Silvana Gamboa Palacios and Jaap Jansen, "Nuclear Energy Economics: An Update to Fact Finding Nuclear Energy." Technology factsheet (Amsterdam: TNO, December 13, 2018); https://publications.tno.nl/publication/34627557/x1eQo8/TNO-2018-P11577.pdf.
48. Many of the arguments in this section can be found in greater detail in Jim Krane, Amy Myers Jaffe, and Jareer Elass, "Nuclear Energy in the Middle East: Chimera or Solution?" *Bulletin of the Atomic Scientists* 72, no. 1 (2016): 44–51.
49. Giacomo Luciani, "Nuclear Energy Developments in the Mediterranean and the Gulf." *The International Spectator* 44, no. 1 (2009): 113–29.
50. Several scholars in the 1970s and 1980s highlighted the "nuclearization" of the state. See: Joseph A. Camilleri, *The State and Nuclear Power: Conflict and Control in the Western World* (Brighton: Wheatsheaf, 1984); Robert Jungk, *The Nuclear State* (London: John Calder, 1979); Michael Flood and Robin Grove-White, *Nuclear Prospects: A Comment on the Individual, the State and Nuclear Power* (London: Friends of the Earth, 1976); Roy Lewis, "Nuclear Power and Employment Rights." *Industrial Law Journal*, no. 7 (1978): 1–15; A. Blowers and D. Pepper, "The Nuclear State—From Consensus to Conflict." In *Nuclear Power in Crisis: Politics and Planning for the Nuclear State*, ed. A. Blowers and D. Pepper

(London: Croon Helm, 1987); G. Donn, "Nuclear Power in Crisis: Politics and Planning for the Nuclear State." Pamphlet (Glasgow: Scottish Council for Civil Liberties, 1982).

51. Camilleri, *The State and Nuclear Power: Conflict and Control in the Western World*.
52. Krane, Jaffe, and Elass, "Nuclear Energy in the Middle East: Chimera or Solution?"
53. UAE prices provided by energy sector official on condition of anonymity, January 2020.
54. Mills, "Appetite and Innovation: Natural Gas in the UAE," 124–5.
55. Author interview with energy sector official on condition of anonymity, January 2020.
56. Farah Elbahrawy and Fahad Alzahrani, "Dubai Utility Gets Record Low Bid to Build Solar-Power Plant." *Bloomberg*, October 13, 2019; https://www.bloomberg.com/news/articles/2019-10-13/dubai-utility-gets-record-low-bid-to-build-solar-power-plant.
57. "Abu Dhabi Solar Record." MEES, Vol. 63, Issue 18, May 1, 2020.
58. Harry Apostoleris et al., "Evaluating the Factors That Led to Low-Priced Solar Electricity Projects in the Middle East." *Nature Energy* 3, no. 12 (December 1, 2018): 1109–14; https://doi.org/10.1038/s41560-018-0256-3.
59. BP estimates that the Middle East holds 38.4% of global gas reserves. Four countries: Iran (16.2%), Qatar (12.5%), the UAE (3%) and Saudi Arabia (3%) hold nearly 25% of those reserves. BP, "BP Statistical Review of World Energy 2019."
60. Mara Hvistendahl, "Coal Ash Is More Radioactive Than Nuclear Waste." *Scientific American*, December 13, 2007; https://www.scientificamerican.com/article/coal-ash-is-more-radioactive-than-nuclear-waste.
61. Author calculation using output formula: (rated capacity * 24 hours * 365 days * capacity factor estimate = yearly expected power production). Capacity factor estimates used from "Chapter 5: Electricity." *International Energy Outlook 2016*, US Energy Information Administration, 2016, p. 89; https://www.eia.gov/outlooks/ieo/pdf/electricity.pdf.
62. Government of the United Arab Emirates, "Energy: The Official Portal of the UAE Government." Government web page (Abu Dhabi, October 23, 2019); https://government.ae/en/information-and-services/environment-and-energy/water-and-energy/energy-.
63. For a discussion on what constitutes "clean coal", see Brad Plumer, "What 'Clean Coal' Is—And Isn't." *New York Times*, August 23, 2017; https://www.nytimes.com/2017/08/23/climate/what-clean-coal-is-and-isnt.html; also: Ian Urbina, "Short Answers to Hard Questions About Clean Coal Technology." *New York Times*, July

5, 2016; https://www.nytimes.com/interactive/2016/07/01/science/what-is-clean-coal.html.
64. Author interviews on condition of anonymity, January 2020.
65. Mitya Underwood, "The Grey Area Over Air Pollution." *The National* (Abu Dhabi), July 29, 2015; https://www.thenational.ae/uae/environment/the-grey-area-over-air-pollution-1.44000.
66. In 2018, Middle Eastern coal production reached only 1.6 million tonnes, roughly 0.02% of the global total. BP, "BP Statistical Review of World Energy 2019."
67. "Construction Begins on New Coal Plant." *Economist Intelligence Unit*, November 18, 2016; http://country.eiu.com/article.aspx?articleid=784825662.
68. The LCOE for Fujairah's recently awarded F3 plant, a 2.4 GW H class CCGT, was 4.57 US cents per kWh, with gas priced at $5mmBtu. The F3 plant's capital investment cost comes in around $450/kW, roughly half the cost of earlier CCGTs in the UAE, such as Sharjah's $900/kW S3 plant. Gas provides other less tangible benefits. The far shorter startup times for CCGT versus coal allow for flexibility to increase solar integration and maximize the cost advantage provided by zero variable cost solar.
69. "DEWA Begins Construction of 2,400 MW Hassyan Clean Coal Power Station." Dubai Electricity and Water Authority (press release), November 10, 2016; https://www.dewa.gov.ae/en/about-us/media-publications/latest-news/2016/11/dewa-begins-construction-of-2400mw-hassyan-clean-coal-power-station. "Levelized Cost of Energy Comparison—Unsubsidized Analysis." *Lazard*, 2018; https://www.lazard.com/media/450784/lazards-levelized-cost-of-energy-version-120-vfinal.pdf. Note that adding CCS to Hassyan would reduce output and add significant cost.
70. "Hassyan Clean Coal Project Symbol of UAE-China Green Partnership." *Xinhua*, July 9, 2018; http://www.xinhuanet.com/english/2018-07/10/c_137313050.htm.
71. Ed Crooks, "The Week in Energy: China's Coal-Fired Outreach." *Financial Times*, June 30, 2019; https://www.ft.com/content/1efe4e16-9b61-11e9-b8ce-8b459ed04726.
72. Aisha Sarihi, "Why Oil- and Gas-Rich Gulf Arab States are Turning to Coal." Arab Gulf States Institute in Washington (blog post), August 21, 2018; https://agsiw.org/oil-gas-rich-gulf-arab-states-turning-coal/.
73. BP, "BP Statistical Review of World Energy 2019."
74. Author interview with Abu Dhabi energy sector executive on condition of anonymity, January 2020.
75. UAE-funded plants have been built or planned in 25 countries, including Saudi Arabia, the UK, Mauritius, Ghana, and Uzbekistan.

76. Jeremy S. Pal and Elfatih A. B. Eltahir, "Future Temperature in Southwest Asia Projected to Exceed a Threshold for Human Adaptability." *Nature Climate Change* 6, no. 2 (February 2016): 197–200; Christoph Schär, "The Worst Heat Waves to Come." *Nature Climate Change* 6 (October 26, 2015): 128.
77. J.-F. Mercure et al., "Macroeconomic Impact of Stranded Fossil Fuel Assets." *Nature Climate Change* 8, no. 7 (2018): 588.

Annex: Future Power Plant Projects in the UAE

Project	*Fuel type*	*Planned capacity (MW)*	*Location*	*Status*	*Expected year online*	*Investment (million USD)*
Ajman 100 MW solar power plant	Solar	100	Ajman	Planned	est. 2019	136
Barakah nuclear power plant	Nuclear	5600	Al Dhafra, Abu Dhabi	Under construction	2020	18,700
Al Warsan waste-to-energy power plant	Biomass	171	Al Warsan, Dubai	Under construction	2020	681
Jebel Ali K Station phase III expansion	Natural gas	590	Jebel Ali, Dubai	Under construction	2020	218
Al Aweer natural gas power plant Unit H phase IV	Natural gas	815	Dubai	Under construction	2020	300
Sharjah 30 MW multi-fuel waste to energy power plant	Biomass	30	Al Saj'ah, Sharjah	Under construction	2020	220
Al Sajah Bee'ah 20 MW solar power plant	Solar	20	Sharjah	Planned	2020	22
RAK FEWA coal fired power plant	Coal	1800	Ras Al Khaimah	Planned	2021	2177
Jebel Ali E Station gas turbine extension	Natural gas	300	Jebel Ali, Dubai	Planned/under construction	2021	53
Al Layyah combined cycle power plant	Natural gas	1026	Layyah, Sharjah	Planned	2021	550
Al Sajah 35 MW waste to energy power plant^	Biomass	35	Sharjah	Planned	2021	39
RAK Utico clean coal power plant	Coal	270	Khorkhowir, Ras al-Khaimah	Planned	2022	400

(continued)

(continued)

Project	*Fuel type*	*Planned capacity (MW)*	*Location*	*Status*	*Expected year online*	*Investment (million USD)*
RAK natural gas power plant	Natural gas	2200	Ras Al Khaymah	Planned	2022	2420
Sharjah 1.8 GW CCGT natural gas power plant	Natural gas	1800	Sharjah	Planned	2022	1000
Hassyan coal power station	Coal	3600	Dubai	Under construction	2023	3400
Hatta Hydroelectric (pumped storage) plant	Hydro	250	Dubai	Planned	2023	523
400 MW pumped hydro storage island in the Gulf	Hydro	400	N/A	Planned	2024	840
Mohammed bin Rashid Al Maktoum Solar Park (MBR solar park)	Solar	5000	Dubai	Partially operating/under construction	2030	13,600
RAK Utico solar power plant*	Solar	40	Ras Al Khaimah	Under construction	N/A	250
RAK Utico hybrid landfill gas-solar-agro power plant^	Hybrid gas-solar-agro	16	Ras Al Khaimah	Planned	N/A	100
Jebel Ali M Station expansion*	Natural gas	700	Jebel Ali, Dubai	Under construction	N/A	400
Umm Al Qaiwain solar power plant	Solar	200	Falaj Al Mu'alla, UAQ	Planned	N/A	N/A
Museum of the future solar power plant	Solar	3	Dubai	Planned	N/A	N/A

(continued)

(continued)

Project	*Fuel type*	*Planned capacity (MW)*	*Location*	*Status*	*Expected year online*	*Investment (million USD)*
Al Dhafra 2 GW solar power plant	Solar	2000	Al Dhafra, Abu Dhabi	Planned	N/A	N/A
RAK FEWA hydro power plant	Hydro	N/A	Ras Al Khaimah	Planned	N/A	N/A
Sajja 80 MW waste to energy power plant	Biomass	80	Sajja, Sharjah	Under construction	N/A	505

*Expected to be online by 2018 based on the most recent source
Source UAE government and company press releases

CHAPTER 4

The Rise of Renewables in the Gulf States: Is the 'Rentier Effect' Still Holding Back the Energy Transition?

Faris Al-Sulayman

Introduction

Ten years ago, one might argue, the story of the rise of renewables in the Arab Gulf states could have gone in a rather different trajectory. Using their oil wealth and unrivaled land and solar resources, these states could have collectively chosen to make a dramatic pivot and become regional and world leaders in renewables deployment. After all, they began the twentieth century as global leaders in another energy resource, with similar investment models. Instead, under the constraints of the rentier state and perhaps in an effort to avoid actively participating in the climate emergency narrative, countries in the region are only now beginning to make inroads into the world of renewables, arguably ceding global energy leadership to countries with often fewer resources.[1] States such as

F. Al-Sulayman (✉)
The King Faisal Center for Research and Islamic Studies, Riyadh, Saudi Arabia
e-mail: f.al-sulayman@lse.ac.uk

R. Mills and L.-C. Sim (eds.), *Low Carbon Energy in the Middle East and North Africa*, International Political Economy Series,
https://doi.org/10.1007/978-3-030-59554-8_4

Germany, Japan, and China, as well as neighbors such as Jordan, made the early risky investments in renewables that helped drive down the cost curve, granting them a privileged position in this emerging global industry.

What explains the slow start? Where are the GCC states now in terms of renewables deployment? And for the countries that have begun making some progress, what explains the difference between them and the others? This will be the focus of this chapter.

A good place to begin understanding the outlook of some of these hydrocarbon-rich states is to look at their approaches to climate change mitigation efforts and renewables development as important tools in that battle. There is a growing literature—addressed in the next section—looking at the behavior of these states in climate change forums; with few exceptions the Gulf states played a historically obstructionist role. If shifting the power and transport sectors away from oil dependence and toward renewables became a solution, the thinking went, then states would be implicitly accepting the premise that oil was the problem. And if oil-rich states began down this road, it would signal the beginning of the end.

In recent years, further down along the cost curve, the economic case for renewables in the power sector has become too compelling to ignore. States in the region have embarked on ambitious renewables development plans, with the UAE taking the lead. In fact, a powerful argument could be made that states in the region were just waiting for a better bargain, and that the energy transformation is not a sprint, but a marathon.

Decreases in government revenues across the GCC states since the oil price decline in 2014 have also exerted stronger pressures for fiscal reforms, and a deeper understanding of the opportunity cost associated with consuming a barrel of oil locally that could otherwise be sold abroad at international market prices. The slashing of wasteful energy subsidies is now also high on the list of priorities. In addition to the obvious economic impetus to engage in price reforms, the low oil price environment has also provided a unique political opportunity to publicly justify the reduction of subsidies, allowing governments to deflect some blame, if and when prices do recover, on market forces now far beyond their reach. There is indeed an argument to be made that such reforms could never have been considered in a stronger fiscal environment. Several member states led by the UAE took advantage of these opportunities, and have lifted subsidies on power and fuel to varying degrees. This has opened some market opportunities, allowing distributed solar energy, in particular, to reach grid parity in a number of tariff segments and markets between 2014 and 2019.

Taking a step back, this chapter will begin by conducting a review of the literature on the topic of renewables deployment in the region, and more specifically in resource-rich states. Though there has been much written journalistically about renewables in the region, more academic analysis of renewables in the rentier states of the Gulf is scarce, particularly through a comparative political lens.

Section "Literature Review" will give a historical overview of renewables deployment in the region over the past decade. This will mostly be a story of ambitious plans but a mixed record of follow through. A survey of current levels of utility-scale deployment will give important context to later discussions, along with an overview of future plans in each of the GCC states and an assessment of the credibility of these plans. The section will conclude with a similar survey of distributed renewable generation and policy across the GCC states.

Section "Renewables Development Over the Last Decade in the GCC" will then look closely at the Saudi case, both because of its size, and because it lies roughly in the middle of the 6 GCC states in terms of fiscal buffers. The early challenges facing utility-scale projects will be examined, as well as the viability of the solutions that have been put in place, and the obstacles that remain a hindrance to achieving the Kingdom's stated goals in the future, including inter-institutional competition and historically weak private sector participation in the energy sector.

The period between 2016 and 2020 has seen the UAE make considerable tangible progress toward renewables targets both at the utility and distributed scales, setting it apart from the other states in the region. Section "What Is the Picture Like Today?" will seek to explain why, despite seemingly similar underlying political economic models, the UAE has been able to surge ahead; and what lessons this offers to the other GCC states.

Literature Review

A starting point of reference for this chapter is the well-established literature on the social contract in the rentier states of the Gulf. Beginning with the work of Beblawi and Luciani and looking particularly at the work of Steffen Hertog,[2] the distributive and clientelistic nature of these states was described, and it is on the basis of this understanding of the way these states function that this chapter seeks to make the case for why renewables deployment was delayed, and then pursued differently across the member states.

More specifically looking at climate policy in the GCC states, Depledge described in some depth the early obstructionist attitude adopted by these states in international forums.[3] Later work by Luomi,[4] Michaelowa and Luomi and Al-Sarihi studied the roots of this obstructionist approach, and the transition that took place in recent years toward a more cooperative one[5]; Sim looked more specifically at the case of Abu Dhabi 'greening' its credentials and the start of a trend acknowledging the soft power potential of projecting an image of sustainability.[6]

Looking directly at renewable energy policy in the GCC states, Doukas et al. were the first to study the issue in some depth in the mid-2000s,[7] assessing the renewable resources region and the rationale for development. AlNaser et al. built on this understanding with an update on regional development,[8] and Al-Maamari et al. continued by looking at the challenges facing adoption in the GCC states.[9] Since 2014 El-Katiri has provided a detailed understanding of the renewable energy landscape in her publication with Husain,[10] and more recently with colleagues in the 2019 IRENA *Renewable Energy Market Analysis: The GCC Region*.[11] Yamada looked more closely at the emergence of the renewable energy agenda with the unveiling of a new wave of Saudi development plans in 2015.[12]

Perhaps most directly related to the scope of this chapter, Alatay et al. looked at renewable energy policy variation across the GCC states, arguing that political leadership and policy transfer explained the early lead then established by the UAE[13]; building on earlier work by Reiche which looked at early renewable energy policies in the GCC states and the opportunities and challenges facing deployment.[14]

What appears to be missing in the literature is an analysis of the 'rentier' effect on renewables energy deployment in the GCC as they seemingly stand on the precipice of a large-scale energy transformation. Apart from the outlier of the UAE, there appears to now be a divergence between a number of states, offering more data points to understand the underlying causes.

Renewables Development Over the Last Decade in the GCC

Early Forays into the World of Renewables

With the exception of a number of small, remote solar installations developed by National Oil Companies (NOCs) and some of the region's militaries, the earliest forays into renewables in the GCC states emerged from a host of newly established research and development institutions in the period between 2006 and 2013. Led by the ambitious plans of Masdar, the sustainable city built on the outskirts of Abu Dhabi, and two institutions established in the name of the late Saudi King Abdullah, the King Abdullah University of Science and Technology (KAUST) and the King Abdullah City for Atomic and Renewable Energy (KACARE), these institutions began conducting research on the viability and suitability of a wide range of renewables technologies to the region.[15] Thereafter, several similar institutions began conducting research and testing in the other GCC states, notably the Kuwait Foundation for Arts and Sciences (KFAS).

The research conducted in these institutions represented the GCC states' first forays into the world of renewables, but had little impact on the political economy conditions of the states in a way that would facilitate wider adoption. The story of KACARE, as an example, is indicative of the broader trend. Emerging from a Royal Decree in 2010, the institution was established as the focal point for renewable and atomic energy deployment in the Kingdom, announcing grandiose plans to deploy 41 GWp of solar and 16 GWp of wind before 2030.[16] Confronted by stiff competition from other state institutions and an unclear mandate, the focus of the institution gradually turned to research and training, at least in the renewables arena. A similar picture emerged in the case of Masdar City in Abu Dhabi. A host of early companies, mostly outgrowths of local conglomerates, were established and shut down as early promises proved to be beyond their institutional reach.[17] In Saudi Arabia in particular, this created a formidable credibility problem for state institutions, which they are still trying to overcome today. The political transition that followed the death of King Abdullah in 2015 ushered in a new period of planning and the creation of a host of new institutions, but also led to an opaque process of decay and relegation for older institutions. In particular, the Ministry of Energy's Renewable Energy

Project Development Office (REPDO), and the PIF would come to play dominant roles in the renewable energy space. And in the nuclear energy space, the King Abdulaziz City for Science and Technology would play an increasingly important role. This phenomenon will be examined more closely in section "A Closer Look at Saudi Arabia".

It is noteworthy that Oman's early experiences with renewables came from a different set of institutions, as their oil and gas sector began deploying solar thermal technology—on a substantially larger scale that its neighbors—for enhanced oil recovery (EOR) as early as 2013. The 1021 MW Miraah project, developed by Petroleum Development Oman (PDO) and Glasspoint Solar in 2017, represented a different kind of early entry into the world of renewables, saving 5.6 trillion BTUs of natural gas per year to be used elsewhere in the industrial and power sectors.[18]

Unlike the other Gulf states, Oman took on some technology risk and chose to enter the world of renewables through a focused high value deployment, with a strong case for financial viability. Despite favorable conditions for renewables deployment in Oman, however, the Miraah project remained a rather unique case of early large-scale deployment, likely driven by the internal corporate incentives of the PDO and not broader political economy conditions in the country.

Nonetheless it would not be until the period of 2016–2019 before the GCC states, led by the UAE, began the process of integrating renewables goals into the highest level development strategies of the state, initiating legislation and endowing institutions with enough clout to create reusable platforms capable of facilitating large-scale renewables deployment.

What Is the Picture Like Today?

Painting a clear picture of the renewables landscape today is a key, if obvious, part of answering the questions outlined in the introduction. Table 4.1, using data compiled in a 2019 IRENA report on the region and complemented using an updated IRENA data set in 2020, details renewables deployment in the GCC states as of end 2019.[19] For consistency, these figures will be used throughout the chapter to give an overview of scale and technology choices across the renewables landscape.

The period between 2014 and 2019, in which more than 75% of the current renewables capacity has been developed, has shown that states in the region have a strong technology preference for solar photovoltaic (PV) deployment, and predominantly at utility-scale. Qatar is a notable

Table 4.1 Renewable energy deployment for power generation in GCC states by end of 2019, in MW of installed capacity

	Solar photovoltaic (PV)	*Concentrated solar power (CSP)*	*Wind*	*Biomass and waste*	*Total renewable energy (RE)*
Bahrain	6	0	1	0	7
Kuwait	43	50	12	0	105
Oman	8	0	0	0	8
Qatar	5	0	0	38	43
Saudi Arabia	344	50	3	0	397
UAE	1783	100	1	1	1885

exception, where most of the renewable energy capacity has been developed as part of a waste to energy plant at the Domestic Solid Waste Management Centre (DSWMC).

Going forward, it appears that states in the region will double down on this technology preference, with solar PV still representing more than three-quarters of short-term planned capacity additions. Countries with strong wind resources, however, notably Saudi Arabia and Oman, are also planning their first large-scale onshore wind deployments for 2020. Oman's plans over the next two years are noteworthy, standing out from other states in the region with a strong focus on solar thermal technology. The latter represents more than 50% of planned capacity additions, though not technically in the power sector. As discussed in the previous section, Oman's deployment of solar thermal for enhanced oil recovery (EOR) is a continuation of a trend that was set in motion as early as 2010, and was made more likely following investments made by the state in its technology partner, Glasspoint, in 2014.[20] The maturity of some of the oil and gas fields in Oman has also undoubtably contributed to their early interest in solar technology for EOR, but this trend may spread to the rest of the region over the coming decade, as other heavy oil wells begin to enter maturity.

Table 4.2 uses data compiled from the 2019 IRENA GCC report and more recent data from various government sources to paint a picture of credible deployment plans in 2020–2021.[21] The term credible is used here to refer to future power projects that are in the final planning stages, either the tendering process or currently under construction.

Table 4.2 Credible short- to medium-term plans, in MW, of planned capacity

	PV	*CSP*	*Wind*	*Biomass and waste*	*Total RE*
Bahrain	100	0	5	0	105
Kuwait	1500	0	0	0	1500
Oman	600	0	200	0	800
Qatar	700	0	0	0	700
Saudi Arabia	2670	0	400	0	3070
UAE	3877	700	0	190	4767

The picture stands in sharp contrast to the one painted in Table 4.1, with all states in the region now seemingly on the precipice of a substantial acceleration in renewables deployment, which is set to see a 10-fold increase in installed capacity in the next two to three years. In many of these states credible installation plans (under construction or in tender process) for the next 18 months exceed the total installed capacity thus far. Despite this, the poor track record of some of these states at meeting previous sets of targets should lead to a healthy dose of skepticism when considering new figures. There are, however, a few structural reasons why this time things may be a little different, some of which we will explore in section "What Explains the Differences".[22] A closer look at the plans of each of the member states at this important juncture is worthwhile.[23]

Bahrain

Bahrain has made two sets of modest commitments for renewables deployment, targeting 5% of electricity production by 2025 and 10% by 2035. As seen in Table 4.2, the short-term credible plans revolve around one 100 MWp solar PV plant. With the smallest grid in the region, and less anticipated growth in energy consumption, Bahraini planners are likely wary of the grid impact of adding significant non-dispatchable power.[24] Though it is noteworthy that the grid of the Dubai Electricity and Water Authority (DEWA) is of similar size and has managed to put forward significantly more ambitious renewables deployment and integration plans.

Kuwait

Kuwait has set one overarching renewables target, looking to develop enough capacity to supply 15% of consumption by 2030. All credible short-term plans are focused on the 1500 MWp solar PV plant set to be built at Al Dibdibah as part of the Shagaya Phase II development. Unlike some of its neighbors, Kuwait has not taken steps to create separate institutions charged with developing its renewable energy strategy, and the Shagaya project is owned by the Kuwait National Petroleum Company. This may be a realistic reflection of the limits of the state's institutional capacity to establish a new entity capable of overseeing such a large capital deployment within the timeframe set of 2021. After a further sustained decline in oil prices following the Covid-19 pandemic, the Kuwaiti cabinet announced in July the cancellation of the 5 main outstanding tenders for the Shagaya Phase II project, casting doubt on the country's ability to make progress towards meeting the overarching targets in the near-term.

Oman

Oman's overarching renewables target is to supply 10% of electricity generation by 2025. An ambitious but manageable goal, as the 800 MWp of capacity categorized as part of their credible short-term plans in Table 4.2, would go a long way toward achieving this target (800 MWp would represent more than 10% of Oman's generation capacity today, although this is offset by the renewables' lower capacity factor).[25] Unlike Kuwait, which also has significant wind resources, Oman is choosing to undertake a diverse development strategy; 200 MWp of wind is set to be developed in Dhofar, with the EPC contract for the first 50 MWp already awarded. The remaining 600 MWp will be developed through two large PV plants.

Saudi Arabia

Saudi Arabia revised its main renewables target upwards at the start of 2019, aiming to develop 27.3 GWp of renewables by 2024 (up from 9.5 GWp), and 58.7 GWp by 2030.[26] The 27.3 GWp figure would represent almost a third of projected capacity in 2023. These are by far the most ambitious targets set in the region, and observers have received these figures with some skepticism. As mentioned earlier in the chapter, the Kingdom had announced plans in 2013 to target 54 GWp of renewables generation capacity by 2032 through KACARE, plans which were later scrapped, and the institution tasked with their execution sidelined. The credibility of these plans has been further called into question due to uncertainty about which government entities were responsible for delivering these targets; while the initial targets and framework for renewable Independent Power Producer (IPP) projects was established through an entity within the Ministry of Energy and Mineral Resources (now known as the Ministry of Energy) called the Renewable Energy Project Development Office (REPDO) and its National Renewable Energy Program (NREP), the Public Investment Fund (PIF) was also announcing that it, along with its partner Softbank, would be developing $200 billion worth of projects in Saudi.[27] By the second half of 2019 these two plans had been consolidated, with state institutions now in agreement that the PIF-Softbank alliance would be responsible for 70% of the renewables target, and REPDO the remaining 30%; the former would be delivering projects through negotiated deals with international partners, as opposed to the competitive tendering process deployed by the latter. In the credible plans short-term horizon outlined in Table 4.2, we have placed a total of 6 projects for which Request For Proposals (RFPs) were released in August 2019, and a further 4 projects with RFPs released in March 2020.

Qatar

Considering the resources available to the state, Qatar has arguably set the most modest renewables target of the group, aiming to build a 700 MWp solar PV plant at Al-Kharsaag, with the first 350 MWp to be completed in 2020. Like the Kuwaiti case, the national oil company, Qatar Petroleum, is a major sponsor of these first large-scale renewables projects. And though a longer-term target to produce 20% of its electricity using solar energy by 2030 is also part of the Qatar National Vision (QNV) 2030, a roadmap to achieve this target has not been outlined. Qatar's abundance of natural gas resources means that it is able to produce relatively clean combustible and dispatchable power domestically at very low prices. This dynamic is an amplified version of the dynamic playing out in other rentier states, where the abundance of low-cost oil and gas resources (opportunity costs aside), has undoubtably delayed the uptake of renewables technologies, and in an atmosphere of particular fiscal abundance in

Qatar, the opportunity cost of exporting these resources at market prices is more easily ignored by planners.

UAE

With the strongest track record thus far in the GCC, the UAE also has some of the most ambitious plans moving forward. The two headline targets at the federal level aim for 27% clean energy by 2021 and 44% of generation capacity by 2050. Credible short-term plans center on a series of solar PV and CSP plants planned for Dubai and Abu Dhabi. Individual emirates also have also set their own targets, with Dubai and Abu Dhabi both targeting 7% renewables capacity by 2020.

Looking at the member states' plans as a whole it is clear that the UAE is still anticipated to retain its substantial lead, though Saudi Arabia and Kuwait are also planning on adding significant capacity, predominantly through large state-backed utility-scale projects, narrowing the large gap that exists today. The UAE's earlier efforts to lift energy subsidies in the period between 2008 and 2014, particularly for commercial and industrial consumers, also allowed it to become the regional leader in the development of distributed solar PV. More recent subsidy reform in Saudi Arabia and Oman, however, which has led to increases in electricity costs for some heavy energy users, will also likely translate into more distributed PV projects in these markets, particularly at the commercial and industrial scale; the next section will look at the potential in these segments in greater detail.

Distributed Renewable Energy in the GCC

It is really at the distributed scale that one sees many of the archetypical effects of the rentier paradigm affecting the development and deployment of renewable energy. Here the distortive effects of energy subsidies on the incentives of the private sector and citizen are laid bare, and the market as it is experienced by players outside of the state—subject to its set utility prices—has insured that private investment in distributed energy resources has been limited till now. In other states that have experienced strong growth in distributed PV over the last 10 years, not only have utility prices been significantly higher, but a variety of incentives have been deployed.

As seen in Table 4.3, the general trend among the GCC states has been to set their highest generally applied electricity tariff brackets somewhere near $0.08/kWh, with the exception of the outliers of Qatar and the UAE. The figure of $0.08/kWh is approximately the average cost of electricity delivery in Saudi Arabia with deregulated fuel prices in the range of $50/barrel, as calculated in a recent KAPSARC report.[28] The DEWA tariff of $0.12/kWh, which includes a fuel surcharge, is also calculated to be a cost reflective tariff. For the sake of this analysis, the range of $0.08–0.12/kWh will be used to describe the approximate real cost of electricity in the GCC states.

Looking at Table 4.3 in greater detail, it is clear that although some energy consumers do pay rates in the cost range highlighted above, most consumers in the region continue to pay tariffs significantly below this range. Industrial consumers in Saudi Arabia, for example, pay a tariff of $0.05/kWh in 2020. Over most of the last decade this has made the economic case for distributed generation—mostly in the form of rooftop

Table 4.3 Highest and lowest electricity tariffs for large energy consumers

	Highest tariff		*Lowest tariff*	
	$/kWh	*Notes*	*$/kWh*	*Notes*
Bahrain	0.08	Commercial tariff	0.08	Same tariff for all large non-domestic energy users
Kuwait	0.08	Governmental tariff, significantly higher than next highest tariff	0.03	Industrial and Agricultural tariff less than half of commercial and governmental rate
Oman	0.17	Cost reflective tariff (CRT), only applied at certain times (TOU), specific to specific regions	0.03	Agricultural tariff, Industrial tariff 0.03 in winter months
Qatar	0.04	Governmental tariff, significantly higher than next highest tariff	0.02	Agricultural tariff
Saudi Arabia	0.09	Governmental tariff, similar to tariff applied to large residential and commercial energy consumers	0.05	Industrial, health care, and education
UAE	0.121	Specific to certain regions	0.01	Agriculture, Abu Dhabi

PV installations—weak. Admittedly this has now begun to change with the levelized cost of energy (LCOE) of rooftop solar at the commercial and industrial scale dropping below \$0.05/kWh.[29]

Despite the fact that developing distributed solar PV is already economically viable for many energy consumers in the GCC states, the size of the savings is subject to some uncertainty, being dependent on the rate of subsidy reform pursued by each state (Fig. 4.1). This means energy consumers are faced with investment decisions characterized by large potential savings over a 30-year period with relatively low risk, but a high upfront capital commitment to an unfamiliar technology, with uncertain project payback periods of around 7–10 years. For many heavy energy users in the commercial and industrial sectors, this is not a convincing investment case. Diverting significant capital away from their core businesses is unappealing, even if internal rates of return (IRR) are likely to be 10–15% or higher over the full project lifetime.

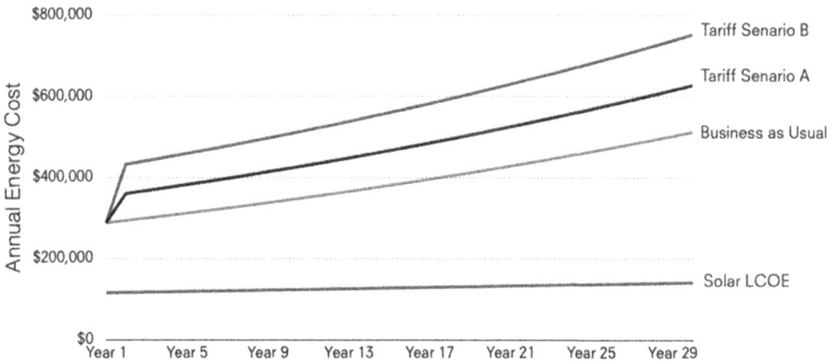

Fig. 4.1 Levelized cost of energy (LCOE) of a typical 2 MWp solar PV system in Saudi Arabia (CapEx discounted over system lifetime) compared to different tariff scenarios (2019) (*Source* SEC, DEWA, Haala Energy); Note on scenarios: BAU: commercial tariff (SAR 0.3/kWp) increases by inflation only, averaging 2% per annum; A: commercial tariff increase by 25%, and then with inflation thereafter; B: tariffs increase by 50% to (SAR 0.45/kWp (current DEWA price) with inflation thereafter; Solar LCOE: The capital cost of a solar EPC discounted over the lifetime of the system, plus the cost of maintenance and cleaning which rises with inflation. The area between the Solar LCOE line and each scenario line is indicative of the return on investment [ROI])

Here we can see the rentier state prohibitively affecting distributed renewables deployment in two distinct ways. The first and more direct effect is caused by the distributive state feeling an obligation to maintain energy subsidies as part of the social contract.[30] This has prolonged the journey of distributed renewable generation toward economic feasibility. The Citizens' Account, a direct cash subsidy program rolled out in Saud Arabia in 2018 with millions of individuals signed on, is meant to mitigate the effects of the then newly imposed VAT and increases in fuel and electricity prices.[31] Once this program is fully functional, the state will likely feel less politically inhibited in further removing subsidies, particularly on residential consumers.

The second is related to the predictability of pricing in the future. With the exception of the UAE and Bahrain, the GCC states have not given clear indications of where electricity pricing is heading, and when it is set to change. From the perspective of the region's rulers, this maintains energy subsidies as a bargaining chip to be wielded when politically expedient. From the perspective of energy consumers considering capital investments in solar PV, for example, this makes the investment case uncertain, as depicted in Fig. 4.1. The absence of strong and credible institutions—albeit in some states more than others—capable of outliving a specific minister or ruler plays an important role in shaping how businesses and individual consumers in the GCC assess long-term investment opportunities in renewable assets.

A Closer Look at Saudi Arabia

Both due to its size, and the fact that Saudi Arabia lies roughly in the middle of the GCC in terms of fiscal buffers, this section will now take a closer look at what explains the current level of renewables deployment in the Kingdom and its future plans. The picture given in the section above of how things currently stand in the Kingdom is one of expansive ambition, but as yet unproven regulatory and policy capabilities.

Within the unveiled plans, and more broadly the rhetoric of the state in international forums, is a clear if belated acknowledgment of the soft power potential that can come from embracing the renewable energy transition, and an understanding that the Saudi market can be a launchpad for national champions. The centrality of the NREP to discussions about the Vision 2030 and the repeated references to the projects by state representatives at international forums and in the media is a testament to this shift. Despite the fact that the Kingdom's climate negotiators still predominantly emanate from the NOC, there has been a notable rhetorical shift. This narrative, unlike earlier and more isolated attempts in 2011–2013, has now been uniformly adopted by all the institutions of the state. The plan is to build a lot of solar, mostly at the utility scale. Just how much is to be built, and by whom, has been the subject of more debate.

The Credibility Gap

At the utility scale, Saudi Arabia's plans include two headline figures: \$200 Billion—the figure the PIF and Softbank have said they are looking to spend on developing solar, storage, and solar related manufacturing in the Kingdom—and 57.8 GWp by 2030—the amount of renewables capacity the state is planning to develop over the coming decade. Both these figures were released before the first utility-scale project in the Kingdom was completed. In fact, as mentioned in the previous section, the 57.8 GWp figure and the closer target of 27.3 GWp by 2024 are figures that have been revised up from more modest targets set in 2018. For reference, the total power generation capacity in the Kingdom in 2019 is 75 GW. The \$200 billion figure also took the renewables world by surprise and was met with a fair amount of incredulity and skepticism, with observers highlighting that that figure would be sufficient to build more than twice as much capacity as is available in the Kingdom in 2019 (75 GW).[32]

The lofty ambitions are commendable, considering the scale of the climate crisis and the ground Saudi Arabia has to cover to make up for lost time. These plans do not exist in a vacuum, however, and come at a time when the Kingdom has struggled to bridge a credibility gap, left over from older institutions and plans that made similar claims earlier in the decade. As discussed in section "Renewables Development Over the Last Decade in the GCC" of this chapter, both KACARE and the SEC had made plans to develop utility-scale solar installations; the latter institution going as far as issuing an RFP and prequalifying companies for a specific set of projects at Rafha and Al Jouf.[33]

A remnant of clientelistic fiefdoms discussed by Hertog and others,[34] these developments mirror the rise and fall of other institutions in the Kingdom. KACARE, for example, an institution named after a former king, clearly fell out of favor once new leadership assumed power in 2015. A similar battle for part of the renewables deployment mandate has played out more recently between the PIF and the Ministry of Energy,

Industry, and Mineral Resources (MEIM), now simply the Ministry of Energy.[35] As outlined in leaked comments to Western financial press agencies, authorities from these very institutions described the two plans as being incongruous. Intervention by the royal court and consolidation of these two sets of plans would take place in 2019, with the PIF receiving 70% of the mandate and only 30% to be managed by MEIM through the competitive development tender process. More recent developments in the first half of 2020, suggesting a rift between the PIF and Softbank, may bring even this arrangement in to question.

All this requires investors both foreign and local, to maintain a detailed and up-to-date map of the institutional arrangements in the Kingdom in order to gauge the viability of the proposed plans. What underlies investors' and observers' ongoing skepticism, however, is an understanding that the causes which lie beneath the early changes and reversals in plans have not been fully addressed. Institutional mandates, and the plans that lie within them, are regularly and unpredictably in flux. The fluidity of these arrangements, and perceptions that they are attached more closely to individuals managing intuitions—at various levels—rather than the intuitions themselves, has likely slowed progress.

The number of institutions involved in the process of forming and implementing policy is indicative of this:

- The Ministry of Energy (MoE), formerly part of the Ministry of Energy, Industry, and Mineral Resources (MEIM)
- The Saudi Electricity Company (SEC)
- The Electricity Cogeneration and Regulation Authority (ECRA)
- The King Abdullah City for Atomic and Renewable Energy (KACARE)
- King Abdulaziz City for Science and Technology (KACST)
- The Public Investment Fund (PIF)
- The Saudi Energy Efficiency Center (SEEC)
- Saudi Arabia's National Energy Services Company (Tarshid)
- Saudi Aramco
- National Grid

The opaque and fluid nature of these relationships and the hierarchies between these entities continue to shape the way policy is formed, reformed, and implemented.

Saudi Arabia's net metering initiative, the 'Small Scale Solar PV Systems Regulations,' has been one notable arena where this kind of inter-institutional competition has played out since 2016. This regulation, first circulated as a white paper in 2017, intended to provide a framework through which businesses and individual energy users could install solar PV on their properties, trade excess generated energy with the grid, and benefit from the credit they accumulated later on in the evenings or during other seasons of the year.[36] The regulations also outlined specific requirements for consultants and contractors looking to qualify to work on these programs, with the distribution service provider, the SEC in this case, managing this process.

The regulation was set to go into effect in July of 2018, but as of Q4 2020 the program has still not gotten off the ground, perhaps because the incentive structures of the main stakeholders are not clearly aligned. The regulations were formulated by the electricity regulator and handed down to the SEC, a nominally profit seeking and partially privatized entity; which is now expected to ignore its economic incentives and assist its customers in replacing power they supply with power from solar PV.

National Champions

Another story that comes out of the Saudi case, and mirrors earlier developments in the UAE, is the emergence of new and powerful constituencies that are driving and shaping the renewables development agenda. Broadly speaking, the constituency consists of entities that are looking to use the Saudi market as a launchpad to compete globally.

The first element of this constituency is ACWA Power, a Saudi company that owns, invests in, and operates, power and water facilities globally. Following an investment in 2018, the company is also now partially owned by the PIF.[37] Established in 2004, ACWA has been accumulating assets in the MENA region and as far afield as Vietnam and South Africa. Its renewable energy unit has taken the forefront in recent years, having won large IPP tenders in Morocco for one of the world's largest CSP plants, and in the UAE for a similarly large PV plant. More recently, and unsurprisingly, ACWA also won Saudi Arabia's first large-scale PV tender for 300 MWp at Sakaka.[38] This has meant that ACWA is now singularly well placed to take advantage of the large opportunities afforded by Saudi Arabia's renewables deployment target of 27.3 GWp by 2024, and to use the portfolio it accumulates through this process to better qualify it to take advantage of opportunities globally. This approach is not new, and many of the largest contenders in international renewable energy tenders are state-owned or state-backed companies; EDF, Engie, Enel, Masdar, and others.

The second and more prominent element of this constituency is the PIF itself. Through its investment in ACWA Power and its more broad interest in the renewable energy space through its partnership with SoftBank, the PIF is also positioning itself to take advantage of—and simultaneously drive forward—the energy transition set to take place in the Kingdom. The pace with which this transition takes place, and the degree to which the PIF is able to leverage these opportunities to tackle others in future developing markets, is now undoubtedly a priority for the PIF. The PIF-SoftBank partnership is also set to include manufacturing and energy storage plans, ensuring that many of the opportunities made available by the energy transition strategy will be within its grasp. In a similar vein, SABIC—the state-owned petrochemical giant—recently announced the launch of a JV with the SCHMID Group to manufacture vanadium redox flow batteries in the Kingdom. All these plans also broadly fit into Vision 2030 plans to encourage local manufacturing.

And as observers will note from recent political developments, the PIF is closely linked to the current leadership of the Kingdom, with its managing director having assumed the position of Chairman of Aramco months before the 2020 IPO. This alignment of interests in the political economy of the state likely bodes well for the progress of Saudi Arabia's renewables plans.

This arrangement mirrors a somewhat similar one that had taken shape in the UAE between 2014 and 2018, as Masdar—a company owned by Abu Dhabi's Mubadala—began to accumulate a solar energy portfolio by winning tenders in Dubai, and using this experience to compete globally.[39] This strategy extended in to the commercial and industrial space as well, as Mubadala invested in Enviromena, a solar project developer that has since become a regional leader.

The late rentier state, characterized by state capitalist tendencies, is now absorbing the renewable energy agenda into its orbit, with state-backed institutions positioning themselves carefully around various parts of the value chain to take advantage of the large number of projects set to take place as part of the energy transition.

What Explains the Differences

The picture painted thus far of renewables development in the GCC states shows that, despite what may be considered a 'rentier handicap'—inhibiting large-scale early adoption of renewable energy—the last five years have seen a noticeable divergence in achievements and ambition in this space.

Rents Are not the Reason for the Divergence

As a group of states, compared to neighbors such as Jordan, it is clear that the availability of low-cost fossil fuel resources inhibited large-scale early adoption of renewable energy at the utility scale. Particularly when rents were increasing and budgets were in surplus—as was the case between 2009 and 2014 when an early adoption strategy might have been implemented—the political economies of the GCC states were not sufficiently sensitive to the opportunity costs associated with burning fossil fuels domestically for power instead of exporting them at international market prices.[40] It is worth mentioning that the opportunity cost calculation is more complex on the ground for policy makers in states like Saudi Arabia, who have millions of barrels of excess daily oil production capacity, and are generally limited by quotas agreed by OPEC or OPEC+. Pierru and Fatih modeled the costs under different scenarios in their informative 2020 paper.[41]

At the distributed scale, where solar PV must compete with subsidized electricity prices, it is the distributive expectations placed on the state by the rentier social contract which has led to persistently low electricity prices and the slow proliferation of the technology on rooftops across Gulf cities.

Within the group of states, however, high rents do not seem to explain either extremes of adoption. The divergence in approaches within the 'Super Rentiers' of Kuwait, Qatar, and the UAE makes this abundantly clear. UAE, on the one hand, has led the region in recent years in renewables development, while Qatar has been a noteworthy laggard. So what does explain the divergence?[42]

Economic Ambition and Dynamism

As discussed in the section looking at national champions in the Saudi case, a recognition of the economic opportunities afforded by the energy transition and the bureaucratic capacity to take advantage of these opportunities seems to be a defining characteristic of the Emirati case and increasingly the Saudi case.

The pursuit of these economic opportunities by state-affiliated entities has created new and powerful clients and constituencies that help ensure targets are ambitious, and that plans materialize. The case of Masdar, and increasingly ACWA Power, using renewable project tenders in their home markets as opportunities to gain portfolio experience and credentials, and then using that experience to compete in international tenders, is an example of this dynamic. Inversely the absence of such economic actors in some of the other GCC states may go some way to explaining the more modest renewable energy targets.

Clients and Rent Seeking Pressures

The political power of constituencies that currently benefit from subsidized energy is also an important factor in determining the pace and extent of subsidy reform pursued by each state.

A salient example of this dynamic is the Kuwaiti National Assembly, which represents both populist and mercantile voices and wields the power to bring down governments. In recent years the Assembly has steadfastly rejected efforts by governments to engage in subsidy reform, even as neighbors have successfully implemented similar measures.[43]

In other markets, the differential between electricity tariff rates for commercial and residential consumers in Saudi Arabia for example—$0.08 and $0.05, respectively—is also indicative of the power of specific constituencies. In the Saudi case, this is evidence of the rigidity of the state's social contract with working-class citizens paying the lowest slab of the residential tariff, and simultaneously, the malleability and weakness of the social contract with the local private sector and business elite.[44] Similarly, the maintenance of low industrial electricity tariffs in Saudi Arabia of $0.05 and low diesel prices (used for off grid generation) is a product of the creation of powerful constituencies in decades past. These constituencies largely consist of industrial players that chose to engage in energy intensive activities in the region with the understanding that the underlying social contract would ensure the continuation of subsidized energy. As D Reiche rightly predicted:

> The energy-intensive industries would fear for their competitive advantage and act as a powerful lobby group against any policies making their business less competitive. It might be necessary to exempt this sector if first steps in the direction of an internalization of external costs are taken.[45]

More specifically, large state-owned entities like SABIC who have developed lucrative energy intensive business units producing and manufacturing steel and aluminum are now likely staunch defenders of subsidized energy in the Saudi industrial sector and also therefore an obstacle to the proliferation of solar PV in that sector.

Comparatively, in the UAE where the social contract has already been altered—or where important political constituencies were protected through targeted policy interventions—subsidies have been lifted to a substantial degree for many heavy energy users.[46] Focusing on the changes to the Emirati social contract would be beyond the scope of this chapter, but they largely consist of providing investors with world-class infrastructure and an inviting business and legal environment while allowing other cost inputs, such as energy, to rise. This, in turn, has allowed for the proliferation of rooftop solar PV in these markets, where the LCOE of solar energy reached grid parity 3–5 years ahead of its neighbors.

Soft Power Projection

Abu Dhabi's 'energy re-branding,' as co-editor Li-Chen Sim put it, proved to be the first iteration of this dynamic, which would take hold in other regional capitals in more recent years.[47] Much in the same way that the Oil Majors engaged in a concerted effort over the past decade to 'green' their image, states in the region have also begun to understand the soft power benefits of being perceived as sustainable energy players.

As with other dynamics, here too the UAE took an early lead, with the establishment of Masdar in 2006, and the establishment of the UN's International Renewable Energy Agency (IRENA) in Abu Dhabi in 2010. The story of Masdar is perhaps indicative of the fact that a number of factors needed to align so that serious progress on renewables development could be made. For the first decade of its life, Masdar wasn't able to garner traction as anything more than proof of concept; a demonstration of what a sustainable city could look like. Even its 10 MWp solar array, the largest of its kind in the region at the time it was built, would be followed by a lull in development as the economics of solar played catchup. It was only really in the period following 2013, when the economic case for renewables became more attractive, that Masdar's profile began to rise again; this time with a focus on its growing renewable energy development portfolio and not the city from which it emerged. This would all seem to suggest that in this political economy, vision and leadership were insufficient on their own, and that a strong underlying economic case for renewables development was always necessary.

In a further acknowledgment of the power of this image shift, since its establishment, Masdar has also been used by the Emirati government to engage in targeted development aid, building a wide range of renewable energy projects in Africa, the South Pacific and in the developing world more generally.[48] Dubai too has engaged in public diplomacy seeking to portray an image of sustainable and future oriented urban development; in a collaboration with National Geographic, Dubai has sought to document and publicize its energy transition.[49]

It is more difficult to assess to what degree the concept of 'greening' their image has played a role in pushing forward renewables development in the other GCC states. The manner in which the renewables agenda is being carried out across these states would suggest that the primary reasons are economic, but that there is increasingly a realization that the credentials gained from this kind of development can be leveraged to project a modernized image of the state; a helpful shift considering decades of negative associations with the role the states have played in hydrocarbon extraction and the climate crisis.

Conclusion

After a slow start it appears that states in the region are finally on the precipice of a more serious effort to transition their energy systems toward a more renewable future.

Collectively, it is clear that the availability of cheap hydrocarbon resources and associated rents delayed the early adoption of renewable energy on a large scale; the abundance of solar and capital resources, and the earlier proliferation of solar PV in neighboring Jordan, support this. This chapter has argued that this 'rentier effect' played out on two levels. At the utility scale, states in the region were able to put off large-scale renewable energy development before 2015 because the period between 2011 and 2015 (when states could have reasonably begun widespread adoption) was marked by high oil prices and relative fiscal abundance. This allowed states to ignore the opportunity costs associated with not exporting hydrocarbon resources at international prices, using them instead for domestic power production. This dynamic came to an end as oil prices declined at the end of 2014, forcing budget rationalization. The second level was at the distributed scale, where distributive expectations placed on the state by domestic constituencies prevented or slowed the removal of energy subsidies. This delayed the point at which solar PV in particular was able to compete against electricity from the grid in a number of segments and markets.

In the period following 2015, however, states in the region, led by the UAE, have begun embarking on plans to develop large-scale renewable energy, with some states setting targets that, if met, would make them global leaders in this space over the coming decade. This chapter assessed the credibility of these targets among the states in the region, arguing that the political economies and regulatory capacities of these states had not been ready in years past to engage in a serious attempt at the energy transition. Looking more closely at the case of Saudi Arabia, however, which has mirrored earlier developments in the UAE, it appears now that the political economy landscape is undergoing structural change; important constituencies of the state, often elements of the state itself, now stand to benefit from the renewable energy agenda, and are helping to shape and ensure the implementation of these plans. The late rentier state, characterized by the state capitalist model deployed in the UAE and Saudi Arabia, has now coopted the renewable energy agenda, setting the stage for a new and accelerated phase in the energy transition of the region.

Notes

1. Mills, Robin. "How Countries Can Learn from Jordan's Renewable Energy Pivot." *The National*, June 9, 2019. https://www.thenational.ae/business/energy/how-countries-can-learn-from-jordan-s-renewable-energy-pivot-1.872412.

2. Beblawi, H. (1987) "The Rentier State in the Arab World." In: Beblawi, H., Luciani, G. (Eds.), *The Rentier State*. Hertog, S. (2006) "Economic Policy-Making in a Segmented Rentier State." Paper Presented at the Annual Meeting of the Midwest Political Science Association, Palmer House Hilton, Chicago, IL. Hertog, S. (2011) *Princes, Brokers, and Bureaucrats: Oil and the State in Saudi Arabia*. Ithaca, NY: Cornell University Press.
3. Depledge, Joanna. "Striving for No: Saudi Arabia in the Climate Change Regime." *Global Environmental Politics* 8, no. 4 (2008): 9–35, https://doi.org/10.1162/glep.2008.8.4.9.
4. Luomi, Mari. "Gulf of Interest: Why Oil Still Dominates Middle Eastern Climate Politics." *Journal of Arabian Studies* 1, no. 2 (2011): 249–266.
5. Michaelowa, Axel, and Mari Luomi. "From Climate Antagonists to Low-Carbon Protagonists? The Changing Role of the Gulf OPEC States in the UNFCCC." *FNI Climate Policy Perspectives* 6 (2012): 1–8. Al-Sarihi, Aisha (2018) "Prospects for Climate Change Integration into GCC Economic Diversification Strategies." LSE Middle East Centre Paper Series (20). LSE Middle East Centre, Kuwait Programme, London, UK.
6. Sim, L.-C. *Place Brand Public Diplomacy* 8 (2012): 83. https://doi.org/10.1057/pb.2011.31.
7. Doukas, Haris, Konstantinos D. Patlitzianas, Argyris G. Kagiannas, and John Psarras. "Renewable Energy Sources and Rationale Use of Energy Development in the Countries of GCC: Myth or Reality?." *Renewable Energy* 31, no. 6 (2006): 755–770.
8. Alnaser, W. E., and N. W. Alnaser. "The status of Renewable Energy in the GCC Countries." *Renewable and Sustainable Energy Reviews* 15, no. 6 (2011): 3074–3098.
9. Al-Maamary, Hilal M. S., Hussein A. Kazem, and Miqdam T. Chaichan. "Renewable Energy and GCC States Energy Challenges in the 21st Century: A Review." *International Journal of Computation and Applied Sciences (IJOCAAS)* 2, no. 1 (2017): 11–18.
10. El-Katiri, Laura, and Muna Husain. "Prospects for Renewable Energy in GCC States—Opportunities and the Need for Reform" (2014).
11. IRENA (2019) *Renewable Energy Market Analysis: GCC 2019*. Abu Dhabi: International Renewable Energy Agency. ISBN 978-92-9260-096-9.
12. Yamada, Makio. "Vision 2030 and the Birth of Saudi Solar Energy." *Middle East Institute Policy Focus* 15 (2016).
13. Atalay, Yasemin, Frank Biermann, and Agni Kalfagianni. "Adoption of Renewable Energy Technologies in Oil-Rich Countries: Explaining Policy Variation in the Gulf Cooperation Council States." *Renewable Energy* 85 (2016): 206–214.

14. Reiche, Danyel. "Energy Policies of Gulf Cooperation Council (GCC) Countries—Possibilities and Limitations of Ecological Modernization in Rentier States." *Energy Policy* 38, no. 5 (2010): 2395–2403.
15. AlYahya, Sulaiman, and Mohammad A. Irfan. "The Techno-Economic Potential of Saudi Arabi's Solar Industry." *Renewable and Sustainable Energy Reviews* 55 (2016): 697–702.
16. "Royal Decree Establishing King Abdullah City for Atomic and Renewable Energy," April 17, 2010. https://www.kacare.gov.sa/en/about/Documents/KACARE_Royal_Decree_english.pdf.
17. "Renewable Energy Initiative Stalls." MEED, September 26, 2017. https://www.meed.com/renewable-energy-initiative-stalls/.
18. "Miraah Solar Thermal Project—Power Technology: Energy News and Market Analysis." Power Technology | Energy News and Market Analysis. Accessed October 20, 2019. https://www.power-technology.com/projects/miraah-solar-thermal-project/.
19. IRENA (2019) *Renewable Energy Market Analysis: GCC 2019*. Abu Dhabi: International Renewable Energy Agency. ISBN 978-92-9260-096-9.
20. https://www.glasspoint.com/about-us/history/.
21. IRENA (2019) *Renewable Energy Market Analysis: GCC 2019*. Abu Dhabi: International Renewable Energy Agency. ISBN 978-92-9260-096-9, Various government sources; and the Middle East Solar Industry Association.
22. IRENA (2019) *Renewable Energy Market Analysis: GCC 2019*. Abu Dhabi: International Renewable Energy Agency. ISBN 978-92-9260-096-9.
23. Note on difference between capacity targets and consumption targets. Important to note the difference here between capacity targets and consumption targets. Given the lower capacity factor of renewable energy technologies (with solar energy only producing power at certain times of the day and contingent on weather) having X% of renewable energy capacity still translates to a significantly lower % of energy generation.
24. IRENA (2019) *Renewable Energy Market Analysis: GCC 2019*. Abu Dhabi: International Renewable Energy Agency. ISBN 978-92-9260-096-9.
25. At peak, the renewable energy would be able to generate its stated generation capacity, but unlike conventional generation capacity, this would normally only represent a fraction of hours in the day. There would therefore be a sizeable proportional difference in a given renewable energy project's contribution to a state's generation capacity and its actual contribution to its annual generation figures in MWh a year, for example.

26. "Saudi Arabia Renewable Energy Targets and Long Term Visibility." MEIM, n.d. https://www.powersaudiarabia.com.sa/web/attach/media/Saudi-Arabia-Renewable-Energy-Targets-and-Long-Term-Visibility.pdf.
27. Meed. "Saudi Arabia Has for a Second Time Set a Mega-Target for the Development of Renewable Energy." Power Technology | Energy News and Market Analysis, January 22, 2019. https://www.power-technology.com/comment/saudi-renewable-energy-targets/. Softbank's Mega Solar Deal in Saudi Arabia Faces a Rocky Future Jason Deign. https://www.greentechmedia.com/articles/read/softbank-mega-solar-deal-saudi-arabia-rocky-future#gs.o7Pp67I.
28. "Reforming Industrial Fuel and Residential Electricity Prices in Saudi Arabia." Murad Anwer and Walid Matar, KAPSARC, July 2017/KS-2017—DP018.
29. Pricing from Haala Energy operations team, a solar EPC based in Saudi Arabia.
30. Krane, Jim. "Stability Versus Sustainability: Energy Policy in the Gulf Monarchies." *The Energy Journal* (2015): 1–21.
31. "CITIZEN ACCOUNT." Ministry of Labor and Social development. Accessed October 20, 2019. https://www.itu.int/net4/wsis/archive/stocktaking/Project/Details?projectId=1514102422.
32. Meed. "Saudi Arabia Has for a Second Time Set a Mega-Target for the Development of Renewable Energy." Power Technology | Energy News and Market Analysis, January 22, 2019. https://www.power-technology.com/comment/saudi-renewable-energy-targets/.
33. Saudi Arabia Cancels Tenders for Solar Projects. https://www.meed.com/saudi-arabia-cancels-tenders-for-solar-projects/.
34. Hertog, Steffen (2011) *Princes, Brokers, and Bureaucrats: Oil and the State in Saudi Arabia*. Ithaca, NY: Cornell University Press.
35. Kerr, Simeon. "Saudi Arabian Infighting Casts Shadow on Solar Deal." *Financial Times*, April 19, 2018. https://www.ft.com/content/7cf9f20a-3f40-11e8-b7e0-52972418fec4.
36. Sutherland, Eversheds. "Saudi Arabia: Small Photovoltaic Solar System Regulation." Saudi Arabia: Small Photovoltaic Solar System Regulation. https://www.eversheds-sutherland.com/global/en/what/articles/index.page?ArticleID=en/global/MiddleEast/Saudi_Arabia_Small_Photovoltaic_Solar_System_Regulation.
37. "Saudi Arabia's PIF Takes 15.2 Pct Direct Stake in ACWA Power." *Thomson Reuters*, July 4, 2018. https://www.reuters.com/article/saudi-fund-acwa-power/saudi-arabias-pif-takes-15-2-pct-direct-stake-in-acwa-power-idUSL8N1U04A8.
38. Ibid.
39. "Abu Dhabi Power Corporation, Mubadala and Masdar Enter into Strategic Partnership." Mubadala Investment Company, Abu Dhabi,

UAE, January 17, 2019. https://www.mubadala.com/en/news/abu-dhabi-power-corporation-mubadala-and-masdar-enter-strategic-partnership.

40. "Fuel, Food and Utilities Price Reforms in the GCC: A Wake-up Call for Business", Glada Lahn, 2016, Chatham House Report.
41. Karinfil, Fatih, and Axel Pierru. "The Opportunity Cost of Domestic Oil Consumption for an Oil Exporter: Illustration for Saudi Arabia." No. ks—2020-dp05. 2020.
42. It is noteworthy that within the UAE, Dubai, which is not a major hydrocarbon producer, took the early lead in renewables development.
43. Kerr, Simeon. "Kuwait's Economic Reforms Face Domestic Opposition." *Financial Times*, September 10, 2019. https://www.ft.com/content/d675f6e8-7d52-11e9-8b5c-33d0560f039c.
44. Faris Al-Sulayman, "State-Business Relations in the Reform Era: Growing Pressures and Diverging Economic Policy Agendas." King Faisal Center for Research and Islamic Studies Special Report, 2018.
45. Reiche, Danyel. "Energy Policies of Gulf Cooperation Council (GCC) Countries—Possibilities and Limitations of Ecological Modernization in Rentier States." *Energy Policy* 38, no. 5 (2010): 2395–2403.
46. More than any other GCC state, the UAE has gone to great lengths to protect its citizens from rising energy costs, creating a tiered system for residential tariffs that differentiates based on whether the consumer is a citizen or expat.
47. Sim, L.-C. *Place Brand Public Diplomacy* 8 (2012): 83. https://doi.org/10.1057/pb.2011.31.
48. Graves, LeAnne. "Masdar Completes Five Solar and Wind Projects in the Pacific." *The National*, May 17, 2016. https://www.thenational.ae/business/masdar-completes-five-solar-and-wind-projects-in-the-pacific-1.202564.
49. Locatelli, Luca. "The World's Most Improbable Green City." *National Geographic*, July 27, 2017. https://www.nationalgeographic.com/environment/urban-expeditions/green-buildings/dubai-ecological-footprint-sustainable-urban-city/.

CHAPTER 5

From Fuel-Poor to Radiant: Morocco's Energy Geopolitics and Renewable Energy Strategy

Sharlissa Moore

Introduction

Realist international relations scholars argue that nation-state politics and bids for power over scarce energy resources trump energy economics and other considerations.[1] Therefore, the international competition over scarce energy resources is a zero-sum game, in which a win for one state's energy security is a loss for another state.[2] In contrast, scholars whose work centers around market liberalization and globalization argue that well-designed institutions and market economics can overcome geopolitical forces and yield win-win energy security outcomes.[3] A third perspective—critical geopolitics—argues that perceptions of geopolitical threats do not entirely reflect objective reality but rather are socially constructed

S. Moore (✉)
Michigan State University, James Madison College, East Lansing, MI, USA
e-mail: moores60@msu.edu

R. Mills and L.-C. Sim (eds.), *Low Carbon Energy in the Middle East and North Africa*, International Political Economy Series,
https://doi.org/10.1007/978-3-030-59554-8_5

by state institutions.[4] To understand the relationship between Morocco's renewable energy policy and the geopolitical environment in the Middle East North Africa (MENA) region, I draw on all three perspectives: conflict over scarce resources, energy markets and economics, and the social construction of energy policy.

It is impossible to understand Morocco's energy policy without examining the effects that resource scarcity has on its state power and economy. However, what realists often overlook is that energy markets, capital investment, and energy prices matter greatly for nation-state power, particularly in low- and middle-income nations in which poverty threatens state security and economic development is necessary for states to gain international power. In much of the MENA region, energy subsidies and services have long been guaranteed to populations in exchange for authoritarian rule, and states are supported by fossil fuel rents rather than taxes.[5] The Moroccan monarchy lacks fossil fuel wealth, but failing to ensure the affordability of energy and the standard of living it provides, as is done in oil-rich states in the region, could threaten state stability.

What is less often examined is that domestic social policy matters for international energy policy. Crafting energy infrastructure is not simply a matter of building hardware. In high-income countries, the construction of energy infrastructure was guided by energy policies shaped by social needs and perceptions.[6] For instance, in the United States, the Jeffersonian ideology of the yeoman farmer as the moral lifeblood of the country led to the creation of the Rural Electrification Administration. The administration subsidized the construction of centralized electricity systems that the private sector would not have otherwise built, and even bankrupted wind companies that provided decentralized power to rural areas.[7] The social shaping of electrical power systems has faded from memory as electrical power systems in the West have developed momentum,[8] and has been replaced with discourses of technological determinism: that the best technology determined the shape of the power system, rather than political, social, and cultural forces.

In Morocco, solving energy challenges relates explicitly to addressing the state's construction of societal challenges. A Moroccan energy vision document states: 'All debates on energy policy become, by definition, a debate on the stakes of the future and returns of the choices of the model of society to which we aspire as a national collectivity.'[9] This chapter argues that the Moroccan government's energy policy is shaped by a conglomeration of competing forces that must be understood in tandem, including achieving domestic sustainable development and industrial policy goals, securing international financing and managing domestic energy prices, and grappling with domestic resource scarcity and complex dynamics among the African Union, European Union, and Algeria. The state must balance the trade-offs among these various goals within its energy policy.

Methods

To understand Morocco's alternative energy policy, I conducted fieldwork and interviews over seven trips to Morocco, as well as document and news analysis. After a scoping trip in June 2012, I conducted 20 interviews and attended energy-related events while living in Salé, Morocco from August to December 2013. The interview sample included officials from Morocco's energy and renewable energy agencies, Morocco's utility company, development bank and financial institutions, as well as researchers and heads of research centers.

In February 2014, I spent one month in Ouarzazate, the first site of Morocco's solar plan, participating in a research project on the social impacts of solar siting. Overall, I made seven trips to Ouarzazate to interview stakeholders. I also co-led four one-month study-abroad trips on sustainable development to Morocco and Spain in 2013–2015 and one trip to Morocco in 2016 in which we met with government officials and stakeholders.[10] In June 2018, a colleague and I conducted 12 interviews on the food-energy-water nexus in Rabat, the Midelt area, and Marrakesh. Near Midelt, we visited the site slated for 800 MW of solar development, as well as nearby stakeholders at farms and energy infrastructure. Finally, I updated my data from 2018 to 2019 through news analysis.

Status of Alternative Energy in Morocco

Morocco's most obvious energy challenge relates to the uneven geographical distribution of natural resources across the globe. The country's only natural resource wealth that provides rents is phosphates—used in fertilizers, animal feed, and detergents.[11] Morocco's lack of resource wealth leads to high external energy dependency and macroeconomic challenges. Morocco's trade deficit averaged −1.780 billion USD from June 2018 through May 2019.[12] Morocco's largest import is petroleum oils ($3.5 billion), and its fifth-largest import is liquefied butane ($880 million).[13] (Morocco must also import coal for its coal-fired power plants, which will be discussed in the section "Fuel Switching and Geopolitics".) In the absence of the fossil fuel rents on which much of the MENA region depends, subsidies provided by the Moroccan government's Caisse de Compensation for butane, diesel, and gasoline have heavily weighed on the state's budget.[14] For example, in 2013, the largest subsidies were for liquified butane, with consumers paying 35% of the market price, followed by diesel, with consumers paying 77.3% of the market price, followed by gasoline, with consumers paying 94.1% of the market price.[15] While butane is cheap, Moroccan consumers pay much more for gasoline than citizens in nearby oil-rich countries, such as Algeria.

A second major challenge is that demand is rapidly growing due to population growth, economic development, and the achievement of universal electrification between the 1990s and 2019.[16] Electricity demand grew by 5.4% per annum between 2002 and 2016, and the national utility company forecasts that Morocco's demand will grow by 4.5–5% per annum through 2030.[17] Water scarcity, which led to protests in 2017,[18] will also increase demand for costly seawater desalination. The country's first desalination facility is under construction in Agadir.[19]

Morocco is one of several countries in the MENA region, including Jordan, Lebanon, and Tunisia, that do not have significant proved reserves of fossil fuels. This is a strong incentive to develop alternative energy. In 2015, resource-poor states led the MENA region in renewable energy development: Morocco and Jordan in renewable energy capacity and Tunisia in energy efficiency.[20]

While utility-scale solar development has received the most attention since 2010, like Jordan, Morocco has considered nuclear power to compensate for fossil fuel deficiency. In the 1970s, King Hassan II announced a nuclear power program that would use the naturally occurring uranium in phosphates and laid the groundwork for the development of a research reactor. Additionally, the national utility company worked on feasibility studies for nuclear power.[21] In 2007, Morocco's 2 MW research reactor, provided with US support, became operational. In 2010, Morocco and France signed an agreement to develop a nuclear power plant. Morocco has been working to develop nuclear expertise through its research reactor and has recently signed nuclear safety agreements with Canada and Spain. In 2017, Morocco joined a long list of developing countries that have signed nuclear power development MOUs with

Fig. 5.1 The 1,872 MW Ludington pumped storage facility in Michigan (Photo by author)

Russia, which suggests the state has not entirely taken the nuclear option off the table.[22]

Morocco's chief focus is its large-scale solar and wind strategy, which is underpinned by strong political will. In 2008, the government developed a renewable energy and energy efficiency plan, which set a goal to reach 42% renewable energy generation capacity (not consumption) by 2020. (Consumption will be lower because of intermittency.) This goal was divided into 14% solar, 14% wind, and 14% hydroelectricity.[23] The Moroccan government also set a goal to reduce energy consumption through efficiency measures by 12% by 2020 and 15% by 2030, compared to business as usual.[24] In 2016, the government increased the target to achieving 52% of capacity from renewable energy by 2030, totaling 10 GW: 20% solar power, 20% wind power, and 12% hydroelectric power. The 12% hydroelectric power goal includes building 950 MW of pumped storage, which is among the cheapest options for energy storage.[25] Water is pumped uphill using surplus energy during off-peak hours of demand and is later released to capture its kinetic energy during peak hours (see Fig. 5.1). Otherwise, the percentage of installed hydroelectric capacity in Morocco's portfolio will go down while installed capacity remains the same. It is necessary to reduce dependency on hydropower because of siltation of the dams and drought impeding electricity production from hydropower facilities, which has required greater electricity imports from Spain.

The government then institutionalized renewable energy policy. Law 57-09 launched the Moroccan Agency for Solar Energy (MASEN), founded in March 2010. The Office National de l'Electricité et de l'Eau Potable (ONEE), the state-owned utility monopoly, became responsible for green power purchase agreements and wind development, in addition to its existing jurisdiction over hydroelectricity and other PPAs outside of those under Law 13-09. Law 16-09 created the Agence Nationale pour le Développement des Energies Renouvelables et de l'Efficacité Energétique to manage solar and wind resource mapping and energy efficiency initiatives. The Research Institute for Solar Energy and New Energies, founded in 2011, is the first competitive research funding agency in Morocco. Finally, law 40-08 established the Société d'Investissements Energétiques, a funding agency for energy development. In 2015, ONEE transferred all wind and hydroelectric responsibilities other than pumped storage to MASEN, which was renamed the Moroccan Agency for Sustainable Energy. In 2010, Law 13-09 allowed independent wind and hydroelectric power producers to sell power to the utility company and allowed for renewable energy export.

Consistent with the critical geopolitics lens, the Moroccan government is reframing Morocco as an energy-wealthy country, awash with renewable energy resources (Fig. 5.2). Morocco's energy leaders frame renewable resources as having latent social and economic benefits that Morocco's institutions will 'valorize,' or unlock, through technological development and commercialization. Resources that interviewees framed as in need of valorization included Morocco's solar and wind deposits (*gisements*), its favorable sites for renewable energy, its geographical position, and its social capital.

Morocco is meeting numerous social challenges through its renewable energy policy including boosting the standard of living, improving equity of opportunity, stemming urbanization, fostering national pride, expanding the research and development (R&D) system, providing opportunities to young college graduates, expanding industrial policy, and developing export commodities.[26] While concentrating solar power

(CSP) plants are more expensive than solar photovoltaic (PV) arrays, CSP serves as a 'charismatic, centralized technology,' or a 'nation-building technology that helps Morocco meet its social goals.'[27] Additionally, interviewees expressed that without achieving the desired socioeconomic benefits from renewable energy, Morocco may as well hire transnational firms to build more fossil generation. Compared to PV, CSP allows for improved outcomes in terms of the following factors: socioeconomic development, local businesses entering the supply chain, and R&D opportunities.

Renewable energy is part of a broader industrialization strategy that focuses on transforming Morocco into an emerging economy.[28] Initiatives also include advanced automotive and aerospace manufacturing, new offshore call centers, and the new Tanger-Med shipping container port and nearby Siemens rotor blade factory that manufactures 'Made in Morocco' wind turbines.[29] In 2016, these initiatives began to pay off as exports of automobiles and ignition wire sets exceeded phosphorus exports.[30]

CSP plants also create more jobs than solar PV. The Moroccan renewable energy plan seeks to address the challenge of youth unemployment—which threatens state stability—by generating fulfilling green jobs for young people. In 2018, 26% of people ages 15–24 and 15.1% of people ages 25–34 were unemployed, compared to 4.7% of people ages 35–44 and 2.4% of people 45 or older.[31] MASEN requires that 30% of CSP materials come from local content and places targets on the percentage of Moroccans and local Moroccans hired on each project. Additionally, MASEN is building power plants in the poorest regions of Morocco to bring socioeconomic development to those regions. In compensation for the purchase of collective land for the Ouarzazate solar power plant, MASEN funded eyeglasses, dentistry, Internet access, and buses and bicycles for children to ride to school.[32]

Climate change is part of Morocco's focus on national pride, although not the primary goal of the renewable energy program. Rather, the government's goal was to secure financing to expand power generation to meet growing demand by tapping into climate change funding provided by industrialized countries to the Global South. Additionally, interviewees took pride in Morocco's moral commitment to and its technological prowess in climate mitigation. Morocco is also engaging in 'host diplomacy.'[33] Most prominently, in 2016, Morocco hosted the COP 22 climate change conference in Marrakesh, which boosted Morocco's international reputation.[34] In March 2019, Morocco announced the $1 million Mohammed VI Prize for the Climate and Sustainable Development at Africa Climate Week.[35] Following COP 22, Morocco joined just seven other non-OECD countries as an International Energy Agency (IEA) Association Country.[36]

Fuel Switching and Geopolitics

Since electrification began in Morocco under the French Protectorate, Morocco has had a prominent renewable energy (hydroelectricity) plan while large quantities of electricity generation from fossil fuels were developed without being publicized by the state.[37] The French Protectorate, and later King Hassan II, projected Morocco's dam-building initiative as its main energy source, in spite of the fact that half or more of installed capacity came from fossil fuels.[38] Today, Morocco's renewable energy strategy does not eliminate fossil fuels but rather reduces their percentage as installed capacity grows. Very little fossil fuel capacity is being retired; rather, the plants are being refurbished and even expanded, as new fossil-fueled plants are being constructed. In 2009, Morocco's installed capacity was composed of 28% hydroelectricity (including pumped storage), 68% thermal electricity (including fuel oil/diesel, natural gas, and coal), and 4% wind.[39] By 2030, Morocco's installed capacity is expected to include 48% conventional thermal energy: 23% natural gas, 21% coal, and 4% fuel oil/diesel.[40]

Coal

Morocco is expanding its coal-fired power plant at Jorf Lasfar by 700 MW, to reach 2,056 MW.[41] Additionally, a Chinese company is building and financing a so-called clean coal plant of 350 MW capacity at Jerada.[42] Even with these expansions, the overall percentage of coal in the portfolio is set to decrease because of increasing installed capacity. Morocco must import almost all of its coal, e.g., 6,490,000-tonnes in 2016 and 6,742,000 in 2017. In 2017, Russia provided about half of Morocco's steam coal imports, or 3,164,000-tonnes, plus 54,000-tonnes of coking coal imports. Coal is typically not a geopolitical resource because of its abundance and varied sources of supply. However, South Africa was a large exporter of steam coal to Morocco in 2016 (2,005,000-tonnes), but exports fell to 600,000-tonnes in 2017 as the two countries butted heads over Western Sahara.[43]

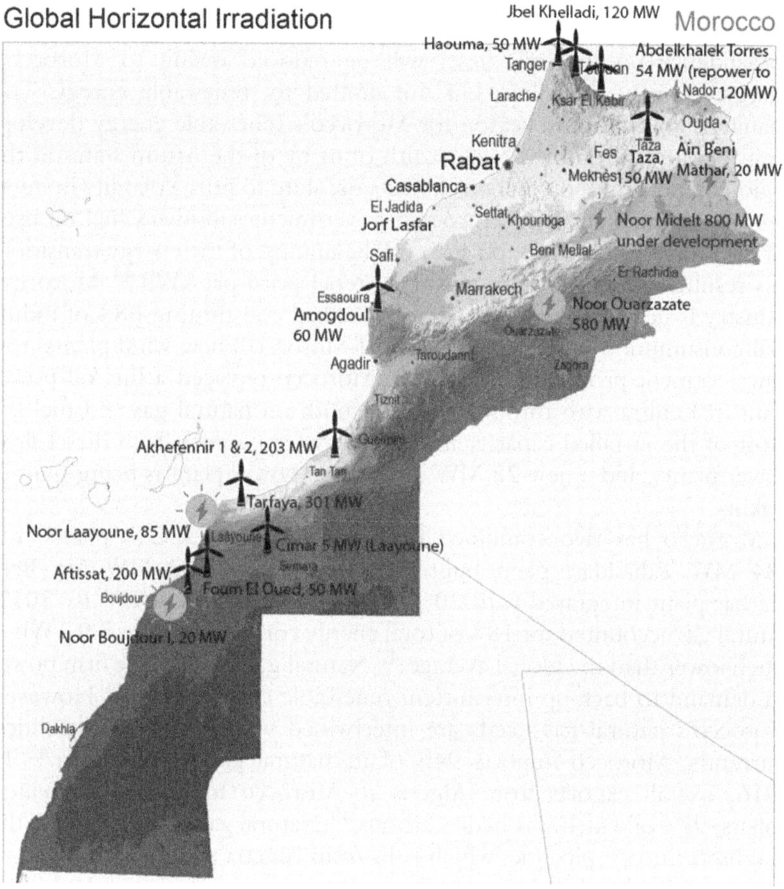

Fig. 5.2 Global Horizontal Irradiation (GHI) in Morocco with existing solar CSP, solar PV, and wind projects labeled by author (*Sources* SolarGIS, Creative Commons license; Wind Icon made by [Good Ware] and solar icon made by [PrettyCons], open source from www.flaticon.com. Note that the GHI measurement applies to solar PV, whereas Direct Normal Irradiation would be used to measure potential for CSP and photovoltaic concentration technology)

Fuel Oil and Natural Gas

Dependence on fuel oil/diesel will be reduced owing to Morocco's energy strategy, including, but not limited to, renewable energy. This change is an important reason for Morocco's renewable energy development because, without the oil wealth of many of the nation-states in the region, dependence on fuel oil subjects the state to price volatility in international oil markets. The Moroccan government subsidizes fuel oil used for electricity production; prior to the beginning of the energy transition, this resulted in a 15% subsidy on the retail price per kWh.[44] Moroccan industry is heavily reliant on petroleum coke, constituting 68% of industrial consumption in 2017.[45] Several of Morocco's new wind plants now power cement production. In 2010, Morocco replaced a fuel-oil power plant in Kenitra with turbines that run both on natural gas and fuel oil. Most of the installed capacity in Western Sahara comes from diesel-fired power plants, and a new 22 MW diesel-fired power plant is being built in Dakhla.

Morocco has two combined cycle gas turbine (CCGT) plants: the 384 MW Tahaddart plant built in 2005 and the 452 MW Ain Beni Mathar plant integrated with 20 MW of CSP built in 2009.[46] By 2017, natural gas accounted for 18% of total energy consumption, or 5.9 TWh—much lower than the global average.[47] Natural gas can provide firm power on demand to back up intermittent renewable energy sources. However, Morocco's natural gas needs are intertwined with complex geopolitics. Currently, Morocco imports 94% of its natural gas from Algeria.[48] In 2016, overall exports from Algeria to Morocco totaled $499 million dollars, 97% of which was hydrocarbons.[49] Natural gas is imported via the Maghreb-Europe pipeline, which runs from Algeria through Morocco to Spain and Portugal.[50] It was built in 1996 with a capacity of 10 billion cubic meters (bcm).[51] ONEE purchases 0.6 bcm of natural gas from the pipeline, and Morocco receives 0.5 bcm as a transit fee.[52] Morocco and Algeria have extended their contract for the pipeline through 2021.

Algeria is the world's sixth-largest natural gas exporter, with the tenth-largest proved reserves of natural gas and the third-largest proved reserves of shale gas.[53] Relations between Morocco and Algeria are poor because of disputes over their border, terrorism, and, most significantly, Western Sahara.[54] According to Larramendi, the Moroccan government sees Western Sahara as a bilateral dispute with the Algerian government, which provides material support to the Sahrawi independence movement.

The Algerian government views the Western Saharan dispute as an issue of decolonization and self-determination for the Sahrawi people. The border is closed, and the governments are building a wall. In 2013, many interviewees noted that Morocco and Algeria cooperate well on energy. Since then, Morocco has rejoined the African Union despite opposition from Algeria. Additionally, in December 2018, Morocco held the first peace talks with the parties involved in the Western Sahara conflict since 2012, after which the UN peacekeeping mission was again extended.

While it is unclear whether the pipeline contract will be extended past 2021, it is in the energy security interest of the European Union (EU) to support the pipeline's continued operation. Increasing imports of natural gas from countries other than Russia is an EU energy security goal. Algeria provides 10.7% of Europe's natural gas.[55] Algeria and Spain are also connected via the MEDGAZ pipeline, and the countries are discussing increasing its capacity.[56] In 2018, Abdelmoumen Ould Kaddour, CEO of Algeria's state-owned oil company Sonatrach, expressed that Algeria had no interest in cutting off exports through the Maghreb-Europe pipeline.[57]

However, in April 2019, Algeria's interim president replaced Ould Kaddour with Rachid Hachichi as Sonatrach's CEO.[58] Large protests in early 2019 had led the president to step down, and the country's political situation is uncertain.[59] Moreover, Algerian natural gas production is declining while domestic consumption is increasing, constraining supply.[60] The government has been slow to approve new projects, and shale gas resources lie in remote areas with low water availability. Furthermore, in 2013, Al Qaeda in the Islamic Maghreb orchestrated a terrorist attack on a large natural gas facility in Tiguentourine, Algeria.[61] While security measures have been increased, the risk of future terrorist attacks remains high given the security situation in the region and the importance of oil and natural gas to the regional and international economy.[62]

Amid this uncertainty and these risks, the Moroccan energy ministry has developed a plan for a Gas-to-Power megaproject that would double or even triple gas consumption.[63] It calls for developing an onshore liquified natural gas (or LNG) terminal at Jorf Lasfar, building two new CCGT plants by 2030 (1,200 MW each), and later potentially building an additional 3,500 MW of CCGT capacity.[64] A new project roadmap is under development.[65] While there is no evidence that Morocco's renewable energy strategy was enacted to gain energy independence from Algeria, it seems likely that the Moroccan government would not want to be dependent on Algeria for 95% of natural gas imports as installed gas capacity grows. Additionally, US shale gas production offers a new opportunity for Morocco to import LNG from a close ally. The Moroccan government also signed a 2018 agreement with Nigeria to develop a new gas pipeline.[66] Through this pipeline, Morocco would become a conduit for natural gas exports from West Africa to Europe, but a Fitch Solutions study found numerous obstacles to feasibility.[67]

Oil

Aside from slightly reducing dependence on fuel oil/diesel for power plants and industry, renewable electricity development does nothing to reduce oil imports, most of which are used for transportation. Electrified train and tram services serve only Morocco's major cities, and electric vehicles are generally neither affordable nor available. In 2016, Morocco's refined oil imports came from 30 country suppliers. Spain (23%) and the United States (19%) are the two largest exporters.[68] From 2009 to 2014, Morocco depended mostly on Saudi Arabia, Iraq, and Russia for oil imports.[69] Algeria only accounts for 8% of Morocco's overall oil and oil product imports.[70] However, an unknown amount of gasoline is smuggled across the Algerian–Moroccan border.[71]

In 2016, the shutdown of all refining capacity harmed Morocco's oil security. Morocco has lost its oil storage capacity and must import all distillates.[72] The government-run SAMIR refinery had gone into service in 1962 to increase Morocco's fuel security.[73] In 1997, SAMIR was taken over by a Saudi company as part of a broader market liberalization initiative.[74] After a long period of insolvency, the Moroccan government provided $500 million to refinance SAMIR in 2014.[75] But the SAMIR refinery was liquidated in March 2016.[76] The Moroccan state is taking SAMIR to court to recover millions of dirhams in unpaid taxes, although the Saudi CEO has left the country.[77] Moreover, an analyst from the Atlantic Council alleges that SAMIR was dealing in stolen crude oil from Nigeria.[78]

Outside Forces and Influences in Morocco's Energy Transition

Although renewable energy development is a project indigenous to Morocco, outside forces play important roles in Morocco's energy transition, including financing from development banks, international climate change negotiations, German energy policy goals, and initiatives to integrate the EU and North African power grids.

Financing

Obtaining financing from private companies, development banks, and climate change initiatives is both a goal of Morocco's renewable energy policy and an outside influence. When Morocco began to expand and transition its electricity sector, it suffered from a lack of capital and foreign direct investment for energy development. Today, capital needs for electricity infrastructure are estimated to be $30 billion.[79] If rents are defined as a source of income for the state from external sources rather than from taxes, all of the external sources of grants discussed in the following, including aid from the Gulf states and the provision of cheap capital to the Moroccan state, are by definition rents.

While the Moroccan government hopes to secure more private funding for energy development, the first major CSP projects have required public funding, with some private funding secured as a consequence of the multilateral development financing.[80] The Noor Ouarzazate CSP plant was financed by KfW Development Bank ($884 million), the European Investment Bank ($473 million), the African Development Bank ($135 million), the European Commission ($122 million), the French Development Agency ($68 million), the World Bank ($400 million), the Clean Technology Fund ($238 million), and the borrower ($357 million).[81] Additionally, the German Federal Ministry of the Environment, Nature Conservation and Nuclear Safety provided EUR 15 million through its International Climate Initiative. According to a MASEN interviewee, the concessional financing interest rate of 3.5%, as opposed to a non-concessional rate of 8%, reduced ACWA Power's bid for the electricity price by 20%. Some people I interviewed from EU countries criticized Morocco for choosing CSP in spite of its higher cost. MASEN has added more solar PV arrays to its solar plan, including Noor Atlas (200 MW), Noor Argana (120 MW), and Noor Tafilalet (200 MW), as well as projects in Western Sahara discussed later.[82] As the price of solar PV has fallen over the past several years, it is possible for the Moroccan government to finance solar PV without concessional financing. However, the plans for CSP are still underway.

Wind has needed much less concessional financing than CSP because of its lower market price. This financing has included equity investment from shareholder companies and debt financing from ONEE. A Moroccan company called Nareva, which is also an independent generator of coal-fired power, has been heavily involved in wind development.[83] European companies, such as Enel Green Power, Siemens, and EDF Renouvelables, as well as TAQA (Abu Dhabi) and Mitsui (Japan), have partnered with Nareva. Morocco has received $148.95 million in financing from the Clean Technology Fund for the Jbel Khalladi wind farm and for energy efficiency initiatives.[84] Financing for Khalladi also came from the European Bank for Reconstruction and Development, the Moroccan BMCE Bank of Africa, and a $960,000 grant from the Sustainable Energy Fund for Africa.[85] In 2012, KfW provided $61,410,500 for the 150 MW Taza wind farm.[86]

The literature on the rentier state typically includes international aid as a type of rent. However, much of this funding is a loan not a grant, which will have to be paid back, and the goal is for this funding to jump-start a renewable energy transition, rather than to provide ongoing rents in the way that hydrocarbons do. Additionally, the funding provided to Morocco for CSP did not focus solely on domestic aid but also on positive externalities at the international scale. According to an interviewee, the World Bank's CSP program sought to bring CSP down the cost curve by experimenting with the technology in areas of North Africa with advantageous geographical resources. Energy prices from CSP decreased from $189 per MWh for Noor I to $140/MWh for Noor II, in spite of a lower level of concessional financing and a switch from wet cooling to dry cooling, which reduces power plant efficiency.[87] Increased storage capacity was added for Noor II, improving the utilization of surplus heat.

The Role of the Gulf States

ACWA Power, a Saudi power and water utility company founded in 2004 with a net income of $245.17 million in 2017,[88] has played a major role in Morocco's renewable energy development. The company built the Jbel Khalladi wind farm in Tangier. ACWA Power's subsidiary, NOMAC, is heading the construction of the Noor Ouarzazate solar complex, and ACWA Power provided part of the capital investment. The company's bid on Noor I was 29% lower than the other bidders.[89] ACWA Power is influential in the MENA region, operating in Saudi Arabia, UAE, Oman, Jordan, and Turkey.[90] The company used Morocco as a testbed for CSP to gain experience that could later be applied in Saudi Arabia.

More broadly, funds from oil-rich states in the Gulf have helped Morocco—and Jordan—balance their budgets and maintain stability since the Arab Spring in 2011. States in the Gulf are concerned about potential Islamist influences in Morocco's policy, particularly as the Islamist Justice and Development Party (or PJD) became the main opposition political party in 2002 and won parliamentary elections in 2011, resulting in the king naming the party's head, Abdelilah Benkirane, as prime minister. Saudi Arabia, UAE, Qatar, and Kuwait pledged to grant Morocco a total of $5 billion between 2012 and 2018, although Saudi Arabia and UAE's grants have fallen short. (These funds were not specifically for energy development.) Additionally, Masdar Clean Energy, an Emirati company, helped Morocco to achieve universal access by deploying small solar and battery systems to the few households that still lacked access in 2017.

In 2017, ACWA Power announced that its price for the new installation in Dubai would be $73/MWh.[91] However, there was conflict between MASEN and ACWA Power over the cost of CSP in its Noor-Midelt I CSP bid.[92] A consortium of EDF Renouvelables, Masdar, and SENER apparently placed a lower bid and won.[93] Reportedly, they bid $71/MWh, a few dollars less than ACWA Power's publicized price of $73/MWh.[94] Public funding has also been announced from the World Bank, the Clean Technology Fund, KfW, the French Development Agency, the European Investment Bank, and the African Development Bank.[95]

EU and Transnational Grid Integration

While the effects are difficult to quantify, EU energy policy has certainly influenced Morocco's renewable energy transition. The EU has agreed to provide energy aid and technical assistance to the 'Southern Mediterranean' in exchange for regulatory and political reform.[96] Numerous multilateral initiatives have focused on developing a common energy policy between the north and south of the Mediterranean since 1995, e.g., the Euro-Mediterranean Partnership, the Euro-Mediterranean

Energy Forum, and the Union for the Mediterranean/the Mediterranean Solar Plan.[97]

Germany has been the most active in promoting renewable energy through its foreign policy. The country aims to spread its *Energiewende*, or energy transition, and climate mitigation policies to developing countries. The German government travels to renewable energy expositions, including in Morocco, to advertise its renewable energy know-how, consulting services, and technology. It also places development officials in positions related to renewable energy within the Moroccan government.

Several private EU-based initiatives have focused on integrating the grids of the North and South Mediterranean and developing renewable energy in North Africa for export. The German-led Desertec Industrial Initiative (Dii)—a consortium of private companies—sought to develop a solar pilot project in Morocco for electricity export to the EU. Elsewhere, I discuss the geopolitics of this plan using the concept of 'renewable energy terroir,' or the politics of the uneven distribution of land most advantageous for CSP generation.[98] Dii's plan to develop an integrated Mediterranean supergrid to achieve 90% renewable energy consumption in Europe and North Africa largely failed for a variety of reasons. These reasons included obstruction from Spain, which was hesitant to become a conduit for renewable energy from Morocco to Germany; accusations in the media that exporting solar electricity from North Africa to Europe was neocolonial; the Eurozone crisis, which reduced the availability of surplus capital for energy investment; and infighting among European project promoters. The realization that electricity demand was rapidly growing in North Africa also affected project planning. The project was originally envisioned to export electricity from North Africa to supposed demand centers in Europe when, in fact, the MENA region's demand is on track to exceed Europe's demand. While demand could be simultaneously met in both MENA and the EU, stakeholders' perceived lack of emphasis on meeting North Africa's demand resulted in negative publicity for the Desertec vision.[99]

Morocco is already connected to Algeria and Spain through transmission interconnection. Algeria and Morocco share three single-circuit 220 kV transmission lines—with one double-circuit 400 kV line potentially under construction.[100] This seems to represent electricity cooperation in the absence of political accord. However, this situation likely stems from a historical trajectory starting under the French Protectorate, which laid the groundwork in the 1940s for Morocco to begin exporting electricity to Algeria in 1956.[101] Exports continued until 1973, when Morocco's petroleum import bill first exceeded its revenue from phosphate exports.[102] In 1988, Algeria began exporting electricity to Morocco because drought had reduced Morocco's hydroelectric production.[103] Today, electrons continue to flow across the otherwise closed border.

Algeria has been less open to electricity integration, particularly with former colonial powers, than Morocco. According to Muzzo, the Algerian state has long associated energy independence with political independence and decolonization. The discovery of hydrocarbons in 1956 prolonged the Algerian War and contributed to resistance from Algerians to dreams of Euro-African integration. By 1967, Algeria had reclaimed its hydrocarbon resources from foreign companies.[104] In contrast, Moroccan interviewees mostly approached electricity interdependence as part of industrial policy and strategic trade relations rather than as a threat to energy independence or a neocolonial scheme. That said, Morocco and Algeria's poor relations have likely impeded further North African or Maghrebi South-South grid integration. Both countries are part of COMELEC, the North African power grid, but little progress has been made on deepening integration, and the Arab Maghreb Union, the regional cooperation organization, has largely failed.

In 1997, Spain became the largest exporter of electricity to Morocco.[105] ONEE and Red Eléctrica de España built the first transmission interconnection between Africa and the EU in 1997. Exchange began in 1998, and an additional line was added in 2007.[106] Electricity imports increased from 4.5% of Morocco's consumption in 2005 to 17% in 2011 due to reduced hydropower generation from drought (see Fig. 5.3).[107]

Transnational grid integration could play an important future role in balancing intermittency from renewable energy sources[108] and could reduce natural gas consumption. Currently, feasibility studies are being conducted for a 1,000 MW transmission cable to Portugal and an additional cable to Spain to allow Morocco to export renewable electricity to Europe by 2026.[109,110]

In 2019, Morocco became a net exporter of electricity to Spain.[111] These low-cost exports originated from the completion of a 1.4 GW coal-fired power plant in Safi in 2018, plus greater hydroelectric output due to increased rainfall.[112] In theory, the Moroccan state could earn rents from the future export of green electricity.[113] Yet, these rents would likely be small. If current models of renewable power plant development are

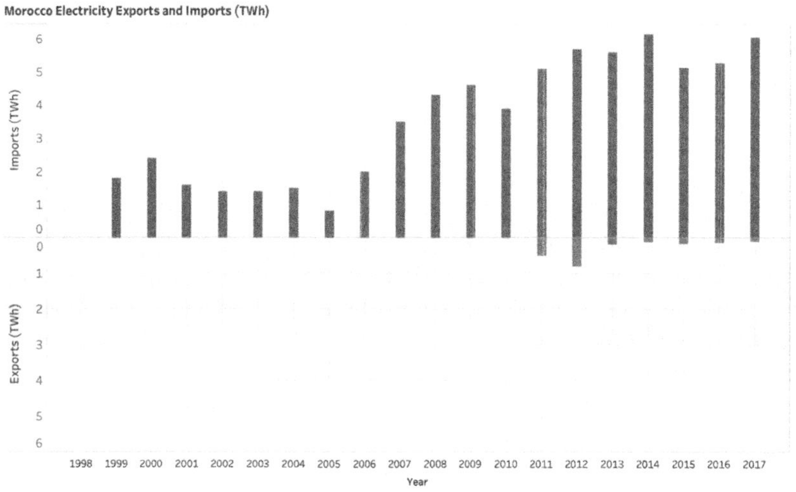

Fig. 5.3 Morocco's imports and exports of electricity, in Terawatt-hours (TWh). Developed in Tableau software using IEA *Electricity Information* data

continued, ACWA Power and other renewable energy developers would secure some of the profits. Dispatchable power from CSP with storage would be ideal for export, but European countries would have to choose to purchase this higher-cost electricity for climate change mitigation and reduction. So far, they have chosen not to do so.

Sub-Saharan Africa

After decades of focusing attention northward toward Europe, the Kingdom is paying greater attention to relations with Africa. When Mohammed VI took the throne in 1999, he sought to increase connections with sub-Saharan Africa.[114] Boukhars refers to Mohammed VI as 'Africa-trotting,' making visits promoting Moroccan businesses, including renewable energy. Additionally, Morocco is competing with Algeria for the leadership role in regional security in the Sahel by promoting a moderate and tolerant version of Islam.[115]

The new 'MASEN partner of Africa' strategy is similar to Germany's foreign policy on renewable energy. MASEN will work with the African Development Bank to establish financing schemes for renewable energy in sub-Saharan Africa, as well as a Desert-to-Power plan to export renewable energy to the Sahel.[116] Like Germany, ONEE emphasizes sharing proven energy expertise and know-how with sub-Saharan Africa.[117]

Despite opposition from Algeria and South Africa, Morocco was readmitted to the African Union (AU) in 2017 after leaving in 1984 over the Western Sahara conflict.[118] In his inaugural speech to the AU in 2017, King Mohammed VI emphasized Morocco's interest in joining the pan-African project and the importance of electricity and natural gas integration with West Africa.[119] He lamented the failed Arab Maghreb Union and gestured toward the idea that regional integration brings security and prosperity. Morocco is seeking to join the West African Power Pool and has discussed building a cross-border transmission line between Dakhla in Western Sahara and Nouadhibou in Mauritania.[120] In theory, this line would connect Morocco to the West African Power Pool, but it is unclear what electricity generation would be exported from Morocco to northern Mauritania. Over half of Mauritania's population lives in Nouakchott, which is 480-km (300-miles) from Nouadhibou.

Western Sahara

The only resource that has provided rents to the Moroccan government is phosphates. Western Sahara's phosphate reserves compose just 10% of Morocco's proved reserves, but this affords Morocco a monopoly on phosphate exports to Europe.[121] South Africa has been trying to block phosphate exports from Western Sahara since Morocco rejoined the AU.[122]

Infrastructural integration has been used by states to foster interdependence with territories. For example, the Soviet Union worked to build a centralized grid across Eastern European and Central Asian Soviet states.[123] Western Sahara Resource Watch (WSRW)—a UK activist group—has been monitoring Morocco's renewable energy activity and the European companies that support it in Western Sahara. WSRW criticizes the 5 MW CIMAR wind farm in Western Sahara, which powers a cement facility, with turbines provided by Spanish company Acciona.[124] WSRW also criticizes Siemens for developing the 50 MW Foum El Oued wind farm in Western Sahara, and the Tarfaya wind farm near the border of Morocco and the disputed territory.[125]

Although two of the five CSP sites in the Moroccan Solar Plan were originally slated for Western Sahara, the government struggled to obtain project financing. At COP 22, the Moroccan government announced a novel green bond financing scheme for 1.15 billion MAD (roughly $115 million).[126] The financing went toward two solar PV plants in Western Sahara, 20 MW Noor Boujdour and 85 MW Noor Laayoune, plus the Noor Ouarzazate IV PV plant (72 MW). Vigeo Eiris—a Moroccan subsidiary of Eiris in the UK and Vigeo in France—certified the green bond, which drew criticism from WSRW.[127] MASEN issued it with investment from Moroccan banks.[128] Noor Laayoune cost approximately $210 million, and it is unclear who provided the remaining financing.[129]

Internal Pressures Maintaining Fossil Fuels, and Challenges of Achieving an Inclusive and Equitable Domestic Energy Transition

Among the foremost internal pressures propping up hydrocarbons is that the state is still drawn to becoming rich in hydrocarbon wealth. In 1992, the government enacted a hydrocarbon code that made Morocco an attractive locale for private oil exploration.[130] In 2000, the government announced the discovery of 12 billion barrels of oil by a Texan company, Lone Star Energy.[131] This led to public exclamations of the new king's *baraka* (blessings), but it was soon realized that the discovery was fake. Lone Star Energy was owned by billionaire John Paul DeJoria, who made his fortune on Paul Mitchell hair products and Patrón tequila.[132] In 2009, a Moroccan court found him guilty of fraud: a finding that was backed up by the US Court of Appeals for the Fifth Circuit in 2015.[133] However, as of late 2018, 12 oil companies were still exploring for hydrocarbons,[134] including off the coast of Western Sahara. (A large natural gas discovery was made off of the southern Mauritanian coast in 2019.) In 2019, a British company reported a gas discovery of 474 billion cubic feet in Tendrara permit area, but it did not achieve commercial flow rates.[135]

Another pressure that could prop up fossil fuels is the discovery of oil shale. Large deposits of oil shale have been discovered near Timahdit and Tarfaya, which are likely to fuel transportation rather than electricity. Modest amounts of shale gas have been discovered, but barriers exist in terms of water availability and infrastructure development.[136] L'Office National des Hydrocarbures et des Mines is offering advantageous terms for private companies to develop these resources.[137]

Another large internal barrier to decreasing dependence on gasoline and butane is public pressure to maintain subsidies. In 2011, the overall subsidies provided by the Caisse de Compensation amounted to 5.5% of GDP: 45 million MAD, or $5.571 million.[138] In 2015, the Moroccan government eliminated the small subsidies on gasoline as well as the moderate subsidies on diesel, which plays an important role in powering irrigation.[139] However, the state has struggled to remove the much larger subsidies for butane gas, which is widely used for residential cooking, water heating, and irrigation. The international price of butane gas fell from $546 per tonne in January 2018 to $374 per tonne in July 2019, which lessened the pressure on the state's budget.[140] Additionally, the Moroccan government is working to phase out electricity subsidies, except for citizens who consume the least per month.

Domestic Social Pressure

The critique of the provision of rents is that it suppresses democracy by removing the general public accountability often linked to taxation. It is impossible to measure whether international funding for renewable energy projects provides a rent that indeed suppresses democracy, although it is clear that Morocco's renewable energy policy seeks to address social challenges that could threaten state stability. Morocco's renewable energy policy is interwoven with fraught social issues and therefore has much more to deliver than electrons. It must also address lack of equity of opportunity and social isolation without providing services from fossil fuel rents as oil-rich states in the region do. Who benefits and who loses from energy and other development is a key social issue in Morocco today. Recent nationwide boycotts against large, transnational corporations have illustrated broad public resistance to economic models that do not result in equitable economic growth, as have controversies around the exploitation of collective land for solar energy development. Thus, the Moroccan government faces immense pressure to achieve an inclusive energy transition that does not perpetuate uneven development.

There have been drawbacks with solar siting processes in terms of lack of sufficient and substantive engagement of local populations, use of water for the first wet-cooled stage of Noor-Ouarzazate, loss of collective grazing land, and benefits that went to the center of the commune rather than the most affected populations.[141] Additionally, apple farmers living near the Noor-Midelt site see the fruits of their labor go to middlemen who control the apple market. They hope that MASEN will help them obtain solar-powered cold storage technologies and solar-powered irrigation that will enable them to gain more control over their market and cope with climate change. World Bank funded projects require the consultation of local populations in project development, and MASEN has initiated local social development projects in the rural areas in which it is working. These do provide accountability mechanisms, but these do not guarantee substantive changes in the state's energy plans.

The 2016 death of Mouhcine Fikri also highlighted the stakes of uneven development. The police confiscated and discarded illegally caught swordfish from Fikri and his business partners. Fikri crawled into the back of the garbage truck to retrieve the valuable fish and was crushed to death in the compactor, allegedly at the behest of the police.[142] His death rekindled the protest movement that began in Morocco's Rif Mountains during the Arab Spring.[143] The Hirak protest movement calls for more equitable access to infrastructure and clean water, employment opportunities, better health care, and the decriminalization of small hashish production.[144] In response, Mohammed VI fired a number of government officials for failing to sufficiently serve the Rif, including the director general of ONEE, Ali Fassi Fihri. *Tel Quel* dubbed this 'the short-circuiting of Mr. Energy by Hirak.'[145] This protest held high-level political appointees accountable, but the king has maintained his overall power.

In April of 2018, Morocco's first boycott gained unprecedented participation. It is unknown who started the boycott, which spread virally on social media using the hashtag #Boycott. Three companies were targeted: Centrale Laitière (a subsidiary of Danon), Sidi Ali and Oulmès bottled water, and Afriquia gas stations. These three companies hold over 50% market share in their respective markets. The Minister of Agriculture Aziz Akhannouch—the majority stakeholder of Afriquia—was among the targets. A Moroccan government report had demonstrated that Afriquia has increased its margins since the liberalization of prices and that the government has been the big winner. The latter was, of course, the goal, but this was of little comfort to people coping with higher gasoline and transportation costs. The boycotters were not boycotting gasoline for renewable energy and electric vehicles, or bottled water for tap water.[146] Rather, they protested liberalization, monopolies, and economic inequality. The boycott had significant economic effects on two of the companies. Danon lost 538 million dirhams ($55.5 million), and Oulmès's revenue dropped by 91% over the previous year.[147] This is an example of consumers holding companies to whom they provide revenue accountable. However, it is not clear whether rents provided for renewable energy development suppressed democracy or lessened public accountability over state funding and priorities.

These examples illustrate that the renewable energy transition must balance multiple and sometimes amorphous goals, ranging from geopolitics and multilateral and bilateral relations, to nation-state pride and power, to socioeconomic inequality and public perceptions. All of these considerations shape energy policy, but energy policy analysts tend to only look at one side or another, based on disciplinary persuasions.

Conclusion

In this chapter, I have drawn on different geopolitical lenses, examining nation-state interests in scarce resources; economics and institutions; and competing social, international, and economic pressures. One perspective suggests that politics trump markets when state security is involved. This can be seen to some extent in Morocco's goals to pursue higher-cost renewable energy from CSP to bolster energy independence, but the goals also seek to meet socioeconomic and industrial policy needs. Simultaneously, Morocco is phasing out fossil fuel subsidies that threaten the macroeconomic stability of the economy. Since the Moroccan state lacks the fossil fuel wealth of its neighbors in the MENA region, it cannot afford to maintain state stability by providing large subsidies on energy services to its population.

Few countries are on track to transition to a 100% renewable electricity system, let alone a renewable energy system. Morocco's 52% of capacity goal is viewed as ambitious. Thus, renewable energy strategy cannot be separated from hydrocarbon geopolitics and overall energy policy. Instead of adding additional fuel-oil capacity to back up intermittent renewable energy supply, Morocco is adding natural gas. While natural gas does not improve energy independence, it will help to power development; back up intermittent renewable energy, particularly in the absence of grid integration; and reduce emissions over fuel-oil or coal. Increasing natural gas generation, however, has geopolitical dimensions due to Morocco's frosty relations with its gas-rich neighbor. Thus, Morocco seeks to gain suppliers in West Africa and the United States.

Finally, I have discussed how Morocco's energy policy is interwoven with its socioeconomic development goals. I have demonstrated that social pressures, scarce resources, international dimensions, and economic pressures are forces bending and shaping Morocco's energy policy. No single force serves as a trump card to the others; rather, the government engages in a balancing act to meet various goals, making trade-offs along the way. These competing forces and goals may cause Morocco's energy policy to seem contradictory, but, in fact, it is necessary to study the variegated parts to understand the whole.

Notes

1. Michael T. Klare, *Rising Powers, Shrinking Planet: The New Geopolitics of Energy* (London: Macmillan, 2009); Ronald Dannreuther, "International Relations Theories: Energy, Minerals and Conflict," POLINARES Working Paper.
2. Klare, 2009.
3. Andreas Goldthau and Jan Witte, *Global Energy Governance: The New Rules of the Game* (Washington, DC: Brookings Institution Press, 2010).
4. Hugh Dyer and Maria Julia Trombetta, *International Handbook of Energy Security* (Cheltenham: Edward Elgar Publishing, 2013).
5. Michael Ross, "Does Oil Hinder Democracy?," *World Politics* 53, no. 3 (2001): 325–61.
6. Clark A. Miller et al., "Narrative Futures and the Governance of Energy Transitions," *Futures* 70 (June 1, 2015): 65–74, https://doi.org/10.1016/j.futures.2014.12.001.
7. Katherine Jellison, *Entitled to Power: Farm Women and Technology, 1913–1963* (Chapel Hill: The University of North Carolina Press, 1993); Robert W. Righter, *Wind Energy in America* (Norman: University of Oklahoma Press, 1996).
8. Thomas Hughes, *Networks of Power* (Baltimore: Johns Hopkins University Press, 1983).
9. Royaume du Maroc Haut Commissariat au Plan, "Prospective Maroc 2030: Energie 2030 Quelles Options Pour Le Maroc?," 2006, www.hcp.ma/file/111440/, p. 4.
10. Mary Jane Parmentier and Sharlissa Moore, "'The Camels Are Unsustainable': Using Study Abroad as a Pedagogical Tool for Teaching Ethics and Sustainable Development," *Teaching Ethics* 16, no. 2 (October 1, 2016): 207–21, https://doi.org/10.5840/tej2016113038.
11. AE Johnston and I Steén, "Understanding Phosphorus and Its Uses in Agriculture" (European Fertilizer Manufacturers Association, n.d.).

12. CEIC, "Morocco Trade Balance [June 2018 through May 2019] [Data & Charts]," CEIC, accessed August 28, 2019, https://www.ceicdata.com/en/indicator/morocco/trade-balance.
13. WITS, "Morocco | Trade At a Glance," World Integrated Trade Solution, 2016, https://wits.worldbank.org/CountrySnapshot/en/MAR.
14. Entreprendre, "Au Maroc la caisse de compensation pèse lourd au budget de l'état," entreprendre.ma, Entreprendre.ma: Portail marocain de l'actualité économique, accessed August 28, 2019, https://www.entreprendre.ma/Au-Maroc-la-caisse-de-compensation-pese-lourd-au-budget-de-l-etat_a4782.html.
15. Paolo Verme, Khalid El-Massnaoui, and Abdelkrim Araar, "Reforming Subsidies in Morocco," Number 134 (Washington, DC: The World Bank, 2014), http://siteresources.worldbank.org/EXTPREMNET/Resources/EP134.pdf.
16. IEA, "Energy Policies Beyond IEA Countries: Morocco 2019" (Paris, France: International Energy Agency, June 20, 2019), https://webstore.iea.org/download/direct/2736?fileName=Energy_Policies_beyond_IEA_Contries_Morocco.pdf.
17. IEA.
18. Hamza Mekouar, "'Thirsty Protests' Hit Morocco Over Water Shortages," PhysOrg, October 15, 2017, https://phys.org/news/2017-10-thirsty-protests-morocco-shortages.html.
19. Janpeter Schilling et al., "Climate Change, Vulnerability and Adaptation in North Africa with Focus on Morocco," *Agriculture, Ecosystems & Environment* 156 (August 1, 2012): 12–26, https://doi.org/10.1016/j.agee.2012.04.021.
20. RCREEE, "Arab Future Energy Index™ (AFEX)," Regional Center for Renewable Energy and Energy Efficiency, 2015, https://www.rcreee.org/content/AFEXRE2015; RCREEE, "Arab Future Energy Index (AFEX) 2016: Renewable Energy," 2016, http://www.rcreee.org/sites/default/files/final_afex_re_2016.pdf.
21. Matthew Adamson, "Peut-on faire une histoire nucléaire du Maroc?" *Afrique contemporaine* 261–262, no. 1 (2017): 85–102. The American Presidency Project, "George W. Bush: Message to the Congress Transmitting a Protocol to the Morocco-United States Agreement on the Peaceful Uses of Nuclear Energy," October 24, 2001, http://www.presidency.ucsb.edu/ws/index.php?pid=73438.
22. Washington Post, "Russian Prime Minister Strikes Energy Deals in Morocco," *Washington Post*, October 11, 2017, sec. Business, https://www.washingtonpost.com/business/russian-prime-minister-strikes-energy-deals-in-morocco/2017/10/11/b661e576-aecb-11e7-9b93-b97043e57a22_story.html.

23. Royaume du Maroc Ministere de l'energie, des mines, de l'eau et de l'environnement, "Les Energies Renouvelables Au Maroc: Stratégie et Plan d'action" (November 20, 2012). http://clusters.wallonie.be/servlet/Repository/ministere-de-l-energie.pdf?ID=28299&saveFile=.
24. Royaume du Maroc Ministere de l'energie, des mines, de l'eau et de l'environnement.
25. Karim Choukri, Ahmed Naddami, and Sanaa Hayani, "Renewable Energy in Emergent Countries: Lessons from Energy Transition in Morocco," *Energy, Sustainability and Society* 7 (September 4, 2017): 25, https://doi.org/10.1186/s13705-017-0131-2.
26. Sharlissa Moore, *Sustainable Energy Transformations, Power and Politics: Morocco and the Mediterranean* (London: Routledge, 2019).
27. Joseph Masco, "Chapter 1: The Enlightened Earth," in *The Nuclear Borderlands: The Manhattan Project in Post-Cold War New Mexico* (Princeton: Princeton University Press, 2006); Moore, *Sustainable Energy Transformations, Power and Politics: Morocco and the Mediterranean.*
28. Moore, *Sustainable Energy Transformations, Power and Politics: Morocco and the Mediterranean*; Royaume du Maroc Haut Commissariat au Plan, "Prospective Maroc 2030: Energie 2030 Quelles Options Pour Le Maroc?"
29. Morocco World News, "First 'Made in Morocco' Wind Turbine Leaves Tanger Med Port," *Morocco World News* (blog), December 13, 2017, https://www.moroccoworldnews.com/2017/12/236258/made-morocco-wind-turbine-tanger-med-port-siemens-gamesa/.
30. WITS, "Morocco | Trade At a Glance."
31. HCP, "Taux de chômage au niveau national selon les tranches d'âge," Haut-Commissariat au Plan du Royaume du Maroc, 2018, https://www.hcp.ma/Taux-de-chomage-au-niveau-national-selon-les-tranches-d-age_a262.html.
32. Julia Terrapon-Pfaff et al., *Social CSP Energy and Development: Exploring the Local Livelihood Dimension of the Noor I CSP Project in Southern Morocco* (Bonn, Germany: Wuppertal Institute; Germanwatch, June 30, 2015), www.wupperinst.org/en/projects/details/wi/p/s/pd/449/.
33. Anouar Boukhars, "Reassessing the Power of Regional Security Providers: The Case of Algeria and Morocco," *Middle Eastern Studies* 55, no. 2 (March 4, 2019): 242–60, https://doi.org/10.1080/00263206.2018.1538968.
34. Liesl Louw-Vaudran, "The Meaning of Morocco's Return to the African Union" (Institute for Security Studies, January 2018), https://issafrica.s3.amazonaws.com/site/uploads/nar-1.pdf.
35. Fondation Mohammed VI Pour la Protection de L'environnement, "Mohammed VI Prize for the Climate and Sustainable Development,"

Mohammed VI Prize, 2019, http://www.prize-fm6e.org/assets/documents/brochureenglish.pdf.

36. "Morocco," International Energy Agency, accessed August 27, 2019, https://www.iea.org/countries/Morocco/.
37. Agnes D'Angio, "L'électrification Du Maroc Vue à Travers l'action de La Société Schneider et Cie (1907-1954)," *Outre-Mers* 89, nos. 334–335 (2002): 317–29.
38. Samir Saul, "L'électrification Du Maroc à l'époque Du Protectorat," *Outre-Mers* 89, nos. 334–335 (2002): 491–512.
39. Royaume du Maroc Haut Commissariat au Plan, "Secteur de l'énergie Chiffres Clés Année 2012 Données Provisoires" (Rabat, Morocco: Royaume du Maroc Haut Commissariat au Plan, 2012), http://www.mem.gov.ma/SiteAssets/PdfChCle1/energie/annuel/chifclesenergie-2012.pdf, p. 22. The Ministry of Energy did not report how its installed thermal capacity broke down by primary fuel.
40. Tarik Hamane, "A Snapshot of Morocco's Power Sector," 2016, https://www.scribd.com/document/457642550/Tarik-Hamane-article.
41. IEA, "Energy Policies Beyond IEA Countries: Morocco 2019."
42. El Mehdi Berrada, "Maroc: 4,7 milliards d'euros seront investis par l'Onee pour l'électricité et l'eau potable," *JeuneAfrique.com*, July 23, 2019, https://www.jeuneafrique.com/807250/economie/maroc-47-milliards-deuros-seront-investis-par-lonee-pour-lelectricite-et-leau-potable/.
43. IEA, *Coal Information 2018 Edition* (Paris, France: International Energy Agency, 2018). The IEA does not report all of the countries from which Morocco imports coal.
44. *Morocco 2014—Energy Policies Beyond IEA Countries* (Paris, France: International Energy Agency/OECD, 2014).
45. IEA, "Energy Policies beyond IEA Countries: Morocco 2019."
46. IEA.
47. IEA.
48. IEA, p. 136.
49. Trading Economics, "Algeria Exports to Morocco," Trading Economics, 2016, https://tradingeconomics.com/algeria/exports/morocco.
50. IEA, "Energy Policies Beyond IEA Countries: Morocco 2019."
51. Carl Dawson, *EU Integration with North Africa: Trade Negotiations and Democracy Deficits in Morocco* (London: I.B. Tauris, 2009).
52. IEA, "Energy Policies Beyond IEA Countries: Morocco 2019," p. 137.
53. Export.gov, "Algeria—Oil and Gas—Hydrocarbons," export.gov, January 31, 2019, https://www.export.gov/apex/article2?id=Algeria-Oil-and-Gas-Hydrocarbons.

54. Miguel Hernando de Larramendi, “Doomed Regionalism in a Redrawn Maghreb? The Changing Shape of the Rivalry Between Algeria and Morocco in the Post-2011 Era,” *The Journal of North African Studies* 24, no. 3 (2018): 506–31, https://doi.org/10.1080/13629387.2018.1454657.
55. Salma El Wardany, “Wars, Coups and Protests Don’t Stop Gas Flowing to Europe,” *Bloomberg.Com*, March 4, 2019, https://www.bloomberg.com/news/articles/2019-03-04/wars-coups-whatever-algeria-never-stops-gas-flows-to-europe.
56. Indrajit Sen, “Exclusive: Saudi Firm in the Lead for Algeria-Spain Gas Pipeline Project,” *Middle East Business Intelligence*, May 13, 2019, https://www.meed.com/exclusive-saudi-firm-lead-algeria-spain-gas-pipeline-project/.
57. Houssam Hatim and Soufiane Chahid, “Maroc-Algérie, si proches, si loin,” https://telquel.ma/sommaire/maroc-algerie-si-proches-si-loin, November 16, 2018.
58. Carla Sertin, “Sonatrach CEO Replaced Amidst Algerian Government Upheaval,” *Oil & Gas Middle East*, April 25, 2019, https://www.oilandgasmiddleeast.com/drilling-production/33821-sonatrach-ceo-fired-in-government-upheaval.
59. El Wardany, “Wars, Coups and Protests Don’t Stop Gas Flowing to Europe.”
60. Jude Clemente, “Will Algeria Be Able to Export More Natural Gas And LNG?,” *Forbes*, May 4, 2016, https://www.forbes.com/sites/judeclemente/2016/05/04/will-algeria-be-able-to-export-more-natural-gas-and-lng/.
61. Larramendi, “Doomed Regionalism in a Redrawn Maghreb?”
62. Derica Lambrechts and Lars B. Blomquist, “Political-Security Risk in the Oil and Gas Industry: The Impact of Terrorism on Risk Management and Mitigation,” *Journal of Risk Research* 20, no. 10 (October 3, 2017): 1320–37, https://doi.org/10.1080/13669877.2016.1153502.
63. Julien Wagner, “Maroc: « Gas to Power est un projet hors-norme en Afrique »,” *JeuneAfrique.com*, January 19, 2018, https://www.jeuneafrique.com/516106/economie/maroc-gas-to-power-est-un-projet-hors-norme-en-afrique/.
64. IEA, “Energy Policies Beyond IEA Countries: Morocco 2019.”
65. Hatim and Chahid, “Maroc-Algérie, si proches, si loin.”
66. IEA, “Energy Policies Beyond IEA Countries: Morocco 2019.” Safaa Kasraoui, “Morocco-Nigeria Pipeline Feasibility Study Is Complete,” *Morocco World News* (blog), January 29, 2019. https://www.moroccoworldnews.com/2019/01/264630/morocco-nigeria-pipeline/.
67. Boukhars, “Reassessing the Power of Regional Security Providers.”
68. IEA, “Energy Policies Beyond IEA Countries: Morocco 2019,” p. 127.

69. Ministère de l'Energie, des mines, de l'eau and de l'environnement, "Secteur de l'énergie Chiffres Clés" (Rabat, Morocco: Ministère de l'Energie, des mines, de l'eau and de l'environnement, 2009), http://www.mem.gov.ma/SiteAssets/PdfChCle1/energie/annuel/chifclesenergie-2009.pdf. See these reports for years 2009–2014.
70. IEA, "Energy Policies Beyond IEA Countries: Morocco 2019."
71. Ian M. Ralby, *Downstream Oil Theft: Global Modalities, Trends, and Remedies* (Washington, DC: The Atlantic Council, 2017), https://www.atlanticcouncil.org/in-depth-research-reports/report/downstream-oil-theft/.
72. IEA, "Energy Policies Beyond IEA Countries: Morocco 2019."
73. A. Mounir Debbarh, "L'Énergie: Développement Énergétique Au Maroc Depuis 1955, Perspectives 2025" (Association Nationale des Collectivities Locales du Maroc, March 20, 2015), http://cndwebzine.hcp.ma/cnd_sii/IMG/pdf/dvp_energetique.pdf.
74. Debbarh.
75. "500 Millions USD Pour Refinancer Samir," *Economie Entreprises*, May 2014.
76. Faiçal Faquihi, "Affaire Samir: Une « cagnotte » de 54,6 milliards de DH pour l'Etat," *L'Economiste*, January 3, 2019, https://www.leconomiste.com/article/1038766-affaire-samir-une-cagnotte-de-54-6-milliards-de-dh-pour-l-etat.
77. Faquihi.
78. Ralby, *Downstream Oil Theft*.
79. Hamane, "A Snapshot of Morocco's Power Sector."
80. Nadejda Komendantova, "Renewable Energies in the Middle East and North African Region: Can Private-Public Partnerships Address Existing Barriers and Risks?," *International Proceedings of Chemical, Biological and Environmental Engineering* 91 (2016): 31–37.
81. The World Bank, "Project Financials: MA-Noor Ouarzazate Concentrated Solar Power Project," The World Bank, accessed August 29, 2019, http://projects.worldbank.org/P131256/?lang=en&tab=financial.
82. Emiliano Bellini, "Morocco Opens 230 MW Solar Tender," *PV Magazine*, July 11, 2019, https://www.pv-magazine.com/2019/07/11/morocco-opens-230-mw-solar-tender/.
83. Khalid Benhamou, "Paving the Way to Large-Scale Wind Power Developments: Morocco's Pre-COP 22 Policies," in *World Wind Energy Conference* (Tokyo: World Wind Energy Conference, 2016).
84. CIF, "Projects in Morocco," Climate Investment Funds, August 25, 2015, https://www.climateinvestmentfunds.org/country/morocco.
85. African Development Bank Group, "Sefa Grant Provides Key Support for Morocco Wind Project," *All Africa*, January 8, 2014, http://all

africa.com/stories/201401081297.html; ACWA Power, "Khalladi Wind Farm Takes Off!," Khalladi wind farm takes off!, December 18, 2017, https://www.acwapower.com/news/khalladi-wind-farm-takes-off/.
86. ACWA Power, "Khalladi Wind Farm Takes Off!"
87. CSP Today, "Morocco Predicts Price Drop at Midelt CSP-PV Hybrid," *CSP Today* (blog), May 18, 2018, http://newenergyupdate.com/csp-today/morocco-expects-price-drop-hybrid-csp-plant-widens-funding-sources.
88. ACWA Power, "Powering Futures: Annual Report," 2017, https://www.acwapower.com/Flip/ACWA%20Power-AR2017-Short-Web/offline/download.pdf.
89. "Plan Solaire Marocain: Masen Sous Pression," *Economie Entreprises*, June 2013, http://economie-entreprises.com/2013/06/01/masen-sous-pression/.
90. OANDA Currency Converter, August 1, 2017.
91. New Energy Update: CSP, "ACWA Power Scales up Tower-Trough Design to Set Record-Low CSP Price," *New Energy Update: CSP*, September 20, 2017, http://analysis.newenergyupdate.com/csp-today/acwa-power-scales-tower-trough-design-set-record-low-csp-price.
92. Julien Wanger, "Maroc: bras de fer entre Masen et Acwa Power sur le prix de l'énergie," *JeuneAfrique.com*, February 15, 2019, https://www.jeuneafrique.com/mag/732051/economie/maroc-bras-de-fer-entre-masen-et-acwa-power-sur-le-prix-de-lenergie/.
93. Wanger.
94. Jose Santamarta, "Noor Midelt winner optimizes Concentrated Solar Power Trough, Storage to Hit Record Price," *HELIOSCSP* (blog), July 6, 2019, http://helioscsp.com/noor-midelt-winner-optimizes-concentrated-solar-power-trough-storage-to-hit-record-price/.
95. Bellini, "Morocco Opens 230 MW Solar Tender."
96. Carlo Cambini and Donata Franzi, "Assessing the EU Pressure for Rules Change: The Perceptions of Southern Mediterranean Energy Regulators," *Mediterranean Politics*, 2013, http://dx.doi.org/10.1080/13629395.2013.809197.
97. Edward Burke, Ana Echagüe, and Richard Youngs, "Energy Challenges in the Middle East and North Africa," ECD2020 (Madrid: FRIDE, October 2008); "Barcelona Declaration and Euro-Mediterranean Partnership," accessed April 30, 2011, http://europa.eu/legislation_summaries/external_relations/relations_with_third_countries/mediterranean_partner_countries/r15001_en.htm.
98. Moore, *Sustainable Energy Transformations, Power and Politics: Morocco and the Mediterranean*.
99. Moore.

100. ENTSO-E, "ENTSO-E Transmission System Map," accessed August 21, 2019, https://www.entsoe.eu/data/map/.
101. Saul, "L'électrification Du Maroc à l'époque Du Protectorat."
102. Debbarh, "L'Énergie: Développement Énergétique Au Maroc Depuis 1955, Perspectives 2025."
103. Debbarh.
104. Marta Musso, "'Oil Will Set Us Free': The Hydrocarbon Industry and the Algerian Decolonization Process," in *Britain, France and the Decolonization of Africa*, ed. A. Smith and C. J. Jeppesen (London: UCL Press, 2017), http://dx.doi.org/10.14324/111.9781911307730.
105. Debbarh, "L'Énergie: Développement Énergétique Au Maroc Depuis 1955, Perspectives 2025."
106. Ramon Granadino and Fatima Mansouri, "A Bridge Between Two Continents," *Transmission & Distribution World*, May 1, 2007, http://www.geni.org/globalenergy/library/technical-articles/transmission/transmission-and-distribution-world/a-bridge-between-two-continents/index.shtml.
107. Royaume du Maroc Ministère de l'Energie, des mines, de l'eau et de l'environnement, "La Stratégie Des Énergies Renouvelables Pour l'autoconsommation Dans Le Secteur de l'industrie" (November 25, 2014), https://nanopdf.com/download/presentation-memee_pdf.
108. Eric Martinot, "Grid Integration of Renewable Energy: Flexibility, Innovation, and Experience," 2016, http://martinot.info/Martinot_AR2016_grid_integration_prepub.pdf.
109. Red Eléctrica de España, "Spain and Morocco Agree on the Development of a Third Interconnection Between Both Countries," Red Eléctrica de España, February 14, 2019, https://www.ree.es/en/press-office/news/press-releases/2019/02/spain-and-morocco-agree-development-third-interconnection-between-both-countries.
110. Soufiane Chahid, "Aziz Rabbah fait marche-arrière sur le Plan Gazier 2021," *Telquel.ma*, January 10, 2019, https://telquel.ma/2019/01/10/aziz-rabbah-fait-marche-arriere-sur-le-plan-gazier-2021_1625100/?utm_source=tq&utm_medium=normal_post?fbrefresh=10.
111. Hassan El Arif, "Electricité: Ce que le Maroc exporte," *L'Economiste*, March 27, 2019, https://www.leconomiste.com/article/1042788-electricite-ce-que-le-maroc-exporte; "Exchanges July 2019," Red Eléctrica de España, July 2019, https://www.ree.es/en/datos/exchanges.
112. Ilias Tsagas, "Spain's Third Interconnection with Morocco Could Be Europe's Chance for African PV—Or a Boost for Coal," *PV Magazine International*, February 20, 2019, https://www.pv-magazine.com/2019/02/20/spains-third-interconnection-with-morocco-could-be-europes-chance-for-african-pv-or-a-boost-for-coal/.

113. Mehdi Rais, "Maroc: Le Pari de l'énergie Renouvelable," *Le Journal International*, June 2013, http://www.lejournalinternational.fr/Maroc-le-pari-de-l-energie-renouvelable_a879.html.
114. Larramendi, "Doomed Regionalism in a Redrawn Maghreb?"
115. Boukhars, "Reassessing the Power of Regional Security Providers."
116. Luchelle Feukeng, "Africa: Masen Partners with IDB to Finance Renewable Energy," *Afrik 21*, April 11, 2019, https://www.afrik21.africa/en/africa-masen-partners-with-idb-to-finance-renewable-energy/; African Development Bank, "Renewable Energy in Africa: African Development Bank and Moroccan Agency Masen Join Forces to Roll out 'Desert to Power' Initiative," African Development Bank, November 7, 2018, https://www.afdb.org/en/news-and-events/renewable-energy-in-africa-african-development-bank-and-moroccan-agency-masen-join-forces-to-roll-out-desert-to-power-initiative-18658.
117. Hamane, "A Snapshot of Morocco's Power Sector."
118. Louw-Vaudran, "The Meaning of Morocco's Return to the African Union."
119. Morocco World News, "Full Speech of King Mohammed VI at 28th African Union Summit," *Morocco World News* (blog), January 31, 2017, https://www.moroccoworldnews.com/2017/01/207060/full-speech-king-mohammed-vi-28th-african-union-summit/.
120. Louw-Vaudran, "The Meaning of Morocco's Return to the African Union"; IEA, "Energy Policies Beyond IEA Countries: Morocco 2019."
121. Lino Camprubí, "Resource Geopolitics: Cold War Technologies, Global Fertilizers, and the Fate of Western Sahara," *Technology and Culture* 56, no. 3 (September 17, 2015): 676–703, https://doi.org/10.1353/tech.2015.0077.
122. Linda Björk, "Battle over Western Sahara Is Moving into Court Rooms," *Sustainalytics* (blog), April 18, 2018, https://www.sustainalytics.com/esg-blog/polisario-front-western-sahara-legal-proceedings/.
123. Sergei Shmatko, "Russia: A Singular Achievement," *Living Energy*, 2013, https://www.energy.siemens.com/co/pool/hq/energy-topics/publications/living-energy/pdf/issue-09/essay-Russia-Living-Energy-9.pdf.
124. WSRW, "The Dirty Green March" (Western Sahara Resource Watch, 2013).
125. Arthur Neslen, "Africa's Biggest Windfarm Sparks Controversy in the Desert," *The Guardian*, November 22, 2016, https://www.theguardian.com/environment/2016/nov/22/morocco-saharan-windfarms-tarfaya-fan-accusations-of-green-plunder.
126. Nina Chestney, "MASEN Issues Morocco's First Green Bond," Masen, March 7, 2017, http://www.masen.ma/en/masen-news/masen-issues-moroccos-first-green-bond.

127. Vigeo Eiris, "Pre-Issuance Verification Statement (Assurance Report)" (Paris, October 4, 2016).
128. ALCBFund, "Understanding the African Green Bond Market," March 5, 2018, http://www.alcbfund.com/wp-content/uploads/2018/03/2018-03-05-African-Green-Bond-Market_Final.pdf.
129. ACWA Power, "Powering Futures: Annual Report," OANDA Currency Converter, August 1, 2018.
130. Debbarh, "L'Énergie: Développement Énergétique Au Maroc Depuis 1955, Perspectives 2025."
131. Marvine Howe, *Morocco: The Islamist Awakening and Other Challenges* (Oxford: Oxford University Press, 2005).
132. Christopher Helman, "Tequila Tycoon Faces $123 M Judgment In Moroccan Oil Deal Gone Wrong," *Forbes*, October 13, 2015, https://www.forbes.com/sites/christopherhelman/2015/10/13/tequila-tycoon-faces-123m-judgement-in-moroccan-oil-deal-gone-wrong/.
133. Helman.
134. "Exploration Activity," Office National des Hydrocarbures et des Mines, accessed August 27, 2019, http://www.onhym.com/en/exploration-activity.html.
135. IEA, "Energy Policies Beyond IEA Countries: Morocco 2019." Sound Energy PLC, "RNS Announcement (TE-10 Well Test Result and Exploration Update) | Sound Energy Plc." In 2019, a British company reported a gas discovery of 474 billion cubic feet in Tendrara permit area, May 21, 2019, https://www.soundenergyplc.com/investors/regulatory-news/rns-announcement/3611771.
136. Christopher Coats, "Shale Gas Flows in Morocco," *Forbes*, accessed December 23, 2019, https://www.forbes.com/sites/christophercoats/2015/06/30/shale-gas-flows-in-morocco/.
137. Gaurav Sharma, "Morocco's Energy Industry in the Midst of a Massive Shakeup," *Forbes*, February 13, 2019, https://www.forbes.com/sites/gauravsharma/2019/02/13/moroccos-energy-industry-in-the-midst-of-a-massive-shakeup/.
138. Entreprendre, "Au Maroc la caisse de compensation pèse lourd au budget de l'état," OANDA Currency Converter, August 1, 2011.
139. Pauline, "Neuf Clés Pour Comprendre La (Dé)Compensation," *Telquel.ma*, June 15, 2015, https://telquel.ma/2015/06/15/neuf-cles-decompensation_1451802/?utm_source=tq&utm_medium=normal_post.
140. Abdelaziz Ghouibi, "Compensation: Le gaz butane décroche de 7% au premier semestre," *L'Economiste*, August 9, 2019, https://www.leconomiste.com/article/1048883-compensation-le-gaz-butane-decroche-de-7-au-premier-semestre.

141. Karen Eugenie Rignall, "Solar Power, State Power, and the Politics of Energy Transition in Pre-Saharan Morocco," *Environment and Planning A* 48, no. 3 (March 1, 2016): 540–57, https://doi.org/10.1177/0308518X15619176; Terrapon-Pfaff et al., "Social CSP Energy and Development: Exploring the Local Livelihood Dimension of the Noor I CSP Project in Southern Morocco"; Moore, *Sustainable Energy Transformations, Power and Politics: Morocco and the Mediterranean*.
142. Al Jazeera, "Fishmonger's Gruesome Death Sparks Protests in Morocco," *Al Jazeera*, October 31, 2016, http://www.aljazeera.com/news/2016/10/fishmonger-gruesome-death-sparks-protests-morocco-161031131330359.html.
143. Rebecca Robinson and Mary Jane Parmentier, "The Arab Spring in North Africa: Still Winter in Morocco?," in *Online Collective Action*, ed. N. Agarwal, M. Lim, and R. Wigand (Springer, 2014); Al Jazeera, "Fishmonger's Gruesome Death Sparks Protests in Morocco."
144. Olmo Calvo, "Social Unrest Boils Over in Morocco's al-Hoceima," *Al Jazeera*, July 29, 2017, http://www.aljazeera.com/indepth/inpictures/2017/07/social-unrest-boils-morocco-al-hoceima-170727090556224.html; Travis Andrews, "Protests Erupt After Moroccan Fishmonger Dies Desperately Trying to Get Back His Confiscated Catch," *The Washington Post*, October 31, 2016, https://www.washingtonpost.com/news/morning-mix/wp/2016/10/31/protests-erupt-after-moroccan-fishmonger-was-crushed-to-death-in-garbage-truck/?utm_term=.084cb74e513a.
145. Telquel, "Ali Fassi Fihri, Le Spécialiste de l'énergie Court-Circuité Par Le Hirak," *Telquel.ma*, October 28, 2017, http://telquel.ma/2017/10/28/ali-fassi-fihri_1566160.
146. El Mehdi Berrada and Fahd Iraqi, "Boycott au Maroc: un « Hirak » numérique," *JeuneAfrique.com*, June 12, 2018, https://www.jeuneafrique.com/mag/564706/economie/boycott-au-maroc-un-hirak-numerique/.
147. El Mehdi Berrada, "Maroc: après le boycott, les Eaux minérales d'Oulmès accusent le coup," *JeuneAfrique.com*, March 13, 2019, https://www.jeuneafrique.com/748871/economie/maroc-les-eaux-minerales-doulmes-accusent-le-coup-du-boycott/.

CHAPTER 6

Byzantine Energy Politics: The Complex Tale of Low Carbon Energy in Turkey

Oksan Bayulgen

A Dangerous Fossil Fuel Dependency

Turkey is addicted to fossil fuels with major implications to the country's economic, geostrategic, and environmental well-being. About 87% of the burgeoning energy demand in the country is met with natural gas, oil, and coal (28, 29, and 30%, respectively). In power generation, the share of fossil fuels is less but still very significant with 68% in 2018. Natural gas by far has played the biggest role in the country since the end of the 1990s. Turkey has been the second country, after China, in terms of natural gas demand percentage growth, growing by 522% from 188,070 terra joules (TJ) in 1999 to 1,170,038 TJ in 2017.[1] Meanwhile, coal has become natural gas' biggest competitor as Turkey accelerated in recent years its reliance on coal for all sectors. Including all coal plants proposed and under construction, Turkey has the largest coal power plant development program in the world, outside China and India.[2]

O. Bayulgen (✉)
University of Connecticut, Storrs, CT, USA
e-mail: oksan.bayulgen@uconn.edu

R. Mills and L.-C. Sim (eds.), *Low Carbon Energy in the Middle East and North Africa*, International Political Economy Series,
https://doi.org/10.1007/978-3-030-59554-8_6

What complicates this picture of heavy reliance on fossil fuels is that Turkey is poor in indigenous fossil fuel resources, except for low-quality coal (lignite), and imports almost all of its oil, natural gas, and hard coal. Between 2007 and 2017, hard coal imports increased by 95.7%, oil products by 160%, and natural gas by 105%.[3] In 2017, domestic fossil fuel production met only 18% of the high energy demand and Turkey was among the largest importers of natural gas, coal, and oil products in the world (5th, 7th, and 7th respectively).[4]

The fact that most of energy consumption is met by imports poses a major energy security problem for Turkey. Rapidly increasing energy consumption means growing import dependency on countries that have complicated relations with it. For instance, in 2015, 11% of Turkey's oil, 56% of its natural gas, and 33% of its hard coal came from Russia alone. Russia's Gazprom was by far the largest single natural gas supplier to Turkey.[5] Iran, Iraq, and Saudi Arabia follow Russia in supplying the majority of Turkey's energy needs. Since 2002, energy imports have also played a major role in the persistent current account deficits Turkey had to grapple with. For example, in 2017, the country paid $37.19 billion for its energy imports, roughly 79% of its account deficit.[6]

In addition to supply security and economic vulnerability concerns, Turkey also faces major environmental challenges as a result of its energy profile. High dependence on fossil fuels and high energy intensity contribute to rapidly increasing greenhouse gas (GHG) emissions. For instance, compared to 1990, power sector emissions were 332% higher in 2018.[7] When non-CO2 greenhouse gases (GHG) are included, Turkey is the world's 20th-largest emitter of greenhouse gases (GHG) and ranks first in terms of emissions growth among Annex I countries since 2006.[8]

As one alternative to fossil fuels, Turkey has accelerated its efforts to develop nuclear energy in the past decade. Even though most Turkish governments have been interested in nuclear energy since the 1960s, the Justice and Development Party (AKP) government signed its first agreement with Russia in 2010 to build Turkey's first nuclear power plant in Akkuyu, on the Mediterranean coast with an estimated capacity of 4.8 gigawatts. A second nuclear project for 4.6 gigawatts in Sinop has also been signed with a Japanese-French consortium in May 2013. The government expects to have at least 10% of the electricity generation from nuclear by 2023, which is unrealistic at this point since construction on the Akkuyu project just started last year and has been encountering many delays since.[9] Aside from the obvious environmental and safety issues associated with it, there is doubt that nuclear energy will in fact lessen Turkey's energy import dependence as nuclear materials would have to be imported, at least initially, and the financing and operation of these power plants would come under the control and management of foreign governments according to the existing contracts.[10] It is argued that Akkuyu would be the first ever nuclear plant in the world on a state's sovereign land, owned and operated by another state.[11]

Given all the problems with fossil fuels and nuclear energy, renewables present an obvious energy alternative for Turkey. Endowed with a favorable climate and geography, Turkey has abundant renewable resources and yet, renewable energy constitutes merely 13% of Turkey's total primary energy supply in 2018. Renewables' share in electricity generation is much higher with 31%, but most of that comes from large hydroelectric dams (20% of all electricity generation).[12] Even though hydropower is a renewable energy, it is regarded by many as less sustainable, and therefore less desirable, given the numerous environmental and social costs associated with it.[13] In the past decade, there was also a rush to develop small hydro resources in Turkey (run-of-the-river facilities with capacities smaller than 10 MW) yet these make up 6% of the country's installed capacity.[14] In 2018, the total share of non-hydro renewables in electricity generation was 12% (with wind at 6.6%, solar at 2.5%, geothermal 2.3%, biofuels and waste 0.8%).[15] Despite the rapid growth of renewables since 2005 (by 93%), fossil fuel supply grew as well, increasing by 71% during the same period.[16] Today, the share of modern (non-hydro, non-traditional biomass) renewables in the overall energy mix—a key measure for sustainable development—remains limited and Turkey is still not close to realizing its vast clean energy potential.

Two-Steps Forward, One-Step Back in Renewable Energy Policy

Turkey is a latecomer to the global scene in terms of formulation of a national renewable energy policy. The distinct policy framework for renewable energy started to emerge with the restructuring and liberalization of the electricity market in the 1990s and reached a major turning point in 2001 with the *Electricity Market Law* (EML) #4628. This law made room for the development of renewables by allowing more competition into the electricity sector. Besides the broad electricity market reform and some specific sector-related laws, there was, however, no legislation directly addressing renewable energy promotion until the introduction of the *Renewable Energy Law (REL)* in 2005. One of the incentives offered with this law was a purchase guarantee, by which each retail licensee was obliged to get a portion of its electricity from Renewable Energy Resource (RER) certified producers. The Law also guaranteed a feed price at which each retail licensee must purchase renewable energy.

Despite this initial progress, the 2005 Law and subsequent amendments failed to adequately jumpstart the non-hydro renewable sector. According to experts, this was mostly due to the uncertainties and limitations in the law and ensuing regulations.[17] For instance, even though the law designed a purchase guarantee scheme, it did not provide any clear guidelines on how the guarantee mechanism would operate in practice. Moreover, the law required all state-owned retail licensee to enter into power purchase agreements with RER certified producers who approached them but it did not impose a similar obligation on private retail licensees. Finally, and perhaps most importantly, the feed in tariff system in the 2005 Law was not flexible enough to distinguish between developers in terms of the type of renewable source, the geographic location or the type of the plant, or the time of production during the day, which could potentially affect a renewable energy plant's ability to sell its output to retail licensees at the guaranteed feed price.[18] In response to criticisms, the government passed new Amendments (Law #6094) on December 29, 2010, in which some of the incentives were increased and differentiated based on the type of renewable source. These payment guarantees to renewable energy generators are done through a pooling of payments (a.k.a. the Renewable Energy Resources Support Mechanism, or YEKDEM).

The renewable energy legislation and the regulations accompanying it took nearly two decades to design and enact. On paper, Turkey now has the ambitious targets and the basic legal and regulatory institutional framework to attract investment and expand the deployment of renewables (especially in the power sector). The *2014 National Renewable Energy Action Plan (NREAP)* calls for a total renewable capacity of 61 gigawatts (GW) by 2023, with 34 GW coming from hydropower, 20 GW from wind, 5 GW from solar, 1 GW from geothermal and biomass each. Moreover, the *2018 National Energy Efficiency Action Plan (NEEAP)* sets out detailed goals for different energy sectors to reduce demand by 14% by 2023 from business-as-usual.[19]

Yet, despite success in growing the installed capacity of certain renewables in recent years, there have been significant regulatory and administrative hurdles and delays in project development, licensing, and grid connection that make further promotion of renewable energy sources difficult and unsustainable. Even though the support mechanisms have become more competitive in recent years when compared to alternative markets in Europe and elsewhere, there is a lot of uncertainty regarding what incentives will be offered when YEKDEM mechanism ends after 2020.[20] A common criticism by investors and industry experts is that the Turkish government has not been genuinely prioritizing renewables and lacks long-term planning and sound implementation roadmap to increase their share in the energy mix.[21] The technology-specific targets it sets out for itself in numerous strategy papers and action plans do not always align and do not go far beyond 2023, the centennial celebration of the founding of the Turkish Republic.[22] Even though the government committed to a target of reducing its GHG emissions by 21% by 2030 in the Intended Nationally Determined Contribution (INDC), it has not yet ratified the Paris Climate Change Agreement.[23] Moreover, there are no legally binding renewable energy targets fixed in legislation. Progress in electricity generation has not yet been accompanied by large-scale efforts to deploy renewables for transportation, heating, and cooling. There is also very little effort put into monitoring and evaluating the plans that are set out.[24] Finally, by making domestically sourced coal the preferred fuel for expanding its electricity capacity and setting a goal to reach 30 GW by 2023, the Turkish government has made plans that are contradictory to achieving a clean energy transition and decarbonization.[25]

What explains this partial progress in clean energy transition in Turkey? What are the external and internal pressures that played a role in jump-starting the renewable energy sector legislation and regulations in the early 2000s? Why didn't those pressures continue to propel the sector to a competitive status vis-à-vis the conventional energy sources? What are the countervailing forces that explain government's interest in prioritizing investments in natural gas, coal, and nuclear energy even though these non-renewable energy sources exacerbate supply insecurity, increase economic and foreign policy vulnerabilities and environmental pollution? The government's contradictory strategy of cultivating renewables while at the same time enthusiastically promoting the dirtier and unsustainable forms of energy is the central puzzle addressed in this chapter. Drawing upon existing literature, government and nongovernmental reports, newspaper articles and more than 35 semi-structured interviews with policymakers, bureaucrats, renewable energy investors, and representatives of civil society organizations, I analyze the drivers of Turkish energy policy in the past two decades.

Cornered by Crises and Pressured by External Actors

It is safe to argue that the Turkish government's interest in and reform efforts to develop renewable energy have had little to do with concerns about climate change and the environmental damage that arises from a high addiction to fossil fuels. Otherwise, how can one explain the Turkish government's rather enthusiastic rush to develop and import coal, the dirtiest fossil fuel, in the past two decades?[26] The development of the renewable energy policy framework in Turkey needs to be seen, instead, as part (and byproduct) of the reaction to the economic and energy crises facing the country since the 1990s and as driven by a pragmatic need to reduce vulnerability to price shocks, energy shortages, and high account deficits. As the political economy literature has extensively shown, crises create urgency for change, disrupt actors' existing incentives, weaken the resistance of those who prefer the status quo, and provide more political space to implement policy reform than had existed before.[27]

High levels of domestic and foreign debt, large fiscal deficits, high inflation, and periodic bank failures caused by weak governance of a series of coalition governments, and the ongoing warfare with Kurdish separatists culminated in three economic crises in Turkey in 1994, 2000, and 2001. The last one especially was very costly in terms of the collapse of output and high unemployment. The real GDP contracted by 7.5%, inflation reached 68.5%, and the Turkish lira depreciated by 115.3% against the US dollar while the insolvent banks increased to 22 by 2003.[28] The 2001 crisis also made it obvious that the government could no longer finance the capacity expansions necessary to meet future energy demand. The state monopolies were unable to provide the investments to increase efficiency in the generation and wholesale markets.[29] The crisis reinvigorated the privatization efforts which had started in the mid-1980s but have been painstakingly slow and unsuccessful.

As a result, the Turkish parliament passed the 2001 *Electricity Market Law* (#4628), which aimed at establishing a financially strong and competitive energy market by unbundling the *Turkish Electricity Generation Transmission Co.* (TEAS) monopoly into three companies responsible for generation, wholesale trading, and transmission; by outlining the major steps to privatize state's distribution and generation assets; and by creating an autonomous regulatory body, namely the *Electricity Market Regulatory Authority (EMRA)* to minimize political interference in market decisions and administer energy production permits in an objective and transparent manner. Along these lines, many other energy reforms, i.e., the *Natural Gas Market Law #4646*, and the *Renewable Energy Law of 2005*, followed.

The crisis also empowered the international financial institutions, which emerged as powerful external anchors for fundamental fiscal and institutional reforms. Confronted with a high unemployment rate and burgeoning external and domestic debt, the Turkish government resorted to International Monetary Fund (IMF) and World Bank financing to avoid a debt default. These donor agencies required power sector reforms and privatization of state assets as a precondition of their assistance packages. A new crisis management program sanctioned by IMF began in April 2001, when the then-Vice President of the World Bank, Kemal Dervis, became the Turkish Treasury Minister. When government changed hands in 2002, IMF continued its pressure by withholding the release of the next loan disbursement. Left with few choices, the new AKP government deepened the IMF structural reforms, which included, among others, further deregulation, privatization, and restructuring of the energy market.

Consequently, the World Bank, International Bank of Restructuring and Development, German Development Bank, and the Council of Europe Development Bank provided substantial financial support for renewable projects in Turkey.[30] US foreign policy and geostrategic interests in keeping Turkey stable in the Middle East in the post 9/11 global environment was also instrumental in getting significant funds and favorable repayment conditions from these international organizations. The unusually favorable global liquidity environment, thanks partly to US Fed's expansionary monetary policy, enabled the AKP government to attract large sums of foreign capital.[31] Availability of cheap loans allowed Turkish capitalists to buy out privatized public assets and build power plants more easily.

It is important to also stress the role of the European Union (EU) in kickstarting the renewable energy industry as the energy reforms were one of the preconditions for Turkey's EU membership. Even prior to membership negotiations, the finalization of the EU-Turkey Customs Union in 1995 accelerated Turkey's neoliberal economic transformation. The EU Council decision in 1999 to declare Turkey as a candidate country for full membership provided significant incentives to governing elites to pursue economic and political reforms. The 2001 economic crisis weakened the resistance of Euro-skeptics and hardened the resolve of reformers. Along these lines, the 2001 market-oriented energy laws were inspired by the EU's 1996 electricity and natural gas directives and reforms.[32] In December 2009, Turkey began to negotiate Chapter 27, the *environmental acquis*, which comprised over 200 major legal acts including water, air quality, waste management, industrial pollution control, among others. Especially the principle of energy sustainability, which emphasized the timely development of renewables, was highly codified in the EU *acquis*, to which Turkey had to align itself in order to be accepted as a member.[33]

Grassroots Resistance and Civil Society Mobilization Against Dirty Energy Projects

In addition to crises and external pressures, it is possible to argue that societal pressures played a role in shaping Turkish governments' energy policies to some extent. Starting in the post-1980 coup context, as the center-right governments embarked on energy-related infrastructural projects such as construction of large coal, hydropower and nuclear power plants, a significant number of local resistance campaigns mushroomed all around the country, drawing attention to environmental and social justice issues associated with those projects and pressuring the government and the private companies to withdraw from them. One of the iconic examples of such local mobilization was seen in Gerze, in the Black Sea region of Turkey, against a proposed coal power plant. Considered one of the ten most successful resistance cases against coal projects in the world by Sierra Club, this local movement brought together villagers, local NGOs, and transnational environmental organizations like Greenpeace to effectively push back against the private company and the government in support of it.[34] A 'No To Coal' meeting was organized in April 2010 with more than 6000 people attending; in March 2010, residents of the village neighboring the proposed plant prevented a public meeting organized by the company, forcing the workers to leave their village. Despite being exposed to police force ordered by the government to protect the private companies' interests, on the night of August 22, 2011, nine village women lay down in front of the drilling machines and successfully prevented the project from going forward. In November 2011, 10,000 people from various provinces and districts of Turkey gathered in the town of Gerze to protest the construction of the plant. Additionally, Greenpeace Mediterranean launched an internet signature campaign in 2011 against the power plant, which gathered over 37,000 supporters.[35] They also successfully targeted the Anadolu Group, the company proposing the power plant which also happened to be the owner of a popular beer brand, EFES. The project was eventually canceled in May 2012 by the Ministry of Environment and Urbanization.

In addition to such grassroots, semi-formal local resistance movements emerging against state-sanctioned, environmentally destructive energy projects around the country, there has also been an increase in the number of formal environmental organizations and climate networks, mostly in urban areas working to educate the public, raise awareness about climate change, lobby the government to participate in international agreements and take action to reduce the country's GHG emissions by investing more on clean energy technologies. In the 2000s, when compared to the previous decades, these civil society organizations enjoyed more opportunities to become involved in the decision-making processes by serving as commission members, preparing and presenting reports when asked by ministries and state agencies, and participating in formulating legislation. Improved funding opportunities for environmental issues—especially thanks to the increased networking capabilities linked to EU membership process—have also improved the capacity of civil society organizations to have some impact on policy. For instance, Greenpeace Turkey, among others, was very active during the formulation of the 2005 Renewable Energy Law by meeting with government officials, organizing demonstrations, and publicizing green energy in media outlets to put pressure on decisionmakers. According to Ozgur Gurbuz, who was the Greenpeace Energy Campaign Director at the time, two weeks after their intense campaigning, the parliament passed the 2005 Renewables Law and the Energy Minister during his speech in the parliament acknowledged specifically the role of NGOs in the preparation of this legislation.[36]

Besides environmental NGOs, part of the domestic pressure for renewables has arguably also come from the new renewable energy producers and their professional organizations/associations. The numerous wind, solar, geothermal, biogas, hydroelectric national associations in Turkey, in addition to providing professional network opportunities for their members, have organized and/or participated in renewable energy conferences and workshops where they regularly met with politicians, government bureaucrats, and foreign investors and presented their views on government policy and challenges of the sector. These increased and increasingly publicized interactions in the 2000s between business associations and the government have contributed to some of the improvements in the renewable legislation.[37]

Despite increased levels of environmental mobilization and resistance against dirtier and unsustainable forms of energy since the 2000s, the extent and impact of grassroots as well as institutionalized civil society pressures on government policy have nevertheless stayed very limited in Turkey. The episodic rises in participation and organizational strength, for the most part, have not translated into coherent and enduring national movements but instead produced short-lived victories or solutions that have done little to change the overall policy structures.[38] Over time due to ideological divisions within the movements, the lack of adequate funding for and membership to these organizations, and the state's heavy-handed efforts to selectively choose and manage the input from them, societal stakeholders had little success in changing the overall direction of government's energy policies.[39]

It also did not help that investors in the renewable sector were, at least initially, inexperienced and opportunistic. Especially in the small hydro and wind energy sectors, many entrepreneurs with no prior experience and knowledge rushed to apply for licenses to trade them at higher profits later as opposed to designing well-planned and thoroughly assessed projects and seeing them through.[40] The field of entrepreneurs was often very diverse with construction companies, appliance producers, real-estate developers, textile companies, and even soccer clubs. These companies often relied on energy brokers, also known as briefcase dealers (*cantaci*), who had access to government resources and received huge commission fees to trade licenses for project sites. As such, many projects changed hands at their early stages and failed to turn into long-term, sustainable developments.[41] In numerous cases, haphazard planning with inadequate feasibility studies generated public outcry and protests, ending in lawsuits, which slowed down or hampered the timely development of resources. Even the more established, traditional energy companies that entered the renewables sector had conflicting motivations as they tried to balance their investments in oil and natural gas with those in renewables. This variety created very different incentive structures and expectations among the players, making collective action needed to push for further reforms extremely difficult.[42]

State Actors as the Drivers of and Obstacles to Clean Energy Reforms

While Turkey's energy pathway is partly shaped by these external and internal pressure groups, it can be more accurately understood in the context of the changing interests and capacity of state actors. In the early 2000s, AKP's unflinching embrace of neoliberalism and commitment to structural reforms provided the first opening for renewable energy legislation in Turkey.[43] As a new party founded fifteen months before the November 2002 election, the AKP capitalized on the dissatisfaction with the established parties during the economic crisis and appealed to wide segments of the population as a reformist party that could bring much-needed economic and political stability to the country. Despite its Islamic and conservative roots, the AKP also understood the importance of constructing a broad-based coalition to avoid the mistakes of its predecessors and stay in power. Its emphasis on market reforms, globalization, and commitment to EU membership was appealing to the liberals and business groups, who traditionally tied the success of the Turkish economy to EU membership, while its concerns with social justice issues, extension of religious and ethnic freedoms attracted formerly marginalized and disadvantaged low- to middle-income groups in rural and metropolitan areas to the coalition.[44]

Despite the early attempts by the AKP governments to create a competitive energy sector, by the end of the 2000s it was clear that they were favoring certain energy projects over others. Renewables continued to have a seat at the table and the government paid lip-service to their importance in official documents and declarations, especially as the concerns with energy import dependency and account deficits increased. Yet, modern renewables, like wind and solar, were treated as the lesser members of the 'national energy' portfolio, where coal and nuclear got the lion's share of attention. Next, I discuss the three reasons for government's insistence on traditional and unsustainable forms of energy despite the pushback from external and domestic actors to more forcefully promote renewables.

Legacy of State-Led Developmentalism

One explanation for the focus on traditional forms of energy can be found in the historical legacy of state interventionism in Turkey that permeates decision-making and makes centralized, state-centric, mega energy projects with little regard for environmental and social costs routine and acceptable. With a long tradition of a highly centralized bureaucracy, Turkish governments have always had the aim of achieving economic development at any cost and as a key indicator of societal progress since the foundation of the Republic in 1923.[45] Rapid economic growth under the tutelage of the state came to dominate Turkish politics and became deeply embedded in the psyche of Turkish people in and outside of the state. Except for a few attempts at decentralization since the 1980s, the strong, paternalistic state tradition in the name of catching up with the advanced industrial nations, achieving capitalist development, and transforming society from above has reigned supreme and unchallenged.

Perhaps no other sector embodies the principles of developmentalism better than the energy sector in Turkey. Regardless of the political orientation of top officials, Turkish governments have historically equated energy with national progress and civilization and most, if not all, energy policies have been underwritten by an economic development imperative. Even though starting in the 1980s, the energy sector became more privatized, the state has kept its central role and dictated the terms of energy development projects. With the exception of nuclear power, projects that require relatively little technical expertise, abundant capital and land that the state has access to, and that can generate large-scale, low-skilled employment have typically been seen as the solution to country's energy challenges.[46]

Along these lines, coal extraction and coal-fueled thermal plants have always been an attractive tool for the Turkish governments to fuel the desired economic growth. Turkey has low-quality but sizeable domestic coal reserves, the technology that is needed for these thermal plants is relatively cheap, coal mines provide huge employment, and coal is affordable for large segments of the population. In the first five-year industry plans of the new Turkish Republic, coal was seen as the most reliable natural resource and the government strategy on energy was mainly constructed around the expansion of coal production in nationalized mining facilities.[47] The AKP's goal of quadrupling coal-fueled power plants by 2020 despite recent coal mining accidents and the increasing reliance on coal imports is illustrative of the continuation of the centrality of this energy source for Turkish economic growth agenda. Having designated 2012 as 'the year of coal,' the AKP government in all its official strategic and development plans highlighted coal as an indispensable, and strategic source of national energy supply, which, in turn, has been regarded as the *sine qua non* of economic growth and development.[48]

Similar to coal, large hydropower has also had a central role in Turkey's modernization project. The Southeastern Anatolian Dam Project (aka GAP) which began in the 1960s with the construction of multiple dams on the Euphrates river was not only envisioned as producing electricity but also as a strategic tool in alleviating regional socioeconomic disparities through improved irrigation systems and agricultural production in 9 provinces, 80 districts, 195 municipalities, and 4,297 villages as well as a foreign policy tool used as leverage against the neighboring countries of Iraq and Syria. In addition to their perceived practical benefits, dams have always been treated as a symbol of improvement and grandeur. Indeed, "just as Nehru claimed that dams were the temples of modern India, Turkish policymakers have aspired to construct impressive visual signs of the catching up of modern Turkey."[49] Ground-breaking and ribbon-cutting ceremonies of dam construction have been common political tools to project the patriotic and modernist image of politicians. The fact that the two of the Turkish presidents were once the heads of the State Hydraulic Works Agency (*DSI* in Turkish) and one of them, Suleyman Demirel, had the nickname of the 'king of dams' demonstrates the centrality of dam construction in the developmentalist ideology of the Turkish state.[50]

When AKP came to power, the emphasis on hydropower as an engine of economic development continued as before. Similar to previous ones, consecutive AKP governments saw environmental degradation and societal dislocations caused by dams as an inevitable and unavoidable result of economic development. They also treated environmentalists who oppose such developmental projects as siding with foreign powers and posing a threat to the Turkish state and nation. This mindset is best reflected in the Turkish president, Recep Tayyip Erdogan's statement that opponents of the controversial Ilisu Dam in southeastern Turkey should be treated as members of the PKK, a militant Kurdish separatist group that is listed as a terrorist organization by the USA and Turkey.[51]

Finally, interest in nuclear power has been a constant in Turkish politics and fits well into the growth-oriented, state-centric developmentalist paradigm that has dominated the public discourse since the founding of the Turkish Republic.[52] First steps for realizing a nuclear power plant were taken in 1956 when the Turkish Atomic Energy Commission (TAEC) was established to oversee nuclear research. With the selection of the Akkuyu as the first nuclear power site in 1974, the decades-long negotiations with foreign investors began. Despite the financial, administrative, and social setbacks for the construction of the power plants, i.e., the difficulty of finding private investors to build and operate them with no government treasury guarantees, lack of administrative and technical capacity, and an active anti-nuclear movement, nuclear power has been a crucial element of national development plans just like the hydroelectric dams.[53] It has been pursued by many governments from the center-left administration of the late 1970s to the center-right governments of the 1980s. The state's desire to build nuclear power did not change when AKP came to power; if anything it gained steam. AKP has been an ardent proponent of a nuclear renaissance, framing it as central to the country's economic growth and competitiveness by reducing dependence on foreign energy sources, diversifying its national resources, and ensuring energy independence.[54]

Obsession with Economic Rents and Political Power

Beyond the pervasive mindset of developmentalism in the Turkish state, politicians' interest in accumulating political power and economic rents can explain their energy choices and the type of energy policies they pursue. Centralized, mega energy projects, and the state agencies that regulate the energy industry offer government elites significant regulatory power and economic benefits. During the 2000s, the AKP governments gave up some of that power thanks to IMF and EU-induced structural reforms and in an effort to broaden the party's support base. The result was reduced government control and a relatively decentralized sector to allow for more competition that was favorable to the development of alternative sources of energy. But by the end of 2000s, the global and domestic context had changed. Emboldened by the impressive economic growth since the 2001 crisis and its increasing political power over the decade, AKP started to act more independently from the demands of external actors. Meanwhile, the increasing opposition to Turkey's membership in Germany and France as well as the stalemate with the EU over the Cyprus issue soured the Turkish public's interest in EU membership. The EU's own economic and political problems in the post-2008 crisis raised questions about the benefits and relevance of EU membership for Turkey and reduced the external pressures for sustaining the reforms. The loss of this external pressure allowed the AKP governments to reverse course on the neoliberal structural reforms of the previous period and embark on a more centralized economic management model where political interests would reign supreme and steer energy policy more in favor of fossil fuel, nuclear and large-hydropower development.

By the end of the 2000s, AKP governments were ready to reestablish authority over the market to appropriate a larger share of the energy rent, which could be used to finance their widespread clientelistic networks that proved vital to their political survival.[55] Resources created and controlled by regulatory agencies, such as the price of electricity, energy production permits, imposition of fines in cases of noncompliance, were seen as too valuable as political tools to be handed over to independent agencies beyond the control of politicians.[56] One of these independent agencies, the EMRA, became subject to increasing political intervention. As government's influence on EMRA grew, so did the spontaneous and arbitrary revisions to licensing procedures and price mechanisms that advantaged certain energy projects over others.

The delay and continuing failure to reduce the state monopoly on natural gas imports and pricing can be seen as another example of politicians' reluctance to give up regulatory power and economic rents. The 2001 Natural Gas Market Law was designed to liberalize the natural gas sector and break the monopoly of the state-owned company, BOTAS, which was responsible for all crude oil transportation, as well as transportation, distribution, import, storage, marketing, trade, and pricing of natural gas. While the privatization of downstream activities—distribution and transmission—proceeded as planned, progress on reducing BOTAS' share in natural gas imports to 20% of the country's total consumption and unbundling the company's upstream activities into separate trading, transmission, and storage companies has been painstakingly slow.[57] Several legislative drafts have been prepared in the past several years; however, a firm timeline for the enactment of the amendment to further liberalize gas imports and restructure BOTAS has yet to be established. BOTAS continues to dominate wholesale gas imports with a market share of about 82% of annual consumption while eight private companies account for the balance.[58] With such a dominant market position, BOTAS also controls natural gas prices and keeps them artificially low to subsidize certain customers in the market. For example, it is reported that in 2013 BOTAS absorbed losses of around US $2 billion, which the government had to reimburse.[59] This resistance to pass the rapid rise in international energy prices to the domestic market in fear of losing political legitimacy makes it harder for the state to be an objective and fair regulator in the energy business.[60]

Clientelism and Populism: Creating Cronies and Co-opting Constituents

AKP governments' energy priorities have also been shaped by their aspiration to create a loyal business class that would legitimize and finance their hold on power. By forging alliances with certain capital owners and ensuring that they accumulate huge sums of wealth, the AKP governments created a loyal bourgeoise that depends on them for lucrative government contracts and favorable regulations.[61] Especially in the aftermath of the 2008 economic crisis, the government turned to large infrastructure (in many cases energy infrastructure) and real-estate projects to generate economic growth, employment, and political rent. Extraction and construction sectors have been of particular importance to AKP since they feed into other subsectors, require low technical expertise and human capital, create vast opportunities for employment, and incidentally are the sectors that are the most vulnerable to political intervention and corruption. This extraction and construction-fueled economic growth model provided the cover for distributing public resources to AKP cronies.

One way the AKP government helped with pro-government capital accumulation has been through privatization deals. Ozcan and Gunduz (2015) in their study of energy sector privatizations—the most extensive sector privatizations in the economy under AKP rule—find that pro-AKP firms, such as Kolin, Calik, Limak, Kazanci, and Cengiz Holdings, won 16 out of 20 electricity distribution tenders across Turkey. Similarly, in the natural gas sector, firms connected to AKP won gas distribution tenders in 15 out of 19 large, 13 out of 18 medium, and 18 out of 29 small size cities.[62] The negotiated and opaque method of auctions as well as the appointment of family members and relatives of government officials to key regulatory agencies have, arguably, made the whole privatization process vulnerable to political intervention.

Another mechanism by which the government enriched and emboldened its own loyal bourgeoise was through the easing of regulations around extraction of energy resources, specifically the relaxation of environmental requirements as well as law enforcement on labor rights and workspace safety inspections. For instance, according to the Ministry of Environment and Urbanization, none of the *Environmental Impact Assessment (EIA)* reports of coal projects have been rejected between 1999 and 2015.[63] These deregulations dramatically decreased the costs for businessowners and allowed them to accrue huge profits in their operations at the expense of workers, the environment, and the well-being of the communities where energy projects are located.

At the same time, AKP governments changed the regulations around land leasing and acquisitions as well as the rules on judicial oversight of these regulatory mechanisms. For instance, the government can use an originally war-time intended administrative procedure, called the *Urgent Expropriation (UE)*, to confiscate private land from farmers and lease them for extended periods to hydropower developers. The use of this procedure skyrocketed under the AKP rule and between 2004 and 2014 the government made 1,785 UE decisions, about 1,500 of them related to energy production.[64] Finally, the government disrupted the energy playing field by providing huge subsidies to fossil fuel producers and investors in the form of tax breaks, discounts on electricity bills, research and development (R&D) support, rehabilitation support, investment guarantees, and electricity purchase guarantees. According to a report, the Turkish government provides US$300 million to US$1.6 billion per year in fossil fuel producer subsidies.[65]

In return for getting lucrative deals and regulatory exemptions from the government, business cronies provided the governing elites with campaign and in-kind donations to the party and party-affiliated charities and disproportionate access to media outlets. For example, an investigative report revealed that the prime minister himself had forced companies such as Cengiz Holding and Kolin to take over the bid for a major newspaper and TV group, Sabah-ATV.[66] Businessmen with strong ties to the ruling party also used part of their profits to support AKP's agenda. State-led capital accumulation has fed the patronage networks organized around the AKP and provided resources for the party's populist, redistributionist policies and appeals to grandeur to attract large number of voters. The energy sector became one of the founding blocks of AKP's regime maintenance.[67]

Other than enabling capital accumulation for government cronies, energy policies have also figured prominently in the clientelist networks that AKP has established in society over the years. For example, the free delivery of coal, which is roughly 500 kg per household, ranks highest among the various goods that the urban poor receive from AKP-controlled municipalities. Since the beginning of the coal aid program in 2003, more than 2 million households have benefitted from this subsidy. Coal also provides much-needed employment for certain regions in the country even though its contribution to overall employment has decreased over time, from 1.3% in 1998 to 0.7% in 2013.[68] The government uses its support for coal projects to obtain votes from coal miners and those living near coal mines and power plants. The popularity of such projects has been shown to be a strong predictor of the party's durability and success across 900 municipal districts in mayoral elections of 2004, 2009, and 2014.[69]

Foreign Policy Interests: Energy Projects for Geostrategic Leverage

Energy choices and priorities can also be understood as an extension of government's foreign policy objectives. Since the collapse of the Soviet Union, successive Turkish governments have been interested in capitalizing on Turkey's geographic position, surrounded by producing countries to its north, east, and south and major consumer markets to its west to become an energy corridor with several oil and natural gas pipeline projects passing through it.[70] It is possible to argue that this obsession with building an extensive pipeline infrastructure was never only about the domestic energy needs of the country. On top of bringing transit fees and construction jobs to the country, these projects offered the potential of increasing Turkish governments' leverage in defining relations with neighbors as well as promoting regional integration and stability. For instance, in the 1990s, the Baku-Tbilisi-Ceyhan (BTC) oil and the South Caucasus, also known as Baku-Tbilisi-Erzurum (BTE), natural gas pipeline projects made Turkey indispensable for the East-West energy corridor that was designed to bypass Russia and limit its traditional influence over the newly independent states in Eurasia. In addition to elevating Turkey's prominence with the West, these projects also enhanced the strategic partnership between Turkey and the Caspian producer states of Azerbaijan, Kazakhstan, and Turkmenistan and cemented the Turkish sphere of influence in Eurasia.

In the 2000s when AKP came to power, pipeline diplomacy accelerated to a whole new level. Criticizing the depiction of Turkey as just an energy 'bridge' or 'transit' country, AKP officials sought a more active role for Turkey and insisted on turning it into an energy 'hub,' which would not only connect the producers to consumers but also establish other upstream and downstream facilities in the country and set the regional price for energy.[71] By the end of 2000s, the AKP governments had some success in realizing their ambitious goals. EU's overdependence on Russia for natural gas and concerns with Russian threats to use the gas weapon led to the formulation of the Southern Gas Corridor (SGC) strategy, in which EU officially acknowledged Turkey's role as a natural energy bridge and energy hub. When the Nabucco pipeline project, which would have transported gas from the Caspian Sea to Europe through Turkey in an effort to bypass Russia, failed due to various commercial and financial issues, Ankara teamed up with the government of Azerbaijan to propose a new infrastructure project, the Trans-Anatolian Pipeline (TANAP). Once the combination of three SGC pipelines, the Baku-Tbilisi-Erzurum (BTE), Trans-Anatolian (TANAP), and the Trans Adriatic (TAP), is operational in 2020, Turkish leaders expect their political leverage vis-à-vis the EU to grow.[72]

Despite its commitment to cooperate with the EU in the SGC project, the AKP government has also not hesitated to participate in a competing pipeline project with Russia.[73] In order to reduce its dependence on the Ukrainian transit route to Europe, Russia has been pursuing alternative pipeline projects; Nord Stream pipeline connecting Russia directly with Germany via the Baltic Sea and the South Stream pipeline to Austria via the Black Sea. When the latter failed to materialize, Russia replaced it with the Turkish Stream project that would transport Russian gas to Turkey under the Black Sea with a total annual capacity of 63 billion cubic meters (bcm), some of which would be used for Turkish domestic consumption. The Turkish Stream is arguably very important for Gazprom: Turkey has become its second biggest customer in Europe after Germany.[74] Sensing this economic importance for Russia, the Turkish government seems to be using the pipeline as a bargaining chip to resolve the serious disagreements between the two countries on a number of issues in Crimea, Georgia, Nagorno Karabakh, and Syria.

In addition to SGC and Turkish Stream projects, the Turkish government has also plans to build or expand on other pipelines in the near future. The discovery of new large natural gas fields in the East Mediterranean region including places like Israel, Cyprus, and Egypt, expansion of the pipeline from Iran (Tabriz-Erzurum pipeline), and the construction of a natural gas pipeline between Turkey and the Kurdish Regional Government in Northern Iraq are keeping the pipeline diplomacy and frenzy alive and well. AKP's ambitious external energy policy, which has already secured significant volumes of hydrocarbons and attracted huge investments for the realization of extensive energy transportation projects, fits squarely with AKP's overall foreign policy objective of expanding Turkey's sphere of influence in the region and making it a key player in world politics. Similarly, the electricity trade, which allows Turkey to establish interconnections with all her neighbors, in the West with Bulgaria and Greece and in the East with Georgia, Azerbaijan, Iran, and Iraq, contributes to the strategic plan of creating mutual interdependencies and cementing Turkey's significance in the region. This 'powerful Turkey' image, in turn, has been conveniently utilized by AKP leaders to project an aura of legitimacy around the regime and ensure its survival.

Yet, it is important to point out the perverse implications of this strategy. The government's geostrategic goal of becoming an energy hub between Europe and Asia ironically contradicts its goal of reducing import dependency and especially dependence on a single country. It is fair to assume that Turkey's overdependence on Russia will continue, as opposed to shrink, in the future. Because of long-term 'take or pay' gas contracts and lack of an extensive storage capacity, Turkey is contractually obligated to pay Russia huge payments for large volumes of gas it does not always use.[75] The completion of the proposed Turkish Stream project and Rosneft (Russian oil and gas company)'s ownership of the planned Kurdistan gas pipeline will only deepen that dependency and so will the Akkuyu nuclear power plant project that Turkey signed with the Russian state company, Rosatom, when it gets built.

And so, not only is the pipeline diplomacy not mitigating Turkey's energy supply vulnerabilities, one can argue that it is also slowing down Turkey's transition to clean energy. Committing large amounts of capital and time for pipeline infrastructure and signing long-term oil and gas contracts with producer countries arguably locks-in Turkey's dependence on fossil fuels for decades to come and makes it more difficult to reduce their share in the energy mix. Being over-contracted to natural gas imports leaves less room for the renewable energy sector to grow. While Turkey's geographical location may be regarded by some to be a geostrategic blessing, it arguably also presents a roadblock for Turkey's clean energy transition.

Changing Institutional Capacity: Concentration of Power and Politicization of Bureaucracy

The political interests of the AKP leaders to build a loyal business class, coopt large segments of the population, and establish Turkish hegemony in the region cannot by themselves explain why certain energy paths prevailed over others in Turkey in the past two decades. We need to also look at the institutional capacity of the AKP governments to pursue and implement their energy agenda. The initial energy reforms that opened the way for renewables were successful not only because AKP embraced (strategically) the neoliberal agenda promulgated by the external actors but also because they *could* carry out the reforms effectively.

Unlike the numerous coalitional governments before it, the AKP government in its first election commanded a comfortable parliamentary majority with 66% of the seats and has ruled as a single party government ever since. The consecutive electoral victories gave Erdogan, the prime minister at the time, enough political capital and institutional capacity to push for reforms with the intensity and commitment he saw fit. Moreover, the party cohesion and discipline under the charismatic and dominant Erdogan established an undisputed system of hierarchy in his cabinet where he acted as the mediator among conflicting ministers but always had the last word. AKP's control of the legislature and executive was also magnified by its control of numerous municipal administrations around the country. Even though the neoliberal reforms of the 2000s decentralized some of the formerly centralized administrative structure in Turkey, AKP's success in local elections allowed it to form and command extensive local networks to implement policies. The consolidation of executive and legislative power for consecutive AKP governments created a high degree of political stability that gave AKP leaders the ability to make credible commitments and draw significant amount of energy investments into the country.

In the past decade, concentration of political power around AKP and especially its leader, Erdogan, increased even further. Erdogan became the president in 2014 and changed the constitution to dismantle the parliamentary system and establish a 'super presidential' regime. By weakening and eliminating judicial veto-players to government economic policies—particularly to privatizations and land confiscations—this new institutional structure allowed the government to politicize energy decisions and protect and enrich its business cronies at the expense of sound energy policies that could develop energy sources in a sustainable and socially equitable manner. By appropriating the energy rents more directly to themselves or through their crony intermediaries, AKP elites were able to generate financial sources to sustain their hegemonic hold on society. The majoritarian politics of the AKP and removal of checks and balances in the system have also made reviewing, questioning, or critiquing of AKP's developmentalist and extractivist policies more difficult and risky over time. What some call 'authoritarian post-neoliberalism,' this new political economic structure increasingly relied on coercive state power as well as legal and extralegal intimidation to discipline and suppress locals who mobilize to stop the construction of contested energy projects.[76]

With more concentration of power, the state bureaucracy has also over time become more dysfunctional and ineffective. Historically, Turkish bureaucracy has been characterized by red tape, delays, inertia, and infighting among various state agencies and ministries.[77] Some of these bureaucratic problems can be attributed to a lack of bureaucratic maturity and competence. It is likely that limited state resources and lack of adequate financial incentives based on performance affected the ability to recruit (and retain) qualified people to bureaucratic agencies and train them to gain specialized knowledge and expertise. For instance, when the State Hydraulic Works Agency or DSI received over 1700 license applications for construction of the Deriner Dam and Hydroelectric Power Plant after the passage of the water use rights regulation in 2003, it was not equipped to examine each project, issue licenses, and monitor compliance in a short period of time. Moreover, private companies were hiring DSI employees experienced in hydro projects for higher wages than what the institution could offer.[78]

Yet, interviews with sector experts and bureaucrats reveal that in the past decade, the problem has been less about bureaucratic incompetence and more about bureaucratic powerlessness and lack of discretion.[79] Bureaucrats lament that there is too much political interference which undercut merit-based performance and that they are usually asked to perform tasks by parliamentarians and government officials that favor clientelist networks instead of being subject to a set of clearly defined, transparent set of objectifiable targets.[80] The fact that the former minister of Energy and Natural Resources and the person who oversaw the operations of EMRA was none other than the son-in-law of President Erdogan and the former CEO of a conglomerate that owns many hydroelectric dams and coal plants, demonstrates the extent of bureaucratic capture in Turkey today.[81] Such lack of insulation of bureaucrats from political pressures undermines the effectiveness of energy policy as preferences of well-positioned private actors and their politician patrons are disproportionately represented in decision-making.

Conclusions

Since the turn of the century, international financial institutions, the EU as well as civil society actors with increased environmental and energy justice awareness, have put pressures on consecutive Turkish governments to reduce dependency on fossil fuels. This chapter argues that despite their efforts, the main driver of energy policies in Turkey has always been—and still is—the Turkish state and its occupants. The AKP governments' insistence on coal, natural gas, nuclear, and even hydropower in the past two decades can be explained by the top-down, state-centric, growth-oriented, neoliberal developmentalist political economy model that AKP inherited from previous governments but brought to a whole new level with much deeper clientelistic networks and more widespread populist policies. AKP's ambitious foreign policy goal of elevating Turkey to become an energy hub has also fed into this fossil-fuel dependent growth path. Finally, the increasing centralization and personalization of political power has weakened bureaucratic capacity and politicized energy policy formulation and implementation. The Turkish case demonstrates the difficulties in implementing and maintaining clean energy reforms in the context of a state-dominated energy market, politicized and weak bureaucracy, opportunistic developers, limited civil society activism, and complicated relations with neighboring countries.

Notes

1. IEA (2019). During the same period natural gas consumption grew by 1,114% in China, 282% in India and 275% in Iran.
2. IEA (2016).
3. IEA (2019).
4. *Enerdata: Global Energy Statistical Yearbook 2018*, https://yearbook.enerdata.net.
5. EIA (2017).
6. "Turkey's Energy Import Bill Up by 37% in 2017," *AA Energy*, February 1, 2018, https://www.aa.com.tr/en/energy/finance/turkeys-energy-import-bill-up-by-37-in-2017/18644.

7. IEA (2019).
8. Saygin et al. (2018). Annex I countries are the industrialized countries that are members of OECD and economies in transition in Russia and Eastern and Central Europe.
9. "Akkuyu: Turkey's Nuclear Dream Overshadowed by Safety Fears," *The National* (August 13, 2019), https://www.thenational.ae/world/europe/akkuyu-turkey-s-nuclear-dream-overshadowed-by-safety-fears-1.897761.
10. Jewell and Ates (2015) and author's interview on May 27, 2019. The nuclear proponents claim that these agreements are economically beneficial for Turkey considering that the risks and the costs associated with construction, operation, fuel provision and waste disposal matters are sub-contracted to foreign governments (Kumbaroglu 2012).
11. Sahin (2011).
12. IEA (2019).
13. "Twelve Reasons to Exclude Large Hydro from Renewables Initiatives," *International Rivers Network*, November 2003, at http://www.rivernet.org/general/hydropower/12reasons.pdf.
14. Erensu (2016).
15. IEA (2019).
16. IEA (2019).
17. Author's interviews on November 15 and 25, 2011 and June 1, 2013.
18. Waheed et al. (2009).
19. Saygin et al. (2018).
20. "Yenilenebilir enerji fiyatları yatırımcıları tatmin etmedi," *Referansgazetesi.com/Gundem*, April 20, 2009. Also, author's interviews on January 12, 2015 and January 23, 2019.
21. Author's interviews on July 2 and 11, 2012, July 2, 2013 and May 28, 2019.
22. OECD (2019).
23. Livingston (2018).
24. IEA (2019).
25. Timperley (2018).
26. Coal supply in Turkey increased by 93% from 2005 to 2018 compared to the 27% growth in world coal supply during the same period. IEA (2019).
27. Baumgartner and Jones (1993), Calder (2012), Karapin (2016), and Baumgartner et al. (2014).
28. Bakir and Onis (2010).
29. Atiyas et al. (2012).
30. In May 2009, the World Bank provided US$600 million from its Clean Technology Fund Financing for the renewable energy investments in Turkey.
31. Onis (2012).

32. World Bank (2015).
33. Carafa (2010).
34. Arsel et al. (2015).
35. "Resistance against coal-fired plant in Gerze," *Bianet*, November 28, 2011, http://bianet.org/english/environment/134340-resistance-against-coal-fired-plant-in-gerze.
36. Author's interview on July 11, 2012.
37. Author's interviews on December 9, 2011, July 11, 2012 and May 28, 2019.
38. Kaygusuz and Arsel (2005).
39. Author's interviews on July 4 and 11, 2012; January 13, 2014; May 24 and 27, 2019.
40. Author's interviews on July 1, 2013, January 23, 2019.
41. Erensu (2018).
42. Author's interview on July 2, 2012.
43. Bayulgen (2013).
44. Onis and Kutay (2013).
45. Ozveren and Nas (2012) and Arsel (2005).
46. Author's interviews on July 10, 2013 and May 24, 2019.
47. Sahin (2016).
48. Author's interview on May 24, 2019.
49. Kaygusuz and Arsel (2005, p. 161).
50. Erensu (2017).
51. "11,000-Year-Old Turkish Town About to Be Submerged Forever," *PRI's The World*, May 22, 2019, https://www.pri.org/stories/2019-05-22/11000-year-old-turkish-town-about-be-submerged-forever.
52. Jewell and Ates (2015).
53. See Sahin (2011) and Aydin (2020). Some have also argued that the Western countries' fear of a transfer of nuclear material and technology from Turkey to third parties prevented the development of nuclear power in Turkey early on (Kibaroglu 1997).
54. Author's interviews on July 11, 2012, July 2, 2013 and May 27, 2019.
55. Kuyucu (2017).
56. Ozel (2012).
57. Biresselioglu et al. (2019).
58. World Bank (2015).
59. Winrow (2014).
60. Author's interviews on July 2, 2012 and May 29, 2019.
61. *Forbes* magazine reported that 82 of 100 richest people of Turkey had active operations in the energy sector in 2013, making the sector the country's most profitable alongside real estate (En zengin 100 Türk'ten 82'si enerjici" [82 of riches 100 Turks are in energy], *Enerji Günlüğü*, May 3, 2014, http://www.enerjigunlugu.net/icerik/7391/en-zengin-100-turkten-82si-enerjici.html#.V8bNm5MrKHo.

62. Ozcan and Gunduz (2015).
63. Sahin (2016).
64. Erensu (2018).
65. "Turkey Subsidies," Climate Scorecard (January 1, 2018), https://www.climatescorecard.org/2018/01/turkey-subsidies/.
66. Ozcan and Gunduz (2015).
67. Author's interviews on July 11, 2012, May 27 and 29, 2019.
68. Sahin (2016).
69. Marschall et al. (2016).
70. According to the Turkish Ministry of Foreign Affairs, Turkey is located in close proximity to 73% of the world's conventional oil reserves and 72% of the proven natural gas reserves (http://www.mfa.gov.tr/turkeys-energy-strategy.en.mfa).
71. Ersen and Celikpala (2019).
72. Bilgin (2015).
73. Demiryol (2013).
74. Ersen and Celikpala (2019).
75. Winrow (2014).
76. Paker (2017) and Erensu (2018).
77. Biddle and Milor (1997).
78. Ocakli (2018).
79. Authors interviews on May 22 and May 30, 2019.
80. Ocakli (2018).
81. Berat Albayrak, son-in-law of President Erdogan, is the current Minister of Finance and Treasury.

References

Arsel, Murat. "Reflexive Developmentalism? Toward an Environmental Critique of Modernization." In *Environmentalism in Turkey: Between Democracy and Development*, edited by Fikret Adaman and Murat Arsel, 29–48. London: Ashgate, 2005.

Arsel, Murat, Bengi Akbulut and Fikret Adaman. "Environmentalism of the Malcontent: Anatomy of an Anti-Coal Power Plant Struggle in Turkey." *Journal of Peasant Studies* 42, no. 2 (2015): 371–395.

Atiyas, Izak, Tamer Cetin and Gurcan Gulen. *Reforming Turkish Energy Markets: Political Economy, Regulation and Competition in the Search for Energy Policy*. Springer, 2012.

Aydin, Cem Iskender. "Nuclear Energy Debate in Turkey: Stakeholders, Policy Alternatives, and Governance Issues." *Energy Policy* 136 (2020): 111041.

Bakir, Caner and Ziya Onis. "The Regulatory State and Turkish Banking Reforms in the Age of Post-Washington Consensus." *Development and Change* 41, no. 1 (2010): 77–106.

Baumgartner, Frank. R and Bryan D. Jones. *Agendas and Instability in American Politics*. Chicago: University of Chicago Press, 1993.

Baumgartner, Frank R., Brian D. Jones and P. B. Mortensen. "Punctuated Equilibrium Theory: Explaining Stability and Change in Public Policymaking." In *Theories of the Policy Process*, edited by C. M. Weible and P. A. Sabatier, 59–103. Routledge, 2014.

Bayulgen, Oksan. "Two-Steps Forward, One-Step Back: How Politics Dim the Lights on Turkey's Renewable Energy Future." *Perceptions* 18, no. 4 (2013): 71–98.

Biddle, Jesse and Vedat Milor. "Economic Governance in Turkey: Bureaucratic Capacity, Policy Networks, and Business Associations." In *Business and the State in Developing Countries*, edited by Sylvia Maxfield and Ben Ross Schneider, 277–310. Ithaca: Cornell University Press, 1997.

Bilgin, Mert. "Turkey's Energy Strategy: Synchronizing Geopolitics and Foreign Policy with Energy Security." *Insight Turkey* 17, no. 2 (2015): 67–81.

Biresselioglu, Mehmet E., Melike Demirbag Kaplan and Evrim Ozyorulmaz. "Towards a Liberalized Turkish Natural Gas Market: A SWOT Analysis." *Energy Sources, Part B: Economics, Planning and Policy* 14, no. 2 (2019): 25–33.

Calder, Kent E. *The New Continentalism: Energy and Twenty-First Century Eurasian Geopolitics*. New Haven: Yale University Press, 2012.

Carafa, Luigi. "How Far Does the European Union Influence Turkey's Energy Sector Reform?" Italian Political Science Association 24th Annual Conference. Venice, 16–18 September 2010.

Demiryol, Tolga. "The Geopolitics of Energy Cooperation Between Turkey and The European Union." *L'Europe En Formation* 1, no. 367 (2013): 109–134.

Erensu, Sinan. "Powering Neoliberalization: Energy and Politics in the Making of New Turkey." *Energy Research and Social Science* 41 (2018): 148–157.

Erensu, Sinan. "Turkey's Hydropower Renaissance: Nature, Neoliberalism and Development in the Cracks of Infrastructure." In *Neoliberal Turkey and Its Discontents: Economic Policy and the Environment Under Erdogan*, edited by Fikret Adaman, Bengi Akbulut and Murat Arsel, 120–146. London: I.B. Tauris, 2017.

Erensu, Sinan. *Fragile Energy: Power, Nature and the Politics of Infrastructure in the New Turkey*. Dissertation submitted to University of Minnesota, 2016.

Ersen, Emre and Mitat Celikpala. "Turkey and the Changing Energy Geopolitics of Eurasia." *Energy Policy* 128 (2019): 584–592.

International Energy Agency (IEA). *Energy Policies of IEA Countries: Turkey 2016 Review*. Paris, 2016. https://www.iea.org/publications/freepublications/publication/EnergyPoliciesofIEACountriesTurkey.pdf.

International Energy Agency (IEA). *World Energy Balances: Turkey 2019*. Paris, 2019. https://www.iea.org/countries/turkey.

Jewell, Jessica and Seyithan Ahmet Ates. "Introducing Nuclear Power in Turkey: A Historic State Strategy and Future Prospects." *Energy Research and Social Science* 10 (2015): 273–282.

Karapin, Roger. *Political Opportunities for Climate Policy: California, New York, and the Federal Government*. New York: Cambridge University Press, 2016.

Kaygusuz, Kamil and Murat Arsel. "Energy Politics and Policy." In *Environmentalism in Turkey: Between Democracy and Development*, edited by Fikret Adaman and Murat Arsel, 149–167. London: Ashgate, 2005.

Kibaroglu, Mustafa. "Turkey's Quest for Peaceful Nuclear Power." *The Nonproliferation Review* Spring–Summer (1997): 33–44.

Kumbaroglu, Gurkan. "Turkiye Acisindan Nukleer Enerji Ekonomisi." In *Nukleer Enerjiye Geciste Turkiye Modeli*, edited by Sinan Ulgen, 82–107. Istanbul: EDAM (Ekonomik ve Dis Politika Arastirmalar Merkezi, 2012.

Kuyucu, Tuna. "Two Crises, Two Trajectories: The Impact of the 2001 and 2008 Economic Crises on Urban Governance in Turkey." In *Neoliberal Turkey and Its Discontents: Economic Policy and the Environment Under Erdogan*, edited by Fikret Adaman, Bengi Akbulut and Murat Arsel, 44–74. London: I.B. Tauris, 2017.

Livingston, David. "Renewable Energy Investments in Turkey: Between Aspiration and Endurance." *Turkish Policy Quarterly* 17, no. 3(2018): 55–67.

Marschall, Melissa, Abdullah Aydogan and Alper Bulut. "Does Housing Create Votes? Explaining the Electoral Success of the AKP in Turkey." *Electoral Studies* 42 (2016): 201–212.

Ocakli, Feryaz. "Reconfiguring State-Business Relations in Turkey: Housing and Hydroelectric Energy Sectors in Comparative Perspective." *Journal of Balkan and Near Eastern Studies* 20, no. 4 (2018): 373–387.

Organization for Economic Cooperation and Development. "OECD Environmental Performance Reviews: Turkey 2019." *OECD Environmental Performance Reviews*. Paris: OECD Publishing, 2019. https://doi.org/10.1787/9789264309753-en.

Onis, Ziya. "The Triumph of Conservative Globalism: The Political Economy of the AKP Era." *Turkish Studies* 13, no. 2 (2012): 135–152.

Onis, Ziya and Mustafa Kutay. "Rising Powers in a Changing Global Order: The Political Economy of Turkey in the Age of BRICS." *Third World Quarterly* 34, no. 8 (2013): 1409–1426.

Ozcan, Gul B. and Umut Gunduz. "Energy Privatizations, Business-Politics Connections and Governance Under Political Islam." *Environment and Planning C: Government and Policy* 33 (2015): 1714–1737.

Ozel, Isik. "The Politics of De-delegation: Regulatory (In)Dependence in Turkey." *Regulation and Governance* 6, no. 1 (2012): 119–129.

Ozveren, Eyup and Selin Efsan Nas. "Economic Development and Environmental Policy in Turkey: An Institutionalist Critique." *Cambridge Journal of Economics* 36 (2012): 1245–1266.

Paker, Hande. "The 'Politics of Serving' and Neoliberal Developmentalism: The Megaprojects of the AKP as Tools of Hegemony Building." In *Neoliberal Turkey and Its Discontents: Economic Policy and the Environment Under Erdogan*, edited by Fikret Adaman, Bengi Akbulut and Murat Arsel, 103–119. London: I.B. Tauris, 2017.

Sahin, Umit. "Country Perspective: Turkey." In *The End of Nuclear Energy? International Perspectives After Fukushima*, edited by N. Netzer and J. Steinhilber, 71–74. Friedrich Ebert Stiftung, 2011.

Sahin, Umit, ed. *Coal Report: Turkey's Coal Policies Related to Climate Change, Economy, and Health*. Istanbul Policy Center Report. Sabanci University, 2016. https://ipc.sabanciuniv.edu/wp-content/uploads/2016/01/Coal-Report-Turkeys-Coal-Policies-Related-to-Climate-Change-Economy-and-Health.pdf.

Saygin, Deger, Max Hoffman and Phillip Godron. "How Turkey Can Ensure a Successful Energy Transition." *Center for American Progress*, July 10, 2018. https://www.americanprogress.org/issues/security/reports/2018/07/10/453281/turkey-can-ensure-successful-energy-transition/.

Timperley, Jocelyn. "The Carbon Brief Profile: Turkey." *CarbonBrief* (May 3, 2018). https://www.carbonbrief.org/carbon-brief-profile-turkey.

US Energy Information Agency (EIA). *Country Analysis Brief: Turkey*. Washington, DC, 2017. https://www.eia.gov/beta/international/analysis.php?iso=TUR.

Waheed, Ayesha K., Ekin Erdogan and Erdogan Fidan. "Turkish Renewable Energy: Blowing in the Right Direction?" *IP Opinion*, February 24, 2009, http://www.lw.com/upload/pubContent/_pdf/pub2585_1.pdf.

Winrow, Gareth. "Realization of Turkey's Energy Aspirations: Pipe Dreams or Real Projects?" The Center on the United States and Europe at Brookings, *Turkey Project Policy Paper*, no. 4 (April 2014), https://www.brookings.edu/wp-content/uploads/2016/06/Turkeys-Energy-Aspirations.pdf.

World Bank. *Turkey's Energy Transition Milestones and Challenges*. Report No. ACS14951. Washington, DC, 2015. http://documents.worldbank.org/curated/en/249831468189270397/pdf/ACS14951-REVISED-Box393232B-PUBLIC-EnergyVeryFinalEN.pdf.

CHAPTER 7

Electricity Sector Developments in Egypt: Toward an Increasingly Clean and Independent Future

Michael Hochberg

Introduction

In developing economies, advancement in renewable energy often occurs when it must. When the perceived costs of maintaining the status quo energy landscape outweigh the projected costs of working toward a

M. Hochberg (✉)
Oxford Institute for Energy Studies, Oxford, UK
e-mail: michael.hochberg@oxfordenergy.org
URL: https://www.oxfordenergy.org/

Hecate Energy, Chicago, IL, USA
URL: https://www.hecateenergy.com

Clean Energy Leadership Institute, Chicago, IL, USA
URL: https://www.cleanenergyleaders.org

Securing America's Future Energy, New York, NY, USA
URL: https://www.secureenergy.org

R. Mills and L.-C. Sim (eds.), *Low Carbon Energy in the Middle East and North Africa*, International Political Economy Series,
https://doi.org/10.1007/978-3-030-59554-8_7

more sustainable generation fleet and modern electric grid, policymakers are driven to action. Power sector decarbonization efforts via renewable energy support policies in developed economies began in the 1990s with the aim of creating a more sustainable sector. Yet the drive toward renewables in developing economies is often motivated by security of supply. With rising electricity demand creating the need for additional generation capacity in recent years,[1] combined with plentiful yet underutilized renewable energy resources, the Arab Republic of Egypt fits this paradigm.

In addition to rising demand, Egypt has experienced electricity supply issues in the recent past, with production shortfalls habitually decreasing the availability of gas for power generation. Egypt also suffers from high transmission and distribution losses and has historically provided large government subsidies for fuel and electricity, contributing to rising electricity demand and fiscal account deficits. While Egypt has undertaken substantial efforts to rectify these issues, domestic political upheaval beginning with the fall of longtime Egyptian President Hosni Mubarak in 2011 helped to decelerate Egypt's energy transition, until the arrival of the current government regime.

The relative political stability during the five-plus years under the regime of President Abdel Fattah el-Sisi has facilitated noteworthy strides in the development of Egypt's renewable energy sector. These developments help to secure the electricity supply that will contribute to economic growth and development and reduce the nation's power sector carbon footprint. To this end, Egypt's updated power sector policies and regulations have already begun to bear fruit, with notable renewable capacity becoming operational. In tandem, the nation is pursuing plans in nuclear energy to provide firm, baseload power to help meet electricity demand, potentially helping Egypt to become an electricity exporter in the future. Egypt's new energy strategy reimagines the sector, removing all energy subsidies by 2022, and introducing a competitive market framework with increased private sector participation.

Drivers of Renewable and Nuclear Power Generation Development

Economic, geopolitical, and environmental factors have driven Egypt to pursue renewable and nuclear energy development. While ensuring security of supply with the most economically efficient set of resources is the main driver of renewable development, geopolitical and environmental considerations are motivators as well. Conversely, while nuclear energy generation does not produce carbon emissions, Egypt's nuclear ambitions are primarily motivated by geopolitics. Nuclear energy is not an economically efficient option for Egypt in the short term, yet the pursuit of nuclear generation is in line with Egypt's desire to diversify its generation mix and expand its base of international support in the form of business and political relationships. The geopolitical angle is highly important for Egypt in the face of a rapidly changing geopolitical landscape in which post-Cold War codes and rules may no longer apply, with a new world order emerging. These drivers are discussed in more detail below.

Security of Supply

With ample sunshine and high wind speeds in many areas, Egypt has superior natural resources for the development of renewable energy generation capacity. Rising power demand and frequent blackouts have helped create the economic incentive for Egypt to maximize these resources. With relative stability in the post-Mubarak era, from 2014 to 2018 the Egyptian economy grew at an average annual rate of 4.6%, and more than 5.3% in 2018 alone. This growth is notably higher than the greater Middle East and North Africa (MENA) region, which experienced annual average economic growth of 2.8% in the same period and 2.4% in 2018.[2] At time of press, the final 2019 economic growth numbers were not yet available, yet forecasted at 5.5% for Egypt and 1.3% for the MENA region as a whole.[3] Power demand is further supported by Egypt's population of nearly 100 million, the third largest in Africa, which is also rising steadily relative to other MENA nations.[4]

Egypt's economic and population growth help apply upward pressure on energy demand in general, and electricity demand in particular, which has been rising at 6% annually.[5] From 2013 to 2017, peak demand increased by more than 30%, from 22.8 gigawatts (GW) in 2009 to 30.4 GW in 2019.[6] As overall electricity demand and peak power demand have increased, new generation development has been necessary to maintain a reasonable reserve margin and enhance the reliability of the electric system. This is particularly important for Egypt, where installed capacity has been steadily increasing, yet may be underutilized due to the aging of units; as of 2016, a third of Egypt's generation fleet was more than 20 years old, and efficiency rates of generation units were 5–8% below the norm[7] (Generation asset utilization is also impacted by issues around fuel quality and hydro's partial dependence on discharged irrigation water rules, defined by the Ministry of Water Resources and Irrigation).[8] Today, Egypt has achieved sufficient generation capacity to maintain reliability, partially through gas-fired combined cycle megaproject that became operational in 2018. Yet, the nation seeks to continue expanding this capacity to both decarbonize its generation fleet, meet anticipated demand and to enhance its status as a regional energy leader.

In terms of hydrocarbon resources, Egypt is Africa's third largest dry natural gas producer, largest non-OPEC (Organization of Petroleum Exporting Countries) oil producer,[9] and fifth largest oil producer.[10] Yet it is also the largest oil and gas consumer on the continent. Despite its reserves, in 2015 Egypt became a net importer of natural gas, due to rising domestic demand coupled with declining gas production (Egypt has since become a net exporter again, discussed below).[11] In addition, the nation's historical dependence on fossil fuels for electricity generation[12] has led to supply shocks in the past, causing hardships such as insufficient gas supply, rerouting gas meant for liquefaction and export to domestic use, and related disputes with international gas companies leading to multi-billion dollar international arbitration. This trend has since been reversed, with Egypt becoming a net exporter again in 2018, as a result of production from the Zohr offshore gas field, discovered in 2015 and the Mediterranean's largest natural gas field to date. (Still, Egypt will require developing further new resources.) As such, Egypt's leveraging of native renewable resources is important not only for economic and societal development, but also enhances Egypt's energy security and geopolitical positioning. Egypt nuclear generation development may also achieve these aims, but at a much greater investment cost, thus increasing fiscal risk as it is a government project.

Geopolitics

Globally, geopolitical rivalries have become increasingly present on the world stage in recent years, returning to a central role in political decision making and international relations. Leveraging alternative energy sources and fortifying relationships through international energy deals and collaboration serves Egypt as it seeks to diversify and deepen alliances. The Gulf nations, particularly Saudi Arabia and the United Arab Emirates, provide billions of dollars in aid to Egypt in the form of loans, grants and oil, and have been critical in helping fund the current Egyptian government. These nations also participate in Egypt's renewable power sector. Saudi-based ACWA Power, partially owned by the Saudi government, is developing multiple solar projects in the country. UAE-based Al Nowais Investments is also developing significant renewable energy capacity in Egypt. In terms of financing, Egypt is also working with a number of multilateral and commercial lenders to bring projects to fruition (discussed further below).

Alternative energy development also creates the opportunity for new and improved commercial terms which allow Egypt to wield additional economic and geopolitical influence. For example, meeting increasing levels of domestic electricity demand with renewable and nuclear sources could permit supplementary liquefied natural gas (LNG) exports either on the spot market, or via long term contracts. To this end, Egypt has already begun to import gas from Israel and Cyprus to make additional domestically produced gas available to the international LNG market.

Excess electric generation that substantially exceeds domestic demand also raises the prospect of exporting additional electricity internationally, which bodes well for relationship fortifying and cross-border economic development. For example, Egypt is already a net exporter of electricity, enjoying interconnections with Jordan and Libya.[13] Egypt has also signed a preliminary agreement with a Cyprus-based firm to lay an undersea 310-kilometer transmission line between Egypt and Cyprus, connecting African and European electric systems.[14] Additional interconnections are under construction with Saudi Arabia, in pilot phase with Sudan and under study with the United Arab Emirates.

While small compared to overall power demand, Egypt's exports to Libya and Jordan are consistent with Egypt's broader regional energy hub ambitions, as are Egypt's plans with Cyprus, Saudi Arabia, the UAE, and Sudan. More specifically, power imports to Libya tie into Egypt's strategy of influencing the outcome of the Libyan Civil War and its postwar oil sector. The interconnection with Sudan also boosts cooperation at a time when Egypt seeks to influence Ethiopia's Grand Ethiopian Renaissance Dam (GERD), which Egypt perceives as a threat to its water security. Egypt seeks Sudan's support in negotiating agreement terms, including minimum water release amounts and longer reservoir filling periods.[15] While small in size, international interconnections can be complex from both technically and politically. Achieving and maintaining these interconnections can help lay the groundwork for deeper regional cooperation and integration.

Climate Change

The impact of climate change domestically is an issue of which the Egyptian government is acutely aware. Egypt is particularly susceptible to the adverse impacts of global warming and its consequences. Approximately 95% of Egypt's 100 million inhabitants live in the Nile Delta and Valley, which comprises less than 5% of the nation's total area. Low lying deltas in general and Egypt's Nile Delta and Valley in particular are highly vulnerable to freshwater availability and sea-level rise associated with global warming. Economic activity in the Nile Delta region makes up more than 20% of Egypt's GDP and employs more than 30% of Egyptians. Agriculture activity in the area accounts for more than 50% of domestically produced crops, and 60% of the nation's fisheries are also in the vicinity. The Egyptian government has already initiated compulsory relocation of inhabitants along zones of the Nile Delta that are particularly vulnerable.[16] As such Egypt has already begun to engage in climate adaptation to both respond to and attempt to mitigate the consequences of climate change to stave off unforeseen domestic crises.

Development Prospects

Accordingly, the Egyptian central government has responded, advancing market reform via regulatory and policy agendas to facilitate investment in alternative electric generation sources. The government has been engaged in electricity market reform for decades, yet has been advancing market liberalization with greater haste since 2014. Through familiar frameworks in which international investors are comfortable operating, these market initiatives allow for augmented private sector participation in developing power generation projects. As a result, increasing renewable generation capacity is beginning to become operational in Egypt. In addition, the nation has been gradually phasing out electricity subsidies to better enable private sector participation and a financially sound and sustainable sector. Yet the nation has a long road ahead in terms of implementing market reforms, attracting investment, maintaining political stability, achieving financing and integrating intermittent capacity into the electric grid, to be able to meet its renewable energy targets and achieve its energy policy objectives and wider goals.

Renewable Energy Targets

Currently, Egypt enjoys more than 56,000 megawatts (MW) of installed generation capacity. Thermal generation accounts for more than 92% of electric generation capacity, with hydro, wind, and thermal solar making up just 6%, 3%, and less than 0.5%, respectively. Together, wind and solar represent just 0.8% of power generated.[17] By 2022, Egypt aims to generate 20% of its electricity from renewable sources with 12% wind, 6% hydro and 2% solar PV; and by 2035, 42% of its electricity from renewable sources with 25% solar photovoltaics, 14% wind, 3% concentrated solar power and 2% hydro. It is also worth noting that the nation aims for 3% of electricity to derive from nuclear power by 2035.[18]

While targets are non-binding policy objectives without enforceable compliance or punitive components, when combined with a solid regulatory framework, market structure and renewable development scheme, targets send an important signal to the market and the international investment community regarding the level of investment that may be required, and the amount of renewable capacity that Egypt may feasibly accommodate on its electric grid. Thus, while current non-hydro renewable energy contribution in Egypt is modest and challenges to exploiting its resources remain, the sector is poised for significant growth. Prior to understanding where Egypt's power sector is heading, it is helpful to briefly review the political context in which the sector exists, the past development of the sector in general, and the evolution of the role of renewable energy in particular.

Domestic Political Context

Egypt's incentive to develop alternative energy resources is clear. Its progress in reforming the sector to allow for private sector participation to help drive renewable power generation development has also been noteworthy. Yet Egypt's energy sector will develop within the greater political environment in which it currently operates. Within this context, domestic stability, national politics, international relations, and geopolitical events provide the foundations on which Egypt's new energy sector will be built and will thus have significant influence on the rules of the game and who comes to play.

Egypt's Recent Transitions of Power

Egypt's internal stability has wavered significantly in recent years. Prior to the Arab Spring, Hosni Mubarak ruled Egypt for nearly thirty years with relative stability, albeit under a repressive human rights regime. After 18 days of public demonstrations against the Mubarak administration in the 2011 Egyptian Revolution, he was ousted and indicted, with the Egyptian military assuming interim rule until Mohamed Morsi of the Muslim Brotherhood was democratically as president in 2012. Morsi was then overthrown in 2013 by a military coup led by Sisi, who has served as president of the country since the successful coup. Sisi has increased the powers of the presidency since taking office, perhaps most notably through a 2019 referendum which approved augmented presidential power over the judiciary and the legislature.[19] The referendum also extended the legal term of the Egyptian president, which could allow Sisi to remain in power until 2030.

Internal Stability

While the Sisi administration is largely perceived as an ally to the West, freedom of expression and public opposition have been further restricted under his rule, with thousands of opposition-related arrests and reports of serious human rights abuses. These alleged abuses may be partially in response to an increase in political violence in Egypt since the 2011 revolution. Since then, the majority of violent attacks in the nation have targeted Egyptian security forces, with violence also targeting key economic sectors including tourism. In response, the Sisi government has enacted national states of emergency on several occasions, granting the federal government far-reaching authority over the citizenry and media. Human rights organizations have deemed the Sisi administration's actions particularly repressive under states of emergency.[20]

Even still, unauthorized protests managed to break out in September 2019 in several cities throughout Egypt including the capital, Cairo, and Alexandria, the nation's second largest city and a major economic center. The protestors seek to end Sisi's rule and oppose the current economic situation, in which fuel and food subsidies have been reduced, while inflation and taxes have increased. Some of Sisi's economic policies, such as subsidy reform and floating the currency, have largely been directed by the International Monetary Fund (IMF). The policies have brought macroeconomic stability and significant economic growth through the imposition of structural reforms and austerity measures.[21] However, the policies have concurrently increased living costs for ordinary Egyptians, who are experiencing stagnant wage growth and rising poverty. As of late September 2019, more than 2,000 people had been arrested in the protests.

Increasing signs of political risk and challenges to the continuity of the Sisi administration could begin to impact the alternative energy investment landscape. For example, Egypt's renewable energy projects thus far have been financed by development finance institutions (DFIs), along with some commercial lenders. In this regard, the International Finance Corporation (IFC) organized a consortium of nine banks to finance a portion of the BenBan Solar Park in the Aswan Governorate in Egypt's southeast. The $653 million debt package included participation from the African Development Bank, the Asian Infrastructure Investment Bank, the Arab Bank of Bahrain, CDC of the UK, Europe Arab Bank, Green for Growth Fund and the IFC, among others. As the sector matures and investments in major energy projects with private sector participation prove successful, such opportunities are de-risked for the international investment community, facilitating the participation of private commercial lenders and affording the sector more capital and growth opportunities. Increasing levels of internal instability and political risk, however, reduce the likelihood of commercial lenders entering the market on a widescale, inhibiting sector growth and dynamism. Political risk can also increase the risk premium on the cost of capital for energy projects, a cost that would ultimately be passed on to electricity retail customers.

The recent protests may be an isolated incident, and it is unlikely that the Egyptian public has the appetite for another revolution. Yet the protests demonstrate the public discontent and potential political risk under the surface. While Sisi is expected to stay in power for the foreseeable future, Egyptian politics have been characterized by unpredictability in recent years, with the staying power of the Sisi administration, and by extension the current alternative energy policy and regulatory agenda, subject to this uncertainty.

Egypt's Military

The Egyptian military has played a role in the nation's economy as an economic manager and administrator for decades, as a means of both reducing the defense budget by shifting costs to non-defense sectors, and providing additional compensation and benefits to senior military officials. Egypt's role as an economic manager and administrator has increased substantially since Sisi came to power in 2014; Sisi had previously spent 37 years in the Egyptian military.[22] The Egyptian military's clout and relevance within national economy is vast, yet does not seem to have exercised outsized influence in promoting or resisting renewable energy. Rather, the military tends to support infrastructure projects, including renewable energy, that are consistent with national policy goals and global price trends. For example, the military has awarded contracts to install relatively small-scale solar capacity of 20 megawatts at its bases and has been in talks with private investors to develop large-scale solar.

Brief Review of the Egypt's Power Sector Evolution

The history of Egypt's power sector can be broken down into four principal stages. The first stage of development of Egypt's power sector primarily involved private electric service companies. The first supply of power on a commercial basis in Egypt began in the 1890s during Egypt's colonial era, under private control of Egypt's electric service companies via concession agreements.[23] The private sector's control of the nation's power sector remained intact for seven decades.[24]

The second stage of the nation's power sector began in 1962, involving comprehensive nationalization and a statist approach to sector management, which lasted through the mid-1990s. All generation, transmission, and distribution assets were nationalized in 1962, largely as a result of the Egyptian Revolution of 1952 and the nationalist and anti-imperialist sentiment that arose thereafter.[25] In this period, all assets and activities across the electricity sector value chain were owned and operated by the state, and primarily administered by Egyptian Electricity Authority (EEA), currently known as the Egyptian Electricity Holding Company (EEHC).

The third stage began in the mid-1990s. In response to pressure from multilateral development lenders (primarily the World Bank) to reform the sector and raise electric rates to achieve a cost-reflective tariff, the Egyptian government alternatively began to introduce private sector participation in the power sector via a single-buyer model. Raising electric rates was perceived as politically unachievable at the time, which created a funding gap due to Egypt's inability to meet lender terms, leading to Egypt's introduction of the independent power producer model with a single-buyer.[26] The reasoning for the external push toward competition and cost-reflective tariffs in Egypt was related to a shift in donor policy and is outlined in a 1993 World Bank policy paper.[27]

In the first iteration of this arrangement independent power producers (IPPs) built, owned, and operated power plants under long-term power purchase agreements (PPAs) with the EEA, the vertically-integrated, government-owned monopoly offtaker. IPPs won long-term contracts through competitive bidding to sell power to the EEA, with the generation assets transferred to the EEA upon contract expiration. The mechanism is known as a build, own operate and transfer (BOOT) agreement. Additional measures including tax incentives, full profit repatriation and protection against nationalization were employed to encourage investment.[28] This third stage of power sector development, in one form or another, has largely continued through the present, yet began to include renewable support policies in 2014.

The fourth stage of Egypt's power sector development further liberalizes the market per the Electricity Law 87 of 2015. The law provides the foundational legal framework for a competitive power sector in Egypt, fundamentally changing the sector's structure. The law, which allows for an eight-year transition period toward a competitive market, introduces increased wholesale and retail competition into the market, as well as enhanced regulatory oversight and an independent market operator.[29] As such, the initiative should ultimately facilitate augmented opportunities for renewable energy investment in the future and will be discussed in greater detail later in this chapter.

Recent Generation Capacity Additions

While peak demand has increased by more than one-third in the last 10 years, installed generation capacity has more than doubled from about 32 GW in 2014 to approximately 56 GW in 2019. This is partially the result of 14.4 GW of new gas-fired combined cycle generation capacity coming online in 2018. The three 4.8 GW plants, which became operational and grid connected in just 27 months after the project began, were completed in record time and developed by the EEHC in a consortium comprised of Siemens and local partners. The project helped Egypt end serious power shortages that negatively impacted industrial activity and economic output. The success of the Siemens project and several smaller projects have increased the country's reserve margin and significantly reduced the likelihood of blackouts.[30] In addition to gas, significant renewable energy capacity has recently become operational, with approximately 1 GW of new solar capacity coming online in 2019.[31]

Sector Governance

To understand Egypt's power sector, it is helpful to review below the primary institutions charged with its governance, and the primary government-owned energy service companies.

Entity	*Function*
Supreme Energy Council	The Supreme Energy Council (SEC) is the highest energy sector policymaking body, which evaluates and sanctions national energy strategy and policy, and tends to strategic sector issues such as major policy initiatives and investment schemes. The SEC is led by the Prime Minister of Egypt along with his team of ministers.[32]
Ministry of Electricity and Renewable Energy	MOERE is the traditional energy policy entity, responsible for policy planning and oversight of generation, transmission, distribution, and all power sector activities.[33] The Egyptian Electricity Holding Company (EEHC), the state utility described below, is a subsidiary of the MOERE.[34]
Electric Utility and Consumer Protection Regulatory Agency	EgyptERA serves as the power sector regulator. It regulates and supervises all electricity sector activities, is responsible for compliance oversight and management, license issuance, tariff approval and establishing and monitoring performance standards, among other responsibilities.[35] It is an autonomous entity.

(continued)

(continued)

Entity	*Function*
New and Renewable Energy Authority	NREA develops commercial renewable energy programs in Egypt under the supervision of the MOERE.[36] The NREA maintains a particular focus on solar and wind technologies.[37] It is also the proprietor of land earmarked for renewable development, with permits for land allocation obtained from the NREA. The NREA is independent from the EEHC but reports to the MOERE.[38]
Nuclear Power Plants Authority	The NPPA is charged with establishing and managing nuclear plants in Egypt, as well as undertaking research required for nuclear power project development.[39] It is the owner and future operator of the El Dabaa Nuclear Power Plant.[40] The NPPA reports to the Ministry of Electricity and Renewable Energy.[41]
Nuclear and Radiological Regulatory Authority	The NRRA is responsible for leading regulatory tasks on nuclear and radiation facilities, activities, and practices.[42] The authority was established as an independent agency reporting to Egypt's prime minister.[43]
Egyptian Electric Holding Company	The EEHC is the successor of the now-defunct Egyptian Electricity Authority, the vertically integrated utility. As a result of unbundling, the EEHC is home to Egypt's 16 state-owned, legally separated electric service companies—9 generation companies, 1 transmission company and 6 distribution companies.[44]
Egyptian Electricity Transmission Company	The EETC is the government transmission company that sits within the EEHC. It serves as the offtaker for private generation projects and the issuer of bids and tenders (in collaboration with the NREA for renewable schemes). The EETC will be removed from the EEHC, becoming the nation's independent system operator, to permit increased competition, per Law 87/2015.[45]

Long Term Contracts for Renewable Support

Within the context of renewable development, several government schemes have been executed to support new generation capacity in Egypt. Almost all development of renewable technologies (excluding hydro) has taken place since 2014, when the government endorsed the Renewable Energy Law (law 203/2014). The law creates two schemes for long-term contracting for renewable energy investment: feed-in-tariffs (FITs) and competitive auctions.[46] Long-term contracts with creditworthy counterparties help provide investors with the confidence to undertake large capital investments, and for markets that are not yet liberalized, FITs and auctions also serve as a step toward increasing competition.

Beginning in 2014, the FIT schemes employed have ultimately experienced success, leading to a substantial pipeline for new solar capacity. The two rounds of FITs held thus far demonstrate that the Egyptian government is responsive to the investment community after a largely unsuccessful first round FIT, in which international arbitration for dispute resolution was disallowed. Egypt's refusal to include terms for offshore arbitration in the FIT contracts represented a major sticking point for investors. This disagreement was exacerbated by currency risk issues (with the instability of the Egyptian pound potentially impacting the government's ability to meet FIT payments),[47] and by the government requirement that 85% of solar project financing and 70% of wind project financing come from abroad in foreign currency.[48] The disagreement over international arbitration caused many project developers and lenders to withdraw from the contest, with only three investors achieving financial close out of the initial 136 qualifying developers. Under a lower tariff and with provisions for international arbitration, round two of the FIT was far more successful. Before the end of 2017, a total of 30 solar PV projects had reached financial close, representing approximately 1.5 GW of new renewable capacity.[49] Round two also reduced currency risk by lowering the minimum foreign currency funding requirement.

The offtaker for FIT projects is the Egyptian Electricity Transmission Company (EETC), which signs 25-year power purchase agreements (PPAs) with developers for solar projects and 20-year PPAs for wind projects.[50] While the duration of the contracts helps investors achieve financing, cost-sharing for grid upgrades, in which grid reinforcement costs to accommodate the new generation capacity are shared between the project developer and the EETC, have led to some delays and can significantly increase financial risk for investors. Even so, project developers receive additional benefits including discounted state-owned land for development, the ability to participate in consortium for multiple projects (as long as a majority equity interest is limited to one project), and other tax incentives. As such, projects from the FIT scheme continue to come online, with clean energy comprising an increasingly larger proportion of Egypt's capacity and generation.

Consistent with global trends, Egypt has moved away from FITs, implementing competitive auctions for renewable support. Egypt's auctions have thus far been successful in incenting efficient price discovery and high levels of competition, facilitating low electricity prices, with reported lowest bids of approximately $28 per MWh.[51] Solar projects receive 25-year PPAs with the EETC. Compared with the round one FIT of approximately $140 per MWh and round two FIT of $84 per MWh,[52] the strike price under the auction system is clearly more favorable, due to both the competitive nature of auctions and the ever-increasing maturity of solar PV technologies. Egypt is likely to continue holding auctions for long-term PPAs with private developers as a primary renewable development policy support tool.

Law 87/2015

Issued in July of 2015, Electricity Law 87/2015 outlines a more competitive path for the future of Egypt's power sector, introducing a partially liberalized market structure, and restructuring the sector to accommodate competition. Such measures can help lead to increased competition and lower power prices, better electric service and reliability, and enhanced sector innovation and economic development. It can also encourage increased investment in renewable energy capacity. The Electricity Law creates opportunities for the private sector in new markets for bilateral contracts and retail choice, grid balancing, ancillary services, and in the regulated market via private ownership of regulated monopoly distribution companies.[53]

Additional Opportunities Within the Updated Sector Structure

Egypt is taking the requisite steps to accommodate the increased competition contemplated in the Electricity Law, as well as laying the foundations for the eventual introduction of a highly competitive electricity market structure complete with markets for bilateral contacts, spot trade, balancing and a host of ancillary services. Importantly, the Electricity Law legally separates the EETC from the EEHC, making the EETC the independent system and market operator, and paving the way for non-discriminatory third-party access (TPA) to electricity network infrastructure, a precondition of competition in wholesale and retail electricity markets.[54]

TPA is critical to mitigate conflicts of interest between the grid operator and the companies that use the grid, making the EETC an impartial entity with respect to its treatment of market participants. The Electricity Law also increases the authority, independence and transparency of the energy regulator (EgyptERA), another key precondition of competition. The unbundling of transmission and the EETC's new role as the independent transmission system operator combined with an increasingly transparent regulator will help provide private sector generators, including renewable energy generators, confidence that they will be able to access the grid to transport power.

Under the Electricity Law, the EETC operates both the competitive market and the traditional regulated market. Within the competitive market qualifying high-voltage customers, which account for 16% of the nation's electricity consumption, purchase electricity directly from generators or electricity marketers, who then pay a transmission wheeling charge to the EETC for the use of the transmission system. In the regulated market, the EETC acts as a clearinghouse between the generators and the distribution companies, matching supply from the generators with demand from the distribution companies who serve customer within their service territories under regulated tariffs.

Bilateral Contracts and Retail Choice

Within this structure, direct contractual negotiations for power supply deals are permitted between qualified customers (which are large electricity consumers) and eligible load serving entities (LSEs). LSEs serve demand (also known as load), and include power generators and authorized suppliers.[55] This will likely permit government-owned generators to compete directly with privately-owned independent power producers for power supply contracts with large load customers. Via the authorized supplier construct, the law will also allow for independent marketers to commercialize electricity, creating opportunities for brand new market entrants exclusively focused on electricity retail, and independent power producers that seek to establish separate retail companies. Authorized suppliers may also find themselves in direct competition with government-owned generators and independent power producers to supply qualified customers.

This new market construct may help facilitate renewable energy development. For example, qualified customers such as large industrial customers (or organizations with corporate sustainability goals) will be able to purchase electricity directly renewable energy developers. Qualified customers will also be able to purchase power from electricity marketers. Renewable developers may elect to overbuild capacity in certain areas, for example, off the back of a contract won via a FIT or an auction, with the expectation of offloading additional generation to qualified users or electricity marketers. This additional flexibility represents a potential boon for renewable energy capacity additions.

Ancillary Services and 'Stabilization Power'

Ancillary services products, which help maintain the stability of the electric grid, will likely emerge in order to help balance the transmission system with generation reserves. This is particularly true given Egypt's planned addition of substantial intermittent renewable energy generation, which may increase the error rates of electricity production forecasts. This can in turn apply stress on the electric system, causing electricity prices to rise and electric reliability to suffer. The Electricity Law contemplates 'Stabilization Power,' which is electricity that would be purchased by the EETC to help compensate any supply-demand imbalances, and stabilize the grid.[56] More diverse and advanced ancillary services related to grid synchronization, flexibility reserves and other products are likely to emerge over time as the market advances and new grid needs emerge. To the extent that renewable energy sources are also able to provide ancillary services to the grid, this may provide additional return on investment, and help incentivize renewable capacity buildout.

Regulated Market

In the regulated market, power is supplied under traditional utility monopoly regulation, with power sold to non-qualified users under tariffs approved by the regulator. The Electricity Law, however, allows for private sector participation in electricity distribution,[57] which may help improve efficiency, especially if there are 'quick win' solutions to increase the profitability and economic efficiency of electric distribution companies, which has been the case in other countries that have allowed for private sector participation in distribution. In Egypt, the private sector would likely participate via concession agreements. If investors are offered a cost-reflective tariff plus a reasonable rate of return that is consistent with international norms for regulated distribution utilities, this would likely be an attractive opportunity.

Nuclear Energy Ambitions

In addition to renewable energy, Egypt seeks to integrate significant nuclear capacity into the grid and currently has a major nuclear project under development.

Development of the El Dabaa Nuclear Power Plant

Egypt's nuclear ambitions date back to the 1950s, when the country inaugurated two nuclear reactors for research purposes. Plans for the El Dabaa Nuclear Power Plant (DNPP), which is currently under development, were first announced in the early 1980s. Yet instability, the complexity and cost associated with nuclear power plant development, access to alternative energy sources like natural gas, and the fallout from the 1986 Chernobyl disaster all contributed to Egypt's lack of progress over the ensuing decades. In 2007, Egyptian President Hosni Mubarak began to move the plan forward again by launching preliminary technical studies, and revising the legal framework to meet international standards for nuclear activity. Following the initial turmoil of the Arab Spring, Egypt re-engaged Russia with respect to the technical and financial aspects of nuclear development.[58]

In 2014, Sisi announced plans to develop the plant in cooperation with Russia. During Vladimir Putin's December 2017 visit to Egypt, Rosatom (Russia's state corporation specializing in nuclear power) signed an agreement with the Egyptian government for the construction of the plant.[59] In addition to financing and construction, Russia's support is likely to include fuel supplies, storage of waste, training, and other nuclear technology-specific expertise.[60] In March 2019, the Nuclear and Radiological Regulatory Authority issued a siting permit for project, an important step, which confirms that the site meets domestic and international stipulations.[61] As such, construction is scheduled to begin in 2020 with the plant becoming fully operational by the end of the decade.

Project Cost

The 4,800 MW project envisages four 1,200 MW nuclear reactors at a cost of $30 billion, with $25 billion financed through Russian loans and $5 billion undertaken by the Egyptian government.[62] While nuclear power will help meet the nation's baseload demand with a reliable and carbon-free energy source, the project presents challenges in terms of its development and cost.

The project is more expensive than other megaprojects and electricity capacity additions in Egypt in recent years, partially due to the high fixed costs associated with nuclear development in general, but also as a result of abundant natural gas resources and favorable renewable conditions. The nation currently enjoys a rapidly growing renewable energy sector and access to extensive natural gas resources, including the Zohr gas field. Discovered in 2015, Zohr is the largest gas field discovery made in the Mediterranean Sea and began producing in less than 3 years from the announcement of its discovery. The success of the Zohr field to date and Egypt's natural gas sector reforms are likely to continue to provide further impetus to sector development. Given Egypt's indigenous gas and renewable energy resources, these solutions are more cost-effective options in meeting Egypt's electricity supply needs when compared with a major nuclear power plant. Still, future major gas discoveries in Egypt are not guaranteed, nor is Egypt's ability to maintain its net exporter status in gas beyond the mid-2020s.

For example, the 14,400 MW gas-fired combined cycle project completed in 2018 resulted in total spend of approximately $7 billion, almost 3 times the capacity of the DNPP, for less than a quarter of the cost. While the marginal generation costs associated with natural gas electricity production are higher than those of nuclear generation, the DNPP is still likely to represent a substantial economic burden for Egypt given its high investment cost. With interest rates of 3%, the Russian loans include favorable terms, yet would add to Egypt's growing external debt. However, developing gas or renewable resources also implies costs for Egypt, either through sovereign debt, increased taxation or higher electric rates. In the case of debt, interest would likely accrue at rate of approximately 5.75%, Egypt's Eurobonds yield. While the Russian loans provide better interest rate terms, the absolute amount paid to finance the nuclear project would likely be greater, due to the high capital costs of nuclear.

Compatibility with Renewables

In addition, conventional nuclear technology is not particularly compatible with electric systems that enjoy high levels of renewable penetration. Nuclear plants are inflexible, meaning that they have little capability to quickly ramp output up or down, and typically run with little to no variation in output, providing baseload generation. As renewable output depends on weather conditions, inflexible nuclear capacity would likely prohibit renewable generation from delivering electricity to the grid, particularly under certain circumstances.

Justifications for the Project

As a result of the supposed weak economic case for the project, the DNPP's perceived value also stems from fostering nationalism and popularity at home, and its utility in gaining an edge and hedging bets in geopolitics and relationship building abroad. Egypt seeks to deepen ties with more international players as the world becomes increasingly globalized and multipolar, and the internal politics of longtime allies and aid benefactors, such as the United States, are increasingly unpredictable. In addition, given criticism against the Sisi administration's human right's record, Egypt may see value in deepening ties with allies that are less likely to require that financial assistance be partially dependent on Egypt's domestic affairs. Egypt also received offers for the nuclear project from China and South Korea prior to selecting Russia.

Looking Toward the Future

With carbon-free electricity generation and energy sector competition both on the rise, Egypt is on the path to a more sustainable and prosperous energy sector. Furthering competitive initiatives in the sector by rolling out the reforms contemplated in the 2015 Electricity Law should help lower power prices and lead to improved market methods for ensuring security of supply, while supporting economic development and a cleaner sector overall.

Yet risks remain. Egypt should anticipate potential unintended consequences caused by sector overhaul and seek to manage these consequences proactively rather than reactively. For example, prudence in the pursuit and management of expensive megaprojects is paramount. While nuclear power may help to achieve perceived prestige or future geopolitical gains, the economic cost of the project could prove troublesome, negatively impact other parts of the energy sector and larger economic. Given Egypt's domestic instability and international geopolitical uncertainty (including recent attacks on a major Saudi oil processing facility), protection of physical infrastructure and large capital projects should be taken seriously.

In addition, the integration of large amounts of intermittent renewable energy generation can also be an issue for grid stability and electric reliability. To this end, appropriate measures and international norms should continue to be adopted and enforced, and a framework for additional market products to help mitigate the destabilizing effects of renewables should be rolled out. Egypt may be served by considering an electricity storage policy support mechanism to better balance supply and demand, thus creating new investment opportunities and positioning itself as an international leader in the nascent power storage market industry. If successful, such an initiative would likely afford Egypt new business relationships and geopolitical power.

Egypt is in the midst of a complex balancing act and faces a trying task. The nation seeks to reap the rewards of private sector participation in renewable energy while ensuring a good deal for the country, while simultaneously developing a costly nuclear plant without overextending itself financially. It also intends to use this new power generation capacity as a geopolitical tool, while meeting IMF-mandated conditions and maintaining stability within the domestic milieu.

Yet however imperfect, Egypt's ability to turn its energy sector woes into opportunities has been noteworthy in recent years. Perhaps most notable is the 14.4 GW gas-fired megaproject that was conceived, developed, and brought to commercial operation in a short time period in order to avoid serious electricity shortages. Egypt's ability to design, plan, and implement feed in tariffs) and electricity auctions have also resulted in clear successes in the form of new renewable capacity at very low prices. If Egypt can continue apply the same dexterity and aptitude within its energy sector and greater policymaking agenda, the nation will be poised for leadership in alternative energy regionally.

Notes

1. Rising demand and the need for additional capacity has helped drive renewable energy policy. However, demand has since slowed, partially due to subsidy reform. The threat of serious power supply crises has also driven installed generation capacity increases. New capacity has created a capacity surplus, mostly as a result of gas-fired generation development.
2. World Bank. *GDP Growth (Annual %)*. 2019. https://data.worldbank.org/indicator/ny.gdp.mktp.kd.zg.
3. World Bank. *Global Growth to Weaken to 2.6% in 2019, Substantial Risks Seen*. June 2019. https://www.worldbank.org/en/news/press-release/2019/06/04/global-growth-to-weaken-to-26-in-2019-substantial-risks-seen.
4. World Bank. *Population Growth (Annual %)*. 2019. https://data.worldbank.org/indicator/SP.POP.GROW.
5. Egyptian Ministry of Electricity and Renewable Energy. *Power Sector Cooperation Planning Survey in Arab Republic of Egypt*. October 2018. https://openjicareport.jica.go.jp/pdf/12321873.pdf.
6. Egyptian Electricity Holding Company. *Annual Report*. 2016/2017. http://www.moee.gov.eg/english_new/EEHC_Rep/2016-2017en.pdf.
7. Norton Rose Fulbright. *A Focus on the Egyptian Power Market*. June 17, 2016. https://www.insideafricalaw.com/publications/a-focus-on-the-egyptian-power-market.
8. Egyptian Electricity Holding Company. *Annual Report*. 2016/2017. http://www.moee.gov.eg/english_new/EEHC_Rep/2016-2017en.pdf
9. U.S. Energy Information Administration. *Country Analysis Brief: Egypt*. May 24, 2018. https://www.eia.gov/beta/international/analysis_includes/countries_long/Egypt/egypt.pdf.
10. International Renewable Energy Agency (IRENA). *Renewable Energy Outlook Egypt*. 2018. https://www.irena.org/-/media/Files/IRENA/Agency/Publication/2018/Oct/IRENA_Outlook_Egypt_2018_En.pdf.

11. U.S. Energy Information Administration. *Country Analysis Brief: Egypt*. May 24, 2018. https://www.eia.gov/beta/international/analysis_includes/countries_long/Egypt/egypt.pdf.
12. Fossil fuels have represented at least of 87% total installed electric generation capacity since 2010.
13. Egyptian Electricity Holding Company. *Annual Report 2017/2018*. 2019 http://www.moee.gov.eg/english_new/EEHC_Rep/2017-2018en.pdf.
14. Cyprus currently has no international electric interconnections, yet the project seeks to connect Israel, Cyprus and Greece.
15. Mahmoud, Khaled. *What Sisi Wants from Sudan*, Carnegie Endowment for International Peace. February 2019. https://carnegieendowment.org/sada/78367.
16. Council on Strategic Risks. *Working Group on Climate, Nuclear, and Security Affairs Nuclear Energy Developments, Climate Change, and Security in Egypt*. May 2019. https://councilonstrategicrisk.files.wordpress.com/2019/06/working-group-on-climate-nuclear-security-affairs-report-three_nuclear-energy_climate-change_security_egypt_2019_06-1.pdf.
17. Ministry of Electricity & Renewable Energy New & Renewable Energy Authority. *Egypt's Renewable Energy Activities and Strategy*. 2019. https://irena.org/-/media/Files/IRENA/Agency/Events/2018/Jan/Geothermal-financing/S6-P3-GEO-EGYPT.pdf?la=en&hash=A19BCEAD5A22A6B070E25204553A132E7F9FE947.
18. Renewable Energy Authority. *Egypt Experience in Renewable Energy Egypt Strategy 2022–2035*. 2019. https://www.worldfutureenergysummit.com/__media/Speaker's%20Presentation/WFES%20Solar/Egypt-Experience-in-Renewable-Energy.pdf.
19. Council on Strategic Risks. *Working Group on Climate, Nuclear, and Security Affairs Nuclear Energy Developments, Climate Change, and Security in Egypt*. May 2019. https://councilonstrategicrisk.files.wordpress.com/2019/06/working-group-on-climate-nuclear-security-affairs-report-three_nuclear-energy_climate-change_security_egypt_2019_06-1.pdf.
20. Ibid.
21. Congressional Research Service. *Egypt: Background and U.S. Relations*. March 12, 2019. https://fas.org/sgp/crs/mideast/RL33003.pdf.
22. Carnegie Middle East Center. *Egypt's Military Now Controls Much of Its Economy. Is This Wise?*. November 25, 2019. https://carnegie-mec.org/2019/11/25/egypt-s-military-now-controls-much-of-its-economy.-is-this-wise-pub-80281.
23. Maria Vagliasindi and John Besant-Jones. *Power Market Structure: Revisiting Policy Solutions*. The World Bank/International Bank for Reconstruction and Development, 2013. https://books.google.com/books?id=oGyXVUfmqrsC&printsec=frontcover#v=onepage&q&f=false.

24. Ministry of Electricity and Renewable Energy. *Development of Electricity in Egypt. 2013.* http://www.moee.gov.eg/english_new/history2.aspx.
25. Oxford Business Group. *The Report: Egypt 2013.* 2013. https://books.google.com/books?id=-dcVBgAAQBAJ&printsec=frontcover#v=onepage&q&f=false.
26. Anton Eberhard and Katherine Nawaal Gratwick. *From State to Market and Back Again: Egypt's Experiment with Independent Power Projects.* University of Cape Town Management Programme in Infrastructure Reform & Regulation. October 2007. https://www.gsb.uct.ac.za/files/Egypt_IPP_Experience_April_2006.pdf.
27. The World Bank Group. *The World Bank's Role in the Electric Power Sector: Policies for Effective Institutional, Regulatory, and Financial Reform.* January 1993. http://documents.worldbank.org/curated/en/477961468782140142/pdf/multi-page.pdf.
28. The World Bank Group. *Assessment of Private Sector Participation in the Power Sector of Egypt.* December 2014. http://documents.worldbank.org/curated/en/820931468188650718/pdf/98547-WP-P149491-Box393173B-OUO-9-P149491.pdf.
29. Sharkawy and Sarhan. *The New Electricity Law.* September 27, 2015. https://www.lw.com/thoughtLeadership/egypt-new-electricity-law-explained.
30. Siemens. *The Egypt Megaproject Boosting Egypt's Energy System in Record Time.* 2019. https://assets.new.siemens.com/siemens/assets/public.1528339867.38ad89c9f4532436a921ed151da1d987a985deec.siemens-egypt-megaproject.pdf.
31. Middle East Economic Survey. *Egypt Solar Soars Thanks To Booming Benban Output.* August 23, 2019. https://www.mees.com/2019/8/23/power-water/egypt-solar-soars-thanks-to-booming-benban-output/8196c620-c594-11e9-960d-4beda73b71f1.
32. International Renewable Energy Agency (IRENA). *Renewable Energy Outlook Egypt.* 2018. https://www.irena.org/-/media/Files/IRENA/Agency/Publication/2018/Oct/IRENA_Outlook_Egypt_2018_En.pdf.
33. Ministry of Electricity and Renewable Energy. *The Ministry: Overview on the Ministry of Electricity and Energy.* 2013. http://www.moee.gov.eg/english_new/define.aspx.
34. International Renewable Energy Agency (IRENA). *Renewable Energy Outlook Egypt.* 2018. https://www.irena.org/-/media/Files/IRENA/Agency/Publication/2018/Oct/IRENA_Outlook_Egypt_2018_En.pdf.
35. Donia El-Mazghouny. *Renewable Energy in Egypt.* Shahid Law Firm. April 3, 2019. https://www.lexology.com/library/detail.aspx?g=799894d0-f8f5-4264-bf61-0cb4e1524b3a.
36. Ibid.

37. International Renewable Energy Agency (IRENA). *Renewable Energy Outlook Egypt*. 2018. https://www.irena.org/-/media/Files/IRENA/Agency/Publication/2018/Oct/IRENA_Outlook_Egypt_2018_En.pdf.
38. European Bank for Reconstruction and Development. *FP039: GCF—EBRD Egypt Renewable Energy Financing Framework*. March 15, 2017. https://www.greenclimate.fund/documents/20182/574760/Funding_proposal_-_FP039_-_EBRD_-_Egypt.pdf/0d64d21a-0bd5-4a8b-8ebf-115c27a8c3ba.
39. Nuclear Power Plants Authority. *NPPA in Brief*. 2019. http://nppa.gov.eg/en/about-us/#overview.
40. Nuclear Power Plants Authority. *Site Approval Permit for El Dabaa NPP Issued*. 2019. http://nppa.gov.eg/en/el-dabaa-npp-project/.
41. Nuclear Power Plants Authority. *Law No. 13 of 1976 on the Establishment of the Nuclear Power Plants Authority for Generating Electricity As amended by the Law No. 210 of 2017*. 2017. https://nppa.gov.eg/wp-content/uploads/2019/06/Law-13-en.pdf.
42. International Atomic Energy Agency. *Egypt*. 2015. https://cnpp.iaea.org/countryprofiles/Egypt/Egypt.htm.
43. Egyptian Nuclear Radiological Regulatory Authority. *Egyptian Nuclear Radiological Regulatory Authority Experience and Its Relation with Technical Supporting Organizations*. October 2014. https://www.researchgate.net/publication/306323713_EGYPTIAN_NUCLEAR_AND_RADIOLOGICAL_REGULATORY_EXPERIENCE_AND_ITS_RELATION_WITH_TECHNICAL_SUPPORTING_ORGANIZATIONS.
44. Egyptian Electric Holding Company. *About the Company*. 2014. http://www.eehc.gov.eg/eehcportal/Eng/Company/History.aspx.
45. Egyptian Electricity Holding Company. *Annual Report*. 2016/2017. http://www.moee.gov.eg/english_new/EEHC_Rep/2016-2017en.pdf.
46. International Energy Agency. *Egypt Renewable Energy Law (Decree No 203/2014)*. September 21, 2016. https://www.iea.org/policiesandmeasures/pams/egypt/name-157164-en.php.
47. KPMG. *Renewable Energy in Egypt: The Green Opportunity*. February 2017. https://home.kpmg/content/dam/kpmg/uk/pdf/2017/03/renewable-energy-in-egypt-the-green-opportunity.pdf.
48. The Economist Intelligence Unit. *Egypt Revises Feed-In Tariff Terms for Renewable Projects*. September 22, 2016. https://country.eiu.com/article.aspx?articleid=1784635962&Country=Egypt&topic=Economy&subtopic=Forecast&subsubtopic=Policy+trends&u=1&pid=1644795948&oid=1644795948&uid=1.
49. ClimateScope. *Egypt Renewable Energy Feed in Tariff by Tender*. 2018. http://global-climatescope.org/policies/4386.

50. International Energy Agency. *Egypt Renewable Energy Law (Decree No 203/2014)*. September 21, 2016. https://www.iea.org/policiesandmeasures/pams/egypt/name-157164-en.php.
51. Institute for Energy Economics and Financial Analysis. *Bids for Egypt Solar Project Come in Under ¢3/kWh*. August 14, 2018. http://ieefa.org/bids-for-egypt-solar-project-come-in-under-%c2%a23-kwh/.
52. Eversheds Sutherland International LLP. *Egypt Announces Second Phase of Feed-In Tariff Programme*. September 12, 2016. https://www.lexology.com/library/detail.aspx?g=08865856-b64c-4634-adc5-fb6d41977bd2.
53. Sharkawy and Sarhan. *The New Electricity Law*. September 27, 2015. https://www.lw.com/thoughtLeadership/egypt-new-electricity-law-explained.
54. Ibid.
55. Ibid.
56. Ibid.
57. Ibid.
58. Council on Strategic Risks. *Working Group on Climate, Nuclear, and Security Affairs Nuclear Energy Developments, Climate Change, and Security in Egypt*. May 2019. https://councilonstrategicrisk.files.wordpress.com/2019/06/working-group-on-climate-nuclear-security-affairs-report-three_nuclear-energy_climate-change_security_egypt_2019_06-1.pdf.
59. Stockholm International Peace Research Institute. *Russia's Nuclear Energy Exports. Status, Prospects and Implications*. February 2019. https://www.sipri.org/sites/default/files/2019-02/eunpdc_no_61_final.pdf.
60. Congressional Research Service. *Egypt: Background and U.S. Relations*. March 12, 2019. https://fas.org/sgp/crs/mideast/RL33003.pdf.
61. Nuclear Power Plants Authority. *Site Approval Permit for El Dabaa NPP Issued*. 2019. http://nppa.gov.eg/en/el-dabaa-npp-project/.
62. Congressional Research Service. *Egypt: Background and U.S. Relations*. March 12, 2019. https://fas.org/sgp/crs/mideast/RL33003.pdf.

CHAPTER 8

Levant: Where Politics Defeat Alternative Energy Disruptions

Jessica Obeid

Overview of the Power Sector

The Middle East has long been characterized by its vast hydrocarbon resources; yet several of its constituents are petroleum-poor, especially in the Levant. Jordan, Lebanon and Palestine, subjects of this chapter, have witnessed significant growth in energy demand attributed to rapid urbanization and increases in population and economic activity. With either negligible or no proved reserves to date, they consequently suffer from a heavy dependence on fossil fuel imports. For example, imported fuels cover 97% of Jordan's energy needs and make up 17.5% of the kingdom's imports.[1] In Lebanon, they accounted for 22.7% of the total imports in 2013.[2] Palestine's energy sector is fully dependent on fuel imports. In

J. Obeid (✉)
Academy Associate-Energy Environment and Resources Programme, Chatham House, London, UK
e-mail: jessica@obeid.re

Non-resident Fellow-Lebanese Center for Policy Studies, Beirut, Lebanon

R. Mills and L.-C. Sim (eds.), *Low Carbon Energy in the Middle East and North Africa*, International Political Economy Series,
https://doi.org/10.1007/978-3-030-59554-8_8

addition to the high reliance on fossil fuel imports, the electricity sector in Lebanon and Jordan is dominated by subsidies, which have negatively impacted the national security and economy, accruing high debts and fiscal deficits in these low-revenue states and threatening to trigger economic collapse, along with an increased vulnerability to politics and regional turmoil.

The electricity sector is at high risk of supply disruption and fuel price volatility. In Jordan, crude oil and products constituted 54% of the primary energy consumption in 2018, followed by natural gas with 35%.[3] In Lebanon, imported oil is the main source of electricity generation, with approximately 91%.[4] Lebanon's most dominant power generation fuels are expensive and polluting heavy fuel oil and diesel oil, which have also displaced natural gas in power generation in Jordan at different periods due to supply disruptions. 92% of Palestine's power comes from electricity imports from Israel.

Electricity and fuel subsidies have prevailed for decades and have chronically strained states' budgets. Citizens have perceived subsidized utilities to be a service. Any hike in electricity tariff or elimination of energy subsidies would require a new social contract, the absence of which could result in political unrest. The more the institutions and entities governing the state were perceived as illegitimate and operating against the national interest, the more citizens were inclined to cheat the system and refuse to pay for services such as electricity. In such environments, non-technical losses, such as non-billing, non-collection, and electricity theft, also became a characteristic of the power sector. This is especially true for Lebanon where non-technical losses are estimated at 26% versus 17% technical losses,[5] and to a lesser extent, Palestine.

Lebanon is a highly indebted economy with a debt to GDP ratio surpassing 150%. The power sector is accountable for 43% of the public debt or the equivalent of $40 billion for the period between the years 1992 and 2019.[6] This is mainly due to the high cost of generation driven by inefficient power plants operating on heavy fuel oil and diesel oil, subsidized electricity tariff and elevated technical and non-technical losses. Despite many plans to switch to the use of natural gas, no infrastructure or gas agreements are yet in place. The electricity tariff has not been adjusted since it was initially set back in 1994, based on the then-oil price of approximately $20 per barrel, and averages $0.095 per kWh. In contrast, the cost of generation has ranged between $0.16 and $0.23 per kWh, depending on fuel prices. The fiscal deficit resulting from the cost of subsidies and the annual losses have averaged $1.6-billion in the past decade.[7] While state officials continuously blame the power sector for the skyrocketing public debt, eliminating the subsidies has been off the table due to the acute shortage in electricity supply. The available generation capacity is 2,060 MW and the peak demand is 3,600 MW. This has obliged citizens to own or subscribe to high-cost private diesel generators, averaging $0.3 per kWh, or suffer from an electricity blackout for 12–18 hours a day. The parliament approved two electricity policy papers, in 2010 and 2019, aiming to increase power generation and eliminate subsidies. The 2010 paper remained largely unimplemented. The 2019 paper is a revamp of the 2010 paper and anticipates a tariff hike of 51% to an average of $0.1438 per kWh, upon reaching 24 hours daily supply of electricity.

Both papers focus on centralized thermal power generation and have been subjected to political bickering, hindering any true reforms, and accruing more debt in a collapsing economy.

The picture is less gloomy in Jordan yet, the energy sector, mainly electricity, has also been, a main driver of the surge in the kingdom's public debt. The kingdom has a power generation capacity of 4,400 MW and a peak demand of 3,200 MW. Energy accounts for 40% of the state's budget.[8] In 2012, petroleum and electricity subsidies stood at 2.8 and 5.5% of GDP respectively.[9] In light of a critical economic crisis then, influx of Syrian and Iraqi refugees increasing electricity demand and rising costs of fuel due to interruption of gas supply from Egypt, the losses in the national electric power company (NEPCO) contributed 19% to the total debt (equivalent to $7.8 billion). Jordan therefore implemented a package of fiscal reforms entailing a phased removal of subsidies for gasoline, diesel, and kerosene, and a partial removal of those for liquefied petroleum gas (LPG). The elimination of the electricity subsidies, which have been a higher fiscal burden on the state, has taken a slower path. This is because until end of 2019, electricity subsidies are safeguarded for the lowest consumers in the residential and industrial sectors. The end-user tariff has become significantly high, as the cost of service in Jordan is at $0.23 per kWh. The government of Jordan has set a cap of $55 per oil barrel for which the electricity tariffs would remain unchanged. Higher oil prices would entail further hikes on electricity tariffs, negatively impacting the economy's competitiveness.

Jordan is also vulnerable to natural gas disruptions, which it has suffered from in the case of imports from Iraq when the latter's war erupted in 2003, and Egypt when the Sinai pipeline attacks happened in 2011. The kingdom took steps to improve the security of gas supply by implementing a Liquefied Natural Gas Terminal (LNG) in Aqaba through a $65 million grant by Kuwait Government. The terminal project, completed in 2015, allows imports from international markets. As of early January 2020, Jordan is importing natural gas from Israel and is met with public backlash rejecting normalization and calling for the cancellation of the agreement, threatening another gas supply disruption. But the kingdom's plans are ambitious as it aspires to switch from a fuel importer to producer through an oil shale program, expected to start operations in 2022. The program has been in discussion since the 1990s, but is yet to be implemented. The program is expensive and polluting, but will provide a local source of fuel to the kingdom.

The electricity tariff in Palestine is relatively high averaging at $0.12–$0.17 per kWh, close to the tariff of Israeli consumers. Yet, the cost of electricity as share of household expenses in Palestine is the highest within MENA countries.[10] The power sector, with a peak demand estimated at 2,600 MW,[11] covered mostly by electricity imports from Israel Electric Company (IEC), also suffers from a fiscal deficit resulting from the high cost of imports, the high technical and non-technical losses, and the expensive cost of the electricity generated in Gaza's power plant.

There is only one thermal power generation plant in Gaza; a 140 MW diesel-fired plant, developed through an Independent Power Producer (IPP) in 2004 on a 20-years Power Purchase Agreement (PPA), with a take-or-pay model; thus, the Palestinian Authority has to pay for the full capacity of the plant regardless of any constraints. Due to the high cost of diesel, the electricity produced by the power plant ranges between $0.29 and $0.46 per kWh.[12] The distribution grid is severely weak resulting in a loss of 25% of the purchased power,[13] and non-paying customers are estimated at 25%, hindering the ability of Palestine Electricity Transmission Limited (PETL) to pay all its purchased power fees.

Palestine's dependence on fossil fuel and electricity imports is one of the outcomes of the Israeli occupations and the prevailing political situation. Yet, this dependence creates a vicious circle and also increases Palestine's susceptibility to foreign politics and regional turmoil, making its energy security very fragile, if at all existent. 100% of the West Bank's electricity supply and almost half of Gaza's are linked to imports from IEC. There's enough power supply in Gaza to meet half of the supply, resulting in 8 hours of blackout for every 8 hours of supply. Although the West Bank has 24-hour supply, any conflict threatens to put the area in the dark. The supply of electricity or lack thereof serves as a tool for political pressure, and is aggravated by Palestine's inability to fully pay its electricity bills to IEC.

Current Status of Alternative Energy

The three countries are investing in alternative technologies at different paces and success rates. Yet, all three are lagging behind on their 2020 renewable energy targets, namely, 20% of the primary energy mix for Jordan,[14] 12% for Lebanon, and 5% for Palestine. For the year 2030, Lebanon has pledged to meet 30% of the total electricity generation from renewable energy sources, a target that Jordan is also considering. Located on the global Sun Belt, the three countries have significant solar irradiance ranging between 1,800 and 2,000 kWh per m^2 per year, and relatively moderate temperatures, creating favorable conditions for solar energy.

Jordan is considered one of the most developed countries in renewable energy deployment in the Middle East, with 7.9% renewable energy of the total electricity generation in the year 2018,[15] up from 2% in 2013. In 2017, the share stood at 6.9% with solar accounting for 4.5% of electricity generation, wind for 2.2%, and biogas and hydropower for 0.2%.[16]

In addition to high insolation, Jordan has significant wind potential showcased in the kingdom's mapping for wind resources conducted first in 1988 and updated by the Ministry of Energy and Mineral Resources (MEMR) in 2007 and identifying six regions comprising potential wind sites,[17] with wind speeds exceeding 7 m/s, considered economically viable. Therefore, Jordan has remarkable renewable energy potential that can drastically change its energy scene.

Lebanon followed the lead and in 2011, Beirut-based CEDRO project by the United Nations Development Programme (UNDP), published a thorough wind atlas identifying potential sites and estimating the country's onshore wind potential at 6.1 GW.[18]

There are currently several streams for the implementation of renewable energy projects, with Jordan providing the most diverse options. These include direct unsolicited proposals, auctions, and competitive tenders for the state's projects, and net-metering[19] and power wheeling policies[20] for distributed generation. Palestine offers the same options, with the exception of the wheeling policy which is restrained by the segregated grid design and its weak status. In Lebanon, both direct unsolicited proposals and power wheeling schemes are not yet available, therefore only the net-metering policy and public tenders have been adopted by the end of 2019.

The sector was making strides in Jordan until early 2019, where the government started halting and delaying projects. Renewable energy installed capacity in 2017 was estimated at 609.4 MWp, namely, 395.5 MWp solar PV, 198.4 MWp wind, and 15.5 MWp hydro and biogas projects.[21] As of end of 2019, there is approximately 1,560 MWp in the pipeline either installed, planned, or under development,[22] the bulk of which is in utility-scale solar and wind farms.

For its first renewable energy tenders, the government of Jordan launched 12 projects of a total of 200 MWp in 2011 through long-term PPA at a fixed tariff of $0.169 per KWh. They were followed by a 52.5 MWp Ma'an solar PV project of $0.148 per kWh. A few years later, the latest off-take prices have averaged between $0.06 and $0.08 per KWh,[23] driven by Jordan's accumulating experience in similar projects and the associated risk reduction for investors, and the global decrease in the cost of technologies.

Apart from renewable energy, the government of Jordan decided in 2007 to invest in nuclear power plants. Following a multi-year series of discussions and agreements with Atomic Energy of Canada Ltd, Korea Electric Power Corp, and other companies to conduct the feasibility assessments, and a parliamentary vote to suspend the program, the Jordanian Atomic Energy Commission announced in 2013 that the Russia's Rosatom would build two nuclear reactors of a 2,000 MW total capacity by the years 2023 and 2025.[24] The deal was scrapped in June 2018 as JAEC found the project to be too costly,[25] and smaller reactors have been under consideration since then. The road ahead for nuclear energy in the kingdom seems bumpier as other challenges are added such as the small grid and the scarcity of water.

In Lebanon, renewable energy stood at almost 9% of the primary electricity demand in 2018, with 7% coming from old hydropower plants, which generated 60–70% of Lebanon's electricity until the 1960s. Nevertheless, renewable energy deployment has been slow. Despite the award of three wind farms and the launch of expression of interests (EOI) for large-scale wind and solar farms ranging between 410 and 700 MWp, the current installed renewable energy capacity is solely through distributed generation. The installed capacity was estimated at 340.87 MW in 2018, of which approximately 284.5 MW are from hydropower plants and

56.37 MWp from solar PV. Of the distributed solar PV, 33.7%, equivalent to 19 MWp, were installed that year.[26] The first wind farms tender was launched in 2013. Due to a lengthy cabinet vacuum lasting for several months and which is typical to Lebanon due to the historic political divide, the absence of an energy regulator for the same political reasons, intermittent policies permitting power licensing, along with other political dynamics, 25-year PPAs were only signed in the year 2018. Three different joint ventures with a total capacity of 212 MWp are to be installed in Akkar, North of Lebanon, and expected to be completed by 2021 at the cost of $0.1045 per kWh for the first three years, and $0.095 per kWh for the remaining period.

Compared to a regional average of $0.06 per kWh, these farms come at a significant cost due to the risk premium that the private sector had to account for. The first round for solar PV farms was launched in 2017, but the contract awarding has not been completed to date. In 2018, a call for EOI for a second round of wind and solar farms was launched, but the bidding process has not started yet. While reasons for the delay haven't been communicated, the economic crisis that hit fall 2019 predicts that moving ahead will be even slower, as attracting investments will be challenging and the cost of debt and risk premiums will be high.

The lowest share of renewable energy among these three countries is recorded in Palestine at only 1% of the primary energy demand. Solar energy is the most prominent renewable resource for Palestine. The installed capacity in Palestine is estimated at 50 MWp, of which 10 MWp are in Gaza and 40 MW in the West Bank. Of the total installed capacity, 20 MWp are of commercial size and the remaining 30 MWp are small-scale distributed systems implemented through the net-metering scheme. However, the sector faces many political, technical, and economic hurdles, including constrained land spaces, limited grid capacity, and low ability to attract investments.

The Oslo Accords, signed in Washington, DC in September 1993, between Israel and the Palestine Liberation Organisation, classified land into three areas A, B, and C, requiring the Palestinian authorities to secure Israeli approval over the usage of the majority of lands. There is significant solar potential of more than 3,000 MW in the West Bank Area C, suitable for solar PV and concentrated solar power (CSP),[27] yet Israel holds control over 61% of area C, questioning the possibility of harnessing this potential. The Gaza Strip has more extreme land restrictions.

To mitigate the land issues, rooftop solar PV has developed as the most common renewable energy projects across Palestine. The potential for rooftop solar is 530 MW in West Bank and 160 MW in Gaza.[28]

Due to the political context, the grid is divided into three unconnected zones and can only handle renewable energy integration up to 5 MWp capacity, therefore hindering large-scale projects. The ability to attract funding and to provide sovereign guarantee for the private sector in PPAs is hindered by the lack of political stability and future certainty. Past experience of the Palestinian Authority in sovereign guarantee provided in 2004 for Gaza's Independent Power Producer (IPP) and resulting in bulky take-or-pay charges, also decreases the Authority's willingness to provide further guarantees to new projects, adding further challenges to future investments in renewable energy.

Opportunity of Challenging the Status Quo

Lebanon: The Spread of the Decentralized Model

Distributed energy generation decentralizes power systems and optimizes the costs by cutting down on the distribution and transmission costs and the otherwise necessary system flexibility measures. The potential is substantial in reducing the losses of the state-owned electricity utility, Électricité du Liban (EDL), which receives hefty treasury transfers to cover the electricity subsidies and the technical and non-technical losses.

Distributed renewable energy models can change the governance structure by strengthening local authority, and can get around the bottlenecks and political conflicts in Lebanon, which have been preventing any improvements in the energy sector in the past two decades.

In the Lebanese context, political power is not monopolized by one entity, but power-sharing is conceptualized through a coalition of political parties in the central government. These parties, however, only share their own aspirations for dividends in terms of influence and/or financial returns, rather than a common vision, which results in chronic bottlenecks and political clashes, hindering the government from executing policies and spilling into the various sectors.

Politics in Lebanon cause a dilemma: Parties in the parliament endorse policies and laws, and the government, which comprises more or less the same parliamentarian representation of parties, fails to execute them, for no declared reason. The power sector is a true illustration of that dilemma. Getting around these bottlenecks therefore requires a dilution of powers and the national centralized focus, while emphasizing decentralization and local authorities.

The sector suffers from a significant shortage in electricity supply since generation capacity of 2,000 MW is overwhelmed by peak power demand estimated at 3,600 MW. While the need for additional thermal power plants to meet the base load is obvious, the last power plant constructed was in 1999, after which the succeeding governments failed to add significant generation capacity due to the non-functional political system blocking any progress. Reforms in the power sector have largely remained on paper. The 2010 policy paper for the electricity sector was approved by the parliament, yet its implementation was obstructed. It was updated in 2019 and endorsed as the 2019 sector's policy paper. The Ministry of Energy and Water (MoEW) is working toward its execution, yet, the chronic political clashes may partially or fully impede it and future policies. The length of the electricity crisis has spurred the development of vested interests across the value chain.

Moreover, the monopoly of the state has historically entailed that the public utility owned and operated power plants with little contribution from the private sector solely through engineering, procurement and contracting and turnkey projects.

Renewable energy started developing as a game changer, taking a different path than conventional thermal generation. The first utility-scale wind farms initially launched in 2013 are a breakthrough in the energy sector as they became the first energy projects to endorse public–private participation through the IPP model.

Some commercial and industrial consumers were among the early adopters of distributed solar generation, especially through hybrid solar photovoltaic/diesel systems, realizing the high benefits and fiscal savings resulting from the reduction in usage of the expensive diesel generators. The availability of the National Energy Efficiency and Renewable Energy Action (NEEREA) financing scheme and the net-metering policy, along with continuous decrease in renewable energy technologies' cost, stimulated the small-scale and rooftop solar market. Yet, the economic crisis and shortage of liquidity might jeopardize that. Unlike centralized systems, the consent of the central government is not required for distributed generation; the typical political bottlenecks and vested interests were therefore circumvented. Decentralization therefore became the core of the renewable energy deployment, and distributed generation spread faster than centralized power plants and utility-scale solar and wind farms.

Jordan and Palestine: The Promise of Reduced Foreign Dependence

Although Jordan's power sector has a better standing than the other two countries, it has remained vulnerable to supply shortage risks. The government of Jordan has turned toward alternative energy following economic and fuel supply shortage crises, and aimed for the diversification of supply sources and the promotion of domestic resources. This mission has launched the kingdom into a new energy era. Jordan's position in the region had never been particularly strong, especially with the kingdom's total reliance on fuel imports. The investment in alternative energy would eventually improve Jordan's political and economic stability and transform the dynamics with the economies in the region.

Prior to the US-Iraq war in the year 2003, Jordan relied on oil imports from Iraq at a concessional rate.[29] The war and the change in administration in Iraq halted Jordan's supply. This, coupled with rising global oil prices, placed a significant burden on the state's budget and electricity supply. An agreement with Egypt was signed to import natural gas for the power sector, and the National Energy Strategy 2005–2020 was issued.

The fragile power sector took another hit from 2011 onward as violent attacks targeted the Egyptian pipeline through Sinai during the Arab Spring, causing an electricity crisis and reducing the country's export capacity.[30] Gas imports to Jordan came to a halt in 2014 and the kingdom had to switch to more expensive fuel imports of heavy fuel oil and diesel. This increased the cost of electricity by multiple folds and resulted in large losses for NEPCO and rising debt on the state. NEPCO losses climbed from $3.2 billion in 2012 to $6.9 billion in 2015.[31] The government redoubled effort to diversify the sources of supply.

The government has been keen on attracting private investments into the sector since the 1990s. It has hence implemented a series of reforms including restructuring the Jordan Electric Authority into a government-owned public joint company NEPCO, under the law No. 316 of 1996 and issuing the General Electricity Law No. 10[32] as a general regulatory framework. NEPCO was unbundled into generation, distribution, and transmission companies in 1997. Currently, the power sector comprises four partially or fully private generation companies (GENCOs), three private distribution companies (DISCOs), and the state-owned shareholding transmission company, which purchases all the produced electricity from the GENCOs and resells it to the various DISCOs.

As a result of the early reforms, MEMR launched the first IPP in 1997 for a 450 MW gas-fired combined cycle plant. The IPP model proliferated since then in conventional generation, prior to the market penetration of renewable energy.

Renewable energy became a central energy policy in 2007 as the kingdom decided to reduce dependence on fuel imports and adopt a target of 7% renewable energy by 2015 and 10% by 2020. The 2015 target was missed despite serious efforts, but renewable energy deployment speeded up right after, driving the government by the end of 2018 to modify the 2020 target from 10 to 20% of primary energy, a target which will also be missed, especially that the kingdom halted all new large-scale renewable energy systems since early 2019 stating the need to upgrade the grid.

With an already significant reserve capacity margin, a fierce commitment to renewable energy would enable Jordan to become an exporter of electricity in the region, with existing potential of exports to Iraq, Lebanon, Syria, and Palestine, if the infrastructure and politics permit. Jordan and Iraq are in talks to build the necessary infrastructure for that. Former negotiations with Lebanon weren't successful as the grid connection between the two countries passes through Syria, which wasn't in favor of permitting wheeling through its transmission lines.

For Palestine, solar energy offers a tremendous opportunity to address the imbalance of power between the two states and reduce Palestine's electricity dependence on Israel in some areas. Since the Israeli authorities hold monopoly of the sector at elevated costs, the Palestinian government is a supporter of solar energy. Yet, the challenges are many and the energy vulnerability is so extreme, that tremendous efforts need to be in place, and the aspiration for autonomy is a long-term one.

Governments' Drive Supported by Donors

The commitment by governments in the Levant to push renewable energy forward was a vital factor in kick-starting and building momentum for renewable energy. This commitment was demonstrated by the adoption of relevant policies and regulations and clean energy targets, although interviews with stakeholders reveal that the governments' drive has faded over time. Nevertheless, international organizations and foreign donors have assisted in realizing the governments' initiatives, especially in the provision of technical support and financing mechanisms. The early supporters among the donors were mostly European countries. The involvement of Gulf funds and institutes is witnessed in utility-scale investments, mostly in Jordan.

Jordan's commitment to clean energy was demonstrated in public policies and regulations. The National Energy Research Center (NERC) attempted to kick-start the sector in the 1980s when it started installing solar thermal systems in various institutions. However, the lack of policy instruments hindered the scalability of the project.

The sector was gaining momentum by 2011–2012 in Lebanon and Jordan; solar photovoltaic systems in the range of 100–300 kWh, back then considered of significant scale in the region, were being implemented. Renewable energy laws, policies, and actions plans were being adopted. For Palestine, this took place in 2015.

Mid-2000, his majesty King Abdullah II bin Al-Hussein, along with a few visionary leaders, found the necessity for energy diversification following the Iraq war. The "Updated Master Strategy of Energy Sector in Jordan for the Period 2007–2020," was issued including for the first time an alternative energy chapter. The required investment in alternative energy, including nuclear energy, was estimated to range between $14 and $18 billion, equivalent to $1.2 billion per year.[33] The discussions following the strategy revolved around mobilizing the private sector and attracting international finance institutions. In 2008–2009, EDAMA initiative was launched to coordinate the efforts.

The kingdom then issued law No. 13—the renewable energy and energy efficiency law (REEEL) of 2012—becoming the first country in the region to develop renewable energy legislation, which provides a legal mandate for the government and a regulatory framework for the technologies' deployment. The law permitted in its article six (6) any person to submit a direct unsolicited proposal to the ministry or the council of ministers in order to develop a renewable energy system in any site, outside the sites being developed through public tenders. The law also enacted the establishment of Jordan's Renewable Energy and Energy Efficiency Fund (JREEEF), which has so far enabled the implementation of more than $70 million worth of renewable energy and energy efficiency projects. The fund's contribution has been $26 million while the remaining amount was covered by donors, especially the European Union, USAID, and project owners.

Moreover, Jordan passed By Law No. 10 of 2013 for tax exemption on renewable energy systems, devices, instruments, and energy-consuming rationalisation, as further incentive instruments.

Renewable energy progress has been slower and more complex in Lebanon. These resources received official endorsement in 2009 at the United Nations Climate Change Conference held in Copenhagen, where the government voluntarily pledged to reach 12% share of renewable energy by 2020. The pledge was further enforced in 2010 when the then-minister of energy and water expressed commitment toward renewable resources through the adoption of clean energy plans, and the intention of completing the necessary feasibility studies for wind and solar, and launching IPP wind farms.

Although the country did not issue a renewable energy law, it developed the National Renewable Energy Action Plan (NREA) and National Energy Efficiency Action Plans (NEEAP) through the Lebanese Center for Energy Conservation (LCEC), based on the Arab Energy Efficiency Guideline adopted by the Arab Ministerial Council for Electricity in 2010. The guideline provided a framework for energy efficiency planning in the Arab region, but Lebanon was first Arab country to officially adopt it. It was at the forefront of this among Arab countries, developing a first NEEAP for the years 2011–2016, and adopting a second in 2016 running to 2020. By contrast, Jordan's NEEAP was developed in 2014. An energy efficiency law is currently in the making in Lebanon. The national financing mechanism—NEEREA—was established in 2014 to leverage private funds for financing small-scale green projects by providing subsidized long-term and low interest loans through the Central Bank of Lebanon with the support of the European Union. In so doing, it has encouraged the distributed solar PV generation market.

Renewable energy became serious in Palestine in 2015, following the adoption of renewable energy and natural resources law and the net-metering scheme in 2015. Palestine NEEAP's was adopted earlier in 2012. The electricity demand growth averages 5.2%, with forecasts that it will reach 8.5% from the year 2025.[34] The growing electricity demand, the dependence on imports from Israel, and the Palestinian Authority's weak record of covering its electricity expenses resulting in accumulated outstanding debt, is pushing the government to fully support renewable energy.

But overcoming the land, grid, and financing challenges is challenging. The Palestinian Energy Authority has put in place a revolving fund, through seed money from Agence Française de Developpement (AFD), allowing the authority to get the money back through the savings accrued by the end-user from the installation of rooftop solar. To ensure mass implementation, the government is seeking to use the available rooftops and connecting them to the local grid. This is happening through targeting the roofs of 500 schools with spaces providing for 50–100 MW. A share of the produced electricity will be used on-site, whereas the remaining share is sold to the distribution grid. The first part of the project comprising 50 schools has been launched.

Furthermore, the PA is pushing 24 ministries to implement rooftop solar systems, but the key hurdle is the funding availability since each ministry will have to finance its own system.

Jordan, Lebanon, and Palestine have adopted net-metering, enabling the surplus of electricity generated from renewable energy systems to be transferred to the utility grid, and allowing customers to offset the cost of electricity consumed from the utility. Jordan took a significant step forward and endorsed power wheeling, which Lebanon is currently discussing, enabling the implementation of renewable energy in one site and offsetting the electricity usage in another site through the usage of the utility's transmission lines.

Donors and international community have provided conditional support linked to the government's commitment toward renewables, to overcome policy gridlock and build momentum. This support took the form of technical support, provision of international experts, development of national studies, and assistance in financing and attraction of private investment.

Given that these countries face high political and economic risk, attracting foreign direct investment and private funding is a challenge, there has instead been a large reliance on remittances and aid. Foreign grants have played a role in pilot projects demonstrating the benefits of renewables across different sectors. They have enabled the deployment in public institutions; schools, health clinics, etc., and provided incentives in terms of subsidized costs for the commercial and industrial sectors early adopters. To name a few, in Lebanon and since 2008, UNDP, through multitude of funds, including Spanish, Dutch, and EU grants, has piloted renewable energy in private industries, public schools, hospitals, and community centers. In 1996, Jordan's first commercial wind farm was implemented in 1996 in Hofa, with the support of the German Government. In 2019, Jordan has implemented the world's first solar-powered large accelerator complex through EU funds. In Palestine, UNDP through a grant from the Japanese government implemented solar systems powering healthcare laboratories. European funds have also supported the implementation of financing mechanisms across the three countries. Foreign donors have also played a major role in building the local non-governmental organizations (NGOs) involvement in the sector and awareness raising.

Gulf institutes and funds have been involved in utility-scale renewable energy projects in Jordan such as the Kuwait Fund for Arab Economic Development involvement in the Ma'an wind farm, and in building host community resilience in Lebanon following the Syrian refugees influx, such as the Saudi Fund for Development support for small-scale solar photovoltaic systems in the North of Lebanon. But politics play a role in the size and scale of their involvements in countries in the region.

These policies, action plans along with donors' support and the private sector engagement and the rise of renewable energy lobby groups, resulted in several utility-scale solar and wind farms in Jordan and the spread of distributed solar energy generation in Lebanon and Palestine.

Botched Execution: Identifying the Shortcomings

The willingness of governments in the Levant to deploy renewable energy is there, but shortcomings in the implementation are common, hindering the attainment of pledged targets. For example, around the period 2012–2014, Ministries of Energy and the public in Jordan and Lebanon had high hopes that the renewable energy train had taken off. With every passing year, the global cost of renewable energy technologies was falling and local competition was increasing with increased local capacity. The technology itself seemed unstoppable, able to disrupt the most complex contexts. However, these hopes have yet to be fulfilled in both countries.

The bet on technological advancements was needed, but not enough. The lack of long-term planning, institutional capacity, and policy consistency has obstructed the renewable energy spree. Vested interests associated with the fossil fuel-based energy sector have also been formidable veto players while potential regional rivalries with regard to electricity exports need to be taken into account.

Lack of Strategy and Long-Term Planning

The most common impediment seems to be depicted in the general lack of strategy and long-term planning. The lack of consistency and security of tenure among government officials and institutions in Jordan, the sectarian and political clashes inside the one cabinet in Lebanon, and the conflicts in Palestine, have driven these economies to trade long-term sustainable planning for short-term—political—gains. Whereas politicians typically favor short-term results over long-term impact, countries that have strong institutions have the advantage of developing and executing long-term plans, despite the changing of leaders or agendas. The three countries mostly lack institutional strength to enable that.

The overall energy modeling and planning to develop different scenarios that permit the assessment of the least cost investments in order to reach the optimal cost-effective, reliable energy mix, seem to have been compromised or dismissed. The pillars dictating renewable energy deployment have become the introduction of targets, then simulating different renewable energy technologies and capacities to reach those targets. Energy policies and strategies are noting the renewable energy share, but they are not integrated within a comprehensive planning approach for the whole power sector.

The biggest consequence is the lack of strategy and clarity on the expected energy mix, the long-term generation capacity expansion, and the necessary infrastructure upgrades in the transmission and distribution networks. The thermal generation expansion is disassociated from the renewable energy plans. The grid network, energy storage, ensuring reliability, flexibility and system balancing, major components of the renewable energy deployment, get the lowest attention.

The lack of long-term planning also demeans the ability to adequately forecast and optimize the cost of energy diversification, especially that the build-own-operate, and build-own-transfer models governing the IPP model incur additional costs to the capital expenditures, in terms of equity, interest and debt servicing, that should be accounted for.

Coordination is also hindered. Fossil fuels, nuclear, electricity, and renewable energy portfolios are treated in a decoupled manner, handled by different departments or committees with separate action plans, and weak coordination.

This problem becomes more obvious as the share of renewable energy increases, illustrated best in the case of Jordan.

The growth of power demand was recorded at a rate of 7.4% annually[35] in the period before 2007. The master energy strategy of 2007 included an energy efficiency target to reduce consumption, but there was no enforcement of this target, and consumers and investors preferred implementing renewables over complex, long-term impact energy efficiency measures. The electricity demand was estimated to maintain its rapid growth, necessitating an additional generation capacity of 4,140–4,020 MW compared to 2007 baseline, in order to meet the demand and replace old power plants.

Faced with the threat of intermittent electricity and supply shortage after the Iraq war, and an accelerating growth in demand, the kingdom doubled down on its efforts to increase power generation. The implementation model entailed awarding rather random long-term thermal PPAs, spanning over approximately 20 years, in non-transparent processes, at relatively expensive rates, with no consideration for the final energy mix, and ensuring flexibility and balancing the systems, necessary for renewable energy penetration.

The race to add conventional generation capacity became an unintentional competitor to renewable energy, resulting in a capacity reserve margin of more than 33%, among the highest in the Middle East, most of which remained thermal. The kingdom was therefore in a significant excess of electricity generation, which will be exacerbated when the 470 MW oil shale plant enters service, originally anticipated for 2020, bound by its long-term unplanned contracts to fully purchase the power produced by IPPs, and unable to reduce the high cost of electricity negatively impacting the overall competitiveness of the economy.

With the prevalence of the single-buyer model, NEPCO would still be losing money even in the scenario where subsidies are eliminated.

The focus on generation wasn't met by a parallel emphasis on the grid network, which remained weak and highly underinvested as the pressure on state budgets and the power sector's fiscal deficit mounted. Toward the end of 2016, the Green Corridor project was initiated to increase the grid capacity allowing the wheeling of power from the south region to consumers in the north and central regions.

The challenge of increasing the share of renewable energy in the mix was suddenly multiplied by the excess of non-consumed electricity and the weak overall grid network, leading the government in early 2019 to halt all large-scale renewable projects.

Lack of Institutional Priority, Capacity, and Consistency

Energy diversification requires significant changes in governance, and a set of enablers including the strength of institutions, the priority rank of alternative energy on governments' agenda, and the policies' consistency.

The renewable energy portfolio is mandated by the cabinets to the ministries of energy, which have a set of portfolios and priorities across the energy spectrum, and where renewable energy does not necessarily rank high.

As its name implies, Jordan's MEMR is in charge of the energy and mineral resources, including the power sector, renewables, and fossil fuels. Past experiences of fuel supply disruptions make the security of this supply a major focus of the ministry. Lebanon's MoEW comprises fossil fuels including imports and exploration, power generation, renewables, and water. Blamed for the economic crisis, the power sector is the focus of the entire country including the ministry. Developing potential offshore petroleum resources is a dominant ambition of the Lebanese politicians, who are banking on the sector to emerge from the debt crisis. The first offshore exploration phase was intended to start at the end of 2019 along with the second round of licensing, but was later delayed to the first quarter of 2020. No commercially viable discoveries have yet been made, but any potential discovery will completely shift the government's focus and possibly derail the renewable energy plans, as has been the case in emerging petroleum producers.

Renewable energy institutions developed with the evolvement of the sector, but they have in general safeguarded the monopoly of one entity, and dismissed a wide range of stakeholders. The global efforts in diversification have showcased the importance of engaging a wide level of actors in reaching a sustainable transition and deploying renewable energy, which is not witnessed in the region.

The Jordanian EDAMA initiative was launched in 2008–2009 as a coordinating umbrella in the sector, but was later on dismissed. NERC along with several NGOs could play a role, but there is not enough current political will to engage them. The sector is managed and operated by MEMR. JREEEF is supposed to provide loan guarantees for renewable energy and energy efficiency systems for small and medium enterprises and the residential sector. In practice, the fund has mainly supported renewable energy systems in schools and for the lowest-consuming residential consumers, and is reported to be politicized, requiring restructuring.

The Lebanese experience is different, but not less complex. LCEC grew from a UNDP project in 2005 into the national sector's umbrella in 2011, becoming the technical arm of the MoEW, where is it lodged, despite having financial and administrative autonomy. The center is registered as an NGO, although it is commonly treated by stakeholders as a government entity, and is dealing with all renewable energy matters; including national policies, technical implementation, procurement, and playing a technical role in NEEREA financing, with insufficient institutional capacity. The NEEREA fund requires a lengthy process that has become more difficult due to Lebanon's escalating economic crisis and liquidity shortage, thus disheartening end-users from tapping into the fund, leaving only the share of consumers that can sustain themselves to consider renewable energy. An assessment of the fund recipients shows that the highest share of the fund went to green buildings.

One major issue limiting the implementation of renewable energy in Lebanon has been the absence of an independent regulatory authority, in charge of issuing licenses. The council of ministers has been granted the authority to issue licenses for two to three-year periods, through different laws: law 288 of 2014, law 54 of 2015, and law 129 of 2019. Upon expiry of these laws, there would be no operating laws enabling private developers to generate electricity, such as the period between the expiry of law 54 in April 2018 and the enactment of law 129 in April 2019, and which obstructed the award and licensing of the first utility-scale solar PV farms.

In Palestine, several authorities share the mandate of supporting renewables: the Energy Authority (PEA), the Palestinian Energy and Environment Research Center (PEC), and the Palestinian Electricity Regulatory Council (PERC).

As renewable energy is cross-sectorial, inconsistency in policies across the value chains has negative repercussions on the sector. The three countries suffer from the lack of taxation policy consistency. Jordan's taxation policy is ever changing; from income taxes, to imports/exports and customs, leaving businesses wary of the government. In Palestine, renewable energy technologies receive an exemption from import duties and Value Added Tax, yet, the process is complicated as materials go through Israeli ports. Renewable energy technologies in Lebanon should be tax exempted but businesses report uncertainty over a recent 3% tax, though there are discussions that it will be waived.

Fueling the Competition

While alternative energy deployment should be hailed as a game changer for highly indebted, net energy-importing economies, changing the outlook of an otherwise extremely costly and monopolized energy market, it would be fueling a direct competition with the traditional electricity utilities, the fossil fuel imports industry, and the informal private generators industry in Lebanon only, and the vested interests in the political economy, and may trigger a regional rivalry or potential collaboration.

Battling with Traditional Utilities

The core of the electricity utility business is impacted by powerful emerging trends and developments including the volatility of fossil fuels, the growing investments in energy efficiency, the pressure to decrease greenhouse gas emissions, accelerating number of prosumers[36] (the traditional consumers, whose role was changed into generating their own electricity needs), and decentralized energy generation.

On the political level, the decentralization concept in general faces opposition across the Middle East, as monopoly and centralized decision-making are key aspects of the prevailing political and governance models.

The electricity utilities in the region, adopting the single-buyer model and subsidies, are accumulating fiscal losses whenever they generate or purchase power. Whereas decentralized power generation decreases the demand from the utility's side, therefore cutting down on these fiscal losses, it also threatens to make the electricity utilities lose their highest paying consumers, and as such, the bulk of their revenues, especially when subsidy reforms are partially or fully implemented and electricity tariffs are hiked.

The most straightforward approach to subsidy elimination for governments has been to increase the tariff for the highest consumers, while safeguarding the vulnerable population and small productive activities. As a result, those high-paying consumers are seeking alternatives, implementing rooftop solar and other distributed generation mechanism.[37]

The threat to the utilities is growing in Jordan and Palestine but is yet to be felt in Lebanon, which has not embarked on subsidy reforms. For NEPCO, the revenues from the highest paying consumers cover a significant share of the losses incurred from the subsidies retained for the lowest consumers, and the utility cannot afford to lose them. Consequently, as reported by interviewees, the Jordanian utility has been hesitant to grant permissions for power wheeling, especially for commercial banks and hotels, blaming the weakness of the grid. Eventually in 2019, the government halted licenses for energy projects of a capacity higher than 1 MW, until grid was reinforced and in an attempt to delay restructuring the power market.

Palestine's distribution companies are the threat to solar energy. These companies purchase power from Israel and make significant profits. Yet, the cost of power from rooftop solar systems currently stands for the end-user at 10% less than electricity purchases, risking deflections from the grid, and major revenue losses for the distribution companies.

Competing with Fossil Fuels

While the competition with the utilities is still nascent, the long history of fuel imports has created vested interests across the value chain that renewable energy threatens.

As these economies are not petroleum producers, there is no concrete obvious internal pressure to maintain fossil fuels' dominance. However, alternative energy creates a wide set of winners and losers, with the latter being led by the fossil fuel industry, casting no doubt that there is a sort of competition, although not easily quantifiable.

Across the value chain, petroleum companies, fuel importers, and distributors, among others, have been making hefty revenues from the fuel dominance in quasi-monopolized economies. The key demonstration of the vested interests is the chronic lack of willingness to change the electricity sector. Despite continuous discussions in Jordan to improve the electricity sector, and deal with NEPCO fiscal deficit, the government has not yet taken any serious efforts. Lebanon's plans to switch to natural gas date back to mid-2000s and have been formalized and adopted by the Lebanese parliament through the 2010 policy paper for the electricity sector, but have constantly been stalled. The plan included the implementation of one Floating Storage Regasification Unit (FSRU), a vital component of LNG supply, but was changed in 2018 to three units to be placed in regions with three different dominant powers and sects, and officials haven't shied away from declaring the move from one to three units is for political reasons. The tender for the procurement of the three units was launched end of May 2018, and the bid offers opening took place in July 2019, but was not yet awarded in the fall of 2020.

Moreover, the fiscal drain caused by the shortage of electricity supply has been acknowledged by the succeeding governments for more than two decades, yet, the sector has never been fixed, and thermal power plants have not been implemented since the year 1999. Only a minor total addition of 270 MW took place in 2017. In addition to the fuel industry, the private diesel generators proliferating due to the shortage of electricity supply since the year 1994 have grown into a $2 billion industry that would lose market shares to renewable energy.

There is however a consensus among interviewees that the vested interests and the competition with fossil fuels are a minor factor hindering the renewable energy progress, compared to the overall inefficiency of the political systems in both Jordan and Lebanon. Across the energy sphere, there's cultural resistance, regardless of educational attainment, to renewable energy, by individuals used to doing things in a certain way, who believe that renewables are too complex to integrate, or worse, that they are a myth. The share of young generation, typically more open to new approaches and technologies, is trivial in government, policy, and decision-making.

Triggering Regional Rivalry

On the regional level, alternative energy may increase the prospects for electricity exchange across interconnected grids, which may also subject these countries to a risk of political instability, and a switch of vulnerability from a supply disruption caused by pipeline wars, to one caused by grid wars. Yet, it may also be a driver of more regional cooperation and mutual interdependence. The opportunity is especially there for Jordan to become an exporter of electricity, provided the infrastructure is developed and the politics permit the power exchange.

With its current excess of power generation, Jordan needs to export electricity to neighboring countries. If this opportunity is presented, the kingdom can leapfrog renewable energy implementation and move from a petroleum importer to an electricity exporter, such as exporting to Iraq. In fact, developing an electricity exchange market will be a major enabler of alternative energy deployment in the region, decreasing the need for expensive better storage, and enabling more stability in the grid and flexibility in the system.

If Lebanon's 2019 policy paper is implemented, and the planned conventional generation capacities are built, then the country will face the same prospect as Jordan, and will need external markets for its electricity in order to further add renewable energy capacity.

Complex regional politics however mean that an Arab electricity exchange market is easier planned than executed. Jordan currently has an interconnected grid with Syria, which is in turn connected to Lebanon suffering from a shortage in electricity supply. It may seem as a match made in heaven, except that for political and economic purposes, Syria would not allow Jordan to wheel power through its transmission grid. Syria, suffering from a liquidity shortage, would rather sell electricity to Lebanon, instead of only wheeling it.

Talks about establishing links between Gulf and Levant countries have been taking place. It remains unclear if such links will start regional grid rivalries or will lead to a more collaborative environment. In early January 2019, following a feasibility assessment, a Jordanian-Saudi technical committee approved the plans of building an interconnection between the two countries through a 170 km transmission line, expected to be completed in 2022. Jordan is also planning a grid connection with Iraq, and Saudi Arabia is also eyeing a connection to Iraq.

Conclusion

Alternative energy would significantly improve the energy security of economies in the Levant by diversifying the sources of supply and enhance the economy by reducing the cost fuel and electricity imports and subsidies. But despite governments' drive, targeted pledges, and policy instruments, the economies have fallen behind their 2020 targets, mostly due to the lack of long-term planning, the weakness of institutions, the inconsistency of policy, and the low ranking of alternative energy on the cabinets' agendas.

The major strength of alternative energy is that it can challenge the status quo and overcome the governance bottlenecks in Lebanon through distributed generation, and decrease dependence on foreign actors in Jordan and Palestine. In fact, Jordan could also move from being an energy importer to becoming an electricity exporter. But aspirations are obstructed by the political context and regional rivalries. Competition with fossil fuels and vested interests across the value chain are present, but are less of an impediment than the overall inefficient political systems.

The political rivalry and clashes across the system, and the opposing forces sharing power, are a major cause of delays in diversification and, as a rule of thumb, across all sectors.

The system beats everything, including alternative energy disruptions.

Notes

1. EDAMA, *Jordan Clean Technology Sector: Report 2016* (Amman, 2016), 10.
2. Ministry of Environment/UNDP, *Fossil Fuel Subsidies in Lebanon: Fiscal, Equity, Economic and Environmental Impacts* (Beirut, 2015), 2.
3. Ministry of Energy and Mineral Resources, *Energy 2019—Facts and Figures* (Amman, 2019).
4. Ministry of Environment/UNDP, *Optimal Renewable Energy Mix of the Power Sector by 2020: Investment Cost Implications for Lebanon* (Beirut, 2015), 1.
5. Ministry of Energy and Water, *Updated Policy Paper for the Electricity Sector* (Beirut, 2019).
6. Jessica Obeid, "The 3-Decade Impossible Power Sector Reforms", Italian Institute for International Political Studies, March 13, 2020, https://www.ispionline.it/it/pubblicazione/lebanon-3-decade-impossible-power-sector-reforms-25377.
7. Ibid.
8. EDAMA, *Jordan Clean Technology Sector: Report 2016* (Amman, 2016), 10.
9. Aziz Atamanov, Jon Jellema, and Umar Serajuddin, "The Cost of Reform in Jordan: Petroleum and Electricity Subsidies", *World Bank* (2015), 2.
10. World Bank/ESMAP, *West Bank and Gaza Energy Efficiency Action Plan 2020–2030* (Washington, DC, 2016), 26.
11. According to a government official, the target of 5% renewable energy of primary demand by 2020 equates 130 MW.
12. World Bank/ESMAP, *Securing Energy for Development in West Bank and Gaza* (Washington, DC, 2016), 5.
13. World Bank, *Electricity Sector Performance Improvement Project: Palestine* (Washington, DC, 2018), 4.
14. Modified by the Government of Jordan upwards in 2018 from the 2007 target of 10%.
15. Data Computed from NEPCO, Bulletin 2018 (2018), 1.

16. Barbara Franceschini, "Scaling Up Renewable Energy Development in Jordan", RES4MED (2019), 4.
17. Ministry of Energy and Mineral Resources, *Wind Map of Jordan* (Amman, 2007).
18. UNDP/CEDRO, *The National Wind Atlas of Lebanon* (Beirut, 2011), 27.
19. Net-metering is an electricity billing mechanism that credits renewable energy system owners for the electricity that is not used on-site and instead is injected into the grid.
20. Power wheeling is the transportation of electricity through transmission lines. In the case of renewables, it allows the implementation of a renewable energy project in a site location, and offsetting the electricity consumption in another site.
21. Barbara Franceschini, "Scaling Up Renewable Energy Development in Jordan", RES4MED (2019), 4.
22. Majd Batarseh, "Wind Energy Production in Jordan", Princess Sumaya University for Technology Jordan (2017).
23. Jessica Obeid, "The Cost of Simplistic Power Purchase", Castlereagh Associates, May 30, 2019, https://castlereagh.net/the-cost-of-simplistic-power-purchase/.
24. Ibrahim Marei, "Revisiting the Regulatory Framework: A Necessary Action to Promote the Deployment of Renewable Energy Sources for Electricity in Jordan", *Renewable Energy Law and Policy Review*, Vol. 7, No. 1 (2016): 47.
25. World Nuclear Association, "Nuclear Power in Jordan", June 2019, https://www.world-nuclear.org/information-library/country-pro files/countries-g-n/jordan.aspx.
26. Lebanese Center for Energy Conservation, *2018 Solar PV Status Report for Lebanon* (Beirut, 2019), 14.
27. World Bank/ESMAP, *Securing Energy for Development in West Bank and Gaza* (Washington, DC, 2016), 9.
28. Ibid.
29. Oxford Business Group, *The Report: Emerging Jordan 2007* (London, 2007), 127.
30. Prior to the pipeline attacks, Jordan relied on imported Egyptian natural gas for 80% of its electricity generation equivalent to 6.8 million cubic meters per day.
31. OECD, *OECD Clean Energy Investment Policy Review of Jordan*, Green Finance and Investment (Paris, 2016), 20.
32. The law was later replaced with the General Electricity Law No. 13 of 1999, and Law No. 64 in 2002.
33. Hashemite Kingdom of Jordan, *Updated Master Strategy of Energy Sector in Jordan for the period 2007–2020* (Amman, 2007).

34. Chen Herzog, Norden Shalabna, and Guy Maor, "Israel Natural Gas Demand Forecast 2017–2040", BDO Consulting (2017), 19.
35. Hashemite Kingdom of Jordan, *Updated Master Strategy of Energy Sector in Jordan for the period 2007–2020* (Amman, 2007), 17.
36. Fereidoon P. Sioshansi, "Decentralized Energy: Is It as Imminent or Serious as Claimed?" in *Distributed Generation and Its Implications for the Utility Industry*, ed. Fereidoon P. Sioshansi (Cambridge, MA: Academic Press, 2014), 4.
37. Jessica Obeid, "Middle East Utilities vs Distributed Generation: a Losing Battle", Castlereagh Associates, June 25, 2019, https://castlereagh.net/middle-east-utilities-vs-distributed-generation-a-losing-battle/.

CHAPTER 9

Governance Amid the Transition to Renewable Energy in the Middle East and North Africa

Paasha Mahdavi and Noosha Uddin

Introduction

Despite its status and reputation as a region dominated by petro-states, the Middle East and North Africa is making strides toward the transition to renewable energy. At the forefront among the oil-exporting states is the United Arab Emirates, which has emphasized the need to reduce reliance on petroleum by adopting new energy technologies that can spur growth and employment. The UAE hosts 79% of the solar photovoltaic capacity in the Gulf and has done so largely without offering subsidies to developers and investors.[1] Its national energy strategy aims to increase the share of clean energy in the country's electricity generation capacity

P. Mahdavi (✉) · N. Uddin
UC Santa Barbara, Santa Barbara, CA, USA
e-mail: paasha@ucsb.edu

N. Uddin
e-mail: noosha@ucsb.edu

R. Mills and L.-C. Sim (eds.), *Low Carbon Energy in the Middle East and North Africa*, International Political Economy Series,
https://doi.org/10.1007/978-3-030-59554-8_9

to 50% by 2050. Likewise, Iran, Kuwait, and Saudi Arabia have sought renewables investments as a means to free up petroleum for export, lower greenhouse gas emissions, and create new jobs and local businesses.

Yet there is broad variation in how successful and effective these investments are in displacing fossil fuels at nontrivial levels, as shown in Fig. 9.1. For example, the share of renewable energy in national electricity generation (excluding hydroelectric power) ranges from less than 0.1% in Bahrain and Oman, to 0.2% in Iran and Saudi Arabia, to a maximum of 2.0% in the UAE. Furthermore, there exists a divide in how renewable energy plays a role in the national economy. In Saudi Arabia and Iran, renewables primarily serve to increase oil exports through efforts such as displacing domestic oil consumption and using renewable electricity for enhanced oil recovery and petroleum processing. In the UAE, renewables serve not just to free up oil for export (rather than domestic

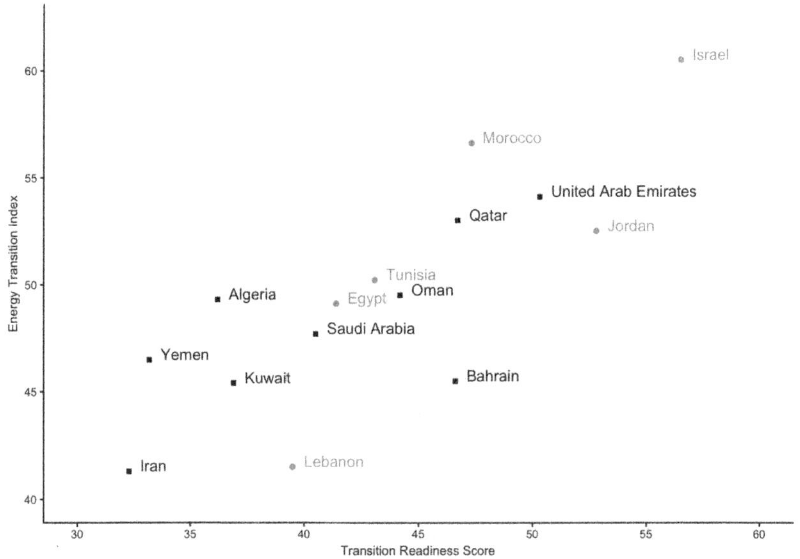

Fig. 9.1 Energy transition indicators in the Middle East and North Africa. Higher values correspond to greater advances and preparedness for making the transition to renewable energy. Major oil and gas exporting states are represented by black square points, non-oil-exporters are represented by gray circles. Data are missing for Iraq, Libya, and Syria (*Data source* World Economic Forum)

consumption), but to the long-term goal of making the UAE a regional hub capable of becoming a major exporter of renewable energy services and technical knowledge. In oil-poor Jordan and Morocco, renewable energy will provide the means to escape from energy shortages and a heavy reliance on imports for total energy consumption—96% in Jordan and 95% in Morocco. In war-torn Yemen, renewable energy is crucial in providing energy access; as of 2019, the country's current generation capacity can only satisfy one-third of its demand.

What explains this variation? And what do these different choices imply for domestic and international politics? In this chapter, we draw on political economy theories to explore the transition from conventional energy to renewable energy in the MENA region. We first establish the theoretical framework in the context of the resource curse hypothesis and the theory of the rentier state. We then apply this framework to provide implications for the transition from conventional to renewable energy. Here, we build an argument that the renewable energy transition will diffuse existing and future societal pressures by increasing youth employment, hindering corruption, and reducing fiscal volatility. Compared to the concentrated political economy of petroleum-reliant states, we argue that the up and coming renewables sector provides an opportunity for these states to broaden and diversify their sources of economic and international political power. We conclude with a set of potential scenarios drawn from best practices in the region to reduce dependence on fossil fuels.

Political Implications of Conventional Energy Resources

Theory of the Rentier State

'No representation without taxation.' This reversal of the American Revolution's byword is the core of the idea that natural resources such as oil and gas hinder democratic governance. In contrast to taxing its citizens to finance state expenditures, a 'rentier state'—defined as a state which generates income by collecting an external rent, such as the sale of petroleum and minerals—has no need for taxing the income of its citizens. As such, rentier states are not dependent on the complicity of their citizens when making fiscal decisions. Instead, according to the rentier state theory, this type of state plays a provisory role, whereby leaders purchase support using rents to provide public goods and patronage, buying off more people with larger packages of money than their non-rentier state counterparts.

While Karl Marx, and to a lesser extent Adam Smith, is widely credited with the appellation of the 'rentier state,' two scholars of the Middle East are cited as the first to apply this moniker to a theory of political economy. The first is Hussein Mahdavy, an Iranian economist, who is best known for making the claim in 1970 that the existence of an external fiscal revenue source, such as oil sales or foreign aid, widens the gap between citizens and their government. In his words, 'a government that can expand its services without resorting to heavy taxation acquires an independence from the people seldom found in other countries.'[2] This assertion has come to be the foundation on which rentier state theory is built.

It took nearly two decades before Mahdavy's work was revisited, this time by the Egyptian economist and onetime Prime Minister Hazem Beblawi, who took up the self-prescribed onus of propagating Mahdavy's theory. In his 1987 book with Giacomo Luciani, *The Rentier State*, Beblawi explores the instrumental value of the theory by applying it to the 'prominence of the oil economies in the Arab region.'[3] Beblawi's most accredited contribution to the rentier state theory is to make the theory more than a simple classification system of the different types of economies in the world. In its most concise form, Beblawi's general hypothesis is that rentier states will suffer 'a serious blow to the ethics of work' that 'pervert[s] the economic system' and leads to an inefficient burgeoning of 'a huge bureaucracy.'[4] In addition to reducing labor productivity, resource rents hinder the development of fiscal accountability and discipline. This was best captured by Luciani's later argument of an 'allocative strategy' of rentier states. In short, Luciani posits that petroleum sales provided the oil-rich MENA countries with the means to spend lavishly on providing public sector jobs and targeted benefits to loyal elites, which increased overall support for incumbent regimes.[5] Non-rentier states, by contrast, lack the fiscal means for such allocation and instead rely on measured redistribution of revenues from taxation.

The Political Resource Curse[6]

These theoretical propositions served as the foundation for a new paradigmatic contract between states and their citizens, and subsequently, for a larger hypothesis regarding the negative development effects of rentierism. The former, now referred to as the rentier social contract, is a transactional civic relationship whereby 'the state provides goods and services to society (such as subsidies on basic commodities) without imposing economic burdens, while society provides state officials with a degree of autonomy in decision-making and policy.'[7]

This channel provided the basis for a theoretical extrapolation to explain why so many oil-rich states suffered from authoritarianism and generally negative governance outcomes, such as corruption, bureaucratic inefficiencies, and targeted repression. The political components were first explicated by Terry Lynn Karl, who proposes that the characteristics of a country's leading export sector tend to influence the state's capacity to promote development.[8] Karl argues that a reliance on petroleum, rather than manufacturing, services, or agriculture, fosters weak institutions that constrains the state's ability to adapt to changing economic market conditions—such as the collapse of commodity prices or the expansion of trade openness. Michael Ross expands this argument to construct a political theory of the resource curse: resources such as petroleum provide rulers with revenues for repression, patronage, and the tools to dampen pressures for accountable government.[9] Thus, oil—and natural resources like it—are posited to hinder democracy and instead provide avenues for the endurance of authoritarian regimes.[10]

This 'curse' in political terms therefore seeks to explain why so few states of the oil-rich Middle East and North Africa did not democratize, have such long-lasting autocrats, and suffer from bureaucratic inefficiency, corruption, human rights violations, and large-scale censorship of the press. In economic terms, oil wealth is linked to unemployment, economic stagnation, stifled innovation, and fiscal imbalances, among myriad other maladies. Jeffrey Sachs and Andrew Warner set the foundations for the broader study of the economic resource curse by showing statistical evidence that countries rich in natural resources have systematically lower levels of economic growth than non-resource-rich countries.[11] Their finding led to rigorous scholarly debate questioning the mechanisms and measures underpinning this correlation—and whether this correlation is spurious or, if not, whether it only applies to the post-1973 period once states had nationalized their oil sectors—and whether it applies to other natural resources, such as metals and minerals.[12] Of particular relevance to the MENA countries is the investigation of the productivity-damaging effects of resource wealth, whereby commodity booms hinder entrepreneurship and instead divert efforts into non-productive, rent-seeking activities.[13] This is partly explained by extreme under-investment in the education sector following resource booms, such that resource wealth effectively crowds out the conditions needed for the development of human capital.[14]

Under What Conditions Are Resources a Curse or a Blessing?

Yet the 'curse' is clearly not ubiquitous: the theory could not explain the emergence of established oil-rich democracies such as the United States, Canada, Norway, and the UK, nor the wave of democratization that hit the oil-rich states of Latin America. Hence the theory shifted to a 'conditional resource curse,' whereby certain pre- and post-resource-discovery conditions mediated the negative effects of petroleum on politics.[15] Thad Dunning, for instance, argues that the interaction between resource wealth and income inequality explains why oil reduced the likelihood for democratization in Angola, Algeria, and Nigeria, but not in Brazil, Colombia, Mexico, and Venezuela.[16] Dunning's argument implies that relatively low levels of income inequality in the MENA, combined with high dependence on resource wealth, made elites wary of democratization for fear of losing these rents to distributive demands. In explaining the persistence of democracy in the UK and the US, Timothy Mitchell argues that fossil fuel production—particularly coal—created a new political base of power in the form of unions and working-class organizations.[17] These provided the means for a classic modernization effect, whereby unions demanded more progressive and inclusive policies from their governments. Oil, by contrast, did not have the same effects given its capital intensity; the death of oil-based labor movements under Thatcher certainly attests to this vision of energy political history.

Much of the basis for earlier claims about the effects of natural resources on politics is that these resources were by and large 'exogenous.' That is, these theories assumed that political forces did not shape the production of resources, but rather that resource endowments were due to chance: some countries were lucky to have oil and therefore could reap its benefits as though they were 'manna from heaven.' This is now known to be a problematic assumption, given the political determinants of whether a country cultivates its natural resource wealth and ultimately becomes reliant on its revenues.[18] Victor Menaldo, for instance, argues that the strength of institutions prior to the discovery of extractive resources determines a country's extraction strategy.[19] Countries with weak institutions—including those left by problematic colonial legacies—were more likely to develop their natural resources without the ability to also foster the human capital for a developed, technically-advanced economy. By contrast, countries with strong pre-discovery institutions could invest in natural resource extraction alongside diversified economies. As such, according to Menaldo, the relationship between the high levels of oil dependence on GDP and bad governance is spurious: weak institutions are to blame for both.

Concerns Beyond the 'Curse'

Reliance on fossil fuels is the basis for a multitude of political and societal ills beyond its effects on accountable government and healthy labor markets. One that is particularly relevant for the MENA states is the persistence of fossil fuel consumer subsidies in the form of below-market prices for gasoline, diesel, natural gas, and other petroleum products. Globally, these subsidies are an enormous fiscal burden for the governments that support them. The World Bank and the International Monetary Fund estimates for fossil fuel subsidies vary from half a trillion to two trillion dollars per year, depending on the choice of alternative definitions, assumptions, and methods.[20] In addition, consumer fuel subsidies are regressive in that the primary beneficiaries are upper-class consumers who own vehicles, although the removal of subsidies disproportionately affects the poor.[21]

Low prices for gasoline are particularly prevalent in the MENA when compared to the rest of the world. The average tax on gasoline outside the MENA across the 2003–2015 period was 58.4 US cents per liter, while among the MENA countries the average tax was *negative*, implying a subsidy of 14.8 cents per liter (Fig. 9.2, top panel). The average is notably pulled down by the region's oil exporters, where gasoline is subsidized at 38.6 cents per liter (i.e., taxed at -38.6 cents per liter), compared to the non-oil-exporters in the MENA, where gasoline is taxed at 34.9 cents per liter (Fig. 9.2, bottom panel).[22] Indeed, the region's oil exporters—Algeria, Bahrain, Iran, Iraq, Kuwait, Libya, Oman, Qatar, Saudi Arabia, Syria, the UAE, and Yemen—maintain some of the lowest gasoline prices in the world.[23] This group of countries are, on average, consistently below the international market price for gasoline during this period, and remain

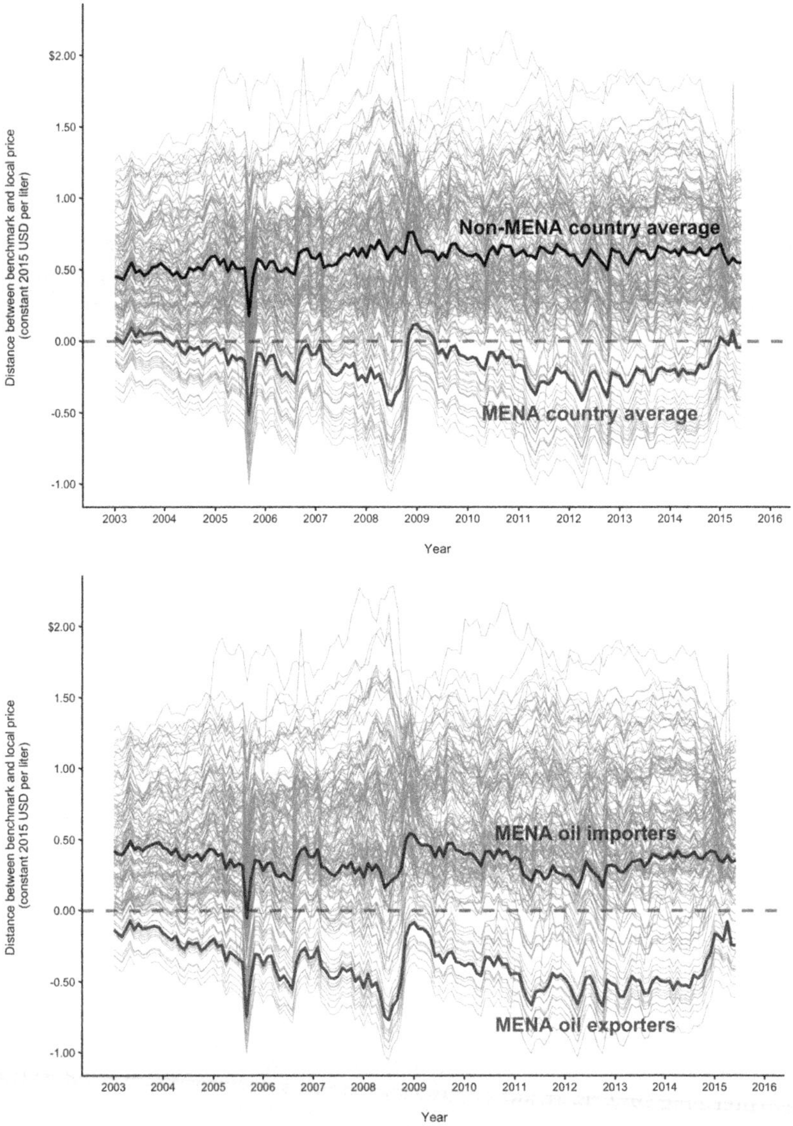

Fig. 9.2 Monthly trends in country-level gasoline taxes and subsidies, 2003–2015. Averages for the MENA countries and non-MENA countries highlighted in bold (top panel); averages for MENA oil exporters and MENA non-oil exporters highlighted in bold (bottom panel). See text for country groupings (*Data source* Ross, Hazlett, and Mahdavi 2017)

so even after several subsidy reforms in the 2015–2017 period of low oil prices.[24] Meanwhile, the region's oil importers—Egypt, Israel, Jordan, Lebanon, Morocco, and Tunisia—maintain relatively low gasoline taxes, especially when compared to European and East Asian states, though are on par with gasoline prices in North America and in emerging markets in Latin America and Sub-Saharan Africa.[25]

The negative fiscal impacts of subsidies vary for countries that are able to produce petroleum and other energy sources at below-market costs, though the net fiscal effects are nonetheless quite impactful. In Saudi Arabia, for instance, the cost of refining gasoline from local oil is far below the international market price for refined gasoline given local oil production costs in the range of $3 to $10 per barrel (compared to market prices at $55 to $75 per barrel). The effective subsidy is nevertheless large if we compare local prices to the opportunity cost of selling domestic oil on the international market, despite a low marginal cost of supply that masks the true fiscal cost of the subsidy, holding production fixed.[26]

Implications for Renewable Energy

In the late 1980s, at the height of the 'oil glut,' oil prices were at their lowest levels since before the Arab Oil Embargo and oil-producers around the world were suffering from severe fiscal (and existential) crises. Governments were suddenly unable to deliver on their spending commitments, facing rising pressure from elite supporters and the broader public. Outside the MENA, once mighty oil-financed regimes collapsed and ushered in more democratic governments. The sustained period of low oil prices in the 1980s and lingering into the 1990s is argued to be a key driver in regime collapses from the Soviet Union to Mexico. Indeed, this spurred broader claims derived from the political resource curse whereby as the price of oil sinks lower, the more resilient is representative government.[27]

MENA leaders by and large escaped this fate, but still suffered from worsening economic conditions, mounting fiscal deficits, and weakening legitimacy in their ability to maintain their end of the rentier social contract. When these leaders ultimately went to the IMF for financial rescue, the consensus advice was that these countries needed to reduce dependency on fossil fuels because of the severe volatility of oil markets.[28] Leaders of the MENA petro-states saw this not as a means to reduce fiscal dependence on these commodities, but rather as a call to establish ever-larger petroleum savings accounts that accumulate wealth in boom periods to cover deficits in bust periods.[29] Of course, few states heeded this advice prior to the oil price collapse of 2014 (with the exception of Iran and the UAE, whose reforms preceded the price shock).

Now the case can be made in terms of life-and-death: advisers and multilateral agencies will argue for the transition before assets are stranded and because it will solve massive unemployment. A 'do-nothing' approach is fiscally unsustainable: international climate policy pressure and rise of low-carbon technology will eventually displace reliance on hydrocarbons, leaving all but the most low-cost extractors out of business.

The volatility-induced fiscal crises of fossil fuel dependency would pale in comparison with the fiscal cliff that awaits because of the transition. The IEA estimates that low demand for oil and gas could lead to losses on the order of 25% to 40% of petroleum revenue over the 2020–2040 period.[30] The sheer magnitude of this pitfall is staggering: according to a Citicorp report in 2015, approximately $100 trillion worth of fossil assets could be stranded by 2050 to stay below 2 °C.[31] The potential loss of one-quarter to two-fifths of government revenue is enough to send shockwaves through society and increase mass pressure for investment in decarbonized solutions.

While this may play out less dramatically in the low-carbon-intensive oil producers—Saudi Arabia, Bahrain, Qatar, Kuwait, and the UAE—it will be particularly problematic for high-carbon-intensive producers, namely Algeria, Iran, Sudan, Yemen, Iraq, and Oman. Algeria, for example, is estimated to have the highest carbon intensity of crude in the world, at 20.3 grams of carbon dioxide per megajoule of crude oil ($gCO_2eq./MJ$) compared to the global average of 10.3 $gCO_2eq./MJ$ and to the astoundingly low 4.6 $gCO_2eq./MJ$ of Saudi Arabia.[32] The carbon tax on an Algerian barrel of oil would be roughly four times that of a Saudi barrel of crude.[33] In an oil-constrained world, any nontrivial price on carbon would all but strand oil assets in places like Algeria and Iran from coming to market. Of course, such a tax would be secondary in terms of fiscal impact than the collapse of global oil prices in a carbon-constrained future. Even a high carbon tax of $100/tonne would only result in a roughly $9/barrel loss of revenues for a state like Algeria, which would pale in comparison with a significant decline in oil prices.[34]

From a purely fiscal-driven understanding of leadership decisions,[35] shifting to renewable energy in the medium- to long-term will maximize political survival and stability. As with the oil-glut era of the 1980s, this loss of revenues will threaten to break the rentier social contract if leaders are no longer able to provide goods and services. Following the logic of the resource curse theory, acquiescence will turn into engaged protest—and the oil-producing countries will likely be unable to weather the storms they escaped during the Arab Spring. Even modest declines in petroleum revenue will result in giving up subsidies, which are known to spark protests even for marginal increases.[36]

However, this will depend largely on the time horizons of leaders and regimes in power in the oil-producing states.[37] Most of the dynastic Gulf monarchies—the Houses of Saud, Nahyan, Khalifa, and Sabah—perceive long and lasting rule and therefore see the inherent value of the transition to renewable energy to ensure future survival.[38] By contrast, conflict-plagued regimes in Iraq, Libya, Syria, and Yemen face shorter odds of durable survival and will not place the same political value on potential revenues in 2050, let alone in 2030. And in between these extremes, rulers in Algeria, Egypt, and Iran all strive toward longevity but realize immediate challenges to their rule by either internal opposition parties or external forces. By this logic—and again, from a strictly fiscal perspective—we would expect the greatest political incentives for renewable investment and decarbonization in the Gulf monarchies and the least incentives for leaders in the conflict- and post-conflict regimes.

For the non-oil-exporting states in the MENA—particularly the non-producing states of Jordan, Lebanon, and Morocco—the transition to renewable energy has more straightforward fiscal gains. The costs of petroleum imports are substantial, especially in Egypt and Tunisia, whether directly through the market or indirectly through subsidized imports by the oil producers in exchange for international political support. Renewable energy investments can also reduce volatility in energy prices by decoupling these states from their reliance on imported oil, gas, and (to a lesser extent) coal.

What Is the Impact of Decarbonization on Governance? Will Renewable Energy Provide the Means to 'Escape' the Resource Curse?

In contrast to the economic concentration of conventional energy systems such as oil and gas, we argue that decarbonized energy systems foster diversified economies that mobilize demands for inclusive governance and democratic institutions. This is due to four important characteristics of renewable energy as compared with non-renewable energy systems:

low rents, diffuse systems, energy security, and increased employment opportunities.

The first differing characteristic is the lack of Ricardian, or differential, rents: that is, profits above and beyond classical income resulting from the gap between world market prices and local production costs plus return to capital.[39] This gap exists primarily because of the scarce nature and inelastic demand of commodities such as oil, which accounts for its excessively large rents compared to other commodities. And in the MENA in particular, the oil sector has particularly high differential rents given production costs are often below $10 per barrel compared to $55 to $75 per barrel market prices, due in part by restraining long-term production growth within the OPEC framework. While renewables based in the MENA could potentially boast lower production costs—given its relative abundance of sunlight and wind potential—the obvious lack of global scarcity for these 'commodities' precludes abnormally high market prices. Further, the need for transporting electricity across long distances adds to overall costs.

This loss of rents will change the fundamental nature of the allocative rentier state.[40] Instead of serving as provider of rent-financed patronage and targeted goods and services, the state in a decarbonized energy system will instead be re-allocative. It will serve to redistribute revenues from taxation to the mass public, just as in the traditional economies of non-oil-rich states, notwithstanding variation in the degree to which this wealth is equitably redistributed.[41] This shift from extractive-based fiscal governance to governance based on taxation of the broader economy—such as income taxes, VAT, tourism, or municipality fees—is what Mick Moore refers to as the 'transition to the status of tax states.'[42] Such a system naturally fosters a negotiated relationship between citizens and government, one which involves bargaining for greater institutionalized societal influence over fiscal matters in exchange for higher and higher levels of domestic taxation and, therefore, government revenues.

A system with inherently lower rents also provides fewer incentives for malfeasance and corruption.[43] Across the renewables value chain, there are fewer opportunities for extortion as compared to the complex and opaque segments of the oil system. This begins with differences in upstream value, where would-be extorters can profit from the fixity of assets, such as oil reservoirs and coal mines, while bureaucrats will find less financial value in extorting prospective bidders on specific parcels of land for solar and wind development. While this will vary across states depending on the scarcity of surface areas available for renewables, recent trends in solar auctions in the Middle East suggest a remarkable high level of pricing transparency. In sum, lower rents will, somewhat paradoxically, improve overall governance in the region by improving incentives for fiscal responsibility and accountable institutions.

The second differing characteristic to note is the diffuse structure of renewable energy systems. In contrast to oil, revenue generation from renewable energy is not geographically or vertically limited to points of extraction.[44] Governments can garner tax revenues across the value chain: taxing power generators, distributors, storage facilities, and retail providers; electric vehicle manufacturers and retailers; and end-use consumers in residential, commercial, industrial, and transportation segments. Within the utilities sector specifically, value can be created (and taxed) across six segments, from planning all the way to decommissioning. Planning, installation, and grid connection all entail short-term value and highly-skilled job creation, while manufacturing, operation, and maintenance offer long-term value creation and opportunities for sustained employment.[45] This decentralized system contains both capital- and labor-intensive segments, such that a decarbonized, electrified system—much like Mitchell's (2011) vision of the coal industry in nineteenth-century England and the US—fosters working-class organizations that press leaders for accountable government. This is especially the case if the system is not just decarbonized but also distributed and peer-to-peer.[46]

Third, there is a gained advantage of greater energy security not only in MENA oil-exporting states but especially for the MENA oil-importing states.[47] Given the latter states' abundance of wind and sunshine in contrast to their lack of fossil fuel resources, the oil-importing MENA states have a clear incentive to develop renewable energy as a solution to threats of possible conventional energy scarcity in the future.[48] Additionally, the increasing volatility of conventional energy prices has resulted in unpredictable energy bills for these importing countries—a trend which will be amplified in a future oil-constrained world until reaching a low-price equilibrium for fossil fuels. The prospect of secure renewable resource assets is also relevant for oil-exporting states, whose conventional oil and gas assets tend to be concentrated and vulnerable to outside threats. The drone attack on Saudi oil processing facilities in September 2019, for example, exposed a key vulnerability that knocked out half of Saudi oil production for several weeks and triggered fears about the future value of the country's petroleum sector.[49]

Fourth, and perhaps the most prominent draw to the renewable energy transition, is the potential boon for widespread employment. This is particularly crucial to alleviate the 'labor resource curse' in that the MENA oil and gas producing countries have a terrible track record in terms of labor productivity when compared to non-oil producers.[50] Youth unemployment in the region stands at 30%, with the highest rates in Palestine (43%), Saudi Arabia (42%), Jordan (36%), and Tunisia (36%).[51] Even where unemployment is relatively low, such as in Qatar, the problem is 'solved' by bloating the public sector with redundant jobs.

Labor force issues are only expected to get worse over time. The region's high youth population ratios have spurred some to label youth unemployment as the Middle East's 'ticking time bomb.' The problem is most acute in Palestine, Syria, and Yemen, where young people (ages 15 to 24) make up over 20% of the population.[52] The IMF estimates that roughly 27 million youths will enter the Middle East labor market by 2023, which will significantly inflate unemployment.[53]

The region also suffers from highly gendered employment challenges: only 15% of women are active in the MENA labor force, and unemployment rates are 80% higher among women compared to men (the global average gender differential is roughly 20%).[54] As with the region's other maladies, this is in part due to the gender inequities inherent in an oil-dependent economic system that crowds out manufacturing and service jobs held by women, though such imbalances are still quite prevalent in the oil-importing states as well.[55] Nonetheless, shifting to the more gender-balanced renewable energy sector would narrow the gender employment differential, which by itself could increase regional GDP by up to 7.1% by 2025.[56]

Within these sectors, there are numerous synergies in transitioning petroleum-sector workers to renewables jobs. Biofuels processing facilities share technical similarities with oil-processing plants, while offshore wind platforms necessitate skilled labor for construction, assembly, and deployment that mirrors development of offshore oil and gas platforms. The key to fostering these synergies is the establishment of a competitive renewables manufacturing industry, something which MENA states have so far struggled within the context of petroleum equipment. The more that these governments can do to create incentives and favorable regulations for renewables manufacturing, the greater the opportunities for developing a balanced and sustainable industry—and not one where unemployment arises anew once installations are complete.

Globally, increased investment in decarbonized energy systems has led to sustained employment increases: the International Renewable Energy Agency (IRENA) estimates 7.3 million jobs created from renewables in 2012, increasing up to 11 million new jobs in 2018.[57] One-third of these jobs are in solar photovoltaics, primarily in China, with bioenergy and wind power combining to make up the remainder of non-hydro renewables employment. These improvements have already been realized in several states across the MENA, where even small-scale renewables investments have increased the share of non-fossil energy while simultaneously providing much-needed employment in the country. In Egypt, the first of 41 planned plants of the Benban solar complex opened in 2019 and employs 650 people; construction of the entire complex is expected to require more than 10,000 workers, and 4,000 for operations and maintenance activities. In Iran, the modest solar photovoltaic industry employs roughly 13,500 workers and the wind sector employs 7,100, despite only accounting for 0.2% of electricity generation. Scaling up installations to levels currently seen in countries such as Germany and China—where in 2015 renewables provided 370,000 and 3.4 million jobs, respectively[58]—would not only boost high-skill jobs but also require labor for large-scale construction. The latter are particularly critical for providing a solution to unemployment among non-educated youth.

This is directly relevant to the fossil-dependent countries, who for decades have struggled with unemployment—which, in part, is a direct consequence of their reliance on fossil industries. The oil and gas sector, for example, is a highly capital-intensive industry, one which requires very little labor. In the United States, the top global oil producer at 3.3 billion barrels per year, the oil industry only employs roughly 170,000 people. Not only that, but fossil fuel dependency actively crowds out jobs in other sectors. This is one aspect of the economic resource curse. Fossil exports cause exchange rates to work against exporters in non-fossil sectors such as agriculture, manufacturing, and services (i.e., the 'Dutch Disease') and governments over-invest in fossil extraction at the direct cost of investing in non-fossil segments of the economy.[59] Shifting away from fossil dependence thus provides a net benefit in terms of national employment, even if this turn is not directed toward decarbonized industries.

Summary of Theoretical Expectations for Variation in the Renewable Energy Transition

The theoretical approaches sketched above imply two relevant variables—fiscal reliance on oil exports and government time horizons—that help to explain variation in renewable energy policies in the MENA. While not a formally articulated set of theoretical expectations, these two generally map onto current country experiences with the transition to renewable energy.

At one end are the oil-importing, long-time-horizon governments that have the greatest incentives and capacity to invest in renewable energy. This would include the monarchies of Morocco and Jordan, along with the stable parliamentary republic of Israel. Similarly incentivized are the oil-exporting, long-time-horizon Gulf monarchies. But here we find some variation based on differences in the urgency with which each government sees the coming transition. The UAE, on the one hand, views the transition as inevitable, and has been a leader in renewables investments among the oil-exporters. On the other hand, the Saudi and Kuwaiti governments have been slower to pivot to renewable energy. This could stem in part from the relatively lower climate vulnerability of these states' low-carbon-intensive oil production, though it could also be the result of both states' low costs of oil extraction and hence less fiscal vulnerability as oil markets become more constrained.[60]

At the other end of the spectrum are states that have shorter political time horizons, either due to conflict or post-conflict dynamics or due to increasing domestic political turmoil. Within the net oil importers, namely Lebanon, Egypt, Turkey, and Tunisia, recent transitions and political turmoil have stymied development plans that are sufficiently forward-looking. This political instability notwithstanding, all four states still recognize the inherent value in transitioning to renewable energy in terms of labor and energy security; as such, these four are roughly in the middle in terms of existing and future commitments to renewable energy policies.[61]

The current laggards in the transition are the oil-exporters with short horizons. Governments in Syria, Yemen, Libya, and Iraq carry little political and economic incentives to make long-term adjustments to existing energy policies, given existing challenges to governance in light of ongoing conflict and post-conflict environments. Likewise, current uncertainties in the long-run political survival of regimes in Algeria and Iran have made renewable energy policy a low political priority.[62] This is particularly problematic for these two states given the bleak outlook of their relatively high-carbon-intensive petroleum sectors in an oil-constrained world.

Potential Scenarios for How the Transition Will Affect Fiscal and Political Stability

Will the Rise of Competitive Renewables from Oil Spark Rivalry Between Competing SOEs? Or Will This Instead Result in a Unified, Transformed SOE?

Reforms that advance the transition to non-hydrocarbon sources of energy will unsurprisingly create political adversaries for incumbent leaders. A major fear among MENA oil producers is the potential for challenges from state-owned oil companies. These fears are not without foundation: shifts to renewable energy in sub-Saharan Africa have prompted backlash from prominent SOEs who seek to thwart a broader transition to renewable energy.[63] The seeds for such backlash may already be playing out in the case of Morocco, where the state-owned utility ONEE is grappling with reforms that prioritize public-private development of renewable electricity generation. Despite serving a major coordinating role in the transition, ONEE is witnessing the disruption of its core business model: with a declining pool of customers, the utility is faced with less revenue from electricity sales and a dwindling capacity to provide credible power purchase agreements to new investors.[64]

SOEs such as national oil companies (NOCs) and sovereign wealth funds (SWFs) have traditionally managed the government's largest revenue flows, such that many MENA producers lack a robust, independent financial sector. They also play a crucial role in the labor market: SOE and SOE-related institutions account for much of the state employment in the MENA, where state employment is already a large portion of overall employment. For example, 30% of the Saudi and Iraqi workforce and 15% of the Kuwaiti labor force is employed by SOEs and other government entities.[65] These numbers are significantly higher when looking at the share of national labor: in Kuwait, for instance, over 90% of the non-expatriate labor force is employed by the state.[66]

But if properly governed, SOEs can thrive in a renewable energy system. NOCs in particular are uniquely positioned to pivot into decarbonized investments because they are not 'boxed in' by private investors.[67] If the government makes the decision to veer investments away from fossil fuels, the SOE has the green light to do so and does not have to worry about shareholder backlash. Kuwait offers an interesting example. The 1.5 GW Al Dibdibah (Shagaya Phase II) utility-scale solar PV project is currently managed by the national oil company, KNPC, who is the only market player large enough and managerially competent enough to own and oversee the $1.2 billion investment.[68] Similarly in Oman, the giant 1 GW (heat output) Miraah solar thermal project is owned and co-operated with GlassPoint Solar by the Petroleum Development of Oman (PDO), the country's NOC.[69]

How Can These Countries Reduce Dependency on Fossil Fuels?

In light of existing and future challenges stemming from a reliance on fossil fuels, what have the oil exporters in the region been doing so far to reduce dependence? In brief, producers have been investing in renewables for electricity generation and hedging with investments in low-carbon petroleum production, petrochemicals, and carbon capture and sequestration.

Sustained global competition over the last decade has dramatically reduced generation costs for renewables when compared to conventionals. Figure 9.3, from IRENA, shows the strikingly low relative costs of large-scale solar electricity generation in the Gulf Cooperation Council (GCC) countries. Figures such as these are commonplace now in the Organization for Economic Cooperation and Development (OECD), where solar or wind beats out coal and gas. But this looks specifically at the source: that is, solar is even cheaper than gas in the cheapest place to produce natural gas in the entire world. IRENA reports that in Saudi Arabia, for instance, the winning bid for the 300 MW Sakaka solar PV farm in Saudi Arabia came in at 2.34 cents per kWh, and at 2.13 cents per kWh for the 400 MW Dumat Al Jandal wind project. However, it is important to maintain perspective: renewables, excluding hydroelectric power, are still only 2% of total installed capacity in even the best case (UAE) and 0% in the worst (Sudan). Of course, the share of renewable capacity will only continue to increase as solar and wind costs only recently reached such low levels.

Aside from minimal, but growing, investments into renewable energy for electricity generation, the MENA oil exporters have also been heavily

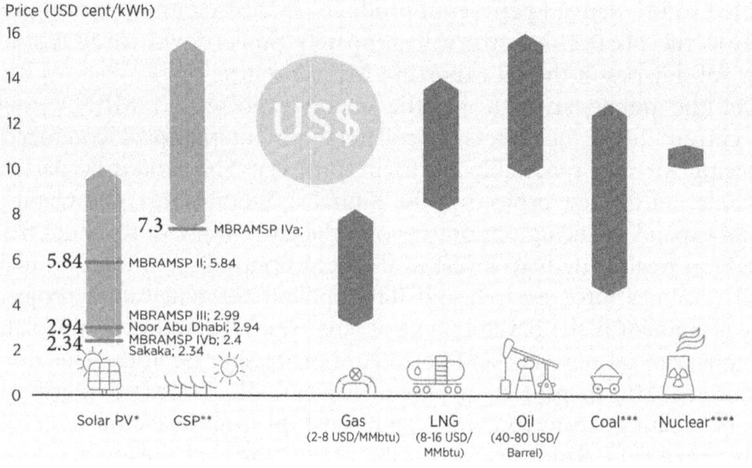

Fig. 9.3 Generation costs in the Gulf Cooperation Council states compared to conventional utility-scale electricity generation (*Image source* IRENA 2019)

investing in petrochemicals. A bet that the oil majors have been making lately to hedge against 'light' decarbonization is increased investment into factories that convert petroleum into plastics and feedstocks, which is a sector that the BP Energy Outlook in 2019 hailed as 'the single-largest projected source of oil demand growth in the next twenty years,' delivering half of global oil consumption growth to 2040.[70] Saudi Arabia's state-owned oil company Aramco, for instance, plans to invest $100 billion by 2030 to converting 2–3 million barrels a day, or 15–25% of total production, into petrochemicals.

But shifting investments from upstream oil exploration to petroleum products is a short-term fix that will not solve the long-term fiscal cliff and unemployment crises that await these countries. Former head of research development for the Abu Dhabi Investment Authority (ADIA), Christof Ruehl, made this argument clear in February 2019 that the possible 'war on plastic' will ultimately flounder long-term demand for oil. This will potentially lead to a 20% reduction in oil demand, larger than the introduction of electric cars to new markets.[71] This has spooked some firms, such as Italy's Eni, into ditching new petrochemicals investments and instead putting their money into bio-petrochemicals using vegetable oil and biomass. While no MENA oil companies have yet pivoted to bio-derived petroleum products, increasing international pressure on the plastics industry will ultimately ripple down to NOCs and their subsidiaries in the oil-exporting MENA states.

On the public-facing front, the energy-exporters in MENA could use current fossil fuel assets as collateral for international commercial financing for new renewable electricity projects. This would be particularly relevant for new projects in the Emirates, Saudi Arabia, and Qatar. It would expand financing options beyond the current use of revenues from sovereign wealth funds to invest in the decarbonized sector and re-invest fossil revenues into research and development for renewables projects. Less prominent is the development of large-scale renewable power plants for enhanced oil recovery and petroleum processing facilities. The aforementioned Miraah project in Oman, for example, is geared specifically toward creating steam to extract additional oil from heavy oil reservoirs in the Amal field. Saudi Arabia, on the other hand, has already developed solar photovoltaic facilities used for powering its oil processing plants.

All states in MENA have in one form or another pitched renewable energy and the decarbonized sector as solutions to build up local industries that can support jobs in ways that the oil industry cannot. This is likely to be the best political strategy to further advance the renewable energy transition particularly in the petro-states, given severe unemployment prospects for the region's youth. And with the 'Arab Spring' uprisings of 2011 still fresh in the memories of the region's leaders, the looming potential for mass youth unemployment—and the social unrest it assuredly brings—could be enough justification to break a century-old business model and seek a new political economy based on renewable energy.

Conclusion

The adoption of renewable energy policies in the Middle East and North Africa invites further analysis into the political and economic implications that may come as a result. These policies can help transform those states in the MENA from their traditional 'rent-seeking' status to one of higher economic development and potential for democratization. Specifically, renewable energy investments have the potential to lower rents, deter corruption at the state level, increase access to energy throughout the region, and implement ample employment opportunities for growing populations. This chapter serves as an introduction to some of these implications and how institutions can promote these developmental goals for the MENA while taking part in the global pursuit divesting from fossil fuels in favor of renewable energy enterprises.

Notes

1. International Renewable Energy Agency (IRENA), (2019), *Renewable Energy Market Analysis: GCC 2019.*
2. Hussein Mahdavy, (1970), "Patterns and Problems of Economic Development in Rentier States: The Case of Iran," in M.A. Cook (ed.), *Studies in Economic History of the Middle East* (London: Oxford University Press), p. 466.
3. Hazem Beblawi and Giacomo Luciani, (1987), *The Rentier State* (London: Croom Helm), p. 50.
4. Hazem Beblawi, (1987), "The Rentier State in the Arab World," in Hazem Beblawi and Giacomo Luciani (eds.), *The Rentier State* (London: Croom Helm), pp. 61 and 66.
5. Giacomo Luciani, "Allocative vs. Production States: A Theoretical Framework," in Giacomo Luciani (ed.), *The Arab State* (Berkeley, CA: University of California Press, 1990), pp. 65–84.
6. Given the chapter's focus on the governance effects of the renewable energy transition, we deliberately limit our discussion of the resource curse to select political components. This, of course, leaves out the broader effects on corruption, civil and interstate conflict, gender and income inequality, and others. For a review of these issues, see Michael Ross (2015), "What Have We Learned About the Resource Curse?" *Annual Review of Political Science* 18: 239–259 and Andrew Rosser (2006), "The Political Economy of the Resource Curse: A Literature Survey," Institute of Development Studies working paper.
7. Quintan Wiktorowicz, (1999), "State Power and the Regulation of Islam in Jordan," *Journal of Church and State*, 41(4): 677–696, p. 680.
8. Terry Lynn Karl, (1997), *The Paradox of Plenty: Oil Booms and Petro-States* (Berkeley, CA: University of California Press).
9. Michael Ross, (2001), "Does Oil Hinder Democracy?" *World Politics* 53(3): 325–361.
10. Benjamin Smith, (2004), "Oil Wealth and Regime Survival in the Developing World, 1960–1999," *American Journal of Political Science* 48(2): 232–246; Michael Ross, (2012), *The Oil Curse* (New York: Princeton University Press); Joseph Wright, Erica Frantz, and Barbara Geddes, (2015), "Oil and Autocratic Regime Survival," *British Journal of Political Science* 45(2): 287–306.

11. Jeffrey D. Sachs and Andrew M. Warner, (1995), "Natural Resource Abundance and Economic Growth," National Bureau of Economic Research Working Paper No. 5398, Cambridge, MA.
12. See van der Ploeg (2011) for a review. On the issue of whether the curse is limited to certain time periods, see Yu-Ming Liou and Paul Musgrave, (2014), "Refining the Oil Curse: Country-Level Evidence From Exogenous Variations in Resource Income," *Comparative Political Studies* 47(11): 1584–1610.
13. James A. Robinson, Ragnar Torvik, and Thierry Verdier, (2006), "Political Foundations of the Resource Curse," *Journal of Development Economics* 79(2): 447–468; Paul Collier and Benedikt Goderis, (2007), "Commodity Prices, Growth and Natural Resource Curse: Reconciling a Conundrum," Centre for the Study of African Economies WP Series #274.
14. Thorvaldur Gylfason, (2001), "Natural Resources, Education, and Economic Development," *European Economic Review* 45(4–6): 847–859.
15. Regarding the institutional conditionality of the economic resource curse, see Halvor Mehlum, Karl Moene, and Ragnar Torvik. "Institutions and the Resource Curse," *The Economic Journal* 116(508): 1–20.
16. Thad Dunning, (2008), *Crude Democracy* (Cambridge, UK: Cambridge University Press).
17. Timothy Mitchell, (2011), *Carbon Democracy: Political Power in the Age of Oil* (Verso Press).
18. Christina N. Brunnschweiler and E.H. Bulte, (2008), "Linking Natural Resources to Slow Growth and More Conflict," *Science* 320: 616–617.
19. Victor Menaldo, (2016), *The Institutions Curse: Natural Resources, Politics, and Development* (Cambridge, UK: Cambridge University Press).
20. Kojima and Koplow (2015), Parry et al. (2014), Coady et al. (2015), Davis (2014, 2016).
21. Jun Rentschler and Morgan Bazilian, (2017), "Reforming Fossil Fuel Subsidies: Drivers, Barriers and the State of Progress," *Climate Policy* 17(7): 891–914.
22. Calculations made based on monthly gasoline price data from Michael Ross, Chad Hazlett, and Paasha Mahdavi, (2017), "Global Progress and Backsliding on Gasoline Taxes and Subsidies," *Nature Energy* 2(16201).
23. Oil exporters are defined here as countries where fuel exports (oil and gas) are more than 50% of total merchandise exports, averaged across the 2003–2015 period. Based on fuel exports (% of merchandise exports) variable from the World Bank World Development Indicators.
24. Note that the UAE simultaneously has the highest gasoline price in the MENA region. See Statistical Appendix of Middle East, North Africa, Afghanistan, and Pakistan REO Update, April 2019, IMF.
25. See Ross, Hazlett, and Mahdavi (2017). Note that the oil-importing MENA states also differ in governance outcomes when compared to the

oil-exporting MENA states, though remain noticeably lower in institutional quality when compared to comparable states in Latin America and Asia. On this debate, see Ross (2012) and Victor Menaldo, (2012), "The Middle East and North Africa's Resilient Monarchs," *Journal of Politics* 74(3): 707–722.

26. Paasha Mahdavi and Michael Ross, (2017), "The Political Economy of Hydrocarbon Wealth and Fuel Prices," UC Berkeley: Center for Effective Global Action.
27. This is a stylized adaptation of the oft-cited "first law of petropolitics," as popularized by the journalist Thomas Freidman in 2009, wherein the "price of oil and the pace of freedom always move in opposite directions." See Thomas Freidman, (2009), "The First Law of Petropolitics," *Foreign Policy* (October).
28. Irfan Nooruddin, (2008), "The Political Economy of National Debt Burdens, 1970–2000," *International Interactions* 34(2): 156–185; Stephen Kretzman and Irfan Nooruddin, (2011), *Drilling into Debt: An Investigation into the Relationship Between Debt and Oil* (Washington, DC: Oil Change International).
29. Benjamin J. Cohen, (2009), "Sovereign Wealth Funds and National Security: The Great Tradeoff," *International Affairs* 85(4): 713–731.
30. IEA World Energy Outlook 2019.
31. Citi GPS: Energy Darwinism II: Why a Low Carbon Future Doesn't Have to Cost the Earth (Citicorp Global Perspectives & Solutions, 2015).
32. Mohammad S. Masnadi, Hassan M. El-Houjeiri, Dominik Schunack, Yunpo Li, Jacob G. Englander, Alhassan Badahdah, Jean-Christophe Monfort et al., (2018), "Global Carbon Intensity of Crude Oil Production," *Science* 361(6405): 851–853. Masnadi et al. (2018) note that roughly 40% of Algeria's high carbon intensity is due to flaring alone, which, in a carbon-constrained world, would be significantly reduced.
33. Much of the difference in estimates arises from lower natural gas flaring at Saudi wells compared to Algerian wells, where routine flaring is substantial.
34. We thank Robin Mills for clarifying this point.
35. Margaret Levi, (1989), *Of Rule and Revenue* (Berkeley, CA: University of California Press).
36. Ross, Hazlett, and Mahdavi, (2017).
37. Paasha Mahdavi, (2020), *Power Grab: Political Survival Through Extractive Resource Nationalization* (Cambridge, UK: Cambridge University Press).
38. Michael Herb, (1999), *All in the Family: Absolutism, Revolution, and Democracy in Middle Eastern Monarchies* (Albany, NY: SUNY Press). The exception would be the House of Thani in Qatar, which do not share the same confident outlook given recent rifts with long-time allies in

the GCC. See Zeina Azzam and Imad K. Harb, eds., (2019), *The GCC Crisis at One Year: Stalemate Becomes New Reality* (Washington, DC: Arab Center Washington DC, Inc.).

39. David Ricardo, (1976 [1871]), *The Principles of Political Economy and Taxation* (London: J.M. Dent and Sons, 3rd edition). See also H. Hotelling, (1931), "The Economics of Exhaustible Resources," *Journal of Political Economy* 39(2): 137–175.
40. Luciani (1990).
41. Of course, lack of access to external rents does not preclude states from pursuing an allocative strategy. Still, decarbonization will remove a key source of revenue typically used for patronage; while these states may continue to adopt such a clientelistic strategy of governance, this will be harder to maintain in the presence of fiscal pressures and redistributive demands.
42. Mick Moore, "Revenues, State Formation, and the Quality of Governance in Developing Countries," *International Political Science Review* 25(3): 297–319.
43. Alberto Ades and Raphael Di Tella, (1999), "Rents, Competition, and Corruption," *American Economic Review* 89(4): 982–993; Rabah Arezki and Markus Brukner, (2012), "Oil Rents, Corruption, and State Stability: Evidence from Panel Data Regressions," *European Economic Review* 55(7). See, however, Pradeep Bardhan and Dilip Mookherjee, (2000), "Corruption and Decentralization of Infrastructure Delivery in Developing Countries."
44. This is not to say there is no value across the rest of the oil supply chain, as several states successfully generate revenues from taxing gasoline and other downstream oil services.
45. International Renewable Energy Agency (IRENA), (2014), *The Socio-Economic Benefits of Solar and Wind Energy.*
46. We thank Li-Chen Sim for this point.
47. This follows a similar rationale for MENA states pursuing nuclear energy though nuclearization is not without its own dependencies (for example, if fuel enrichment is completed abroad).
48. Montassar Kahia, Mohamed Safouane Ben Aïssa, and Charfeddine Lanouar, (2017), "Renewable and Non-renewable Energy Use-Economic Growth Nexus: The Case of MENA Net Oil Importing Countries," *Renewable and Sustainable Energy Reviews* 71: 127–140.
49. Andrew England, Ahmed Al Omran, Najmeh Bozorgmehr, and Demetri Sevastopulo, (2019), "Why Saudi Attacks Changed the Calculations on Regional Security," *The Financial Times*, 20 September 2019. This is not to say that renewable energy systems are without their own vulnerabilities, particularly to long-term transmission lines and highly-concentrated power plants.

50. Simone Tagliapietra, (2019), "The Impact of the Global Energy Transition on MENA Oil and Gas Producers," *Energy Strategy Reviews* 26(100397): 1–6.
51. *Youth Employment in the Middle East and North Africa: Revisiting and Reframing the Challenge*, Brookings Doha Center, February 2019.
52. "Youth Unemployment: The Middle East's Ticking Time Bomb," *Stratfor*, 28 February 2018.
53. Andrew England, (2018), "Middle East Jobs Crisis Risks Fueling Unrest, IMF Warns," *The Financial Times*, 12 July 2018.
54. Ibid.
55. Michael Ross, (2008), "Oil, Islam, and Women," *American Political Science Review* 102(1): 107–123.
56. International Labor Organization, (2016), *World Employment and Social Outlook: Trends for Women 2017*.
57. IRENA, (2019), *Renewable Energy and Jobs Annual Review*.
58. Sharan Burrow, (2015), "How Will Climate Change Affect Jobs?" World Economic Forum.
59. Graham A. Davis, (1995), "Learning to Love the Dutch Disease: Evidence from the Mineral Economies," *World Development* 23(10): 1765–1779.
60. It is interesting to note that Kuwait has struggled with new oil-sector developments as well, pointing to a larger potential problem of state capacity and management of the energy industry.
61. For a more complete assessment of the impact of political instability on the energy transition in Egypt and Turkey, see Hochberg (2021) and Bayulgen (2021), respectively, in this volume.
62. On current instability in Algeria, see Geoff Porter, (2019), *Political Instability in Algeria*, Council on Foreign Relations Contingency Planning Memorandum No. 35. For renewables and political uncertainty in Iran, see Mohammad Hazrati and Zeynab Malakoutikhah, (2019), "An Unclear Future for Iranian Energy Transition in Light of the Re-imposition of Sanctions," *Oil, Gas and Energy Law* 17(1). Note that the shortened government time horizons in these cases also affect state investment in oil and gas exploration, which similarly yields long-term rather than short-term rewards.
63. Alan David Lee and Zainab Usman, (2018), "Taking Stock of the Political Economy of Power Sector Reforms in Developing Countries," World Bank Policy Research Working Paper 8518.
64. Zainab Usman and Tayeb Amegroud, (2019), "Lessons from Power Sector Reforms: The Case of Morocco," World Bank Policy Research Working Paper 8969.
65. Tagliapietra (2019).
66. OBG, (2018), *The Report: Kuwait 2019* (London, UK and Dubai, UAE: Oxford Business Group).

67. Valerie Marcel, (2019), "National Oil Companies of the Future," *Annales des Mines - Responsabilité et environnement* 95: 133–136.
68. IRENA, *Renewable Energy Market Analysis: GCC 2019*. See p. 53.
69. This is a particularly natural fit since the steam from the plant will primarily be used for enhanced oil recovery (EOR), potentially displacing up to 80% of the natural gas currently used for EOR at the heavy Amal oil field. See Steven Moss, "Solar Energy Isn't Just for Electricity," *Scientific American*, 19 April 2019.
70. Nicholas Newman, "The Plastics Backlash Has Some Oil Giants Worried," *Rigzone*, 4 July 2019. See also Christof Ruhl, "The War on Plastic Will Dent Oil Demand More Than Anticipated," *Financial Times*, 17 February 2019.
71. Ruhl (2019). Note that this is based on forecasts of future oil use; petrochemicals currently make up only 10% of demand.

CHAPTER 10

Powering the Middle East and North Africa with Nuclear Energy: Stakeholders and Technopolitics

Li-Chen Sim

Introduction

Between 2000 and 2017, the consumption of electricity in the Middle East and Africa grew from 786 terra-watt hours (TWh) to 1700 TWh. This 116% increase was the largest rise in the world after the Asia-Pacific region (184%) and far ahead of that recorded by third-placed South and Central America at 29%.[1] Electricity demand in the Middle East and North Africa (MENA) is expected to continue, albeit at a more moderate pace of over 3% per annum down from 5.6% between 2007 and 2017.[2] To meet this demand, over $500 billion worth of power projects were ongoing/planned in 2019, with the focus on gas and renewable energy.[3]

L.-C. Sim (✉)
Khalifa University of Science and Technology, Abu Dhabi, United Arab Emirates
e-mail: li-chen.sim@ku.ac.ae

R. Mills and L.-C. Sim (eds.), *Low Carbon Energy in the Middle East and North Africa*, International Political Economy Series,
https://doi.org/10.1007/978-3-030-59554-8_10

Less heralded is the contribution of nuclear-fuelled electricity to electricity demand. According to the International Atomic Energy Agency (IAEA), the 17 TWh or 2.1% of total electricity production currently produced by nuclear power plants in the Middle East and Africa may rise to 163–316 TWh or 6–12% of total electricity production by 2050.[4] Joining Iran's Bushehr unit 1 (1 gigawatt or GW of installed generation capacity) will be MENA's newest nuclear plant in the United Arab Emirates (5.6 GW), which began commercial operations in 2020. Other nuclear newcomers include Turkey (4.8 GW) which is in the early stages of construction at Akkuyu and Egypt (4.8 GW) which has awarded tenders for phase one of the El-Dabaa project but is still in the pre-construction phase. Elsewhere, Saudi Arabia and Jordan are drawing up plans for nuclear power.

The logic of using nuclear energy to power growth in MENA deserves closer attention for several reasons:

- It appears to be somewhat counter-intuitive on several grounds. A new nuclear plant is characterized by long lead times and high financial costs compared to utility-scale solar or wind. Its contribution to environmental sustainability is ambiguous; although it emits the lowest level of greenhouse gas among all major energy production options, it faces significant waste and water withdrawal issues.[5] Nuclear energy promises to provide relative energy independence but could result in increased dependencies on the vendor in host countries without indigenous manpower to operate nuclear plants.
- Enthusiasm for nuclear energy cuts across traditional political, economic, and social cleavages in MENA. These include net energy importers versus exporters, income level, population size, type of political system, degree of economic diversification, and attitudes towards political Islam. Turkey, for example, is a net energy importer with a population of 80 million, a gross domestic product (GDP) per capita of $10,500, and an electoral democracy dominated by the Islamist Justice and Development Party (AKP). In contrast, the United Arab Emirates (UAE) is a net energy exporter with a population of 9.4 million, a GDP per capita of $40,700, and an absolute monarchy. The leadership of both countries, however, desire an indigenous nuclear power capability.
- The choice of reactor vendor and fuel supplier has geopolitical implications. This is because several nuclear newcomers in the region,

which are traditionally American allies, are interested in engaging the leading vendor, Rosatom of Russia. Consequently, Tristan Volpe and Nicholas Miller argue that the US must be more constructive in engaging newcomers like Saudi Arabia because 'Russia and China use trade in civil nuclear technology to gain influence in regions of strategic value'.[6]

This chapter will use the well-established framework known as multi-level perspective (MLP) to analyse why and how a niche technology like nuclear power was adopted in some countries (Iran, UAE, Turkey, and Egypt), seriously under consideration in others (Saudi Arabia and Jordan) but rejected in Kuwait. After all, decisions about nuclear energy took place within shared landscape and niche level environments in MENA. Countries in MENA are also shaped by fossil-fuel-based energy regimes that are strongly embedded in the region's political, economic, and social fabric. While the Gulf monarchies are 'archetypal' rentier states heavily reliant on hydrocarbon revenues, corporations run by well-connected businessmen and military personnel in north African states like Egypt or Tunisia have vested interests in perpetuating energy subsidies.[7]

The first part of the chapter will provide a brief overview of the MLP methodology, including the niche, regime, and landscape levels as they pertain to nuclear energy in MENA. The second part of the chapter will explore interactions between the three levels of analysis through an in-depth case study of the UAE, whose Barakah nuclear plant began operating in 2020. The intention is not to claim that the UAE is representative of the MENA experience in adopting nuclear power. Rather, the detailed case study of the UAE is aimed at understanding and applying the MLP framework; it also facilitates a comparative study of nuclear power in other MENA countries. The third part examines the efficacy of strategies deployed by the UAE and other countries in MENA to sustain the commitment of stakeholders in favour of nuclear energy. Finally, the chapter will weigh the likelihood of the appearance of more nuclear newcomers in MENA in future.

Multi-level Perspective: An Analytical Framework

MLP has been widely used to analyse the sustainability of transitions in food, transport, housing, water, and energy systems. Scholarship on the latter include transitions related to specific technological innovations such as heat pumps, gasifiers, and electric vehicles, as well as to broader changes in energy systems such as the rise of renewable sources like solar and wind, and resistance to change from hydrocarbon-based energy regimes.[8] Although the overwhelming majority of these case studies is Europe-centric, the framework has been used to explore the uptake of renewable energy in the MENA region and in Saudi Arabia and Jordan.[9]

MLP distinguishes between three levels of analysis—niche (micro), regime (meso), landscape (macro)—to understand the extent to which incumbent regimes can be destabilized as a result of developments and processes in other levels. The niche is inhabited by novel innovations as well as the actors and institutions that champion them. In this regard, nuclear-fuelled electricity does not appear to be a niche technology, particularly in the industrialized world. One-tenth of the world's electricity is generated by 450 nuclear reactors located in 30 countries. Around 20 countries including France, South Korea, Russia, Finland, Czech Republic, UK produce at least one-fifth of their electricity from nuclear energy while Italy and Denmark import significant shares of nuclear-fuelled electricity from their neighbours. Nuclear energy is an established, albeit controversial, technology which has even been endorsed by the United Nations' Intergovernmental Panel on Climate Change to keep global warming below the two degrees scenario.

Nevertheless, as far as the MENA region is concerned, nuclear power is a niche technology. In 2019, nuclear power accounted for a mere 0.4% of electricity generation (see Fig. 10.1), making MENA the region with the lowest share of nuclear in total primary energy supply in the world.[10] Several countries host research reactors at academic institutions but these only engage in small-scale niche research into topics such as irradiated barley varieties suited for desert conditions or production of radioisotopes for industrial and medical purposes, and also for training of personnel.

The landscape lies outside the direct control of niche and regime levels. It is the domain of slow-moving long-term trends including climate change, migration, demography, oil demand, and economic ideologies like the Washington Consensus. It also includes unanticipated short-term shocks such as the collapse of the Soviet Union, natural disasters, fluctuations in oil prices, and the financial crisis of 2008.

The regime level features the network of actors, institutions, rules, habits, material infrastructure, business models, and societal expectations that have evolved alongside, locked in, stabilized, and perpetuated the incumbent energy regime. In the case of the Gulf for example, the energy

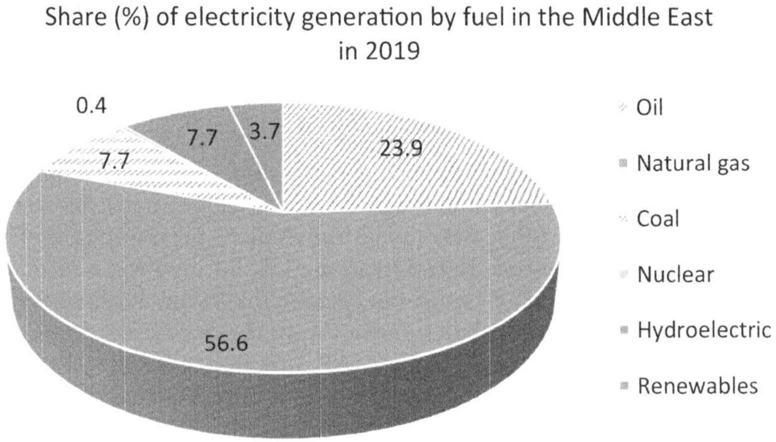

Fig. 10.1 Share of electricity generation by fuel in the Middle East (including Egypt and Turkey) (*Source* BP Statistical Review of World Energy, 2020)

regime includes a local variant of capitalism known as *Khaleeji* capitalism, the *kafala* system for sponsoring foreign labour, the rentier mentality, energy subsidies, state-owned hydrocarbon companies, and petrochemical industries.[11] A systemic, energy regime change is rare but can occur if major coalitions of actors align their behaviour with disruptive impulses at the landscape and niche levels. In most cases, the pathways of regime change are incremental.[12]

The shortcomings of the MLP framework have been discussed elsewhere. Nevertheless, as noted by Dennis Kumetat, its strength lies 'in its explanatory power, which captures the systemic change on these three analytical scales as well as the interplay between them'.[13] MLP also offers an elegant opportunity to focus on the significance of regime agency in facilitating or hindering a niche breakout by nuclear energy; it is precisely this agency that informs much of the analysis in this chapter, in line with calls to bring politics back in.[14] This is because changes at the landscape and niche levels are not merely functional or linear; it is 'interpretive actors' at the niche and regime levels who 'fight, negotiate, search, learn, and build coalitions as they navigate transitions'.[15] While MLP has guided discussions of nuclear energy in the US, Asia, and Europe,[16] to the best of the author's knowledge it has not been applied specifically to nuclear energy in the Middle East.

Nuclear at the Landscape Level

The niche level is usually assumed to be the source of pressure on the regime in favour of radical, innovative change that threatens the status quo; this explains why the regime usually resists niche breakthroughs. The rise of distributed renewable electricity in the US, for instance, is meeting resistance from some utility companies because the former challenges the influence, networks, and revenues derived from the pre-existing centrally dispatched electricity model.[17] In the UAE, however, a nuclear advocacy network was in its infancy as the country had no prior experience with the technology, unlike Egypt and Iran that had experimental research reactors and which had sent students abroad for training prior to breaking ground on a civilian nuclear programme. In this regard, the interaction between landscape and regime levels played a particularly significant role in the UAE in explaining its nuclear energy policy.

The key landscape-level factor which informed the UAE's nuclear energy policy was the gradual interest in and acceptability of nuclear energy at the regional and global levels by the dawn of the twenty-first century. Partly to address Russia's 2005 agreement with Tehran to fuel the reactor at Bushehr,[18] one of the last remaining steps to a fully operational unit that would enhance Iran's regional clout, Saudi Arabia commissioned a study for a nuclear power plant that would serve members of the Gulf Cooperation Council (GCC). The latter was created in 1981 as an anti-Iran, US-backed organization comprising six Arab Gulf member states namely, Saudi Arabia, the UAE, Bahrain, Kuwait, Oman, and Qatar. The intention to develop a joint programme for peaceful nuclear energy was announced at a GCC meeting in December 2006 during which Iran's ambition of a weapons programme was also denounced. Thereafter, the group embarked on consultations in 2007 with the IAEA.

The UAE's leadership assessed, correctly, that the GCC plan to jointly develop nuclear energy was unworkable. This was because of historical sensitivities over sovereignty, as underlined by the failure of regional initiatives like a GCC gas grid or common currency as well as the lack of interoperability between the GCC's military forces.[19] Taking a cue from the legitimization of nuclear energy at the regional level, the

UAE, Kuwait, and Bahrain drew up plans accordingly. Inspired by the UAE's progress on nuclear energy (discussed below), Kuwait's leaders declared that 'if nuclear was going to happen in the UAE, then we should do it too'.[20] The advisor to Kuwait's Nuclear Energy Commission, Adnan Shihab-Eldin, noted that 'we considered the Emirates as an example, although we were four or five decades ahead of them in terms of nuclear experience. We had also worked with the same consultants used to develop the program in the Emirates'.[21] As for Bahrain, it announced that it would cooperate with the US to operate nuclear plants in the Gulf state by 2017.

The regional legitimacy of nuclear energy was an echo of the global nuclear renaissance at that time, prompted by sustained increases in crude oil prices since the early 2000s on the back of insatiable demand from Asia.[22] During this period, the administration of George W. Bush in the US was offering multi-billion dollar subsidies to encourage the building of new nuclear plants in the country by 2010, Prime Minister Gordon Brown of the UK proposed in 2008 the building of eight new nuclear plants that would feed electricity into the national grid by 2017, and construction began on additional nuclear reactors in Finland and France based a new European pressurized reactor design.

The link between oil prices, energy import bills (since gas is often indexed to oil prices), and interest in nuclear energy informed decisions in energy importing states. In Jordan, where 96% of energy needs are imported, nuclear energy was seen as a way to reduce the financial burden in the long run; energy imports rose from 9% of GDP in 2003 to 16% in 2013, and even after the oil price crash were 10% in 2016.[23] This link also motivated oil exporters to maximize export revenue. For Kuwait, where 64% of electricity generation capacity is from oil,[24] it made financial sense to free up oil for export. A senior Kuwaiti policy participant explained it as follows: 'each time there was an increase in the price of oil, there was a debate in Kuwait about why we were burning oil for electricity. This was an opportunity cost and we should have been exporting oil to earn its high value, as well as consider producing electricity from cheaper energy sources, such as nuclear energy. The price of oil increased on three occasions, and on each occasion, Kuwait attempted to have a nuclear power program (1976–1980; 1985–1986; 2007–2011)'.[25]

This gradual acceptability of nuclear energy at the regional and global levels in turn provided the impetus at the regime level to consider how nuclear energy could meet what the UAE leadership considered to be one of the key domestic policy challenges—the shortfall in energy requirements to power its twenty-first-century economic development. The interaction between landscape and regime level considerations is discussed in a later section.

What of the geostrategic motivation, in particular that civilian nuclear energy was a hedge against another landscape-level development, namely, Iran's bellicosity and alleged ambition to acquire nuclear weapons?[26] Competition over regional hegemony between Iran and the Gulf has intensified since 1979, manifested through sectarian, ethnic, strategic, and territorial rivalries. These tensions were underlined by the continuing Iranian occupation of three UAE-claimed islands, formation of the GCC, by the latter's financial support for Iraq during its eight-year war with Iran, by proxy wars fuelled by Arab fears of an ascendant Iran-led Shia crescent in Iraq, Syria, and Lebanon,[27] and by suspected Iranian-backed attacks on civil infrastructure in the Gulf. The UAE's ambassador to the US argued in 2010 that 'the UAE is most vulnerable to Iran. Our military wake up, dream, breathe, eat, sleep the Iranian threat. It's the only conventional military threat our military plans for, trains for, equips for…it's very much in our interest that Iran does not gain nuclear technology'.[28] Some scholars have also asserted the existence of a robust link between national security considerations, nuclear weapons, and civilian nuclear energy programmes.[29]

For the UAE, however, while Iran's nuclear programme was certainly a huge source of concern, it was not the driving force behind Barakah. The UAE's adoption of the 'gold standard' of non-proliferation eliminated any possibility of a domestic capacity for advanced uranium enrichment required for a weapons programme. Although the UAE's bilateral agreement with the US—Section 123 of the Atomic Energy Act of 1954—contains a provision that should the US negotiate a more favourable 123 agreement with another country in the Middle East, the 'gold standard' can be renegotiated, the UAE is highly unlikely to do so. The global goodwill, respect, prestige, and 'soft power' earned through its management of the nuclear programme is invaluable; the UAE leadership would be loath to give this up. This is not to say there was no political calculation about symbolically pushing back against Iran's nuclear hegemony, only that it was not a driving force. As reiterated by its Minister of Foreign Affairs, the country's nuclear programme was also an 'opportunity to drive positive change at the international level' in terms of widely-shared global aspirations such as non-proliferation, security, transparency, and multilateral cooperation.[30]

In comparison, the weight of the Iran factor in Saudi Arabia's decision to acquire nuclear civilian energy is more ambiguous and informs an approach characterized as nuclear 'hedging'.[31] On the one hand, the weak economic rationale for nuclear energy, the country's refusal to sign the IAEA's Additional Protocol to allow more intrusive verification of its nuclear programme, and its close ties with nuclear-armed Pakistan suggest that geopolitical calculations loom large.[32] Echoing his late father and other senior princes, Saudi Crown Prince Mohamed bin Salman famously declared in 2018 that the kingdom 'does not want to acquire any nuclear bomb, but without a doubt if Iran developed a nuclear bomb, we will follow suit as soon as possible'.[33] On the other hand, bearing in mind that the Crown Prince has staked his legitimacy on modernizing the Saudi economy and society, the success of which is in part dependent on foreign investment and support, it is arguable that per Ethel Solingen, 'internationalizing' domestic stakeholders in the kingdom may have little incentive to use nuclear power as a cover for developing nuclear weapons.[34] In any event, the point here is that landscape-level factors do not have a homogenous effect on the regime level; Iran's geopolitical challenge resulted in the pursuit of distinct nuclear programmes by two countries in the Gulf.

Nuclear at the Niche Level

For the UAE, it quickly became clear that nuclear as a niche technology offered a partial yet innovative solution to the energy supply problem on several counts—price volatility, political stability of suppliers in the fuel cycle, and delivery schedule. The price of uranium is much less volatile than oil or gas; in this regard, nuclear offers a 'valuable tool in countering the risk of price volatility inherent in use of fossil fuel-based technologies'.[35] Because of the cost structure of nuclear power generation, with high upfront capital expenditure and comparatively low variable fuel costs, the cost of generating electricity from a nuclear power plant is much more predictable than that of gas or oil for baseload power generation. For instance, fuel costs for nuclear and combine-cycle gas power stations are around one-quarter and three-quarters of total costs or $0.85 per MMBtu and $3.45 per MMBtu, respectively.[36] Consequently, unlike hydrocarbons subject to the vagaries of economic conditions, demand forecasts for uranium depend largely on installed and operable capacity. For the UAE 'with an economy that is still relatively undiversified, that relative absence of price volatility for nuclear fuel is actually quite valuable in making industrial policy plans and strategies for the future'.[37]

Other inherent advantages of nuclear are associated with the fuel cycle. Uranium is mined in relatively stable countries like Kazakhstan, Australia, Canada, and Namibia; these top four suppliers account for over three-quarters of global uranium production.[38] Enrichment is offered by facilities in UK, Germany, the Netherlands, and the US through URENCO (which has a one-third share of the global market), in Russia through TENEX (45%), and in France (12.7%).[39] As for fabrication into fuel rods, Russia's TVEL (18% market share), France's Framatone (21%), and US's Westinghouse (24%) are market leaders.[40] The fact that nuclear fuel rods can be easily stockpiled and that their delivery to refuel a nuclear plant is usually required only once every 24–36 months are also advantageous since the vulnerability of host countries like the UAE to supply disruptions is minimized. In brief, while not as numerous as hydrocarbon suppliers, there seems to be enough diversity in the suppliers of the fuel cycle and reactor construction to preclude over-dependence on a single supplier.

Finally, this niche technology is well-suited to Abu Dhabi's grid size and geography. The emirate has an installed electricity generating capacity of 16.6 GW. Given that each reactor at Barakah generates 1.4 GW of electricity, this is well within IAEA's recommendation that a single reactor should not account for more than 5–10% of an electricity grid to maintain grid stability in the event of reactor maintenance or shut down. In addition, Abu Dhabi's long coastline provides ample siting opportunities for a water-intensive nuclear power plant. In the case of Jordan, however, its initial plan to acquire two 1 GW reactors was questionable on technical grounds alone, given the country's installed system capacity of 3.2 GW.[41] Its small territory and population density of 115 persons per square kilometre (compared to 48.9 in Abu Dhabi emirate) also resulted in competing land use between nuclear plant site and tribal lands. For a country that is one of the five most water-scarce in the world, the lack of availability of cooling water also disincentivized conventional nuclear plants.

Disadvantages related to nuclear as a niche technology were understood by the UAE's leaders but were not regarded as deal breakers. For instance, given that new nuclear plants take 10–19 years or more between planning and operation,[42] this implied that nuclear energy would be unable to meet electricity demand in the UAE in a timely manner. Nuclear plants are also prohibitively expensive, costing at least three and a half times more per megawatt hour than a solar PV plant and two and a half times more than a combined gas cycle plant on a whole life-cycle basis [43] Indeed, when asked in 1992 about nuclear energy in Egypt and the $18–20 billion estimated cost for three or four reactors, Egyptian President Hosni Mubarak cautioned that he 'would be leaving a debt for the citizens, a burden on the people. I cannot do this. I do not want to add more burdens than the people can endure'.[44] Under Abdel Fattah el-Sisi, however, Egypt was swayed by Russia's offer of a low-interest loan that would cover 85% of total construction costs of $28.75 billion, with repayments commencing only after the commissioning of the last of four reactors at the El-Dabaa plant. The economics of nuclear energy have also been prohibitive for Turkey and account in part for its previous failure to attract bids through international tenders. Its current nuclear plant project at Akkuyu was only made possible by an intergovernmental agreement with Russia, whose state-owned company, Rosatom, will finance the construction estimated at $20 billion.

In the eyes of the UAE's energy regime, however, the high oil price environment after the mid-2000s meant that revenues from oil exports could easily underwrite the plant construction cost of over $24 billion. The country's GDP of $254 billion in 2009 when the reactor construction project was awarded was clearly in excess of the minimum GDP of $50 billion for non-nuclear weapon countries that have ever built a nuclear power plant.[45] Moreover, gas was (and still is) very affordable since it was being imported into the UAE at below market prices; the Dolphin Gas Project importing gas from Qatar fixed prices at US$1.30 per MMBtu although market prices were US$6–10 per MMBtu by the time actual deliveries began in 2007.[46] Taking into account the project lead time and high costs of $5–9 MMBtu for developing its domestic sour gas resources, the purchase up to one-third of gas requirements to make-up for the electricity shortfall while waiting for the nuclear plant to come online seemed financially sensible.

The externalities associated with nuclear energy were also not an overriding concern for the UAE. One study found that these health and pollution costs amounted to an improbably high 8.63 cents per kilowatt hour on whole life-cycle basis; this is less than coal or oil, but more than gas or solar.[47] Another study estimated the social costs of nuclear electricity in Europe at just over €20 per megawatt hour which was less than all fossil fuel-based sources of electricity but higher than utility-scale solar energy.[48] The point here is that the energy regime forged on the basis of oil was largely unfazed since there were few incentives at the international level for the UAE to embrace costly adaptation or mitigation measures. To be sure, Masdar, the subsidiary of the Mubadala sovereign wealth fund tasked to promote renewable energy and to create a zero-carbon city in Abu Dhabi among other mandates, had been created in 2007. But, as wryly noted by its co-founder, Steven Geiger, 'virtually everyone outside Mubadala considered it a daft idea. With [CEO of Mubadala and Chairman of EAA] Khaldoon Al Mubarak's and Mohamed bin Zayed's visible support, there were no direct attacks, but surely there were many snide whispers in the majlises'.[49] In this connection, a researcher found 'no profound environmental awareness among most UAE citizens' during the first decade of the twenty-first century, the country was referred to as the 'worst case scenario' within the GCC in 2008 in terms of addressing environmental degradation, and its per capita emissions of carbon dioxide of 21 metric tons in 2009 were the sixth highest globally, surpassing even Saudi Arabia or the US.[50]

Nuclear at the Regime Level

Following the death of his father in 2004, the Crown Prince of Abu Dhabi, Sheikh Mohamed bin Zayed, became the dominant policy entrepreneur in the emirate. Not content with the traditional practice of recycling petro-dollars in Europe and North America, the Crown Prince directed that some of these revenues be invested within Abu Dhabi to create a diversified economy with indigenous sources of growth. The task was given to the newly created Mubadala, the emirate's sovereign wealth fund, of which he was the Chairman. This change of development philosophy, subsequently institutionalized as Abu Dhabi Vision 2030, 'presaged a massive increase in energy requirements and came with a huge energy price tag…It became absolutely clear that to continue along this economic diversification trajectory would require a lot more energy than what we had at the moment'.[51]

Based on a cumulative demand growth of 9% per annum between 2007 and 2020, gas would only be able to meet 40–50% of the country's peak electricity demand by 2020.[52] The severity of the power shortage was underlined in 2007 when the UAE, which was almost entirely dependent on gas to fuel its power stations, became a net gas importer for the first time. This was a result of decisions by the leadership to subsidize electricity and water produced in gas power plants (hence resulting in wasteful over-consumption) as part of the 'ruling bargain' in exchange for political acquiescence, to inject gas into mature oil fields to enhance oil recovery and increase oil revenues, and to provide cheap gas to energy-intensive industries as fuel and feedstock to encourage diversification away from oil.[53] Consequently, a shortage of gas imperiled these three major objectives along with the regime legitimacy that came with economic progress.

This quest for energy security was not unique to the UAE. It is replicated in energy-poor and energy-rich MENA countries, as the country studies in this volume show. High rates of growth in electricity demand are largely a consequence of subsidized electricity and desalinated water. Accounting for 5% of GDP in MENA (the highest among all regions),[54] energy subsidies are perceived to contribute to regime stability by buying political acquiescence and distributing patronage. Even though subsidies account for as much as one-third of electricity demand (because low prices encourage wasteful consumption),[55] reducing or removing them is politically tricky, as social unrest in Iran and Jordan has demonstrated. Similarly, although energy efficiency is the 'invisible fuel' that could reduce consumption by over 20%, implementation is challenging in the short run due to high upfront financing costs of retrofitting buildings, lax enforcement of efficiency standards, and disincentives arising from energy subsidies.[56] Supply-side management of energy security, of which nuclear energy is only one possible approach, therefore appears to be a relatively easier fix for the regime.

To address the issue of energy supply, an interagency energy task force was created in 2007, led by the newly established Executive Affairs Authority (EAA) of Abu Dhabi. The latter was set up by Mohamed Bin Zayed to provide him with strategic advice. The aim of the energy task force was to develop an all-options evaluation of increasing energy supply and security. The recruitment of Ambassador Hamad Al Kaabi, the UAE's first nuclear engineer who had just completed his studies at that time, as Associate Director at EAA and his role in the team was another milestone for nuclear energy. The committee was technology-agnostic about how to meet the shortfall in demand for electricity, but Al Kaabi's presence on the committee ensured that there was an advocate for nuclear energy.

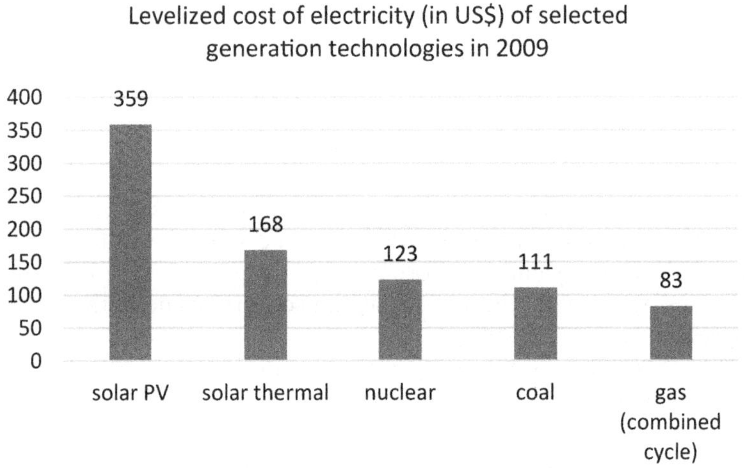

Fig. 10.2 Levelized cost of electricity of selected generation technologies in 2009 (*Source* Levelized Cost of Electricity Analysis, Lazard, 2019)

The process eventually resulted in a White Paper on the Evaluation and Development of Peaceful Nuclear Energy in April 2008. Other niche technologies did not make much headway in the task force because the technology was extremely costly at that time (solar) or the resource was inadequate (wind); coal, though relatively cheap, did not meet the committee's criteria on emissions (see Fig. 10.2). The mandate of Abu Dhabi's Water and Electricity Agency, the emirate's sole buyer of water and electricity, to procure the most cost-efficient technology for water and electricity further cemented the decision to adopt nuclear over solar for baseload energy requirements.

Political Management of the Nuclear Commitment

In between the White Paper of 2008, the award of the Barakah project to a South Korean-Westinghouse consortium in December 2009, through the start of construction at Barakah in July 2012 and beyond, state entities in the UAE worked tirelessly to forge enabling political coalitions. The latter was deemed necessary to sustain commitment since the plant would take over a decade to complete. After all, reactor units at the Zwentendorf nuclear plant in Austria and Kalkar in Germany were finished but then decommissioned even before going into operation. The Zarnowiec nuclear plant in Poland had been under construction in the 1980s but then abandoned in the 1990s. More recently, Vietnam, which had broken ground on its first-ever nuclear plant in 2014 after nearly a decade of planning, scrapped plans for two nuclear plants and removed nuclear power from the country's future energy mix at the end of 2016. Work was also halted in 2017 on the two additional reactor units at VC Summers in South Carolina despite having already incurred costs of $9 billion. Other countries including Australia, Ghana, Ireland, Kuwait, and Singapore planned for but never built their nuclear plants.

In this regard, the political management of a sustained nuclear commitment in the UAE is crucial and the subject of the following section.

Create New Actors in Favour of the Niche Technology

The first task was the creation of new actors at the regime level with a vested interest in nuclear-fueled electricity. The aim was to create positive and institutionalized 'policy feedback' to make it harder to dismantle or dilute nuclear energy policy.[57] These actors included an independent regulatory body (Federal Authority for Nuclear Regulation or FANR), a nuclear plant owner (Emirates Nuclear Energy Corporation or ENEC) and operator (Nawah), a nuclear technology centre to spur innovation on safety systems, nuclear engineering and other related training courses at Abu Dhabi's Khalifa University, and hundreds of trained Emirati nuclear engineers and specialists. The GCC Interconnection Authority, which was established in Saudi Arabia in 2001 to promote cross-border electricity trade, is another example of an actor that has increased its profile and ambition of late. Having completed the GCC Interconnector in 2011, an increase of 20% was recorded in cross-border trade although absolute volumes remain tiny. Nevertheless, the capacity of the Interconnector to export and hence stabilize national grids that have excess nuclear and renewable electricity, such as the UAE's or Saudi Arabia's in winter, could enhance GCCIA's future relevance as an actor supportive of nuclear energy at the regime level.

In contrast, Kuwait was much less successful in creating new pro-nuclear actors. Even though the National Nuclear Energy Committee was headed by the Prime Minister, the Committee was well aware of the weak autonomy of the government. This is because Kuwait's political system, in particular, the popularly-elected National Assembly and its power over budgetary allocations, discouraged large, ambitious projects, such as a civilian nuclear plant, that had a direct impact on the immediate benefits enjoyed by Kuwaiti citizens.[58] Regime resistance against a niche breakthrough was hence formidable.

Elsewhere in MENA, the King Abdullah City for Atomic and Renewable Energy (KACARE) was established in 2010 to spearhead the kingdom's civilian nuclear programme while Turkey and Jordan created new, pro-nuclear actors, in the form of the Turkish Atomic Energy Agency (TAEK) and Jordan Atomic Energy Commission (JAEC), respectively. However, as discussed below, TAEK and JAEC lacked credibility and ended up being sources of negative policy feedback, which added to the difficulties of implementing and sustaining nuclear energy programmes in these countries. As for KACARE, it has not made significant progress in nuclear's legal and regulatory development.[59]

Co-benefits of Nuclear and Fossil Fuel Energy Regimes

A second aspect of building an enabling coalition was to pre-empt potential 'regime resistance' by reinforcing the co-benefits of adopting a niche technology.[60] One of the staunchest supporters of nuclear energy in the UAE was the gas industry since nuclear power freed up and facilitated the monetization of gas by substituting nuclear for gas in the electricity grid. Exporting gas or injecting it into oil fields for enhanced oil recovery or using gas as industrial feedstock is more valuable, in terms of revenue and economic diversification, than consuming gas domestically at subsidized prices. Nuclear energy—together with subsidy reductions, intensive exploitation of gas deposits, and energy efficiency measures—was perceived as a key contributor to the UAE's goal of gas self-sufficiency and thereafter of becoming a net gas exporter.[61] ENEC also courted other regime-level actors such as industry and businesses, which traditionally relied on spending by the hydrocarbon sector. As of October 2018, ENEC awarded contracts worth $3.8 billion to over 1500 local businesses including Emirates Steel, Dubai Cable Company, and National Cement for procurement of nuclear-grade reinforcing steel bars, cables, and cement respectively.[62] The co-benefits to local businesses also extended more generally to the wider economy since every dirham spent by an average nuclear energy plant results in the creation of 1.04 dirhams in the local community and about 1.87 dirhams in the country's economy.[63]

Nuclear power, with its dispatchable energy, large utility-scale operations owned by the state, centralized production, distribution and transmission systems, replicates the infrastructure of conventional fossil fuel, as well as the implications for top-down, state-society relations. It does not upend incumbent regime networks as much as the 'soft' nature of variable, distributed, decentralized renewable energy systems with its consequences for grassroots democracy.[64] In this way, nuclear energy segues with the 'modernizing autocracy' narrative in the UAE and the wider Gulf, where technology and technical management are perceived as instrumental in solving agricultural, environmental, and economic obstacles to development. Dams, irrigation, drainage, and desalination have contemporary equivalents in carbon capture and storage, zero-carbon cities, solar parks, hyperloops, and space travel. In this connection, nuclear energy confers onto Abu Dhabi's ruling elites increased legitimacy from its citizenry.

The co-beneficial relationship between niche and incumbent regimes is also evident in other MENA countries. Turkey's first-ever nuclear plant at Akkuyu, together with a new airport in Istanbul, additional hydroelectric dams, the world's longest suspension bridge, and the world's first three-storey tunnel are all part of Prime Minister Recep Erdogan's ambitious Vision 2023 plan to make the country one of the top 10 economies in the world. Having broken ground in April 2018, TAEK and Russia's Rosatom, which is building Akkuyu, have committed (improbably) to completing the plant by 2023 to mark the centenary of the proclamation of the Turkish republic. Nuclear electricity will help to perpetuate current control of the energy sector by Erdogan's relatives and friends as well as loyalists of his AKP party.[65]

Pre-empt Negative Policy Feedback

A third aspect of coalition building involved disarming potential negative policy feedback effects. In the UAE, potential critics of nuclear energy from health and environmental circles were co-opted as board members of FANR. The role of the Environment Agency Abu Dhabi (EAD), whose Managing Director is on FANR's board, is particularly interesting. Originally established in 1996, it had been stretched thin as a 'do-it-all' entity; a re-constitution in 2005 re-focused its expertise on policy and regulatory, instead of operational, matters. As an environmental regulator for the Barakah nuclear plant, EAD was tasked with reviewing and approving licence applications for site preparation, construction, and operation.[66] Although tensions between environmental regulators and nuclear operators are common, ENEC had a 'very positive' working relationship with EAD.[67] For example, ENEC undertook design modifications to the original reactors to ensure a thermal discharge environmental limit of no more than five degree Celsius to protect marine flora and fauna around Barakah; it constructed a much longer breakwater than the reference plant in South Korea to minimize thermal recirculation in the shallow Arabian Sea; it also created artificial reefs to grow new areas for sea life by way of compensatory activities. Consequently, EAD had no cause to delay or block nuclear energy in the UAE.

The UAE was also proactive in disarming negative policy feedback from abroad.[68] The leadership was fully cognizant that the security risks of its nuclear programme would be under the global microscope, thanks to earlier developments at the landscape level. These included the participation of Emirati citizens in 9/11, concerns about the impact of DP World's acquisitions on port security in the US, and possible lapses in export control as underlined by AQ Khan's illicit nuclear network in Dubai.[69] Consequently, Abu Dhabi placed a high priority on winning the confidence of external stakeholders. It made sure the credibility of its nuclear regulator was unquestioned.[70] The board of management of the UAE's FANR is appointed by a Cabinet resolution thus avoiding direct ministerial control over nuclear safety regulation; Turkey's TAEK reports to the Prime Minister, who appoints members for a fixed four-year term. This means that FANR's board members are better protected from discretionary removal from duty. FANR derives part of its budget from licensing fees and is hence more financially independent than TAEK, which depends on annual appropriations from the Prime Minister's office. In the UAE, regulatory and promotional responsibilities are carried out by separate entities—FANR and ENEC respectively—to avoid conflicts of interest, such as pressure to speed up approvals.[71] In Turkey's case, TAEK, which was established in 1982, combines both roles; a regulatory agency was never created although one was envisaged under the country's Nuclear Law of 2007.

Abu Dhabi also did not shy away from hiring foreigners with vast experience in the nuclear industry, particularly in safety and non-proliferation. They included William Travers and his successor at FANR, Christer Viktorsson; Hans Blix, the UN's former chief weapons inspector and former head of the International Atomic Energy Agency, was appointed as Chairman of the UAE's International Advisory Board. In comparison, the heads of the regulatory agencies in Egypt, Turkey, and Jordan are local citizens; this raises questions since all three host countries are nuclear newcomers albeit with limited experience of research reactors in the case of Egypt and Turkey. Leveraging on the European Union's stature as Turkey's trading partner and foreign director investor, the European Parliament even recommended the termination of Akkuyu's construction.

To further assuage foreign concerns, Abu Dhabi became a signatory of all basic and additional protocols for acquiring civilian nuclear technology. It even voluntarily agreed to a rare 'gold standard' whereby prohibition against uranium enrichment and reprocessing is enshrined in the country's legal code, a move that earned the UAE worldwide praise and respect. Iran, by contrast, is the only country in the world with a major nuclear project that is not a member of the Convention on Nuclear Safety.[72] The difference of the UAE's approach with that in Saudi Arabia is striking. The Kingdom has defended its right to enrich domestic uranium resources, despite the high costs and lengthy lead time of an indigenous uranium programme and availability of multiple suppliers of enriched uranium.[73] Coupled with bin Salman's infamous declaration, discomfort about Saudi-Pakistani nuclear ties, and Saudi refusal to sign the IAEA's Additional Protocol, it is little wonder that the Saudi programme has encountered a much higher level of negative policy feedback from external audiences. In any event, not all external stakeholders were on board about Barakah. Qatar, for example, decried the lack of cooperation with Gulf neighbours over disaster planning.[74]

Build Domestic Public Support

The fourth aspect of coalition building focused on the UAE public. ENEC and FANR have been proactive in engaging with the wider public through regular information sessions even prior to the Fukushima nuclear incident in 2011. The result has been consistent and overwhelming support of over 80% for the country's nuclear energy programme; among residents of the Al Dhafra region where the Barakah nuclear power station is located, support is even higher at 94% in 2018.[75] To put these numbers in perspective, it is worth noting that public support for nuclear energy stands at 38–50% in the G7 countries, almost 60% in South Korea, and over 70% in Russia.[76] Public receptivity to information sessions was positive partly because 'the Emirates is an engineering-intensive society, much more so than other places in the world where a service economy dominates. A lot of the population here are engineers of one form or another and that has an impact on their ability to consume information about technical topics. And that translates into a high level of support'.[77] Consequently, even Fukushima was not able to derail the nuclear project in the UAE.

Public support and the aforementioned successful courting of domestic stakeholders meant there was no significant competing narrative about nuclear energy in the UAE. In Turkey and Iran, however, alternative narratives were offered by nuclear detractors and elite groups with ambivalent views. The latter are not opposed to nuclear power per se in a country's energy mix, only the way safety issues or financing or vendor selection are managed.[78] For instance, concerns were raised that Turkey's 'double dependence' on Russia—for gas and nuclear power—ran counter to the energy security promised by nuclear energy. The membership and role of the nuclear ambivalent public partly explain the weakness of sustained opposition to nuclear power in these countries.

In other MENA countries, the deficit in public support stems from wider dissatisfaction with government in general. In Jordan, for instance, the lack of trust in government feeds into negative public perceptions of the country's nuclear energy programme. With a Trust in Government index of 3.5–3.9 out of 7 between 2010 and 2017 for Jordan compared to 5.6–6.3 for the UAE, it is little wonder that the prevailing sentiment is that 'in Jordan we have witnessed fraudulent elections, a fraudulent Parliament; it is not out of the realm of possibility that at the end of the day we will receive fraudulent studies' about the feasibility of nuclear energy.[79] With a mandate to promote and implement nuclear energy, the JAEC led by Khaled Toukan has tried to raise public awareness and acceptance of nuclear energy through outreach on social and conventional media. However, Toukan has been dogged by allegations of corruption, use of misleading or fraudulent data and influence capture of the regulator. A parliamentary vote to suspend the nuclear programme in 2012 was ignored by the King and the programme continues under Toukan.

To a much greater degree than the UAE, prestige and identity play an important role in sustaining nuclear energy adoption in other countries although it is not the sole consideration. In the case of Jordan, its resolute determination to develop nuclear power in the face of multiple challenges has been explained by its contribution to regime legitimacy; the latter is credited with resisting pressure to bandwagon with the US's policy preference, as has traditionally been the case.[80] As for Iran, despite an earlier announcement in 1979 that the unfinished units at Bushehr would be used as silos to store wheat, Ayatollah Khomeini reversed his stance against weapons of mass destruction in the mid-1980s and ordered that work be resumed at Bushehr.[81] His regime and subsequent ones thereafter recognized that nuclear technology could be usefully framed as a civil religion to mobilize the Iranian population to make sacrifices to combat arch-enemy Iraq or to assert sovereignty in the face of international sanctions by the West. For Iran's leaders, therefore, it appears that spending billions to fix ageing transmission lines, through which 15% of the country's generated electricity is lost, is less visible and legitimacy-inducing than acquiring a civilian and military nuclear programme.[82]

The Future of Nuclear Energy in MENA

Having applied the MLP framework to examine the decision-making and implementation process behind nuclear energy in the UAE and other MENA countries, the chapter will now consider variables that may prompt a niche breakthrough elsewhere in MENA in the near future.

At the landscape level, the continued evolution of the composition, ownership, and capacities of nuclear reactor vendors since the 1980s will shape competition among them to supply purchaser countries in MENA. Russia's Rosatom is the region's (and world's) front runner by far. It is the only vendor that is a one-stop shop for the full nuclear cycle, including fuel take-back arrangements. It offers extremely attractive financing terms to purchasers, as the earlier examples of Egypt and Turkey demonstrate, because it can draw up to 10% of its funding from one of Russia's sovereign wealth fund, the National Wealth Fund.[83] This is particularly helpful for developing countries since lenders like the World Bank have effectively placed a ban on financing new nuclear projects. Russia also places less stringent legal obligations with regard to export controls on clients than the US, and it has leveraged the anti-US mood in some MENA countries to push Rosatom's reactors and fuel services.[84]

In contrast, the reorganization of French reactor vendors has not halted their declining fortunes and reputational damage. The Flamanville nuclear plant in France is seven years behind schedule while the Olkiluoto 3 plant in Finland is 10 years late and both are over budget by three times the original estimate. In the US, the ever-increasing financial costs of nuclear power plant construction, especially post-Fukushima, the withdrawal of credit by the US Export-Import Bank, the pre-requisite of concluding 123 agreements, and low prices of hydrocarbon and renewable energies have burdened and even bankrupted privately-owned US vendors. As for the nuclear industry in South Korea, its credibility was damaged by the scandal over sub-standard nuclear components. It also lost its top cheerleader when President Lee Myung-Bak completed his term; the current president Moon Jae-In is more ambivalent about nuclear power.

Consequently, Rosatom is almost the only game in town for cash-strapped purchasers in MENA as well as in Iran, a market that other vendors have exited on pain of US sanctions. For Russia, nuclear inroads into former and current US allies have bolstered its military and diplomatic return to a Middle East that has been an American lake since the dissolution of the Soviet Union. Rosatom's success is also a showcase for President Vladimir Putin's vision of a modern Russian economy that is trying to move away from being the world's raw materials appendage to one that produces world-beating nuclear and hypersonic technologies. Thanks partly to its 'nuclear diplomacy', Russia appears to be an indispensable broker in the region's conflicts today where once its preferences could be politely ignored by regional stakeholders.[85]

Comparatively, the rise of Russia's Rosatom did not shape the UAE's motivations to adopt nuclear energy. This was partly because the UAE possessed strong financial capacity and partly because Russia was in the midst of a massive reorganization of over 100 nuclear-related entities.[86] Rosatom was created as a legal entity only in December 2007; it was too preoccupied with internal consolidation to submit a bid in August 2008 for the Barakah project. In any case, Rosatom is one of six suppliers that will provide enriched fuel to Barakah for the first 15 years.

On closer analysis however, the sustainability of Russia's reactor export model is in jeopardy from several sources: competition from China, foreign policy adventurism, domestic economic crises, and new niche developments (see below). Having developed indigenous reactors through reverse engineering earlier imported technology from Russia and the US, China's state-owned nuclear companies are looking for opportunities in developing countries that have signed up to its massive Belt and Road Initiative. In MENA, China has concluded preliminary agreements with Iran, Egypt, Sudan, and Turkey to 'buy lasting influence in regions supplying raw materials and draw historically pro-Western countries further into the Chinese camp'.[87] In so doing, Chinese companies will inevitably compete with Rosatom; China's far greater financial clout will allow it to offer better financial terms than Rosatom to compensate for China's relatively less established track record abroad. MENA countries interested in acquiring a civilian nuclear power plant may be forced to choose between Russian or Chinese nuclear technology that could 'lock-in' long-term bilateral cooperation.

Other challenges for Rosatom emanate, ironically, from Russia itself. Russia's foreign policy such as the annexation of Crimea, supporting a separatist war in eastern Ukraine, and election meddling have also resulted in blowback in the form of ever-increasing financial and investment sanctions on the oil, defence, and banking sectors. According to one estimate, Russia's economy would have been 6% larger in 2018 if it were not for sanctions.[88] Although the nuclear sector has been excluded from sanctions, Rosatom may nevertheless find it difficult to borrow money from Western banks to finance its expansion; it will also be hard pressed to find partners with whom to form a consortium to bid for foreign projects due to a potential expansion of the sanctions regime. Recurrent domestic economic crises, due largely to unreformed structural rigidities in the Russian economy and a poor business climate, also render Rosatom vulnerable to reduced levels of state funding, without which developing country clients would not be able to purchase nuclear reactors.

The speed of the global low carbon transition, facilitated perhaps by images of starving polar bears or fire tornados in Australia, is the other noteworthy landscape-level development. The sooner a global carbon tax regime or other stringent restrictions on emissions come into being and the larger the carbon tax, the more destabilizing the impact on incumbent hydrocarbon-based energy regimes in MENA. In turn, this will allow niche breakthroughs of nuclear and other low carbon energy technologies.

At the niche level, one significant variable for the uptake of nuclear energy concerns small modular reactors (SMRs). These are reactors with not more than 300 MW of power generating capacity compared to the 1000 MW and more offered by conventional large reactors, which can be constructed modularly (i.e. in factories) for assembly on-site. The advantages offered by SMRs include lower construction costs, minimal cooling requirements, mobility, lower technical demands on grid capacity, faster build times, a flexible modular system that can grow with electricity needs, lower investment costs due to this modularity, and potentially inherently higher safety and proliferation resistance (depending on the design).[89]

Jordan is seen as a particularly good fit for SMRs; it has signed cooperation agreements with SMR developers based in US, Russia, Argentina, South Korea, and China. Saudi Arabia is equally enthusiastic about SMRs for stand-alone desalination plants; in this regard, it recently agreed to license for use in the kingdom the SMART SMR built by South Korea and to jointly build a prototype. However, no commercially operational SMR exists yet, with the earliest starting up only after 2025 at best; potential purchaser countries are also disinclined to be the guinea pig even for this new and promising technology. The fact that the most advanced SMRs in terms of licensing approvals originate in the US adds another layer of complication for states like Jordan and Saudi Arabia since they have been reluctant to conclude 'gold standard' 123 agreements with the US.

The other niche level development that will impact nuclear newbuild in MENA is the cost of alternative energy options. Thanks to the precipitous fall in prices of solar modules, for example, nuclear expert Ali Ahmad opined that 'nuclear power, large and small, does not meet the criterion of economic competitiveness...nuclear electricity is already more expensive than that produced by solar technologies. The coupling between renewables and natural gas offers Saudi Arabia the most economically optimal option'[90]; a similar recommendation was made for Jordan. Ever lower bid prices for solar and wind projects in MENA, the increasing experience of homegrown developers like ACWA Power and Masdar, and the availability of low-cost financing will enhance the attractiveness of non-nuclear alternatives. Another example of a competing niche technology is battery storage for solar or wind projects, which will overcome generation variability and essentially transform them into dispatchable baseload power similar to fossil fuels or nuclear energy. Although the costs of lithium-ion batteries have fallen from $1100 per kWh in 2010 to $156 per kWh in 2019, they need to fall much further to be cost-competitive beyond short-term storage requirements.[91]

Conclusion

For the UAE, the disruption at the landscape level caused by the increasing acceptability of nuclear power was instrumental in opening a timely policy window. This coincided with the new, post-Zayed hyper-development mantra at the regime level that required energy not readily and cost-effectively available in the UAE. At the same time, some of the inherent features of nuclear technology lent themselves to easy alignment with regime level motivations. The combined result was a niche breakout for nuclear power in the UAE. The innovation offered by nuclear energy was perceived as an 'add-on' or 'fix' to the existing hydrocarbon-based energy regime, instead of as a technological substitution that would destabilize existing domestic stakeholders. Its adoption therefore posed little significant threat to material and ideational interests of established networks at the regime level.

More broadly, the cross-country comparisons in this chapter strongly suggest that security-related motivations are much less of a driving force for nuclear newcomers in MENA today, compared to established nuclear powers such as the US, UK, France, Russia, and China. The rise of SMRs further chips away at this link between the proliferation of nuclear weapons and nuclear energy programmes. Security considerations do exist, but they function more as fringe benefits or hedging potential rather than as driving forces. For MENA countries interested in nuclear power, enhancing energy security is the primary driver bar none. Consequently, in addition to the institutional and financial capacity of a state to host a nuclear plant, 'you need a society that politically and publicly can stick with the decision to go nuclear – a commitment that spans decades or centuries, rather than just lasting years'[92] due to lengthy project lead times, the 60-year operating lifetime of a plant, decommissioning, and waste disposal. The differences in stakeholder management highlighted in this chapter therefore contributes to understanding why some nuclear energy programmes in MENA are more successful than others.

Notes

1. IEA Data and Statistics, *Electricity Consumption* (Paris: International Energy Agency).
2. APICORP cites a figure of 3.8% CAGR between 2018–2023 whereas IHS Markit forecasts growth of 3.3% per annum until 2035. See APICORP, *MENA Power Investment Outlook* (Dammam: Arab Petroleum Investments Corporation, 2019), p. 6, http://www.apicorp.org/Research/InvestmentOutlook/APICORP_MENA_ANNUAL_ENERGY_INVESTMENT_OUTLOOK_2019.pdf; and Siemens, *Middle East Power: Outlook 2035* (Abu Dhabi: Siemens, 2018), p. 4, https://assets.new.siemens.com/siemens/assets/public.1515594707.c2f5a6e2ab8cb3f50b1f8df1ce67ac4069710a86.middle-east-power-outlook-2035.pdf.

3. See Robin Mills, "Overview: Creating a Low Carbon Economy," *Middle East Economic Digest: Energy in the 21st Century* (2019), p. 8, https://www.meedmashreqindustryinsight.com/wp-content/uploads/2019/04/Mashreq_Energy-Report_Middle-East-Energy-in-21st-Century.pdf.
4. IAEA, *Energy, Electricity and Nuclear Power Estimates for the Period Up to 2050* (Vienna: International Atomic Energy Agency, 2018), https://www-pub.iaea.org/MTCD/Publications/PDF/RDS-1-38_web.pdf.
5. Michaja Pehl et al., "Understanding Future Emissions from Low-Carbon Power Systems by Integration of Life-Cycle Assessment and Integrated Energy Modelling," *Nature Energy* 2 (2017), https://doi.org/10.1038/s41560-017-0032-9; and Tianyi Luo, Arjun Krishnaswami, and Xinyue Li, *A Methodology to Estimate Water Demand for Thermal Power Plants in Data-Scarce Regions Using Satellite Images* (Washington, DC: World Resources Institute, 2018), https://www.wri.org/publication/methodology-estimate-water-demand-thermal-power-plants-data-scarce-regions.
6. Tristan Volpe and Nicholas Miller, *Geostrategic Nuclear Exports: The Competition for Influence in Saudi Arabia* (Washington, DC: Carnegie Endowment for International Peace, 2018), https://carnegieendowment.org/2018/02/07/geostrategic-nuclear-exports-competition-for-influence-in-saudi-arabia-pub-75472.
7. Adeel Malik, "A Pyramid of Privilege: Crony Capitalism in the Middle East," accessed 19 September 2019; Tim Niblock and Monica Malik, *The Political Economy of Saudi Arabia* (London: Routledge, 2007), p. 19.
8. See, for example, Geert Verbong and Frank Geels, "The Ongoing Energy Transition: Lessons from a Socio-Technical, Multi-Level Analysis of the Dutch Electricity System (1960–2004)," *Energy Policy* 35 (2007); Karoline S. Rogge, Benjamin Pfluger, and Frank Geels, *Transformative Policy Mixes in Sociotechnical Scenarios: The Case of the Low Carbon Transition of the German Electricity System (2010–2050)* (Germany: Fraunhofer, 2017), https://www.econstor.eu/bitstream/10419/167650/1/896044947.pdf.
9. See, for example, Bernhard Brand and Thomas Fink, "Renewable Energy Expansion in the MENA Region: A Review of Concepts and Indicators for a Transition Towards Sustainable Energy Supply" (paper presented at the 4th Asia-Africa Sustainable Energy Forum, Oran, Algeria 2014), https://epub.wupperinst.org/frontdoor/index/index/docId/5421; Muatasim Ismaeel, "Transformation Toward Clean Energy in the Middle East: A Multilevel Perspective," in *Climate Change and Energy Dynamics in the Middle East*, ed. H. Qudrat-Ullah and A. Kayal (Cham: Springer, 2019); Katrine Wiulsrød Ratikainen, "Transitioning to Renewable Energy in Saudi Arabia: A Multi-Level Perspective Analysis of the Saudi Renewable Energy Policies" (University of Oslo, 2017), https://www.duo.uio.no/bitstream/handle/10852/58462/Rat

ikainen_M-NA4590.pdf?sequence=1&isAllowed=y; Georg Holtz et al., *Case of Jordan: The Sustainable Transformation of Energy Systems* (Germany: Wuppertal Institut, 2018), http://library.fes.de/pdf-files/bueros/amman/15492.pdf.

10. WEC, *World Energy Scenarios 2019* (London: World Energy Council, 2019), p. 129, Table 10, https://www.worldenergy.org/publications/entry/world-energy-scenarios-2019-exploring-innovation-pathways-to-2040.
11. On Gulf and Arab economies, see Adam Hanieh, *Money, Markets, and Monarchies: The Gulf Cooperation Council and the Political Economy of the Contemporary Middle East* (Cambridge: Cambridge University Press, 2018); Steffen Hertog, "Is There an Arab Variety of Capitalism?," in *Crony Capitalism in the Middle East: Business and Politics from Liberalization to the Arab Spring*, ed. Ishac Diwan, Adeel Malik, and Izak Atiyas (Oxford: Oxford University Press, 2019).
12. For a discussion of different models of change, see Frank Geels and Johan Schot, "Typology of Sociotechnical Transition Pathways," *Research Policy* 36 (2007).
13. Dennis Kumetat, *Managing the Transition: Renewable Energy and Innovation Policies in the UAE and Algeria* (Abingdon, Oxon: Routledge, 2015), p. 25.
14. See James Meadowcroft, "What About the Politics? Sustainable Development, Transition Management, and Long Term Energy Transitions," *Policy Sciences* 42, no. 4 (2009), http://dx.doi.org/10.1007/s11077-009-9097-z; and Phil Johnstone and Peter Newell, "Sustainability Transitions and the State," *Environmental Innovation and Societal Transitions* 27 (2018), http://dx.doi.org/10.1016/j.eist.2017.10.006.
15. Jonathan Köhler and Frank et al. Geels, "An Agenda for Sustainability Transitions Research: State of the Art and Future Directions," *Environmental Innovation and Societal Transitions* 31 (2019): 8–9, http://dx.doi.org/10.1016/j.eist.2019.01.004.
16. Phil Johnstone and Andy Stirling, "Comparing Nuclear Trajectories in Germany and the United Kingdom: From Regimes to Democracies in Sociotechnical Transitions and Discontinuities," *Energy Research & Social Science* 59 (2020), http://dx.doi.org/10.1016/j.erss.2019.101245; Keith Baker, "Power Failures: Metagoverning a Revival of Nuclear Power in Britain," *International Journal of Sustainable Development* 15, no. 1/2 (2012); and Aleh Cherp et al., "Comparing Electricity Transitions: A Historical Analysis of Nuclear, Wind and Solar Power in Germany and Japan," *Energy Policy* 101 (2017), http://dx.doi.org/10.1016/j.enpol.2016.10.044.
17. See Eric Hittinger, "Why Solar Power Doesn't Threaten Electric Utilities," *Slate*, 4 March 2016.

18. Russia took over the construction of Bushehr from Siemens after 1979. Its agreement to fuel Bushehr was premised on the assumption that this would preclude the need for Iran to create facilities to enrich uranium domestically; Russia was not keen for neighbouring Iran to develop nuclear weapons.
19. Cinzia Bianco, *Intra-GCC Relations: Between Cooperation and Competition Stands Sovereignty* (Istanbul: Al Sharq Forum, 2018), http://dailysom.com/wp-content/uploads/2018/11/Intra-GCC-Relations-Between-Cooperation-and-Competition-Stands-Sovereignty.pdf.
20. Adnan Shihab-Eldin, *Author's Interview with Dr Adnan Shihab-Eldin, Director-General of the Kuwait Foundation for the Advancement of Sciences and Former Advisor to the Kuwait National Nuclear Energy Committee* (2019).
21. Ibid.
22. In 2008, the CEO of a consulting group commented that 'not a day goes by without talk of a nuclear renaissance' n.d., *Driving the Nuclear Renaissance—Nuclear Power in Canada* (MZ Consulting, 2008), p. 46, http://www.mzconsultinginc.com/NuclearBusinessMZCarticle.pdf. For other examples of the nuclear renaissance, see Michael White, "Brown Calls for Eight New Nuclear Plants," *The Guardian* (UK), 14 July 2008, https://www.theguardian.com/environment/2008/jul/14/nuclearpower.gordonbrown; Bob Evans, "The Nuclear Renaissance Moves Forward," *Power Engineering*, 1 December 2008; Michael Sauda, *The Atomic Age Enters a New Dawn*, 11 July 2008 ed., *Spiegel online.*
23. Andrea Gamba, *New Energy Sources for Jordan: Macroeconomic Impact and Policy Considerations* (Paris: International Monetary Fund, 2015), p. 3, https://www.imf.org/external/pubs/ft/wp/2015/wp15115.pdf; JT, "Energy Cost Ratio to GDP Down to 10% Last Year," *The Jordan Times*, 14 January 2017, https://www.jordantimes.com/news/local/energy-cost-ratio-gdp-down-10-last-year.
24. KISR, *Kuwait Energy Outlook: Sustaining Prosperity through Strategic Energy Management* (Kuwait City: Kuwait Institute for Scientific Reseach, 2019), p. 35, https://www.undp.org/content/dam/rbas/doc/Energy%20and%20Environment/KEO_report_English.pdf.
25. Shihab-Eldin.
26. See, examples cited by Stasa Salacanin, "Arab States and Nuclear Energy: Necessity or Geopolitical Status Symbol?," *The New Arab*, 22 August 2018, https://www.alaraby.co.uk/english/indepth/2018/8/22/nuclear-energy-necessity-or-geopolitical-status-symbol.
27. As noted by Sanam Vakil, *Iran and the GCC: Hedging, Pragmatism, and Opportunism* (London: Chatham House, 2018), https://www.chathamhouse.org/sites/default/files/publications/research/2018-09-13-iran-

gcc-vakil.pdf, relations between the states of the GCC and Iran are not homogenous.

28. Cited by Gregg Rickman, "Iran's Nukes: Uae's Ambassador Endorses Preemptive Bombing of Iran," *The Cutting Edge*, 16 June 2010.
29. See, for example, Benjamin K. Sovacool and Scott Victor Valentine, "Introduction," in *The National Politics of Nuclear Power* (London: Routledge, 2012); Christian von Hirschhausen, *Nuclear Power in the Twenty-First Century—An Assessment* (Berlin: DIW Berlin, 2017), https://d-nb.info/1154940853/34; Andy Stirling and Phil Johnstone, "A Global Picture of Industrial Interdependencies between Civil and Military Infrastructures," *Nuclear Monitor*, 23 October 2018. A counter-argument is provided by Matthew Kroenig, *Exporting the Bomb: Technology Transfer and the Spread of Nuclear Weapons* (Ithaca, NY: Cornell University Press, 2010).
30. Abdullah bin Zayed Al Nahyan, "Why Go Nuclear? A Perspective from the United Arab Emirates," *Bulletin of the Atomic Scientists* 64, no. 4 (2008).
31. Nicholas L. Miller and Tristan A. Volpe, "Abstinence or Tolerance: Managing Nuclear Ambitions in Saudi Arabia," *The Washington Quarterly* 41, no. 2 (2018); Yoel Guzansky, "Saudi Arabia Nuclear Hedging," *New Atlanticist*, 13 December 2011.
32. See Ali Ahmad, *Economic Considerations of Nuclear Power Deployment in Saudi Arabia* (Washington, DC: Nuclear Policy Education Center, 2018), http://npolicy.org/Articles/Ahmad_Saudi_Arabia.pdf; Robin Mills, "Saudi Arabia Energy Needs and Nuclear Power," in *Avoiding a Nuclear Wild, Wild West in the Middle East*, ed. Henry D. Sokolski (Arlington: Nonproliferation Policy Education Center, 2018); Simon Henderson, *Money for Missiles? Reassessing the Saudi Visit to Pakistan* (Washington, DC: The Washington Institute, 2019), https://www.washingtoninstitute.org/policy-analysis/view/money-for-missiles-reassessing-the-saudi-visit-to-pakistan; Colin H. Kahl, Melissa G. Dalton, and Matthew Irvine, *Atomic Kingdom: If Iran Builds the Bomb, Will Saudi Arabia Be Next?* (Washington, DC: Center for a New American Security, 2013), https://www.files.ethz.ch/isn/161866/CNAS_AtomicKingdom_Kahl.pdf.
33. As cited by Steven Mufson, "Why Does Saudi Arabia Want to Spend Billions to Enrich Its Own Uranium?," *The Washington Post*, 19 March 2018, https://www.washingtonpost.com/business/economy/why-does-saudi-arabia-want-to-spend-billions-to-enrich-its-own-uranium/2018/03/19/1ce87608-2225-11e8-badd-7c9f29a55815_story.html.
34. Ethel Solingen, *Nuclear Logics: Contrasting Paths in East Asia and the Middle East* (Princeton: Princeton University Press, 2009).

35. Abdullah bin Zayed Al Nahyan et al., "Why Go Nuclear?," *Bulletin of the Atomic Scientists* 64, no. 4 (2008): 17, https://doi.org/10.2968/064004005.
36. From John Parsons, "What Does Nuclear Power Really Cost?," *World Economic Forum Agenda*, 26 May 2015, https://www.weforum.org/agenda/2015/05/what-does-nuclear-power-really-cost/; and Lazard, *Lazard's Levelized Cost of Energy Analysis—Version 13.0* (2019), p. 18, https://www.lazard.com/media/451086/lazards-levelized-cost-of-energy-version-130-vf.pdf.
37. David Scott, *Author's Interview with Mr David Scott, Senior Director, Executive Affairs Authority Abu Dhabi* (2019).
38. See Cindy Vestergaard, *Governing Uranium Globally* (Copenhagen: Danish Institute for International Studies, 2015), p. 23, Figure 4, https://www.econstor.eu/bitstream/10419/144724/1/848318978.pdf.
39. WNA, *Uranium Enrichment* (London: World Nuclear Association, 2020), https://www.world-nuclear.org/information-library/nuclear-fuel-cycle/conversion-enrichment-and-fabrication/uranium-enrichment.aspx.
40. WNA, *Nuclear Fuel and Its Fabrication* (London: World Nuclear Association, 2020), https://www.world-nuclear.org/information-library/nuclear-fuel-cycle/conversion-enrichment-and-fabrication/fuel-fabrication.aspx.
41. Ali Ahmad, "Economic Risks of Jordan's Nuclear Program," *Energy for Sustainable Development* 29 (2015), http://dx.doi.org/10.1016/j.esd.2015.09.001.
42. Mark Jacobson, *100% Clean, Renewable Energy and Storage for Everything* (Cambridge: Cambridge University Press, 2020, in press).
43. Lazard, 2. The levelized cost of energy (LCOE) is a useful, albeit imperfect, measure of the cost of electricity generated through different technologies. With variable renewable energy comprising a significant part of the energy mix in many countries, a system LCOE that accounts for balancing and grid costs on top of LCOE is required.
44. Quoted in Robert Mason and Gawdat Bahgat, *Civil Nuclear Energy in the Middle East: Demand, Parity, and Risk* (Washington, DC: The Arab Gulf States Institute in Washington, 2019), p. 18, https://agsiw.org/civil-nuclear-energy-in-the-middle-east-demand-parity-and-risk/.
45. Jessica Jewell, "Ready for Nuclear Energy? An Assessment of Capacities and Motications for Launching New Naitonal Nuclear Power Programs," *Energy Policy* 39 (2011), http://dx.doi.org/10.1016/j.enpol.2010.10.041. Information on the UAE's GDP in current US$ is from World Bank Data.
46. Justin Dargin, *The Dolphin Project: The Development of a Gulf Gas Initiative* (Oxford: Oxford Institute for Energy Studies, 2008), p. 9,

https://www.oxfordenergy.org/wpcms/wp-content/uploads/2010/11/NG22-TheDolphinProjectTheDevelopmentOfAGulfGasInitiative-JustinDargin-2008.pdf.
47. From Benjamin K. Sovacool, "Critically Weighing the Costs and Benefits of a Nuclear Renaissance," *Journal of Integrative Environmental Sciences* 7, no. 2 (2010): 118, Table 4, https://doi.org/10.1080/1943815X.2010.485618.
48. Ecofys, *Subsidies and Costs of Eu Energy* (Brussels: European Commission, 2014), p. 37, https://ec.europa.eu/energy/sites/ener/files/documents/ECOFYS%202014%20Subsidies%20and%20costs%20of%20EU%20energy_11_Nov.pdf.
49. Steven Geiger, *Author's Interview with Mr Steven Geiger, Co-Founder of Masdar* (2014).
50. See Pernilla Ouis, "'Greening the Emirates': The Modern Construction of Nature in the United Arab Emirates," *Cultural Georgraphies* 9 (2002): 342, https://doi.org/10.1191/1474474002eu252oa; and Andy Speiss, "Developing Adaptive Capacity for Responding to Environmental Change in the Arab Gulf States: Uncertainties to Linking Ecosystem Conservation, Sustainable Development and Society in Authoritarian Rentier Economies," *Global and Planetary Change* 64 (2008): 242, http://dx.doi.org/10.1016/j.gloplacha.2008.10.008. Data on carbon dioxide emissions are from CO2 emissions (metric tons per capita), World Bank Data.
51. Cited by Li-Chen Sim, "Re-Branding Abu Dhabi: From Oil Giant to Energy Titan," *Place Branding and Public Diplomacy* 8, nos. 83–98 (2012).
52. See UAE, *Policy of the United Arab Emirates on the Evaluation and Potential Development of Peaceful Nuclear Energy* (Abu Dhabi: 2008), https://www.uae-embassy.org/sites/default/files/UAE_Policy_Peaceful_Nuclear_Energy_English.pdf.
53. Krane estimates that energy subsidies account for one-third of energy consumption in the Gulf monarchies. See Jim Krane, "Political Enablers of Energy Subsidy Reform in Middle Eastern Oil Exporters," *Nature Energy* 3, no. 7 (2018), http://dx.doi.org/10.1038/s41560-018-0113-4. For an excellent review of the Gulf's gas shortage, see Laura El-Katiri and Bassam Fattouh, *A Brief Political Economy of Energy Subsidies in the Middle East and North Africa* (Oxford: Oxford Institute for Energy Studies, 2015), https://www.oxfordenergy.org/wpcms/wp-content/uploads/2015/02/MEP-11.pdf.
54. David Coady et al., *Global Fossil Fuel Subsidies Remain Large: An Update Based on Country-Level Estimates* (Washington, DC: International Monetary Fund, 2019), p. 22, Figure 15, https://www.imf.org/~/media/Files/Publications/WP/2019/WPIEA2019089.ashx.

55. Krane, p. 549.
56. The figure cited is for the US and based on a business-as-usual scenario by 2020. See McKinsey, *Energy Efficiency: A Compelling Global Resource* (New York: McKinsey & Company, 2010), p. 5, https://www.mckinsey.com/~/media/mckinsey/dotcom/client_service/Sustainability/PDFs/A_Compelling_Global_Resource.ashx. For a discussion of barriers to implementing efficiency measures in the Gulf, see Joshua P. Meltzer, Nathan Hultman, and Claire Langley, *Low-Carbon Energy Transitions in Qatar and the Gulf Cooperation Council Region* (Washington, DC: Brookings Institution Press, 2014), pp. 26–39, https://www.brookings.edu/wp-content/uploads/2016/07/low-carbon-energy-transitions-qatar-meltzer-hultman-full.pdf.
57. For a more comprehensive discussion of policy feedback and stability, see Cameron Roberts et al., "The Politics of Accelerating Low-Carbon Transitions: Towards a New Research Agenda," *Energy Research & Social Science* 44 (2018), http://dx.doi.org/10.1016/j.erss.2018.06.001.
58. Juergen Braunstein, "Domestic Sources of Twenty-First Century Geopolitics: Domestic Politics and Sovereign Wealth Funds in GCC Economies," *New Political Economy* 24, no. 2 (2019), http://dx.doi.org/10.1080/13563467.2018.1431619.
59. Charles Ebinger et al., *Models for Aspirant Civil Nuclear Energy Nations in the Middle East* (Washington, DC: Brookings Institution, 2011), pp. 47–54, https://www.brookings.edu/wp-content/uploads/2016/06/0927_middle_east_nuclear_ebinger_banks.pdf.
60. Frank Geels, "Regime Resistance Against Low-Carbon Transitions: Introducing Politics and Power into the Multi-Level Perspective," *Theory, Culture and Society* 31, no. 5 (2014), https://doi.org/10.1177/0263276414531627.
61. See WAM, "Adnoc Seeks to Expand Strategic Partnerships, Pursue Smart Growth, Drive Responsible Production: Al Jaber," *WAM*, 9 October 2019, https://wam.ae/en/details/1395302793437.
62. NEI, "UAE Companies Benefit from Barakah Work," *Nuclear Engineering International*, 15 October 2018, https://www.neimagazine.com/news/newsuae-companies-benefit-from-barakah-work-6801296.
63. ENEC, "US$ 2.5 Billion in Contracts Awarded to Local Companies Participating in UAE Nuclear Energy Program," Emirates Nuclear Energy Corporation, https://www.enec.gov.ae/news/latest-news/us-2-5-billion-in-contracts-awarded-to-local-companies-participating-in-uae/.
64. The concepts of a hard or soft energy path and their implications was first introduced by Amory Lovins, *Soft Energy Paths: Towards a Durable Peace* (New Yrok: Harper & Row, 1976).
65. Oilprice.com, "Turkey's Opaque Private Energy Sector," *Oilprice.com*, n.d., https://oilprice.com/Energy/Energy-General/Turkeys-Opaque-Pri

vate-Energy-Sector.html; and Gül Berna Özcan and Umut Gündüz, "Energy Privatisations, Business-Politics Connections and Governance under Political Islam," *Environment and Planning C: Government and Policy* 33 (2015), http://dx.doi.org/10.1177/0263774X15614659.

66. For a list of licenses filed by ENEC with regulatory authorities including EAD, see ENEC, "Regulatory Licenses," Emirates Nuclear Energy Corporation, https://www.enec.gov.ae/regulation/regulation-and-review/regulatory-licensing/.
67. Scott.
68. See Bryan R. Early, "Acquiring Foreign Nuclear Assistance in the Middle East: Strategic Lessons from the United Arab Emirates," *The Non-Proliferation Review* 17, no. 2 (2010), http://dx.doi.org/10.1080/10736700.2010.485427.
69. Scott Montgomery and Thomas Graham Jr., *Launching a New Nuclear Power State: The United Arab Emirates, Seeing the Light: The Case for Nuclear Power in the 21st Century* (Cambridge: Cambridge University Press, 2017).
70. Izak Atiyas, *A Review of Turkey's Nuclear Policies and Practices* (Istanbul: EDAM Center for Economics and Foreign Policy Studies, 2015), http://edam.org.tr/wp-content/uploads/2015/08/A-Review-of-Turkeys-Nuclear-Policies-and-Practices.pdf; and Christer Viktorsson, "First Steps of a Brand New Regulator," *Nuclear Engineering International* (9 May 2011), https://www.neimagazine.com/features/featurefirst-steps-of-a-brand-new-regulator.
71. See Kareem Shaheen, "Nuclear Watchdog Resists Deadline in Abu Dhabi Plant Evaluation," *The National*, 4 November 2010, https://www.thenational.ae/business/nuclear-watchdog-resists-deadline-in-abu-dhabi-plant-evaluation-1.554327.
72. Mason and Bahgat, 8.
73. Rania El Gamal and Katie Paul, "Saudi Arabia Should Not Forfeit 'Sovereign' Right to Enrich Uranium: Senior Prince," *Reuters*, 21 December 2017, https://www.reuters.com/article/us-saudi-nuclear-turki/saudi-arabia-should-not-forfeit-sovereign-right-to-enrich-uranium-senior-prince-idUSKBN1EF287; Ali Ahmad, Reem Salameh, and M.V. Ramana, *Localizing Nuclear Capacity? Saudi Arabia and Small Modular Reactors* (Beirut: Issam Fares Institute for Public Policy and International Affairs, 2019), https://www.aub.edu.lb/ifi/Documents/publications/working_papers/2018-2019/20190708_localising_nuclear_capacity_KSA.pdf.
74. See also Paul Dorfman, *Gulf Nuclear Ambition: New Reactors in the United Arab Emirates* (Nuclear Consulting Group, 2019), https://www.nuclearconsult.com/wp/wp-content/uploads/2019/12/Gulf-Nuclear-Ambition-NCG-Dec-2019.pdf.

75. ENEC, *National Poll Shows Strong Support for UAE Peaceful Nuclear Energy Program* (Emirates Nuclear Energy Corporation, 2018).
76. Charles Digges, "Nuclear Power Wildly Popular in Russia, Independent Poll Shows," *Bellona*, 10 April 2018, https://bellona.org/news/nuclear-issues/2018-04-nuclear-power-wildly-popular-in-russian-independent-poll-shows; Reuters, "South Koreans' Support for Nuclear Projects Deals Blow to Government Energy Plan," 20 October 2017, https://www.reuters.com/article/us-southkorea-nuclear/south-koreans-support-for-nuclear-projects-deals-blow-to-government-energy-plan-idUSKBN1CP06F.
77. Scott.
78. Nima Gerami, *Leadership Divided? The Domestic Politics of Iran's Nuclear Debate* (Washington, DC: The Washington Institute, 2014), https://www.washingtoninstitute.org/policy-analysis/view/leadership-divided-the-domestic-politics-of-irans-nuclear-debate; Emre İşeri, Defne Günay, and Alper Almaz, "Contending Narratives on the Sustainability of Nuclear Energy in Turkey," *Environment and Planning C: Politics and Space* 36, no. 1 (2018), http://dx.doi.org/10.1177/2399654417704199.
79. Data on Trust in Government is from GovData360, *Public Trust in Politicians*; the quote is from a member of a Jordanian non-government organization as cited by Kane Chen, "Are Jordan's Nuclear Ambitions a Mirage?," *Bulletin of the Atomic Scientists* (16 December 2013), https://thebulletin.org/2013/12/are-jordans-nuclear-ambitions-a-mirage/.
80. Imad El-Anis, "Explaining the Behaviour of Small States: An Analysis of Jordan's Nuclear Energy Policy," *Cambridge Review of International Affairs* 29, no. 2 (2016), http://dx.doi.org/10.1080/09557571.2015.1018136.
81. See Michael Eisenstadt and Mehdi Khalaji, *Nuclear Fatwa: Religion and Politics in Iran's Proliferation Strategy* (Washington, DC: The Washington Institute for Near East Policy, 2011), https://www.washingtoninstitute.org/uploads/Documents/pubs/PolicyFocus115.pdf; and Nazila Fathi, "An Old Letter Casts Doubts on Iran's Goal for Uranium," *The New York Times*, 5 October 2006.
82. Ali Vaez and Karim Sadjadpour, *Iran's Nuclear Odyssey: Costs and Risks* (Washington, DC: Carnegie Endowment for International Peace, 2013), https://carnegieendowment.org/2013/04/02/iran-s-nuclear-odyssey-costs-and-risks-pub-51346.
83. Valdai, *Prospects for Nuclear Power in the Middle East: Russia's Interests* (Moscow: Valdai Discussion Club, 2016), p. 58, http://cenessrussia.org/data/doc/REPORT_ENG_prospectsfornuclearpowerME.pdf.
84. See Li-Chen Sim, "Economic Diversification in Russia: Nuclear to the Rescue?," in *Economic Diversification Policies in Natural Resource Rich Economies*, ed. Sami Mahroum and Yasser Al Saleh (Abingdon, Oxon: Routledge, 2017); Stanislav Martínek, "Sovereign Wealth Funds: Driving

Growth of the Nuclear Power Sector," *Energy Strategy Reviews* 18 (2017), http://dx.doi.org/10.1016/j.esr.2017.09.018; Reuters, "Russia May Use National Wealth Fund to Finance Egypt Nuclear Plant: Siluanov," *Reuters*, 18 October 2018, https://www.reuters.com/article/russia-economy-funds-egypt/russia-may-use-national-wealth-fund-to-finance-egypt-nuclear-plant-siluanov-idUSR4N1SL007.

85. Li-Chen Sim, "Russia and the UAE Are Now Strategic Partners: What's Next?," *Lobelog*, 7 June 2018, https://lobelog.com/russia-and-the-uae-are-now-strategic-partners-whats-next/.
86. For the origins of Rosatom, see Sim, in *Economic Diversification Policies in Natural Resource Rich Economies*.
87. Sam Reynolds, "Why the Civil Nuclear Trap Is Part and Parcel of the Belt and Road Strategy," *The Diplomat* (2018), https://thediplomat.com/2018/07/why-the-civil-nuclear-trap-is-part-and-parcel-of-the-belt-and-road-strategy/.
88. Cited by Natasha Doff, "Russia Still Paying Price for Crimea Five Years after Annexation," *Bloomberg*, 17 March 2019, https://www.bloomberg.com/news/articles/2019-03-17/russia-still-paying-price-for-crimea-five-years-after-annexation.
89. For a comparison between SMRs and large reactors, see Benito Mignacca and Giorgio Locatelli, "Economics and Finance of Small Modular Reactors: A Systematic Review and Research Agenda," *Renewable and Sustainable Energy Reviews* 118 (2020), https://doi.org/10.1016/j.rser.2019.109519.
90. Ahmad, *Economic Considerations of Nuclear Power Deployment in Saudi Arabia*, p. 10.
91. GCC, "Bnef Annual Li-Ion Battery Price Survey Finds Prices Fell 13% from 2018 to Average $156/Kwh in 2019," *Green Car Congress*, 4 December 2019, https://www.greencarcongress.com/2019/12/20191204-bnef.html.
92. Shihab-Eldin.

CHAPTER 11

Climate Change Policy in the Arab Region

Mari Luomi

Introduction: Comparing Arab Countries' Climate Policies

Will Arab countries always remain global laggards in domestic climate policy? Do they still deserve the title of obstructionists in international climate change negotiations? What differences are there in climate change policy in the Arab region at different levels and in different structural contexts?

While there is a nascent literature examining the climate change policies of individual Arab countries and their behaviour in international climate change negotiations, there has so far not been a consistent effort to examine these in a regional comparative setting, from a social science perspective, which is what this chapter sets out to do.

This chapter focuses on three questions: first, why are recent years' changes in domestic climate change policy in many Arab countries often not reflected in policies at the international level? Second, are there

M. Luomi (✉)
Abu Dhabi, United Arab Emirates
e-mail: mari.luomi@gmail.com

R. Mills and L.-C. Sim (eds.), *Low Carbon Energy in the Middle East and North Africa*, International Political Economy Series,
https://doi.org/10.1007/978-3-030-59554-8_11

discernible differences in policy choices adopted by oil exporters versus non-oil-exporting Arab countries, and what explains these differences—the rentier paradigm, leadership agency or something else? And third, is a convergence of domestic rhetoric, domestic policy and international policy positions on the horizon for the region and its countries?

In order to answer these questions, the chapter compares four Arab countries that have been active in either domestic or international climate change policy, or both. Two are net oil exporters and classifiable as rentier economies: Saudi Arabia and the United Arab Emirates (UAE). The other two are net oil importers and have the largest renewable energy capacity among the Arab countries: Egypt and Morocco.

Changes and Continuities

Arab countries have come a long way in domestic climate change policy over the past decade. A 2009 report by the Arab Forum for Environment and Development concluded that 'virtually no work is being carried out to make the Arab countries prepared for climate change challenges'.[1] The report found a near-absence of records of climate patterns and a dearth of systematic data gathering and research on both physical and socioeconomic impacts of climate change climate change.

Since then, a lot has changed. Scientific understanding of physical vulnerabilities has improved[2] and, at the time of writing, in early 2020, 18 out of the 22 countries had ratified the Paris Agreement and developed related medium-term climate change plans. Despite vastly different socioeconomic profiles, many have in place domestic renewable energy targets and demonstrate at least some level of policy development in the two key areas of climate action, mitigation (emission reductions) and adaptation. Some are in the process of developing long-term low-emissions strategies or climate change laws.

At the same time, the Arab Group's positions in the United Nations (UN) climate change negotiations seem to have remained remarkably stable. In 2009, environmental non-governmental organisations (NGOs) described Arab countries in the UN negotiations as being mainly 'focused on protecting oil exports rather than preserving the planet'. They accused Saudi Arabia for 'using its political weight in the region as well as divisions among other Arab governments to push through its interests'.[3]

A decade later, at the 2018 UN climate conference, it seemed much had not changed: Saudi Arabia and Kuwait, along with two other major oil producers the US and Russia, prevented the UN from 'welcoming' a report by the Intergovernmental Panel on Climate Change (IPCC) on the impacts of 1.5 °C of global warming and related emissions pathways, instead calling for merely 'noting' the report. This was widely perceived as an effort to undermine related science and policy discussions to push back the global peak in oil consumption, as keeping global temperature rise below 1.5 °C would require even more radical and rapid cuts to global fossil fuel consumption than staying below 2 °C—both targets enshrined in the Paris Agreement.[4]

In simplified terms, the Arab Group's long-standing position in international climate negotiations can be characterised as being based on a static, binary worldview: it portrays all Arab countries, both rich and poor, oil-exporting and non-oil-exporting, as developing countries (as opposed to developed) that are highly-vulnerable to both the physical impacts of climate change and the impacts of international mitigation measures (i.e. cutting fossil fuel use). It also involves a view that none of the Arab countries—all of which are classified as developing countries under the UN Framework Convention on Climate Change (UNFCCC)—bears notable responsibility for reducing global emissions.

There are apparent disparities in Arab countries' present and historical contributions to climate change: the six Gulf Cooperation Council (GCC) member countries' emissions account for 2.5% of present-day global emissions—compared to a collective share of 3.0% by the other 15 Arab countries.[5] Historically, the oil exporters bear an even higher responsibility: a study from 2014 calculated that the state-owned oil companies of Saudi Arabia, Kuwait, the UAE and Algeria are jointly responsible for more than 5% of global cumulative carbon dioxide (CO_2) and methane emissions between 1751 and 2010.[6] As for the impacts of climate change, while all Arab countries indeed are highly vulnerable to various direct and indirect negative impacts, their capacity to adapt to these impacts, including in infrastructure, urban settlements, agriculture, food and water security and health, is highly varied.

Also typically, although some Arab countries have demonstrated leadership and eagerness for more ambitious domestic climate action, including in other international fora, such views have not been reflected in the Arab Group's views.

Absence of a Two-Level Game

What then drives policy at these two levels in the Arab countries? And why do they seem so disconnected? In the fields of International relations and political economy, it is generally accepted that domestic and international politics deeply influence each other and, as Putnam has noted, there are 'powerful incentives for consistency between the two'.[7] In his seminal article from 1988, Putnam described international negotiations as a two-level game:

> At the national level, domestic groups pursue their interests by pressuring the government to adopt favorable policies, and politicians seek power by constructing coalitions among those groups. At the international level, national governments seek to maximize their own ability to satisfy domestic pressures, while minimizing the adverse consequences of foreign developments.[8]

Perhaps what then explains the observed discrepancies between the domestic and international levels in Arab countries' climate change policies is a combination of weak domestic constituencies that favour ambitious international climate policies (such as environment ministries or NGOs) and low institutionalisation of regional cooperation and coordination mechanisms. In other words, a 'low domestic political cost' of siding with conservative positions at the international level means that negotiators are more likely to support positions that are promoted by oil-exporting country delegations, which often are better-funded, have stronger negotiating capacity and wield more power in the region overall. The chapter will test whether these two factors explain the 'absence' of a two-level game in Arab climate change policy.

Different Domestic Challenges

Climate change of course is a multidimensional policy challenge for many countries of the Arab region. All Arab countries will need to find ways to adapt to the physical impacts and socioeconomic risks of climate change, such as abnormal weather, migration and food insecurity. A second major challenge is the decarbonisation of energy systems, which in many Arab countries are still heavily dominated by fossil fuels.

Climate change for the region's oil exporters has a third dimension, commonly referred to in UN jargon as 'response measures'. These are actions taken by other countries to reduce or limit their fossil fuel consumption, which is ultimately expected to lead to a decline in global coal, oil and natural gas demand and, through this, low prices for the exporters. Arguably, the higher the economic reliance on oil revenue and the larger a country's oil reserves, the more vulnerable it will be to the negative impacts of climate change response measures. Based on International Monetary Fund estimates, oil revenue in ten Arab oil-exporting countries accounted for 19–63% of the GDP and approximately 45–95% of fiscal revenue in 2014. In the region's three top oil-exporting countries, these figures were as follows: Saudi Arabia 43 and 75%, the UAE 34 and 65% and Kuwait 63 and 80%.[9] These three countries, along with Iraq and Libya, also rank in the global top-10 in proven crude oil reserves, with Saudi Arabia and the UAE accounting for 18 and 7% of total world reserves, respectively.[10]

For the non-oil-exporting (or net-importing) countries, the challenge compared to the oil exporters is different in two ways: on the one hand, the structural economic transformation needed will not be as wide-reaching as in the oil-exporting countries. On the other, non-oil economies generally have lower levels of income to spend in adapting to climate change and transforming their energy systems. Climate action also requires new technologies and human and institutional capacities that less wealthy countries cannot afford to purchase, develop or import in a similar way to higher-income ones.

Oil rent, therefore, is both a handicap and an enabler from a climate policy perspective. But are there any specific characteristics in Arab oil-exporting countries' emerging domestic climate change policies compared to Arab non-oil-exporters? Is it possible to identify structural factors that influence climate policy in each case? And what is the role of agency, such as leadership figures or ministers, and, related to this, institutional set-ups in domestic climate change policy outcomes? The chapter will examine these questions through the four case studies.

From Post-oil Rhetoric to Present-Day Climate Action

Recently, the region's oil exporters have made bold statements about the post-oil era. In 2015, Crown Prince of Abu Dhabi Sheikh Mohammed bin Zayed Al Nahyan declared that the UAE would celebrate the export of its last barrel of oil in a few decades' time if it invested now in the right sectors.[11] In 2016, Saudi Arabia's Crown Prince Mohammed bin Salman

Al Saud opined the country had developed 'a case of oil addiction' but could live without it by 2020.[12]

Gulf oil exporters' development plans demonstrate some degree of aspiration with regard to a more systematic transition to more sustainable economies. The most ambitious ones, in this regard, have been the UAE, Saudi Arabia and Qatar. They all have in place detailed and dynamic longer-term visions, which in most cases are carried forward through shorter-term strategic plans. What is common in these strategies, however, is that they largely represent an intensification of policies the countries have considered or had in place for years, if not decades, which have so far not yielded transformative change.[13] In addition to accelerating the implementation of incremental policies that have a proven track record (such as fossil fuel pricing reform and stricter emission standards and laws), transformative policies (such as carbon pricing and ambitious policy targets and implementation plans) will be crucial for the Gulf/Arab oil exporters if they wish to maintain socioeconomic development in an era of intensifying climate change impacts and global energy transitions.

A further question this chapter therefore will explore is whether a beneficial convergence of domestic rhetoric, domestic policy and international policy positions is on the horizon for the oil exporters as well as the Arab countries as a negotiating bloc.

Climate Change Policy in the United Arab Emirates

This section examines climate change policy in the UAE as follows: it starts with an examination of the UAE's role in international climate change negotiations, followed by a description of the evolution and main elements of the country's current climate change policy and institutional framework. The section concludes with an analysis that speaks to the three questions outlined at the beginning of the chapter, namely: is the country's domestic policy aligned with the international level positions and, if not, why? What are the main drivers of the country's approach to climate change? And are there signs of transformative policies to come? The three other country case studies in this chapter follow the same structure.

Role in the UNFCCC

The UAE has traditionally been a quiet player in the UN climate change negotiations, which makes analysing its role difficult. The country rarely takes the floor in formal or semi-formal (contact group and informal consultation) negotiating settings, and it rarely issues independent written submissions of views (similarly to most other Arab Group countries).

The UAE's positions are broadly in line with those of the developing countries' main negotiating bloc, the Group of 77 and China (G-77/China), and the Arab Group, which both participate actively in the negotiations through issue-based country coordinators and make written submissions of views. The G-77/China generally emphasises issues around developed countries' responsibility to lead, need for further climate finance for developing countries, importance of adaptation (and adaptation finance) and alignment with developing countries' poverty alleviation and broader sustainable development efforts.[14] The Arab Group, in addition, has consistently stressed issues related to response measures, calling for assistance to its members' economic diversification efforts and expressing opposition to any 'unilateral trade measures in the name of climate change' (such as emission trading systems or carbon taxes) that could impact exports from developing to developed countries.[15]

In the first half of the 2010s, the UAE was one of only two Arab countries, alongside Lebanon, participating in the Cartagena Dialogue, a bridgebuilding forum for progressive countries from various regions. Also differentiating itself from many other Arab countries, the UAE did not join the conservative Like-Minded Developing Countries (LMDCs) group, formed in 2012 as a response to pressure felt by many emerging and middle-income economies to do more from groups including the EU, Alliance of Small Island States and Least Developed Countries.[16] At the same time, the UAE has also not spoken out against the LMDCs' views, which in many instances coincided with those of the Arab Group in the negotiations in the run-up to the 2015 Paris Agreement and in the negotiations on its rulebook that ended in 2018.

Domestic Policy Evolution and Main Elements

Climate change emerged on the UAE's policy agenda in a significant way in the late 2000s, following the establishment of Abu Dhabi's Masdar

Initiative (2006) and the UAE's successful campaign to host the headquarters of the International Renewable Energy Agency (IRENA) in 2009.[17] Policy milestones have included: a 7% renewable energy power generation capacity target by 2020 by Abu Dhabi; a 25% renewable power target by 2030 by Dubai; and a federal Energy Strategy 2050, which contains a 44% renewable power capacity target by 2050 and targets for energy efficiency and CO_2 emissions that are relative to a business-as-usual (BAU) scenario. In 2012, the government announced a federal-level Green Growth Strategy, which includes a several climate change-related initiatives for 2030. The UAE has also launched a National Climate Change Plan for 2050, which outlines priorities in three areas: mitigation, adaptation and economic diversification. It also outlines a number of priority actions, including an emissions monitoring system, systematic adaptation planning and measures to support the private sector. Since 2018, the UAE has been working on a climate change law, which will provide a more robust institutional and policy framework for a government response to the challenge.

The UAE's first Nationally Determined Contribution (NDC, medium-term domestic climate change plan) submitted to the Paris Agreement in 2015, is framed in the context of economic diversification, in line with Article 4.7 of the Agreement (on mitigation co-benefits resulting from economic diversification plans qualifying as mitigation outcomes)—a concept promoted by a number of GCC countries since 2012. The NDC contains a 24% power sector 'clean energy' generation target, which was raised in 2016 to 27%. Achieving the target is assumed to depend on Abu Dhabi's four nuclear reactors being online by 2021—the reactors, with a total capacity of 5.6 GW, are expected to supply 'up to 25%' of the UAE's electricity needs once operational.[18] In 2018, the UAE had a renewable electricity capacity of 0.6 GW,[19] equal to 2% of the total generation capacity, with plans to raise this to 1.7 GW by 2021.[20]

In 2020, as a party to the Paris Agreement and given its early NDC target year (2021), the UAE is required to announce a new NDC, which by the Agreement's rules must be more ambitious than the previous one. The government has indicated that the new NDC would be based on the federal Energy Strategy's 50% by 2050 clean energy target.[21] However, at the time of writing it was still unclear whether it would also include a more medium-term target year, such as 2030 or 2035, similar to most other countries.

Institutional Framework

The institutional landscape for climate change policy in the UAE is relatively well-developed, even if some gaps exist. At the federal level, climate change was explicitly added to the mandate of the Ministry of Environment and Water in 2016, and the ministry, originally established in 2006, was renamed Ministry of *Climate Change* and Environment (MoCCAE) when a Directorate of Energy and Climate Change (est. 2010) was transferred over from the Ministry of Foreign Affairs in an effort to consolidate both domestic and international climate change policy under one government entity. The MoCCAE is tasked with leading on the UAE's federal climate change policy, and it coordinates with various stakeholder entities at both federal and emirate levels on related matters. Even the UAE's UNFCCC delegation is composed of delegates from a large number of government stakeholder organisations.

Reporting and policy work on energy-related emissions, which form 87% of the UAE's GHG emissions,[22] however, is under the mandate of the Ministry of Energy and Industry. In Abu Dhabi, the Environment Agency—Abu Dhabi (EAD) has undertaken pioneering work on climate change research, data and policy and in Dubai, the municipality has been working on a climate change adaptation strategy. In the five smaller emirates, municipalities (and an environmental authority in Sharjah) govern environmental protection, but there are no records of ongoing emirate-level climate change policy work, and representatives from these five entities do not generally attend UN climate change negotiations.

The UAE has only one non-governmental (NGO) organisation, Emirates Nature (the local chapter of the environmental NGO WWF), that actively engages in policy-oriented work on climate change. Unlike local WWF chapters elsewhere, however, Emirates Nature's board is composed of UAE government officials. It mainly focuses on working with the government and informing policymaking, and does not play an environmental watchdog role. Neither does the local chapter work on issues related to the UAE's UNFCCC policies.

Alignment, Drivers and Future Prospects

The UAE has sought to be seen as a regional leader in climate action since the early 2010s through hosting IRENA and a number of high-profile climate change-related events, including the annual Abu Dhabi Sustainability Week and preparatory meetings for the UN Secretary-General's Climate Summits in 2014 and 2019. This objective remains an important policy driver, alongside being seen as a good global citizen through exerting 'active global responsibility'—an objective enshrined in the UAE Foreign Ministry's strategy.[23] The UAE's top leadership is fully supportive of these objectives and the Crown Prince of Abu Dhabi, Sheikh Mohammed bin Zayed, in particular has been perceived as the driving force behind the UAE's decision to place sustainable energy and climate policy as key elements in the country's economic policy.

Two policy misalignments are, however, observable in this regard: first, there is a disconnect between the UAE's rhetoric outside the UNFCCC and its positions within the UNFCCC, where its positions are not well-defined. In non-UNFCCC fora, the UAE often applies an opportunities-oriented rhetoric. On the eve of the 2019 Climate Summit preparatory meeting, the UAE's Climate Change and Environment Minister announced 'a green and clean future is good for the economy… in the UAE, we have proven that climate action leads to more jobs, more growth, and more resilience and prosperity'.[24] At the same time, when the positions of the Arab Group in the UNFCCC negotiations seem to be out of line with that of a country seeking to be a role model and voice for ambitious climate change policy in the Gulf and Arab region, the UAE often acquiesces.

As for domestic policy, despite the fact that the UAE has conducted significant policy work and is taking action to reduce emissions and resilience in ways that go beyond those described in this chapter, the overall levels of policy ambition and implementation are still relatively modest and should be significantly accelerated in the coming years.

Based on this track record, the UAE deserves its self-promoted title of a leader in climate change policy in the Gulf region. Much, however, still remains to be done. The policies currently in place, if implemented, will only result in incremental change, which does not meet the scale of the challenge for a country that still receives a third of its GDP and two-thirds of government revenue from oil. First, there are no emissions-related/renewable energy targets that go beyond the power sector. Electricity and heat production account for 36% of the UAE's total GHG emissions[25]—meaning that two-thirds of the UAE's emissions are not yet covered by a quantitative climate change policy target. Second, some of the plans, including the Abu Dhabi 2020 target and the 2050 federal energy strategy have not been accompanied by (publicly-available) implementation plans or, in the latter case, a baseline scenario. Third, the 2050 climate change plan does not include any quantitative emission reduction targets. The plan also does not refer to any processes for setting such targets despite an article in the Paris Agreement (4.19) stating that all countries 'should' develop long-term low GHG emission development strategies that align with the goals of the Agreement.

Climate Change Policy in Saudi Arabia

Role in the UNFCCC

Saudi Arabia has since the 1990s been the most active, skilled and dominant Arab country in the UN climate change negotiations. In addition to the Arab Group, it has been active in the LMDCs and G-77/China. In an observation-based study published in 2008, Depledge examined the Saudi positions through the concept of obstructionism, arguing that obstructionists join negotiations 'because they fear the agreement that others might reach'.[26] She argued that the Saudi UNFCCC positions were driven by 'its fears over the potential negative impacts of climate change mitigation policies on its economy' and supported by 'powerful oil and coal lobbies within industrialized countries'.[27]

Much of the positions emphasised, and tactics employed, by the Saudi delegation in UNFCCC and IPCC meetings in the 1990s and 2000s are still visible in present-day negotiations. These include an emphasis on the costs of mitigation action and on the negative impacts of response measures on oil-exporting countries' economies. Saudi Arabia has also consistently sought to slow or water down negotiating processes and politically-negotiated documents that relate to climate science and IPCC reports, in particular with regard to staying below 1.5 °C of global warming. Many of Saudi Arabia's skilful negotiators, with a few exceptions, come from the Ministry of Energy and many have remained in the process for a long period of time—characteristics highlighted also by Depledge in her 2008 article.[28]

In the negotiations, the Arab Group holds preparatory meetings in the run-up to UNFCCC meetings and coordinates twice a day during the negotiating sessions. Saudi Arabia is the de facto lead country of the Group, and its national positions are visibly reflected in those of the Arab Group (discussed in the UAE section above). Egypt is another country that occasionally formally speaks for the Group. Kuwait and Qatar often voice their support of Saudi Arabia's views in semi-formal negotiating settings—the latter seemingly less since the 2017 embargo.

It is difficult to ascertain to what extent other Arab countries' inputs, views and interests are aligned and/or reflected in the Arab Group's positions. This is due to many Arab countries' low degree of formal articulation of their international policy positions (e.g. in single-country written submissions or public policy statements) and low levels of active participation in formal and semi-formal negotiating settings in the UNFCCC (which, unlike country group coordination meetings, are open to observers and which the author has regularly attended since 2008).

Despite being perceived as a difficult player in the negotiations, Saudi Arabia is not a heavyweight like the US or China and cannot therefore decide alone on the rise or fall of major decisions. It did not publicly oppose the adoption of the Paris Agreement in December 2015, for example. Many long-term observers also suggest that Saudi Arabia has softened its rhetoric in the past decade compared to the previous two, after a change of the lead negotiator. It was also among the first few Arab countries to ratify the agreement. The fact that the Saudi ratification happened exactly a day before the agreement's entry into force, in November 2016, could however either be interpreted as a more constructive approach to global climate action or merely further evidence to support the obstructionism argument.

Domestic Policy Evolution and Main Elements

In the past decade, policies that support emissions reductions directly or indirectly have emerged on the Saudi domestic policy agenda. Similarly to the UAE, Saudi Arabia began engaging in the UNFCCC Clean Development Mechanism (CDM) to pursue monetisation of some of its emissions reductions projects through the sale of carbon credits. In 2003, the government launched its first National Energy Efficiency Program, followed in 2010 by the establishment of the Saudi Energy Efficiency

Center (SEEC) to guide related programming. An energy conservation law was also under development in 2019.[29]

Saudi Arabia does not have a national climate change plan, economy-wide mitigation or adaptation strategies or absolute emissions targets. Despite its significant contribution to domestic emissions the national oil company Saudi Aramco has not set any quantitative targets aimed at reducing emissions across its operations. The Saudi National Renewable Energy Program, from 2016, contains domestic renewable power targets of 3.45 GW by 2020 and 9.5 GW by 2023. (The targets were later revised upwards to 27.3 GW by 2023 and 57.8 GW by 2030.[30]) A 30% renewables and 70% natural gas power sector target for 2030 has also been announced.[31] In addition, Saudi Arabia has nuclear energy-related plans, but capacity targets have kept shifting over recent years.[32] As of 2019, the government had not yet embarked on constructing nuclear energy, and Saudi Arabia's total renewable energy power generation capacity stood at 0.1 GW, equal to 0.2% of total capacity.[33]

Saudi Arabia's first Paris Agreement NDC, like that of the UAE, is framed in the context of economic diversification-related co-benefits. It contains an emissions avoidance target of 130 million tons of CO_2 equivalent by 2030 (albeit the absence of a baseline makes it impossible to evaluate the actual emissions trajectory this would translate into), which is conditional 'on the Kingdom's economy continuing to grow with an increasingly diversified economy and a robust contribution from oil export revenues to the national economy'.[34] Similarly to the UAE, Saudi Arabia does not make its NDC mitigation target conditional on external financing.

Given that Saudi Arabia's NDC target year is 2030, it is not legally required to update its NDC until most likely 2025.

Institutional Framework

According to Al-Sarihi, challenges facing Saudi domestic climate change governance include 'a lack of quantitative data, consistency, and certainty; absence of a climate action plan; heavy involvement of the Ministry of Energy and the energy industry itself in addressing climate-related matters; and fragmentation of climate-related policies and efforts'.[35] While the involvement of the energy industry in climate action should arguably not be seen as a problem, its dominance of climate change policy could be. Saudi Arabia's climate change policy is exclusively led from the Ministry of Energy. An environment ministry, the Ministry of Environment, Water and Agriculture, was only established in 2016.

Further institutional landscape characteristics can be identified via a comparison to the UAE where the governance of energy is highly fragmented: management of the export-oriented oil and gas sector (under the national oil companies and Abu Dhabi's Supreme Petroleum Council) is separated from the domestic policy and management of renewables (emirate-level energy authorities and utility companies), nuclear energy (Federal Authority for Nuclear Regulation, Emirates Nuclear Energy Corporation and Abu Dhabi government) and energy supply (Ministry of Energy and Industry and emirate-level authorities).

In Saudi Arabia, in a move that some perceive as potentially beneficial for renewable energy deployment, energy sector governance has been in recent years increasingly consolidated under the Ministry of Energy. The ministry is in charge for both fossil fuel and renewable energy policy, as well as electricity. A Renewable Energy Project Development Office at the Ministry of Energy has been tasked with the implementation of the 2023 renewable energy target. It has oversight of 30% of the country's renewable energy target via auctions, while the remaining 70% falls under the Public Investment Fund via direct negotiations with developers. A multi-sectoral Supreme Committee for Energy Mix Affairs for Electricity Production and Enabling Renewable Energy chaired by Crown Prince Mohammed bin Salman was formed in April 2020 to support coordination and promote implementation of the target.[36] The King Abdullah City for Atomic and Renewable Energy (KA-CARE) leads on nuclear energy regulation. The SEEC has a mandate to develop energy efficiency policies and regulations, and a separate regulatory authority, the Electricity and Cogeneration Regulatory Authority, sets non-residential electricity tariffs.[37]

Similar to the UAE, Saudi Arabia does not have a culture of environmental activism or broader civil society activism. A 2017 expert workshop described environmental issues as mainly featuring in Saudi elite discussions, with low interest among other parts of society. There is a limited number of environmental NGOs and, according to the experts, 'academia and think tanks play no relevant role' in the areas of environmental and natural resource conservation.[38]

Alignment, Drivers and Future Prospects

Saudi Arabia has displayed a remarkable consistency in its international negotiating positions and tactics over the past decades. Its role is perceived negatively by many players, including small island states, environmental NGOs and most Western countries. In recent years, Saudi Arabia has taken some steps that seem to be aimed at softening its public image in the UNFCCC context. These include sponsoring GCC pavilions at UNFCCC conferences, which feature regular presentations showcasing research and technological development and pilot projects undertaken in the Kingdom. The Ministry of Energy also develops web content featuring Saudi Arabia's national actions and UNFCCC conference side events.[39]

In the domestic context, Saudi Arabia has demonstrated high levels of interest in both energy efficiency and clean energy, but nevertheless seems still reluctant to present these as elements of a national climate change policy. Major question marks remain around why the Saudi government displays such reluctance, but the centralisation of climate change-related matters under the Ministry of Energy offers a plausible explanation: in its strategic calculations the Ministry continues to place more emphasis on the negative impacts of international climate change mitigation efforts to Saudi Arabia's oil revenues and economic competitiveness than on the negative impacts of dangerous climate change on the global economy as a whole.

Energy efficiency and increasingly also renewable energy (through its increasing cost-effectiveness) are seen as sensible domestic policy options from the perspectives of economic efficiency and energy supply security—but not so much from a climate change mitigation perspective.

This separation of climate change from energy policy is reinforced by the Ministry of Energy's near-exclusive leadership of both international climate change policy and domestic energy governance. Going forward, the role of the ministry, in the absence of broader stakeholder inclusion in policymaking, could therefore continue to hinder the development of a cross-sectoral approach to climate change governance and policy.[40] The plans and targets around energy efficiency and renewables are positive first steps, given that the energy sector contributes 89% of Saudi Arabia's CO_2 emissions.[41] Nevertheless, Saudi Arabia still seems far from developing a comprehensive domestic climate change policy, pledging transparent emissions-related targets to the UN or revisiting its ultimate objectives in global climate governance.

Climate Change Policy in Morocco

Role in the UNFCCC

In the international climate negotiations, Morocco is best known for having hosted two sessions of the UNFCCC Conference of the Parties (COP), in 2001 and 2016, both in Marrakesh. In its role as the President of COP 22 in 2016, Morocco both sought to demonstrate its national commitment to climate action and to draw attention to African countries' priorities and needs. At COP 22, the Moroccan government was perceived to be giving greater emphasis to Africa and other vulnerable developing countries than Arab countries—partly understandable as this was Africa's hosting turn in the rotation schedule of COP Presidencies.[42]

In addition to G-77/China (to which all Arab countries are members), Morocco is part of both the Arab Group and African Group. The African Group's positions have traditionally centred around the vulnerability of its members to the negative impacts of climate change and seeking robust finance arrangements and commitments from developed countries. In addition to the response measures issue, which is not generally a priority for the African Group, another difference between the Arab and African Groups is that many of the latter's members have demonstrated a high level of ambition in the UNFCCC context, including through individual pledges of action pre-2020 and by participating in the progressive High Ambition Coalition (HAC), which has members from various regions and was instrumental in the endgame of the Paris Agreement negotiations in Paris in December 2015.[43] Morocco has in the past signed statements of the HAC. At the time of writing, in 2019, it also co-chaired with France the UN Group of Friends of Climate.[44]

Moreover, Morocco (along with Comoros, Lebanon, Palestine, Sudan, Tunisia and Yemen) is also part of the close to 50-member Climate Vulnerable Forum (CVF), originally established in 2009 but with growing membership and prominence since 2015. The CVF has positioned itself as a voice of the most vulnerable calling for ambitious climate action. It is also a strong supporter of limiting global warming to 1.5 °C. At COP 22, members of the CVF pledged to update their NDCs before 2020, prepare long-term low GHG emission development strategies (Paris Agreement

Article 4.19) by 2020 and strive towards 100% renewable energy production between 2030 and 2050.[45] The CVF countries have also launched, in 2015, the Vulnerable Twenty (V20) Group of Finance Ministers, which describes itself as 'a dedicated cooperation initiative of economies systemically vulnerable to climate change'. The V20 has been active in engaging multilateral development banks in discussions on climate risk insurance and finance.[46]

Domestic Policy Evolution and Main Elements

Morocco has been a regional frontrunner in renewables (alongside Egypt). In 2009, Morocco launched a National Energy Strategy for 2020 and, a year later, established the Moroccan Agency for Solar Energy (later renamed as Moroccan Agency for Sustainable Energy, MASEN). At the core of the strategy were renewable energy capacity targets for solar, wind and hydropower of 2 GW each by 2020—amounting to a 42% share of the power generation capacity. In 2015, this target was raised to 52% by 2030.[47] With a total installed renewable electricity capacity of 3.3 GW in 2018 (an increase of 1.7 GW since 2009) and projects in the pipeline, the country was well on track to achieving its 2020 targets.[48]

Morocco has also passed several important pieces of legislation to support upscaling of renewables, including a law from 2009 obliging the national utility to purchase electricity produced by the private sector and a law from 2015 introducing net-metering for intermittent renewables.[49] According to the International Energy Agency, energy efficiency, despite being a policy priority, has suffered the 'most significant implementation challenges' owing to a weak mandate and insufficient funding allocated to the Moroccan Agency for Energy Efficiency, in charge of implementing related programmes.[50]

The country's first National Plan Against Global Warming, dating back to 2009, contained a 'portfolio of actions [and] programmes for mitigation and adaptation'.[51] A Climate Change Policy was launched in 2013 outlining strategic priorities and setting several goals with a 2030 timeframe. In 2009, Morocco was also among the few Arab countries that submitted a 'nationally appropriate mitigation action' (NAMA) in support of the Copenhagen Accord. NAMAs have been a vehicle for developing countries to submit their mitigation plans to the UNFCCC and seek implementation support pre-2020.[52]

As of 2019, Morocco had submitted two NDC documents: the first intended NDC, submitted in 2015, was updated as an NDC in 2016. Both documents were developed through extensive multi-stakeholder consultations. The intended NDC contained a conditional, economy-wide GHG emissions reduction target of 32% relative to business as usual by 2030. In the NDC, the conditional target was raised to 42% (including reductions from land use and forestry). The NDC also raised Morocco's unconditional target of −13% compared to business as usual by 2030 to −17%. The NDC is underpinned by 55 sectoral strategies and targets. It contains baseline calculations for the emissions scenarios, which demonstrate that achieving the −42% target would equate to maintaining Morocco's emissions at approximately 2010 levels—a significant achievement for a developing country that is expected to add more than 10 million people to its population between 2010 and 2030. The NDC estimates the costs of the conditional component (25% deeper reductions) at US$24 billion. In total, the adaptation and mitigation programmes envisaged in the NDC are estimated to cost US$85 billion between 2010 and 2030.[53]

Although Morocco already updated its NDC in 2016, the country has signalled its intent to do so again in 2020, in line with the CVF pledge and joining the COP 25 Presidency's Climate Ambition Alliance as one of only four Arab countries, together with Comoros, Lebanon and Tunisia.[54] The country's 2016 NDC indicates that the government is also preparing a low-carbon development strategy (in line with Paris Agreement Article 4.19) to serve as the coordinating point for all sectoral mitigation targets.[55]

Institutional Framework

Morocco's climate change governance has strong multi-stakeholder participation from both government and non-state actors. It is led by the Secretary of State in Charge of Sustainable Development at the Ministry of Energy, Mines, and Sustainable Development (which until 2016 was called the Ministry of Energy, Mines, Water and Environment). The Ministry coordinates and engages with other ministries on issues related to climate policy, including the implementation of the Paris Agreement. Prior to 2016, the Ministry had a central directorate in charge of climate change, biodiversity and the green economy tasked with climate change mainstreaming into government policies, in consultation with respective ministries—the status of this function currently is unclear.[56] The Ministry of Foreign Affairs and Cooperation also participates in the international aspects of Morocco's climate change policy.[57]

Morocco has also set up a National Committee on Climate Change, which convenes the main public stakeholder institutions and representatives from the private sector and civil society, and an expert-based National Scientific and Technical Committee on Climate Change. The Interministerial Monitoring Committee, which has participants from 20 different ministries and government agencies, oversees technical studies and policy plans developed for the UNFCCC, including national communications and NDCs.[58]

In the energy sector, the implementation of Morocco's renewable energy plans is delegated to MASEN, and energy efficiency policies are coordinated by the Moroccan Agency for Energy Efficiency (AMEE) under the Ministry of Energy, Mines and Sustainable Development.

Unlike the UAE and Saudi Arabia, Morocco has actively sought international climate financing and has consistently ranked among top recipients in the region. In 2003–2016, Morocco was the MENA's top recipient of multilateral climate finance, having received 59% of the total approved financing in this period, or US$671 million, mostly for renewable energy.[59] Between 2016 and mid-2019, Morocco secured an additional US$800 million through the Green Climate Fund (GCF) alone. Morocco's GCF Designated National Authority (DNA, official contact point) is hosted by the Ministry of Energy, Mines and Sustainable Development.[60] (Most Arab countries, at the time of writing, had DNAs—the UAE and Qatar being the notable exceptions.)

Alignment, Drivers and Future Prospects

Morocco is considered a climate policy leader internationally: in 2018, the Climate Change Performance Index, published by three NGOs and think tanks, ranked Morocco as Africa's leader in addressing climate change. It was lauded for demonstrating that 'economic development in the southern countries can also focus on a mitigation approach'.[61] The Climate Action Tracker ranks Morocco's NDC as one only two Paris Agreement-compatible NDCs included in its assessment.

Morocco's domestic renewable energy policy is driven by economic and energy independence considerations: ranking among the largest energy importers of the MENA region, its energy import bill in 2017 totalled approximately US$7.2 billion.[62] In addition to becoming an electricity exporter, the government also sees great potential in serving as a transit country for electricity trade between Africa and Europe and seeks to pitch itself as a source of renewables-related expertise for Africa.[63] This has led the government to take on active roles in promoting interconnectivity between the two regions in various international fora.

In 2018, Morocco, France, Germany, Portugal and Spain signed the 'Sustainable Electricity Trade Roadmap', aimed at accelerating renewable electricity trade between Morocco and the European energy market.[64] Morocco has also been actively pursuing financing from Europe—and beyond—for its sustainable energy plans. Over the recent years, it has secured tens of millions of Euros via the EU's Neighbourhood Investment Facility, for example.[65] In 2019, press sources reported that the government was seeking US$30 billion in investments to its energy sector through 2030, primarily renewables and liquefied natural gas infrastructure, from investors in Europe, Asia and the Middle East.[66]

In 2016, as part of its role as the COP 22 host, Morocco launched the Adaptation of African Agriculture to Climate Change initiative, which attracted participation by 33 African countries and has as its stated aims promoting innovative solutions and advocating for adaptation financing for the region's priority needs. Also in 2016, Morocco drove the establishment of the Climate Commission for the Sahel Region, centred on leveraging climate financing for this region, and has pledged to conduct feasibility studies for the Commission's investment plans and provide capacity building support to its member countries.[67]

The fact that Morocco's foreign strategic energy interests are largely oriented towards Europe and Africa has meant that its UNFCCC participation has similarly straddled between these two continents: it has signed onto groups that have a strong European backing, such as the High Ambition Coalition, while also participating in the African Group and CVF, which unite many of its African neighbours around concerns relating to vulnerability to climate impacts and calls for further climate finance.

Consequently, while Morocco is the most progressive and active Arab country in terms of climate action both domestically and in its foreign policies, it has not invested in deeper regional cooperation with its Arab peers—neither within or outside the negotiations.

Climate Change Policy in Egypt

Role in the UNFCCC

Egypt, the most populous Arab country, is known for its well-trained diplomats. In the UN climate negotiations too, Egypt often takes on a coordinating role for one of its peer groups. In 2018, Egypt acted as the Chair of the G-77/China in the UN and UNFCCC, and in 2019, Egypt held the seat of the chair of the African Group of climate change negotiators in the UNFCCC.[68]

Egypt also often acts as an issue coordinator of the Arab Group and has in the past coordinated for the entire group. Abdel Gelil has observed that Egypt has played 'a mediating role within the Arab group between the oil exporters led by [Saudi Arabia] and the most vulnerable countries such as Sudan and Morocco'.[69]

In his study of Egyptian climate change policy in the 1990s and 2000s, Abdel Gelil explains changes in Egypt's participation in the UNFCCC through shifts in cabinet and environmental authorities' leadership, as well as institutional capacity. In the first part of the 1990s, due to low capacity at of the environmental authorities and a perception that climate change 'was mainly an energy issue', the Ministry of Petroleum was delegated as the lead in the negotiations.[70]

In the second half of the 1990s, policy leadership shifted to environmental authorities and Egypt emerged as an active negotiator, providing legal support to the Arab Group and coordinating with the African Group. In this period, Abdel Gelil has identified two sub-groups within the Arab Group: 'hard-liners', or oil-producing countries led by Saudi Arabia, which perceived climate change as a 'plot' to harm their economies; and those 'most vulnerable to climate change', including Egypt, Sudan and Morocco, which sought to 'push the negotiations process forward in order to address climate change risks'.[71]

A similar dynamic in the 1990s was also present in an Arab League committee that was assigned the task of following the evolution of climate science. Saudi Arabia—as opposed to Egypt, for example—sought to focus attention primarily to response measures. Another Arab League committee, 'the OAPEC committee', was also formed in this period to 'protect the economic interests of... Arab oil producers' in the negotiations.[72]

In the run-up to the 2009 Copenhagen conference, Egypt emerged again as an active player in the negotiations, with a broader set of stakeholder organisations joining the delegation. (A similar pattern is observable in the UAE's UNFCCC delegations at this time.) From 2009 at least through 2012, the Egyptian delegation was chaired by the Ministry of Foreign Affairs, which further intensified the country's participation in the negotiations. In this period, Egypt also played a leading role in coordinating an Arab position for the UNFCCC, through the League of Arab States' Council of Arab Ministers Responsible for the Environment. According to Abdel Gelil, 'pushed by Egypt', in this period, the Arab group also 'started to coordinate its position away from the OPEC group'.[73]

At the same time, in the early 2010s, Egypt joined the newly-established and more conservative Like-minded Developing Countries' (LMDCs) group, which emerged from the 2011 Durban COP as a counterweight to developing countries holding more progressive views on emissions reductions (see the UAE section of this chapter), and has remained a member since.

Domestic Policy Evolution and Main Elements

As North Africa's major energy consumer, Egypt's energy sector policies will have an important impact on the sub-region's future emissions. The country has the highest renewable electricity capacity in the Arab region, at 4.8 GW in 2018, significantly up from 2016 to 2017 when renewable power capacity, at 3.7 GW equalled to 8% of its total generation capacity.[74] A large share of this capacity is from hydropower. Electricity demand, as in most parts of the Arab region, keeps growing at high rates.

Egypt's first renewable energy target, of 5% by 2000 was set already in 1982, and its first climate change action plan dates to the mid-1990s. In 2008, Egypt set a national renewable energy generation target of 20% by 2020. The renewables target was maintained in the 2016 Integrated Sustainable Energy Strategy, which also includes a 42% target for 2035. In addition, the strategy envisages an energy efficiency improvement target of 8% by 2022, compared to 2006–2007 levels.[75]

The country has also engaged in fossil fuel/energy subsidy reform, announcing a gradual price reform in 2014, which would include an elimination of energy subsidies by 2022.[76] It has also announced a nuclear energy programme, including four Russian-built reactors with a total capacity of 4.8 GW but, as of 2019, no plants were yet under construction.[77]

The country's latest national communication to the UNFCCC, from 2016, refers to a National Strategy for Climate Change, but does not provide details. The only publicly available post-2010 policy document is a UNDP-sponsored National Strategy for Adaptation to Climate Change and Disaster Risk Reduction, from 2011.[78]

Despite Egypt being among the few Arab countries to submit a NAMA support of the Copenhagen Accord around the year 2010 (see also the section on Morocco), the country's NDC from 2015 does not contain any quantitative economy-wide emissions-related targets. Instead, the NDC contains a number of descriptive sectoral adaptation and mitigation actions and policies, to which the document assigns a total price tag of US$73 billion in the period 2020–2030.[79] Given the 2030 timeframe, it could be interpreted that Egypt is not obligated to communicate a new, more ambitious NDC until most likely 2025.

Institutional Framework

The Egyptian Environmental Affairs Agency (EEAA), the executive arm of the Ministry of Environmental, serves as the focal point vis-à-vis the UNFCCC.[80] The same institution also leads on climate change policy and chairs the National Climate Change Committee, which was established in 1997 and restructured in 2007. The Committee has representatives from several government agencies, including the Ministries of Foreign Affairs, Petroleum and Electricity and Energy. It prepares, reviews and activates climate change-related plans and strategies, and coordinates international financial and technical assistance to climate action projects.[81]

In the energy sector, the Supreme Energy Council headed by the Prime Minister oversees national energy policies. The Egyptian Electricity Holding Company (previously Egyptian Electricity Authority) and the New and Renewable Energy Authority (established back in 1986) are responsible for implementing the renewable energy plans.

Experts attribute an important share of Egypt's climate change-related institutional capacity to external support. For example, according to Sowers, the EEAA was created in 1982 by 'local experts with donor assistance'.[82] In 2008–2013, a US$4 million UN/World Bank project led to the establishment of a CDM unit at the EEAA, an energy efficiency unit at the Ministry of Energy and a national Energy Efficiency roadmap.[83] International donors have similarly supported institutional development for climate change governance in many other MENA countries. This unfortunately tends to create discontinuities through unsuccessful knowledge transfer and lack of follow-up mechanisms. Another common characteristic shared by Egyptian and MENA environmental authorities, also pointed out by Sowers, is that 'environmental ministries are widely viewed as "weak" compared with the money and power concentrated in the governmental ministries of the interior, industry, mining, oil and gas'.[84]

Abdel Gelil has described Egypt's climate change policy framework as 'relatively mature', noting that this has played 'an instrumental role in attracting donor funding' for climate change vulnerability and adaptation assessments, capacity building and participation in the Kyoto CDM.[85] As of 2019, Egypt was the Arab country with the highest amount of registered CDM credits, totalling 4.193 million CERs. By comparison, the UAE had 1.163 million registered CERs (each equivalent to 1 tonne of CO_2/year), Saudi Arabia 0.576 million and Morocco 1.740 million.[86] Also, by 2019, Egypt had secured a total of US$830 million from the GCF for building climate finance markets, scaling up renewable energy and private sector participation and building resilience to sea-level rise.[87]

Non-state actors' participation in Egypt's climate change governance is not well-documented. Some environmental NGOs work on domestic climate change policy—many with an international link, either belonging to a global NGO network (such as 350.org or Greenpeace) or supported by foreign donors (e.g. the Cairo Climate Talks forum).[88]

Alignment, Drivers and Future Prospects

Egypt's climate change policy has been driven, as Abdel Gelil has affirmed, by its energy policy requirements and its perceived vulnerability to climate change.[89] Regarding the former, the 2016 energy strategy and its renewable energy and efficiency targets are part of a broader domestic energy supply diversification strategy. Notably, in the early 2010s, Egypt suffered from a severe natural gas shortage, and the Grand Renaissance Dam constructed by Ethiopia is feared to potentially affect Egypt's future hydropower generation capacity. With domestic energy demand growing and solar (and wind) technology costs falling, renewables have become an attractive energy diversification option for many Arab countries—including the ones studied in this chapter. Despite this, as in other Arab countries, little is happening in Egypt to support the expansion of renewables beyond the electricity sector, into transport and heating and cooling. And despite its location in between Europe and Africa, unlike Morocco, Egypt has not yet seriously explored renewable electricity exports or sought to position itself as source of policy leadership in its neighbourhood.

Egypt's vulnerability to climate change impacts, especially with regard to sea-level rise and water resources, have been stressed in government documents since the early 2010s. Awareness about the country's physical vulnerability to climate change, and in particular its impacts on agricultural production and food security, can also be seen reflected in its active participation in the African Group in international negotiations.

In the UNFCCC context, Egypt's diplomatic prowess has led it to take on an active role in all its core peer groups: the Arab Group, African Group and G-77/China. As a result, Egypt's primary role in the negotiations has shaped up to be that of a coordinator, rather than a leader or a laggard.

At the same time, while Egypt has not always agreed with Saudi Arabia on all UNFCCC positions and tactics, its strong emphasis on adaptation (over mitigation) and on developed countries' responsibility (over developing countries) has undoubtedly shaped and strengthened the Arab Group's conservative orientation in the negotiations. It has also participated in the emerging economy-dominated LMDCs group which, according to an Egyptian diplomat in 2012, came together from a mutual perception of being pressured to take on more responsibilities despite still struggling with significant development challenges.[90]

Conclusions

The first of the three questions laid out at the start of the chapter asked: why are recent years' changes in Arab countries' climate change policy not reflected at the international level?

The chapter has confirmed that the prevailing view of the Arab countries acting as a unified group in the negotiations led by Saudi Arabia is only partially correct: first, Egypt has actively participated in coordinating and shaping the group's views since the 1990s. Second, Morocco and Egypt also participate actively in the African Group, through which they can pursue priorities that are not catered for though participation in the Arab Group. Third, seeking to broaden their partnerships with more proactive countries, Morocco and the UAE have joined dialogue fora promoting ambitious action beyond the UNFCCC.

The two-level game hypothesis presented at the beginning of the chapter—namely that the domestic-international policy disconnect is the result of weak domestic constituencies favouring ambitious international climate policies and low institutionalisation of regional cooperation and coordination mechanisms—does seem to hold. However, this chapter has also shed light on a much more subtle two-level game and highly-diverse ways of participating in the UNFCCC. Differentiating features and characteristics in this regard include:

- Strength of UNFCCC negotiating capacity (Saudi Arabia and Egypt being the strongest);
- Weight of oil industry interests and scepticism of climate science (Saudi Arabia as the most vocal);
- Pursuit of an active role in peer groups (the UAE being the only inactive one in this regard);
- Role of different authorities in shaping the country's position (Morocco and the UAE with multi-stakeholder participation, Egypt led by two ministries and Saudi Arabia by one);
- Projection of domestic ambition in the UNFCCC (Morocco being by far the most active); and
- Role vis-à-vis international climate finance (Egypt and Morocco actively seeking foreign assistance and Saudi Arabia and the UAE seeking to avoid being considered as donors).

The chapter has identified several discrepancies between the domestic and international level policies of the countries studied, which lead to unlocked opportunities. The UAE's domestic policy ambitions and the regional leadership role it has been seeking are not coupled with equally ambitious domestic implementation or proactive UNFCCC participation. Saudi Arabia's ambitious domestic energy policies, which could form the basis of a more overarching climate change policy, are held back by the tight leadership of its energy ministry and its emphasis on the costs of mitigation action both domestically and globally over their benefits.

In Egypt, an active diplomatic apparatus has engaged it in the work of four major negotiating blocs, but at the domestic level, despite a long institutional history and ambitious renewable energy targets, climate change policy seems to be stagnating. Morocco's climate change policies are perhaps the best-aligned of all Arab countries: its renewable energy policies and domestic governance framework are among the region's best-performing ones, while its strategic positioning between Europe and Africa is largely reflected in its UNFCCC policies.

The second question concerned the differences in policy choices between oil exporters and non-oil exporters, and whether either the rentier or leadership agency paradigm can help explain policy outcomes. Surprisingly perhaps, the chapter has provided most support for Arab countries' domestic climate change policies being driven by domestic energy diversification ambitions and to some extent existing natural resource endowments—and not so much by entrenched rentier state interests (with the clear exception of Saudi Arabia) or top leadership members. Morocco's and Egypt's hydropower has given them a head-start in renewable electricity, and they also face high fossil fuel import bills, which create an urgent incentive for energy diversification. In Saudi Arabia and the UAE, in turn, the pressure to scale up renewables has not been as urgent, but an added incentive for investing in domestic capacity has been the role of renewables in decreasing the opportunity costs of burning fossil fuels at home below international market prices.

At the international level, as demonstrated by the list above, policies are explained by a broad range of institutional capacity and legacy factors, which intermingle with how the country's leadership sees its role in the region and internationally.

The third question related to a possible future convergence of domestic rhetoric, domestic policy and international policy positions both at a country and regional level. At the time of writing, in a global comparison, the four Arab countries analysed were at various stages of domestic ambition. In 2019, the Climate Action Tracker group ranked the Moroccan NDC among only two that are compatible with the most ambitious goal of the Paris Agreement, of staying below 1.5 °C of global temperature rise. It rated the UAE's NDC as 'highly insufficient', compatible with a 3–4 °C world, and that of Saudi Arabia 'critically insufficient', compatible with a 4 °C+ temperature rise.[91] Another ranking, the Climate Change Performance Index, by Germanwatch, rated Morocco's performance as 'high', Egypt's 'medium' and Saudi Arabia's 'very low'.[92]

In an international context, the Arab countries are united by their vulnerability to climate change impacts and their developing country status. Climate change adaptation solutions are often local and context-specific, but multidimensional risks related to migration, social unrest and shared water resources, if addressed proactively, could create a new basis for regional-level cooperation and a more representative engagement in the UNFCCC as well through the Arab Group. The interpretation of what being a 'developing country' in the UNFCCC entails has in some cases generated obstacles to a more proactive approach to ambitious climate action. While this is an issue that generates strong feelings, many developing countries, including Morocco, have demonstrated that taking on a more proactive role in the UNFCCC is not a slippery slope to further obligations but can facilitate important strategic interests, as in the case of Morocco and its role as a crucial intermediary between Europe and Africa.

Notes

1. Mostafa K. Tolba and Najib W. Saab, *Arab Environment: Climate Change: Impact of Climate Change on Arab Countries* (Beirut: Arab Forum for Environment and Development), ix.
2. See, e.g., the 'RICCAR' Arab Climate Change Assessment Report project by UNESCWA.
3. Germanwatch, IndyACT and tcktcktck, 'Saudi Arabien schwächt die Position der Entwicklungsländer auf den UN-Klimaverhandlungen', press release, 8 October 2009, https://germanwatch.org/de/2163.
4. IISD Reporting Services, 'Summary of the Katowice Climate Change Conference', *Earth Negotiations Bulletin* 12, No. 747, 18 December 2018, http://enb.iisd.org/vol12/enb12747e.html; see also Claire Stam, 'UN Climate Talks End Amid Major Questioning of Landmark 1.5C IPCC Report', *Euractiv*, 28 June 2019, https://www.euractiv.com/section/climate-environment/news/un-climate-talks-end-amid-major-questioning-of-landmark-1-5c-ipcc-report/.
5. Data for Palestine was not available. Total GHG Emissions Including Land-Use Change and Forestry—2014. World Resources Institute, *CAIT Climate Data Explorer*, accessed in August 2019, http://cait.wri.org/historical/.
6. Richard Heede, 'Tracing Anthropogenic Carbon Dioxide and Methane Emissions to Fossil Fuel and Cement Producers, 1854–2010', *Climatic Change* 122, Nos. 1–2, January 2014, https://link.springer.com/article/10.1007/s10584-013-0986-y.
7. Robert D. Putnam, 'Diplomacy and Domestic Politics: The Logic of Two-Level Games', *International Organization* 42, No. 3, Summer 1988, 434.
8. Ibid.
9. International Monetary Fund, *Economic Diversification in Oil-Exporting Arab Countries*, Manama, April 2016, 8.

10. OPEC, 'World Proven Crude Oil Reserves', *Annual Statistical Bulletin 2019*, https://asb.opec.org/index.php/interactive-charts/oil-data-upstream.
11. The National, 'Sheikh Mohammed bin Zayed's Inspirational Vision for a Post-Oil UAE', 10 February 2015, https://www.thenational.ae/opinion/sheikh-mohammed-bin-zayed-s-inspirational-vision-for-a-post-oil-uae-1.8710.
12. Samia Nakhoul, William Maclean and Marwa Rashed, 'Saudi Prince Unveils Sweeping Plans to End "Addiction" to Oil', *Reuters*, 25 April 2016, https://www.reuters.com/article/us-saudi-economy/saudi-prince-unveils-sweeping-plans-to-end-addiction-to-oil-idUSKCN0XM1CD.
13. Kinninmont observes this in the case of Saudi Arabia's Vision, which targets, among other things: increasing the size of the economy, private sector contribution to the GDP and foreign direct investment overall; raising the share of non-oil exports and non-oil GDP; increasing non-oil government revenue; increasing the Saudiization rate in the oil and gas sector; and increasing the assets of the Public Investment Fund. Jane Kinnimont, *Vision 2030 and Saudi Arabia's Social Contract Austerity and Transformation*, Research Paper, London: Chatham House, July 2017, 2 and 11.
14. See, e.g., G-77/China, *Statement on Behalf of the Group of 77 and China… at the Joint Opening Plenary of the 24th Session of the COP to the UNFCCC (COP 24); the 14th Session of the CMP; and the Third Part of the 1st Session of the CMA*, 2 December 2018, https://www4.unfccc.int/sites/SubmissionsStaging/Documents/201812022326---G77%20Katowice%20opening%20statement.pdf.
15. See, e.g., Arab Group, *Arab Statement Opening of ADP*, 29 April 2013, https://unfccc.int/sites/default/files/adp_2_arab_group_29042013.pdf?download.
16. The LMDCs' membership has been somewhat fluid, but it has included a large number of Arab countries. It has generally supported a more hard-line interpretation of the 'common but differentiated responsibilities' principle of the Convention, which has included an emphasis on a binary set of differentiated rules and obligations for developed and developing countries. On the LMDC's members, see, e.g., Third World Network, *TWN Info Service on Climate Change (Oct 12/05)*, 24 October 2012, https://www.twn.my/title2/climate/info.service/2012/climate20121005.htm; LMDCs, *Submission on Elements of the 2015 Agreed Outcome*, 8 March 2014, http://unfccc.int/files/documentation/submissions_from_parties/adp/application/pdf/adp_lmdc_ws1_20140309.pdf.
17. See, e.g., Mari Luomi, *The Gulf Monarchies and Climate Change: Abu Dhabi and Qatar in an Era of Natural Unsustainability*, London: Hurst, 2012.

18. Emirates Nuclear Energy Corporation, 'Barakah Nuclear Energy Plant', accessed in July 2019, https://www.enec.gov.ae/barakah-npp/.
19. IRENA, *Renewable Energy Market Analysis: GCC 2019*, Abu Dhabi, 2019, 14.
20. UAE Ministry of Energy and Industry, *United Arab Emirates 4th National Communication Report*, 2018, 22.
21. WAM, 'Al Zeyoudi Wraps Up Successful Participation in UN Climate Action Summit in New York', accessed in January 2020, https://www.wam.ae/en/details/1395302790094.
22. UAE Ministry of Energy and Industry, *4th National Communication*, 45.
23. UAE Ministry of Foreign Affairs and International Cooperation, 'Strategy of the Ministry of Foreign Affairs 2017–2021', accessed in July 2019, https://www.mofaic.gov.ae/en/The-Ministry/The-Strategy.
24. @MoCCaEUAE, 'HE Dr. Thani Al Zeyoudi welcomes #ClimateAction thought leaders & decision makers…', tweet, 26 June 2019, https://twitter.com/MoCCaEUAE/status/1143836989118132224.
25. UAE Ministry of Energy and Industry, *4th National Communication*, 45, 47.
26. Joanna Depledge, 'Striving for No: Saudi Arabia in the Climate Change Regime', *Global Environmental Politics* 8, No. 4, November 2008, 10.
27. Ibid., 12.
28. There some discontinuities too, however, most saliently the unconditional support that Saudi Arabia currently gives to the adaptation agenda in the UNFCCC (highly-prioritised by all developing countries), as opposed to the 2000s when, according to Depledge, it sought to link the response measures and adaptation agendas and make progress on the latter conditional on progress on the former. Ibid., 16.
29. Aisha Al-Sarihi, *Climate Change and Economic Diversification in Saudi Arabia: Integrity, Challenges and Opportunities*, Policy Paper #1/2019, Washington, DC: The Arab Gulf States Institute in Washington, 2019, 11–12.
30. NREP, 'Saudi Arabia's Ministry of Energy, Industry and Mineral Resources Launches Round Two of Renewable Energy Programme', press release, 29 January 2019, https://www.zawya.com/mena/en/press-releases/story/Saudi_Arabias_Ministry_of_Energy_Industry_and_Mineral_Resources_launches_round_two_of_Renewable_Energy_Programme-ZAWYA20190129082200/.
31. IRENA, *Renewable Energy Market Analysis: GCC*, 58–59.
32. Designated National Authority of Saudi Arabia, *The First Biennial Update Report (BUR), Kingdom of Saudi Arabia*, March 2018, 52; World Nuclear Association, *Nuclear Power in Saudi Arabia*, updated April 2019, https://www.world-nuclear.org/information-library/country-profiles/countries-o-s/saudi-arabia.aspx.

33. IRENA, *Renewable Energy Market Analysis: GCC*, 14.
34. Government of Saudi Arabia, *The Intended Nationally Determined Contribution of the Kingdom of Saudi Arabia Under the UNFCCC*, Riyadh, November 2015, 1.
35. Al-Sarihi, *Climate Change and Economic Diversification*, 1.
36. MEED, 'Riyadh Forms Renewable Energy Body', 9 April 2020.
37. Partly from: IRENA, *Renewable Energy Market Analysis: GCC*, 59; Al-Sarihi, *Climate Change and Economic Diversification*, 14; DNA of Saudi Arabia, *First BUR*, 47–52.
38. Jan Hanrath and Wael Abdul-Shafi, *Environmental Challenges in a Conflictive Environment: Iranian and Saudi Perspectives on the Risks of Climate Change and Ecological Deterioration*, Brief 8, CARPO and East West Institute, 2017, 5.
39. MEIM/Saudi Arabia, 'KSA Climate' portal, accessed in July 2019 when the website's content was focused on COP 24, https://ksa-climate.com/.
40. A similar argument has been made by Al-Sarihi, *Climate Change and Economic Diversification*, 17.
41. DNA of Saudi Arabia, *First BUR*, 20.
42. Based on author's communications at COP 22 and North Africa Post, 'King Mohamed VI to Pay for Travel Expenses of Tropical Islands Delegations Attending COP 22', 10 October 2016, http://northafricapost.com/14507-king-mohammed-vi-pay-travel-expenses-tropical-islands-delegations-attending-cop22.html.
43. On pledges, see, e.g., World Resources Institute's Twitter campaign #stepup2020 @wriclimate #sb50bonn, accessed in August 2019. Few Arab countries have signed onto the HAC, Morocco representing one of the few exceptions.
44. Permanent Mission of France to the UN in New York, 'The Group of Friends of Climate: 2019 Is a Pivotal Year', press release, 22 April 2019, https://onu.delegfrance.org/The-Group-of-Friends-of-Climate-2019-is-a-pivotal-year.
45. Climate Vulnerable Forum, 'Climate Vulnerable Forum Commit to Stronger Climate Action at COP22', press release, 18 November 2016, https://unfccc.int/sites/default/files/cvf_declaration_release_en.pdf.
46. V20, 'Vulnerable Countries and Partners to Climate-Proof Economic Growth', press release, 11 April 2019, https://www.v-20.org/vulnerable-countries-and-partners-to-climate%C2%AD-proof-economic-growth/.
47. MASEN, website, accessed in August 2019, http://www.masen.ma/en/.
48. Climate Action Tracker, 'Morocco', accessed in August 2019, https://climateactiontracker.org/countries/morocco/.
49. Meriem Houzir, Mustapha Mokass and Liane Schalatek, *Climate Governance and the Role of Climate Finance in Morocco*, Heinrich Böll Stiftung, 2016, 82–83.

50. IEA, *Morocco 2019—Energy Policies Beyond IEA Countries: Executive Summary*, 5.
51. Houzir et al., *Climate Governance in Morocco*, 39.
52. UNFCCC, *Compilation of Information on Nationally Appropriate Mitigation Actions to Be Implemented by Developing Country Parties*, FCCC/SBI/2013/INF.12/Rev.3, 45–47.
53. Morocco, *Intended Nationally Determined Contribution (INDC) Under the UNFCCC*, 5 June 2015; Morocco, *Nationally Determined Contribution Under the UNFCCC*, 19 September 2016; UN DESA, 'World Population Prospects 2019', accessed in August 2019, https://population.un.org/wpp/.
54. Chilean Government, 'Climate Ambition Alliance', press release, 23 September 2019, https://prensa.presidencia.cl/comunicado.aspx?id=102021.
55. Morocco, *Nationally Determined Contribution*, 4.
56. NDC Partnership, *NDC Country Outlook: Morocco*, November 2017, 3; Royaume du Maroc, *Premier Rapport Biennal Actualisé du Royaume du Maroc*, April 2016, 19–20; website of the Ministry of Energy, Mines and Sustainable Development, accessed in August 2019, http://www.mem.gov.ma/.
57. Houzir et al., *Climate Governance in Morocco*, 35.
58. Royaume du Maroc, *Premier Rapport Biennal*, 19.
59. Sejal Patel, Charlene Watson and Liane Schalatek, *Climate Finance Regional Briefing: Middle East and North Africa*, Climate Finance Fundamentals 9, Climate Funds Update, ODI and Heinrich Böll Stiftung, November 2016.
60. Green Climate Fund, 'Morocco', accessed in August 2019, https://www.greenclimate.fund/countries/morocco.
61. UN Environment, 'Morocco Ranked Second in Climate Change Performance Index 2018', blog post, 20 December 2018, https://www.unenvironment.org/news-and-stories/blogpost/morocco-ranked-second-climate-change-performance-index-2018.
62. IEA, *Morocco 2019*, 5.
63. See, e.g., MASEN, website.
64. IEA, *Morocco 2019*, 7.
65. European Commission, 'European Neighbourhood Policy and Enlargement Negotiations—Morocco', accessed in August 2019, https://ec.europa.eu/neighbourhood-enlargement/neighbourhood/countries/morocco_en.
66. Deena Kamel, 'Masdar Wins Tender to Build 800 MW Solar Project in Morocco', *The National*, 23 May 2019.
67. AAA Initiative website, accessed in August 2019, http://www.aaainitiative.org/; Congo Basin Forest Partnership, 'Climate Commission for the

Sahel Region, A Shining Example…', press release, 13 March 2019, http://pfbc-cbfp.org/news_en/items/shining-example.html.

68. Demonstrating deep engagement with the African Group, the 2019 Egyptian chair Mohamed Ibrahim Nasr has coordinated the group on several UNFCCC negotiating issues since 2009 and has also served as Africa's lead negotiator in other multilateral environmental and trade processes, including the Sendai Framework for Disaster Risk Reduction, and UNCTAD. UNFCCC, *2018 SCF Forum, Mr. Mohamed Nasr*, accessed in August 2019, https://unfccc.int/sites/default/files/resource/Mr.%20Mohamed%20Nasr%20-%20Egypt%20-%20SCF%20member.pdf.
69. Ibrahim Abdel Gelil, *History of Climate Change Negotiations and the Arab Countries: The Case of Egypt*, Research Report, Issam Fares Institute, July 2014, 30.
70. Ibid., 18.
71. Ibid., 20.
72. Ibid., 21.
73. Ibid., 26–27.
74. IRENA, *Renewable Capacity Statistics 2019*, 2019; Egyptian Ministry of Electricity and Renewable Energy, *Egyptian Electricity Holding Company Annual Report 2016/2017*, 17.
75. IRENA, *Renewable Energy Outlook: Egypt*, 2018, 31–32.
76. Ibid., XV.
77. World Nuclear Association, 'Nuclear Power in Egypt', updated April 2019, https://www.world-nuclear.org/information-library/country-profiles/countries-a-f/egypt.aspx.
78. Egyptian Cabinet Information and Decision Support Center and UNDP, *Egypt's National Strategy for Adaptation to Climate Change and Disaster Risk Reduction*, 2011.
79. Arab Republic of Egypt, *Egyptian Intended Nationally Determined Contribution*, 2015.
80. Egypt's Ministry of State for Environmental Affairs (MSEA) and EEAA, *Egypt Third National Communication*, March 2016, 22.
81. MSEA and EEAA, *Egypt's Third National Communication*, 22–23; Abdel Gelil, *The Case of Egypt*, 17.
82. Jeannie Sowers, 'Environmental Activism in the Middle East and North Africa', in Harry Verhoeven (ed.), *Environmental Politics in the Middle East*, Oxford: Oxford University Press, 2018, 27–52.
83. MDGIF, 'Egypt: Climate Change Risk Management in Egypt', accessed in August 2019, http://mdgfund.org/content/climatechangeriskmanagementegypt.
84. Sowers, 'Environmental Activism'.
85. Abdel Gelil, *The Case of Egypt*, 6.

86. Jørgen Fenhann, *CDM Pipeline*, UNEP DTU Partnership, 1 August 2019.
87. Green Climate Fund, 'Egypt', accessed in August 2019, https://www.greenclimate.fund/countries/egypt.
88. See, e.g., Sowers, 'Environmental Activism'.
89. Abdel Gelil, *The Case of Egypt*, 6.
90. Author conversation in the run-up to COP 18, autumn of 2012.
91. The Tracker did not rank Egypt. Climate Action Tracker, accessed in August 2019, https://climateactiontracker.org/.
92. The Index did not rank the UAE. Germanwatch, 'Climate Change Performance Index 2019', accessed in 2019, https://www.climate-change-performance-index.org/.

Index

R. Mills and L.-C. Sim (eds.), *Low Carbon Energy in the Middle East and North Africa*, International Political Economy Series, https://doi.org/10.1007/978-3-030-59554-8

L

M

N

U

W

The manufacturer's authorised representative in the EU is Springer
Nature Customer Service Centre GmbH, Europaplatz 3, 69115 Heidelberg,
Germany. If you have any concerns regarding our products, please
contact ProductSafety@springernature.com

Printed and bound by CPI Group (UK) Ltd, Croydon, CR0 4YY
30/09/2026
02225459-0017

Index

A

B

C